The Health Economy of London

The Health Economy of London

The Health Economy of London

Seán Boyle and Richard Hamblin

Published by
King's Fund Publishing
11–13 Cavendish Square
London W1M 0AN

© King's Fund 1997

First published 1997

ISBN 1 85717 156 X

A CIP catalogue record for this book is available from the British Library

Distributed by Grantham Book Services Limited
Isaac Newton Way
Alma Park Industrial Estate
GRANTHAM
Lincolnshire
NG31 9SD

Tel: 01476 541 080
Fax: 01476 541 061

Printed and bound in Great Britain by Intertype

Cover photograph: Richard Bailey

Contents

Appendices

Acknowledgements

This report has benefitted from the help and advice of so many colleagues and friends that it would be invidious, and probably impossible, to attempt to list them. We owe a debt of gratitude to all of you.

A special mention is due to the Department of Health which has allowed such full and open access to the data sources upon which this report has drawn.

We would like to thank the members of the London Commission for their encouragement and comment, and the Secretary to the Commission for her, at times, rapacious reading of this monumental volume.

When Samuel Johnson famously said, '... *when a man is tired of London, he is tired of life ...*', London was a much smaller city. Had this report been written then, it may have been commensurately sized. Nevertheless, we never tired of it.

As ever, any errors of fact or interpretation belong to ourselves alone.

Summary

The London population

- Twenty per cent of the population of London belong to minority ethnic groups; the diverse range of ethnic and cultural backgrounds has substantial implications for the level of need for certain services, and the form, manner and cost of delivery.

- Over the next 20 years, the proportion of older people in London – those aged 75 years and over – is projected to increase less rapidly than in England as a whole, but the following 20 years will witness a rapid expansion in the older population of the capital.

- The health of the population of London as a whole is broadly similar to that of the rest of England, though it is substantially worse for people aged under 65 years. There is great diversity in London with areas of high deprivation, and hence poor health status, alongside relative affluence.

- The standardised hospitalisation rate for acute specialties in London as a whole is virtually identical to that of England at 168 finished consultant episodes (FCEs) per 1,000 resident population; however, the rate in deprived areas of the capital, at 170, is much lower than the average of 207 in similar areas elsewhere in England, a substantial change from the picture five years previously, in 1989/90, when the rates were almost identical.

- The psychiatric hospitalisation rate in London as a whole is eight per cent less than the England figure; however, the rate in deprived areas of the capital is higher than average, though equivalent to that in similarly deprived areas elsewhere in England.

- There has been a significant increase in the net use of acute hospital care in London hospitals by non-residents, mainly from the south east of England, from 9.5 per cent of total volume in 1988/89 to around 12 per cent in 1994/95: inward flows are greatest for the former Special Health Authority and single specialty hospitals where almost half of care produced is delivered to non-London residents.

- London health authorities account for 17.5 per cent of total Hospital and Community Health Services (HCHS) expenditure, which is less than the 19 per cent accounted for by London providers, reflecting the export of care from London providers to the rest of the country.

- On the basis of the Department of Health formula designed to distribute monies equitably between different parts of England, taking account of differences in levels of need and in the costs of providing services, the allocation of resources to London as a whole would be less than the England average. However, actual budget allocations are greater, reflecting historical levels of expenditure as well as special responsibilities.

- HCHS expenditure accounted for by London DHAs, per capita resident population, is £460, 30 per cent greater than the average of £353 in the rest of the country. In London and similar areas outside the capital, the difference in expenditure per capita increases with the level of deprivation.

- London residents as a whole make greater use of pay-beds in NHS hospitals, though this amounts to only one per cent of activity for Londoners in NHS hospitals.

- There are parts of London where independent sector hospitalisation rates are particularly high. This adds significantly to overall hospitalisation rates in these areas.

The nature of London hospital provision

- A higher proportion of the care provided by London hospitals is elective than is the case in England as a whole – 54 compared with 51 per cent; however there is variation across sectors of London: the east has a higher proportion of emergencies and the north-west has more elective care than average.

- There is a higher proportion of day case activity in London hospitals than is the case in the rest of the country – 31 compared with 26 per cent. The day case rate has grown more quickly in London than in the rest of England since 1989/90 when there was a common rate of 18 per cent.

- However, in the more specialised London hospitals the higher proportion of day case activity relates mainly to the greater proportion of elective work; often the proportion of this which is day case is less than average.

- Since 1982 there has been a rapid reduction in the number of acute beds in London hospitals, from 4.1 per 1,000 resident population to 2.4 in 1994/95, while bed availability has fallen less quickly in England.

- The excess of acute beds in London as a whole over the rest of England has fallen from 40 per cent in 1982 to just seven per cent in 1994/95.

- The value of land occupied by trusts in London is 21 per cent of their total fixed assets compared with 13 per cent for non-London trusts. One-third of the total value of land occupied by trusts in England is accounted for by London trusts.

- London trusts employ a greater proportion of medical and administrative or clerical staff than average, and commensurably less nursing staff: in some acute trusts in inner-deprived London the ratio of nurse to doctor is closer to three than the national average of almost five.

- London providers as a whole spend a similar proportion of their budgets on staff to those in the rest of England, although more in absolute terms: however agency staff account for a greater proportion of staff expenditure in London than in the rest of England – six per cent of staff expenditure compared with two per cent.

- Average cost per member of staff in London is £22,400, some 25 per cent more than the rest of England figure of £17,900. The difference reflects higher wages costs in London, greater agency staff costs per member of staff, and, perhaps, a greater proportion of more highly paid employees in London.

- London providers account for 19 per cent of national HCHS expenditure compared with 16 per cent of FCE activity; 14 per cent of England's population is in London: these differences reflect both the use of services by non-residents and higher costs.

- The provision of health services accounts for 80 per cent of London provider income; 20 per cent comes from other sources such as education, training and research funding. By contrast, services income accounts for 90 per cent in the rest of the country.

Efficiency

- London has a higher in patient length of stay, but this is matched by a greater day case rate and a turnover interval some 18 per cent less than that of the rest of England.

- Hence, London hospitals produce episodes of care slightly more efficiently than those elsewhere in the country: London as a whole has a throughput of 76 FCEs per bed, including day cases, compared with 75 in the rest of England. There is some variation across London with a considerably greater throughput of 86 in the south, reflecting both a high day case rate and a low in-patient length of stay.

- Bed occupancy rates can be both a measure of efficient use of resources and an indicator of pressure on scarce resources. London as a whole has a higher occupancy rate for combined acute and geriatric beds than the rest of England – 86 compared with 79 per cent.

Cost per unit

- Average cost per acute episode is 20 per cent greater in London than in the rest of England; average cost per psychiatric episode is over 40 per cent greater. However, there is considerable variation across London with an average cost per acute episode of £1,194 in the north-central sector, over 50 per cent greater than the average of £762 in the east.

- Average cost per out-patient attendance is 17 per cent greater in London than in the rest of England: again there is variation, from £57 in the south to £82 in the north-central sector of London.

- The average cost of staff relative to total FCEs delivered is considerably higher in London than in the rest of England. This is particularly true of medical staff: the cost of consultants is 40 per cent more per FCE in London compared with the rest of the country; the cost of non-consultant medical staff is 58 per cent more.

- Trusts are expected to achieve a six per cent return on their net assets. In 1994/95 a quarter of London trusts failed to achieve this target: the proportion of trusts failing to achieve a six per cent return on net assets was greater in London than in the rest of England.

- The provision of privately-funded health care is particularly significant in London, although still small relative to the size of publicly-funded NHS provision.

Community and Primary Care in London

- London residents use GP services more than average: the GP contact rate per resident population is 17 per cent higher in inner London than outer London, and some 12 per cent higher than the England average.

- London has as many GPs per capita resident population as other parts of England but on a number of measures – standard of GP premises, availability of practice nurses, proportion of single-handed practices – the quality of general practice in London remains worse than average. The pattern is not uniform throughout the capital: on most measures the south and south-east sectors perform well relative to the rest of London.

- London residents use less prescribed drugs than average: this is particularly true of deprived areas of the capital where the number of prescriptions per capita resident population is 24 per cent less than in similarly deprived areas elsewhere in England.

- Family Health Services (FHS) expenditure in London, at £141 per capita, is four per cent more than the average of £136 in the rest of the country, excluding administration costs and GP fundholder expenditure on hospital care. Average per capita expenditure varies between £130 in high-status areas of London and £158 in inner-deprived areas.

- However, there is less expenditure per capita on pharmaceutical services in London, and by contrast, expenditure on General Medical Services (GMS) is more in the capital than in the rest of the country.

- There appears to be great variation in the level of provision of community health services across sectors of London: in the capital there tend to be more contacts per individual patient episode than is the case in the rest of the country.

- The demand for ambulance services in London is 60 per cent greater than in the rest of England. The London Ambulance Service had performed consistently worse against response targets for emergency calls than services in the rest of England but a substantial improvement has occurred recently. By March 1996 compliance with the 14 minute target of 95 per cent response had reached 89 per cent compared with 68 per cent in 1994/95.

Social services

*   London has a greater provision of all forms of community-based care relative to population than the rest of the country. Thus London as a whole, in terms of resident population, provides twice as much day care, almost 30 per cent more home care and twice as many meals as the rest of England.

*   There is considerably less provision of residential care in London, especially inner-deprived London, per capita resident population, compared with the rest of England. This is reflected in a lower admission rate to homes in London per capita resident population. The admission rate to residential care in London for older residents of the capital is just 60 per cent of the England average; it is less than 50 per cent in inner-deprived London.

*   On the other hand, in London as a whole, local authorities support a similar number of older people, per capita resident population aged 75 years and over, in residential care, as the rest of England, though not necessarily in homes in London. Local authorities in inner-deprived areas of the capital support a greater number than similar areas elsewhere: 40 compared with 32.

*   There continues to be a significant difference in the balance between residential and community-based care in London when compared with the position in England as a whole: a similar situation to that in 1990/91.

*   The independent sector is increasingly important to the provision of social care. The provision of residential care for older people has declined by approximately 20 per cent in London between 1985 and 1995, but increased by a similar proportion in the rest of England. Local authority provision has decreased throughout England but has not been compensated by increased independent provision in London, as elsewhere.

*   Forty per cent of meals in London are provided by the independent sector, compared with 47 per cent in England as a whole. In inner-deprived areas of London the proportion of meals provided by the independent sector is twice that of similar areas elsewhere.

*   London as a whole has 40 per cent less provision of nursing home places per capita resident population than the rest of England; in inner-deprived London there are just 20 per cent of the places available in similar areas outside the capital.

- Total gross social services expenditure per capita resident population in London is 60 per cent greater than that in the rest of England – £229 compared with £142; the average in inner-deprived London is 82 per cent greater than that in similar areas elsewhere.

- Gross social services expenditure on older people per capita resident population aged 75 years and over is over 50 per cent more in London than in the rest of England.

- Almost half of gross social services expenditure on older people in the rest of England is accounted for by residential or nursing care compared with 39 per cent in London as a whole; on the other hand, London spends 37 per cent on community-based care compared with 29 per cent in the rest of the country.

- Despite the different balance of expenditure, London local authorities spend more per capita on most types of care for older people: the exception is nursing care where the London average is 13 per cent less than that of the rest of England.

Introduction

The Health Economy of London provides a comprehensive review of the health and health care of the population of London, based on a variety of published and unpublished data sources. The report considers London in three ways: first, by providing comparisons between different parts of the capital; second, by comparing areas of London with similar areas in the rest of England; and, finally, and less completely, by considering changes since the report of the first King's Fund London Commission in 1992 (King's Fund, 1992).

It is intended that, as far as possible, the material is presented in a purely factual manner with, therefore, a relatively sparse commentary. There is no conscious attempt to provide a thematic story: rather this is a source of reference. Much of the analysis and many of the findings just scratch the surface of the underlying relationships, and often the text points to directions for future analysis and research.

The information presented here should be of value for all involved in the planning and delivery of health services in London. We believe it is the first time that this broad range of information concerning health and health services in London has been available in one publication. We have had access to numerous data sources, both published and unpublished, mainly from the Department of Health. These are listed in individual chapters.

London sectors

In this report, London is defined as the area covered by the 16 London District Health Authorities (DHAs). These are listed in Appendix 1. Data are most commonly presented in terms of two aggregations of London districts: by geographic sector of London; and, by a grouping of London DHAs into three clusters of similar socio-economic type. For the purposes of comparison, similar groupings are also provided for other parts of England.

The geographic sectors of London are defined as east, south east, south, north west and north central. These correspond roughly to the spheres of influence of the five groupings of medical schools in London extended out to the borders of the capital. A list of constituent DHAs is provided in Appendix 1. A list of the membership of the second grouping of London DHAs, by socio-economic type, and their England comparator groups, is also provided in Appendix 1. These groupings are based on a statistical classification of DHAs, which clusters DHAs together according to their similarity on a number of socio-economic and demographic characteristics derived from the 1991 Census. Three types of area are identified in London: inner-deprived, mixed-status and high-status; similar comparator groups are identified throughout the rest of England.

Guide to the report

The report consists of ten chapters. Chapter 1, *'Health and Health Needs'*, provides an analysis of the demographic structure of London including future population projections.

Broad indicators of health status such as Standardised Mortality Ratios (SMRs) and measures of healthy life expectancy are also provided. The chapter concludes by considering some aggregate measures of socio-economic deprivation and need for health services.

The following four chapters provide an analysis of hospital-based activity. Chapter 2, *'Hospital Admissions'*, is a comprehensive review of in-patients and day cases from a London provider perspective, including more detailed information on the distinction between FCEs and admissions – the phenomenon known as 'episode inflation', on transfers from other hospitals, discharge destination and operative procedures. Chapter 3, *'Hospital Utilisation',* provides a demand-side perspective on the use of London hospitals. An analysis is provided of hospitalisation rates for London residents, both at DHA and individual electoral ward level. A detailed analysis of flows of patients into London hospitals from the rest of the country is also developed.

Chapter 4, *'Other Hospital-Related Issues'*, considers other aspects of hospital-related services. Included are out-patient, A&E, NHS day care and ambulance activity, and the physical and human resources available to London's health care providers. Chapter 5, *'Independent Hospital Provision'*, describes the provision of private hospital care in London, both in NHS pay-beds and in independent hospitals. This includes a consideration of the use of private care by Londoners, and details of human and physical resources available to the independent sector.

We then turn to services provided outside the hospital. Chapter 6, *'Community Health Services',* considers the volume, pattern and location of community-based activity by health professionals such as district nurses and health visitors. Chapter 7, *'Family Health Services'*, considers aspects of General Medical Services, including indicators of the quality of physical resources, and provides an outline of Pharmaceutical and General Ophthalmic Services in the capital. Chapter 8, *'Social Services',* details health-related community and residential social services care in London, whether provided by local authorities themselves or the independent sector.

Chapter 9, *'Financial Resources',* examines the financial framework underlying health services in London. An analysis is provided of Hospital and Community Health Services (HCHS) expenditure from both a purchaser and a provider perspective, together with a more detailed analysis of provider finances using trust summarised accounts, and some discussion of DHA, FHS and social services expenditure. Finally, Chapter 10, *'Measures of Efficiency'*, considers efficiency indicators, both financial and non-financial. The former includes cost per case, and trust performance against financial targets; the latter includes utilisation of hospital beds and performance against Patient's Charter standards.

An overall summary of the report is provided. Each chapter also presents, first, a summary of key issues and findings, and second, a set of key facts comparing London with the rest of England.

Chapter 1

Health and Health Needs

Summary

Population

- London's population of just under seven million is 14 per cent of the England population. Of London residents, approximately two million live in inner-deprived areas, 2.7 million in mixed-status areas, and 2.3 million in high-status areas.

- London in general has a younger population than average: this is especially true of inner-deprived DHAs such as East London and the City where 72 per cent of residents are aged under 45. High-status areas tend to have a relatively older population.

- The contrast between London and England is expected to increase over the next 20 years. The proportion of the population aged 75 and over in England and Wales is projected to grow from seven to eight per cent by 2011, while falling from 6.5 per cent to 5.5 per cent in London over the same period.

- Twenty per cent of Londoners belong to minority ethnic groups. The DHAs with the largest minority ethnic populations are East London and the City, and Brent and Harrow with 37 per cent and 36 per cent respectively.

- Both these DHAs have large Asian populations, accounting for 21 per cent of the local population in East London and the City and 23 per cent in Brent and Harrow. The largest Black populations are found in Lambeth, Southwark and Lewisham (19 per cent) and East London and the City (15 per cent).

- The minority ethnic population in London is expected to increase by the year 2011: Black populations by 55 per cent and Asian populations by 35 per cent. By contrast, the White population of London is expected to decrease.

Health indicators

- All-cause, all-age SMR in London DHAs varies from 87 in Bromley to 109 in East London and the City. London as a whole has an SMR four per cent below the England average.

- SMRs increase with the level of deprivation. Inner-deprived areas of London have an SMR of 103 compared with 93 in high-status London. However, each type of socio-economic area in London has a lower SMR than comparable areas elsewhere in England.

- The relative position changes when SMRs for those aged under 65 are considered. London has an SMR of 104 compared with 99 in the rest of the country. This difference is driven by inner-deprived London which has an SMR of 128. Mixed-status and high-status London have a lower SMR than their counterparts in the rest of England.

- SMRs for heart disease and stroke are lower than those for cancers throughout London. No London DHA has an SMR greater than 100 for heart disease, implying that deaths from heart disease are less common throughout London, given its demographic structure, than is the case in England and Wales as a whole.

- Life expectancy varies across local authority areas in London, as does expected years of ill health. In Tower Hamlets male life expectancy is 70 years, of which 11 are expected to be spent in ill health. By contrast, men in Bromley can expect to live for 75 years and to be in ill health for only eight of them.

- Londoners have a similar life expectancy to non-Londoners. However, they have fewer expected years of ill health. This is particularly true of inner-deprived and mixed-status London when compared with similar areas in the rest of the country.

- The proportion of residents of London DHAs reporting long-term limiting illness ranges from nine per cent in Kingston and Richmond to 13 per cent in East London and the City, and is clearly related to the level of deprivation in an area.

Socio-economic indicators

- Deprivation, as measured by the UPA8 score, is greatest in eastern areas of London, stretching from the north of Lambeth and Southwark, through Tower Hamlets, Newham and Hackney to the eastern half of Haringey. Twenty-eight per cent of wards in London have UPA8 scores of over 30 – the threshold above which GPs in the area attract deprivation payments for their patient lists.

- In 1991, deprivation, as measured by the UPA8 score, was greater in London than in the rest of England.

- Highly deprived areas are not necessarily similar. Thus, the most deprived ward in London, Spitalfields in Tower Hamlets, has high minority ethnic, unemployment and overcrowding scores, while the second most, Liddle in Southwark, has very high lone parent household and unskilled worker scores.

- The need for hospital services, as measured by the Department of Health's acute and psychiatric needs indices for the allocation of financial resources to DHAs, follows a similar geographical pattern to measures of deprivation.

- In half the London local authority wards the acute needs index is above the national average; the need for acute services in London as a whole is close to that of England. However, 60 per cent of London wards have greater than average psychiatric need, implying the relative need for psychiatric care in London is greater than that for acute care.

Key Facts

Population	*London*	*Rest of England*
Population by age-group (1994 mid-year estimate):		
• Total	6,969,000	41,738,000
• 0-14	1,342,000 (19%)	19%
• 15-44	3,278,000 (47%)	42%
• 45-64	1,401,000 (20%)	23%
• 65+	948,000 (14%)	16%
Population by ethnic group (1991):		
• White	5,493,000 (80%)	96%
• Black	559,000 (8%)	1%
• Asian	708,000 (10%)	2.5%
• Other	126,000 (2%)	0.5%

Health indicators

	London	Rest of England
All-cause, all-age SMR (1989-1994):	96	100
All-cause, 0-64 SMR (1989-1994):	104	99
Male healthy life expectancy:	63.9 years	63.9 years
Male unhealthy life expectancy:	9.2 years	9.6 years
Female healthy life expectancy:	67.6 years	70.2 years
Female unhealthy life expectancy:	11.6 years	11.9 years
Performance against Health of the Nation mortality rate targets (1993) (targets for the year 2000 in parenthesis):	*per 100,000*	*per 100,000*
• Coronary Heart Disease, under 65 (**35** per 100,000)	49	51
• Coronary Heart Disease, 65-74 (**619** per 100,000)	729	840
• Stroke, under 65 (**7.5** per 100,000)	12.3	11.2
• Stroke, 65-74 (**155** per 100,000)	199	222
• Lung Cancer, over 75 (**42** per 100,000)	38	37
• Suicide (**9.4** per 100,000)	7.6	7.9

Socio-economic indicators

	London	Rest of England
Mean UPA8 score (1991):	11.9	5.5
Population in wards with UPA8 scores of 30 and above (1991):	1,900,000 (28%)	–
Population in wards with acute need index above England average (1991):	3,400,000 (49%)	–
Population in wards with psychiatric need index above England average (1991):	4,000,000 (58%)	–

1 Introduction

This chapter considers the population of London, in terms of:

- demography;

- health indicators such as the Standardised Mortality Ratio (SMR), healthy life expectancy, and mortality and morbidity data, including comparison with Health of the Nation targets; and,

- broader socio-economic indicators such as the Jarman UPA8 scores and the acute and psychiatric needs indicators used in Department of Health (DoH) resource allocation formulae.

Data are presented by District Health Authority (DHA) area, and by classification by type of socio-economic area: the latter allows comparison with similar areas in the rest of England. The composition of socio-economic groupings for London and England, together with geographic sectors of London are presented in Appendix 1. Where data are accessible, time series and projections are presented.

2 Data sources

Data on London's population, by age-group, are taken from the Office for National Statistics (ONS) 1994 mid-year estimates of DHA populations. However, London Research Centre (LRC) estimates are used in the analysis of minority ethnic groups, and LRC projections are used in considering projected changes by age- and ethnic group. Health indicator data are from a variety of sources. Figures on SMRs, causes of death and performance against Health of the Nation mortality and morbidity indicators are from the Health Service Indicators for 1993/94 (DoH, 1995a). Data on healthy life expectancy are from '*Health Expectancy and its Uses*' (Bone *et al*, 1995*)*. The UPA8 index, calculated by the Department of General Practice at St. Mary's Medical School, is based on 1991 Census data. Acute and psychiatric needs variables are calculated from the DoH resource allocation formula using 1991 Census data.

3 Population

Our analysis of the health needs of Londoners commences with a consideration of London's population. This is analysed by age- and ethnic group. Projections to the year 2011 are provided for age-groups and ethnic groups.

Age-groups

Table 1 shows the population by age-group in the 16 London DHAs. London has a younger population than the rest of England. This is particularly true in inner-deprived London: a quarter of the population of East London and the City DHA are aged under 15 and nearly three-quarters under 45. In contrast outer London DHAs have an older population: less than 60 per cent of Bromley's population is aged under 45.

Table 1: Population by DHA, by age-group, London, 1994 mid-year estimate

DHA	0-14	15-44	45-64	65-74	75-84	85+	Total
Camden and Islington	61,847	181,227	68,974	25,470	15,312	5,472	358,302
East London and the City	143,008	285,170	99,910	39,043	21,003	7,067	595,201
Kensington, Chelsea and Westminster	46,262	176,886	72,737	24,230	15,401	5,742	341,258
Lambeth, Southwark and Lewisham	147,135	366,328	127,156	51,628	29,602	9,667	731,516
Brent and Harrow	91,639	212,586	96,950	31,313	19,880	7,363	459,731
Ealing, Hammersmith and Hounslow	122,067	318,608	127,729	44,020	26,768	9,770	648,962
Enfield and Haringey	92,462	222,719	95,786	32,880	20,673	7,984	472,504
Merton, Sutton and Wandsworth	107,959	303,144	119,901	45,222	28,897	11,508	616,631
Redbridge and Waltham Forest	91,620	206,845	91,957	34,362	22,196	8,478	455,458
Barking and Havering	73,973	156,843	84,375	37,397	18,792	5,905	377,285
Barnet	58,577	139,572	63,326	24,051	16,485	6,218	308,229
Bexley and Greenwich	89,365	189,403	91,533	35,633	20,969	6,888	433,791
Bromley	51,398	120,117	70,771	27,763	16,218	5,904	292,171
Croydon	65,084	149,359	69,978	23,947	13,791	4,970	327,129
Hillingdon	46,705	110,236	51,451	18,886	11,504	3,878	242,660
Kingston and Richmond	52,656	138,870	68,131	24,576	17,064	6,196	307,493
London	1,341,757	3,277,913	1,400,665	520,421	314,555	113,010	6,968,321

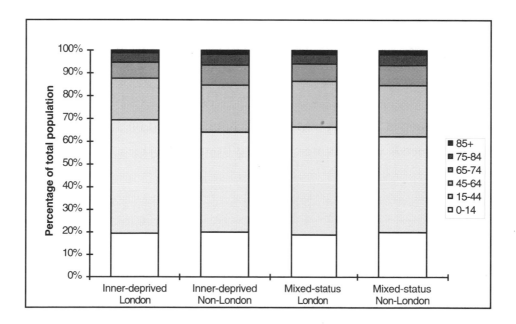

Figure 1: Proportion of population, by age-group, London and England, inner-deprived and mixed-status areas, 1994

Figures 1 and 2 show London has a greater proportion of young people, especially in the 15-44 age-group, when compared with the rest of England. By contrast, the proportion of the population aged between 45 and 64 is less in London than in the rest of the country. This is the case for all types of socio-economic area but is particularly so for the more deprived areas. High-status areas in London have only a slightly younger population profile than high-status areas in the rest of the country. The significant impact of this age profile on London's population twenty years hence is shown in the section on projected changes in London's population by 2011.

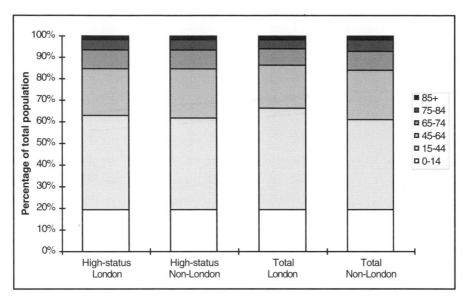

Figure 2: Proportion of population, by age-group, London and England, high-status areas and total, 1994

Projected changes in age composition

Figure 3 shows projected percentage changes in population between 1991 and 2011, by type of London socio-economic area, based on an analysis by the LRC. The age-groups projected to increase are 0-14, 45-64 and 85+. By contrast, the largest age-group, 15-44, is projected to fall slightly, and those aged 65-74 and 75-84, to fall by 14 and 23 per cent respectively.

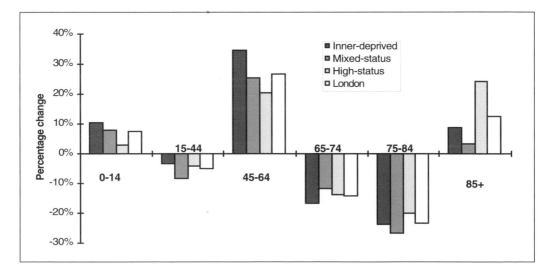

Figure 3: Projected percentage changes in population, between 1991 and 2011, by age-group, London

Changes in older age-groups are explored further in Figures 4 and 5. These contrast projected changes in the 75+ and 85+ age-groups in London with those of England and Wales. Figure 4 shows that in 1991, 7.1 per cent of the resident population of England and Wales was in the 75+ age-group compared with a figure of 6.5 per cent in London. However, these proportions are projected to diverge: by 2011, the London proportion is projected at 5.4 per cent whereas the England and Wales figure is 7.9 per cent.

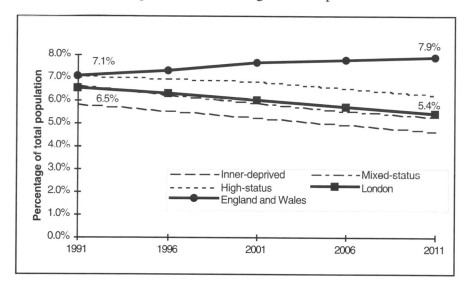

Figure 4: Change in the proportion of total population aged 75 years and over, between 1991 and 2011, London and England and Wales

Figure 5 shows the position for the 85+ age-group. Again, London is projected to behave differently to England and Wales where there is a steady growth as the proportion of the population aged 85+ increases from 1.7 per cent in 1991 to 2.4 per cent in 2011. In London, on the other hand, there is a projected increase from 1991 to 1996, but the proportion of the total population aged 85+ then levels off at around 1.6 per cent. The proportion of the population in both the 75+ and 85+ age-groups is greater in high-status than in inner-deprived areas. This is consistent with Figures 1 and 2 above.

These different trends over time have implications for London's future health services. To a large extent trends are driven by the different age structure in London currently. Figures 1 and 2 showed that in London, and particularly inner-deprived and mixed-status areas, the proportion of the population in the 45-64 age-group was much less than that of England as a whole. It is unsurprising therefore that the 75+ age-group is projected to be a relatively smaller proportion in London in 20 years time. By contrast, the greater proportion of younger age-groups suggests that, even if people leave the capital as they get older, London may have a faster growth in the 75+ age-group than the rest of England over a 40- or 50-year period. This illustrates the difficulty in planning for health services well into the future and shows the need for flexibility.

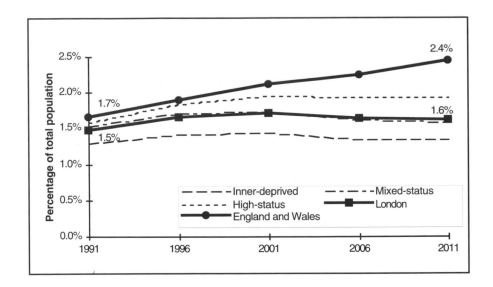

Figure 5: Change in the proportion of total population aged 85 years and over, between 1991 and 2011, London and England and Wales

Ethnicity

(Technical note: the LRC categorises population data by ten ethnic groups. For ease of presentation here, Black Caribbean, Black African and Black Other have been grouped as 'Black'; Indian, Pakistani, Bangladeshi, Chinese and Asian Other have been grouped as 'Asian'.)

Table 2: DHA Population, by ethnic group, London, 1991

DHA	White	Black	Asian	Other	Total
Camden and Islington	289,558	28,633	28,215	8,833	355,239
East London and the City	363,572	85,809	120,839	11,185	581,405
Kensington, Chelsea and Westminster	269,549	23,200	21,338	13,537	327,624
Lambeth, Southwark and Lewisham	537,599	136,270	36,998	13,678	724,545
Brent and Harrow	287,258	48,733	104,812	11,569	452,372
Ealing, Hammersmith and Hounslow	477,542	41,604	112,396	15,514	647,056
Enfield and Haringey	376,059	52,679	36,722	9,453	474,913
Merton, Sutton and Wandsworth	517,328	40,343	41,666	9,112	608,449
Redbridge and Waltham Forest	343,306	34,570	64,528	6,476	448,880
Barking and Havering	361,223	5,635	10,238	1,578	378,674
Barnet	244,591	10,749	38,456	6,149	299,945
Bexley and Greenwich	392,880	14,973	21,485	4,049	433,387
Bromley	280,936	4,630	6,823	2,322	294,711
Croydon	262,970	24,218	25,830	6,170	319,188
Hillingdon	207,556	3,917	22,629	2,654	236,756
Kingston and Richmond	280,904	2,609	14,578	3,703	301,794
London	5,492,831	558,572	707,553	125,982	6,884,938

Table 2 shows the distribution of ethnic groups across London. The largest Asian populations are in East London and the City, Ealing, Hammersmith and Hounslow and Brent and Harrow DHAs. There are large Asian populations throughout East London and the City: these include a Bangladeshi community of 40,000 in Tower Hamlets, a quarter of the borough's population and over a third of the entire Bangladeshi population of London; and an Indian population of 30,000 in Newham. There are large Indian populations in both

Ealing and Hounslow (45,000 and 30,000 respectively), and in Brent and Harrow (43,000 and 33,000). The largest Black populations are in Lambeth, Southwark and Lewisham and East London and the City. Lambeth and Hackney in particular have Black populations of 56,000 and 42,000 respectively.

Projected changes in ethnic composition

Figure 6 shows, between 1991 and 2011, a projected decrease in the proportion of London's population which is White. All other groups are expected to increase. The greatest projected increase is in the Black population, particularly in high-status areas, although these start from a low absolute number – less than three per cent of the total population.

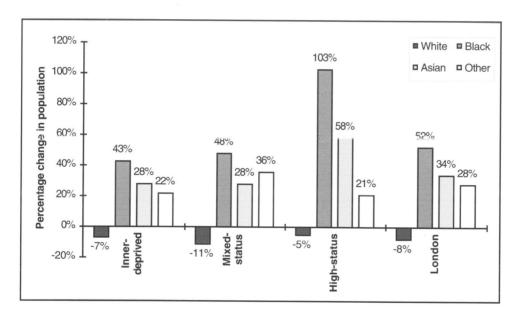

Figure 6: Projected percentage changes in population, between 1991 and 2011, by ethnic group, London

4 Health indicators

In this section we consider some broad indicators of the health of the population of London compared with other parts of England. Sections are included on mortality, healthy life expectancy, morbidity and Health of the Nation targets.

Standardised Mortality Ratio (SMR)

The SMR is a measure of mortality which compares the actual number of deaths in an area with the expected number given its demographic profile, if it had the same death rates as some reference population: in this case England and Wales. Hence, the SMR for England and Wales is 100. Scores of less than 100 indicate fewer deaths than might be expected, while scores of over 100 indicate more. SMRs have been calculated using mortality data for the period 1989 to 1994, unless otherwise indicated. The method of calculating SMRs is provided in Appendix 2.

All-cause, all-age SMR

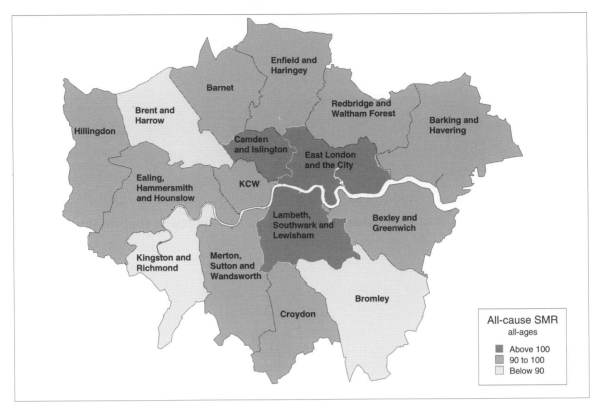

Map 1: All-cause, all-age SMR, London, 1989-1994

Map 1 shows that a majority of London DHAs have an all-cause, all-age SMR, for 1989-1994, less than the England and Wales average of 100. East London and the City has the greatest SMR at 109, followed by Lambeth, Southwark and Lewisham, 105, and Camden and Islington, 102 – all three DHAs are part of inner-deprived London. The lowest SMR, at 87, is for Bromley; Brent and Harrow and Kingston and Richmond also have SMRs of less than 90.

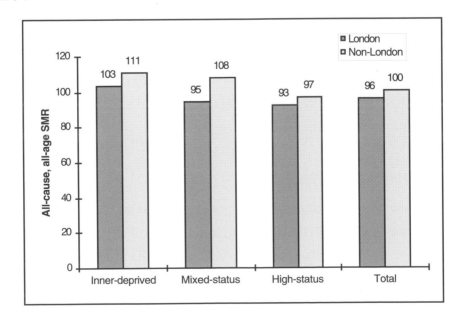

Figure 7: All-cause, all-age SMR, London and England, 1989-1994

Figure 7 shows a lower all-cause, all-age SMR in London than in similar areas in the rest of England. London as a whole has an all-cause, all-age SMR of 96, compared with 100 for the rest of the country.

All-cause, under 65 years SMR

However, as Figure 8 shows, London fares significantly worse when the SMR for those aged under 65 is examined. In this case, London has a *greater* SMR than the rest of England – 104 compared with 99. This is particularly true of inner-deprived areas of the capital where the SMR is 128. The all-age SMR reflects a lower SMR for people aged 65 and over. It is possible that Londoners suffer ill-health at a younger age than people in the rest of the country. More detailed further analysis would be required to confirm this.

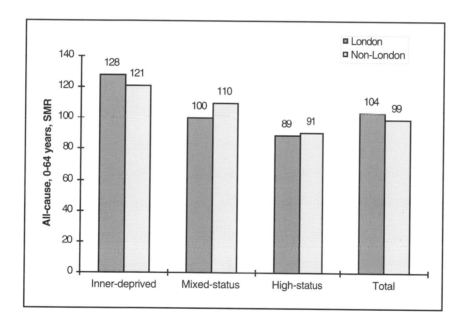

Figure 8: All-cause, under 65 years SMR, London and England, 1989-1994

Individual-cause, all-age SMR

Turning to the cause of death, the Health Service Indicators provide SMRs for the following individual causes: heart disease, lung cancer, all cancers, stroke, suicide and road accident. The first four causes are each responsible for many deaths a year in each DHA, the latter two rather fewer. Indeed, cancer, stroke and heart disease between them account for over 50 per cent of all deaths in London. This section considers the first four causes only.

Maps 2, 3, 4 and 5 show clearly that SMRs tend to be lower in London for heart disease and stroke than for cancers, particularly lung cancer. Indeed, half of the London DHAs have SMRs for lung cancer of over 100. By contrast, none have an SMR of over 100 for heart disease.

Figure 9 shows, for each type of socio-economic area, differences in cause-specific SMRs between London and similar areas in the rest of England. SMRs in London are less than in

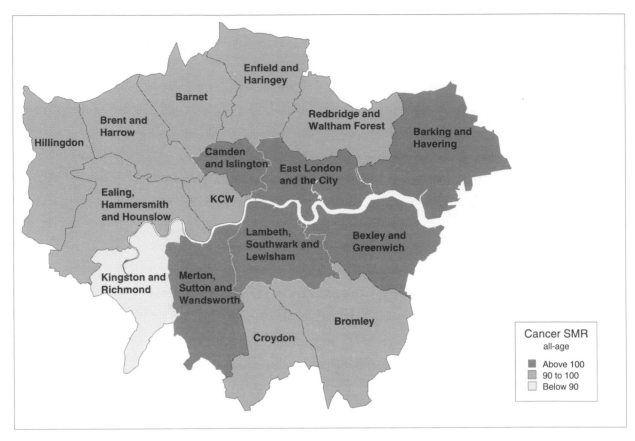

Map 2: All cancers SMR, London, 1989-1994

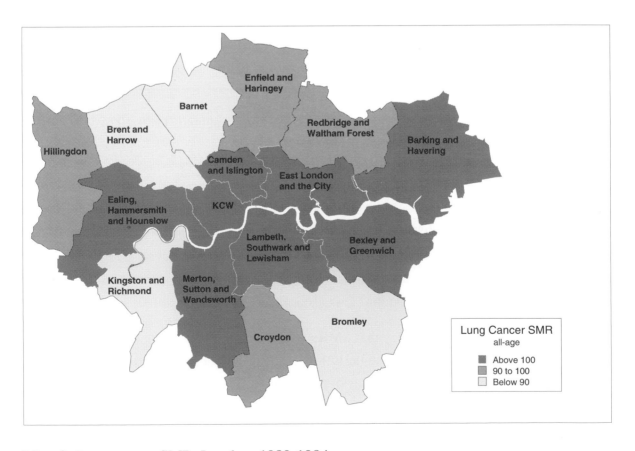

Map 3: Lung cancer SMR, London, 1989-1994

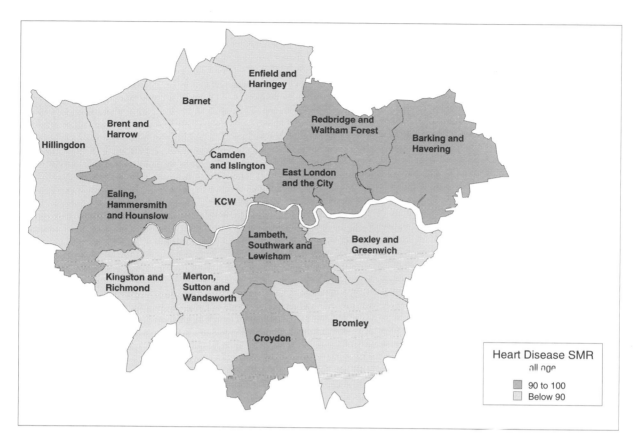

Map 4: Heart disease SMR, London, 1989-1994

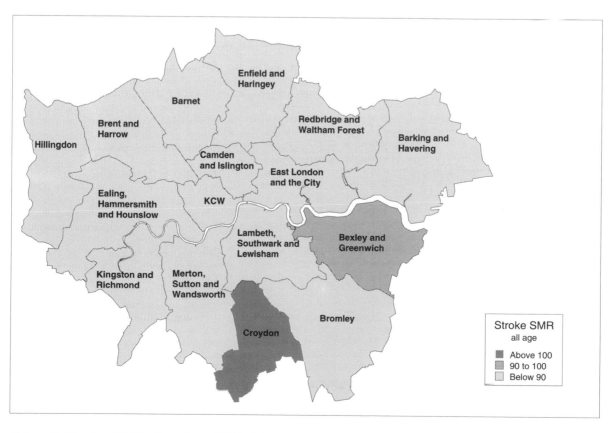

Map 5: Stroke SMR, London, 1989-1994

similar areas in the rest of the country for each cause, with one exception: comparing lung cancer in high-status areas. Greatest differences between similar areas in London and the rest of England occur for heart disease and stroke.

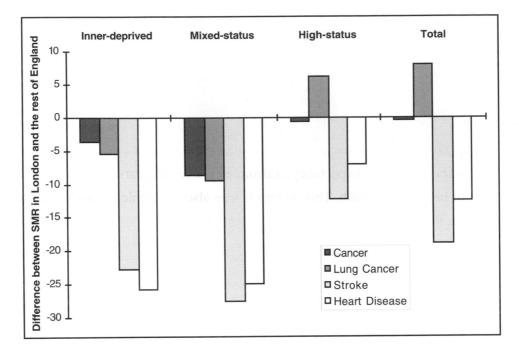

Figure 9: Differences between types of socio-economic area in London and comparable areas in the rest of England, by cause-specific SMR, 1989-1994

Causes of Death

It is possible to consider the most common causes of death for residents of London, using Health Service Indicator data for 1994. As Figure 10 shows, and it is no surprise given that London has lower SMRs for heart disease and stroke than comparable areas in the rest of the country, a smaller proportion of all deaths in London are from these causes than is the case in the rest of the country. This holds for all types of socio-economic area in London.

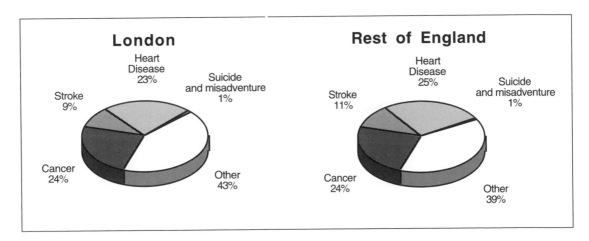

Figure 10: Proportion of all deaths, by cause, London and the rest of England, 1994

Healthy life expectancy

Bone *et al*, in *'Health Expectancy and Its Uses'* (Bone *et al*, 1995), present life expectancy and expected years of ill health, by sex, for each local authority borough in England and Wales. Healthy life expectancy is calculated using age-specific long-term limiting illness rates as a measure of disability. A detailed description of the method is provided in the reference. Table 3 shows considerable variation across London boroughs, both in life expectancy and years of ill health. High-status London areas have a longer life expectancy of which less is expected to be years of ill health. Lower life expectancy seems to coincide with an expectation of more years of ill health. For example, male life expectancy in Tower Hamlets is approximately 70 years at birth, with an expectation of just over 11 years of ill health. By contrast, male life expectancy in Bromley is over 75 years, with an expectation of just over eight years of ill health. This pattern is true also of female residents: for example, Hackney has both the lowest life expectancy and the highest number of unhealthy life years.

Table 3: Life expectancy and years of ill health, by London local authority

Local Authority	Male Life Expectancy	Male Years of Ill health	Female Life Expectancy	Female Years of Ill health
Harrow	75.5	8.3	81.2	11.1
Barnet	75.2	8.1	80.3	10.5
Bromley	75.1	8.1	80.9	10.4
Sutton	75.0	8.2	80.0	10.5
Bexley	74.9	8.6	80.1	10.6
Kingston upon Thames	74.9	7.6	80.2	9.6
Merton	74.5	8.5	80.0	10.8
Richmond upon Thames	74.5	7.6	80.7	9.7
Havering	74.4	8.4	80.0	10.7
Enfield	74.2	8.7	80.2	11.1
Hillingdon	74.2	8.2	79.8	10.6
Croydon	74.0	8.4	79.3	10.6
Redbridge	73.9	9.1	79.7	11.4
City of London	73.4	9.2	80.3	13.0
Brent	73.4	9.8	79.5	12.4
Hounslow	73.3	8.8	79.6	11.3
Waltham Forest	73.2	9.7	78.9	12.2
Haringey	73.0	10.0	78.8	13.0
Kensington & Chelsea	73.0	7.9	80.1	10.3
Ealing	72.7	9.2	79.1	11.7
Westminster	72.5	8.6	79.6	11.1
Greenwich	72.4	9.7	78.7	12.1
Barking & Dagenham	72.2	10.1	78.6	12.5
Lewisham	72.1	9.9	78.6	12.4
Wandsworth	71.8	9.2	78.2	11.7
Newham	71.4	10.9	78.1	13.8
Camden	71.3	9.5	79.0	12.0
Hackney	71.0	11.5	77.2	14.8
Islington	70.9	10.3	78.1	13.3
Lambeth	70.6	9.9	77.9	12.7
Southwark	70.4	10.1	77.4	12.5
Tower Hamlets	70.4	11.1	78.5	13.7
Hammersmith & Fulham	70.2	9.4	78.2	11.9

(Table 3 is ordered by male life expectancy.)

Figures 11 and 12 compare types of socio-economic area in London with similar areas in the rest of England. Life expectancy increases as level of deprivation decreases, both in London and the rest of the country. However, comparing inner-deprived and mixed -status areas of London with comparable areas elsewhere, life expectancy in the capital tends to be higher. This is combined with less years of ill health. However, London as a whole has lower life expectancy than the rest of England. This is due mainly to the effect of higher life expectancy in resort and retirement areas which affects the rest of England figure but not the non-London comparator groups.

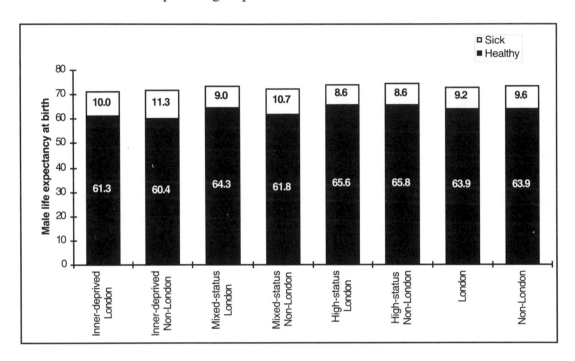

Figure 11: Male life expectancy at birth, London and England

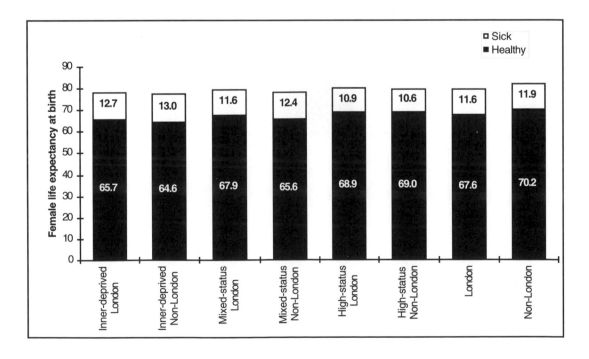

Figure 12: Female life expectancy at birth, London and England

Long-term limiting illness

One useful measure of the health status of an area is the reported prevalence of long-term limiting illness (LTLI). This section considers the LTLI for the total population and for older people, based on data from the 1991 Census. The prevalence of LTLI is greater among older people. However, the proportion of people with LTLI that are under 65 is a useful measure of poor health status, as it reveals areas where the population reports ill health at a younger age.

Total population

Map 6 shows the proportion of the total population in London reporting long-term limiting illness is greatest in inner-deprived areas. The exception is Kensington, Chelsea and Westminster where just ten per cent of the total population report such illness, one of the lowest proportions in the capital. On the other hand, in East London and the City, over 13 per cent of the total population report LTLI. By contrast high-status areas tend to have the lowest rates: for example, just nine per cent of the population in Kingston and Richmond. An exception is Barking and Havering, where 12 per cent of the population reports LTLI, the fourth highest rate among London DHAs.

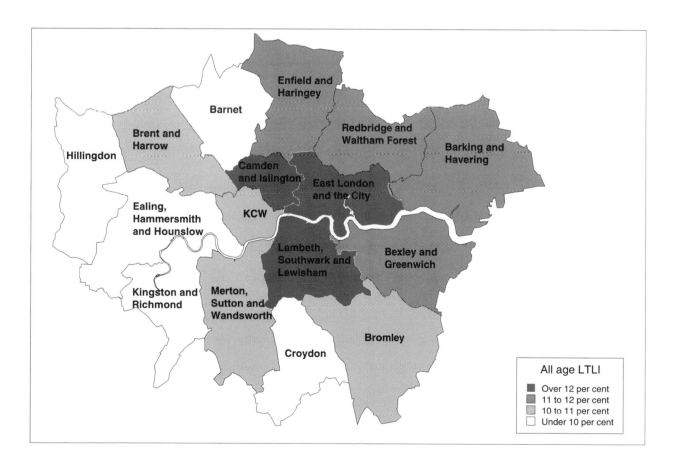

Map 6: All-age long-term limiting illness, London, 1991

Older people

Map 7 reveals a similar pattern among older people as for the total population. In this case older people are taken to be those of pensionable age, i.e. men aged 65 years and over and women aged 60 years and over. Again, the highest prevalence is in inner-deprived London with 38 per cent overall and the lowest in high-status areas with 34 per cent. There is some variation across London with a figure of 42 per cent recorded in East London and the City but just 32 per cent in Kensington, Chelsea and Westminster.

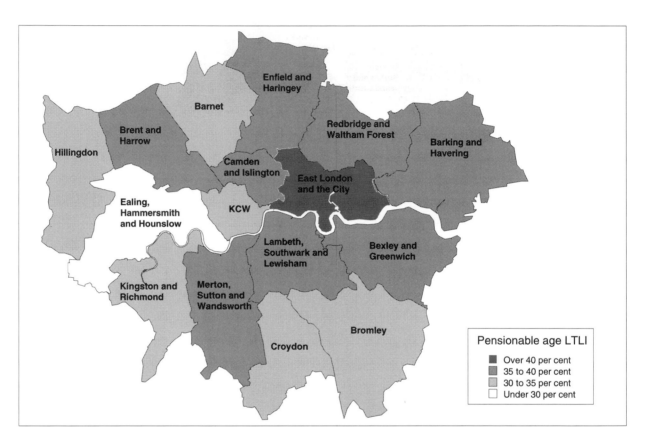

Map 7: Pensionable age long-term limiting illness, London, 1991

Map 8 shows the proportion of the population reporting LTLI who are of pensionable age. In inner-deprived areas, where the overall prevalence is higher, a greater proportion of those reporting LTLI are in the younger age-groups. For example, 13 per cent of the total population report LTLI in East London and the City, but just 45 per cent of these are of pensionable age. By contrast, in Kingston and Richmond where just nine per cent of the total population report a long-term limiting illness, 62 per cent of these are older people. Thus, the population of inner-deprived areas of London is not only more likely to report long-term limiting illness than those living in more affluent parts, but is likely to report it at a younger age.

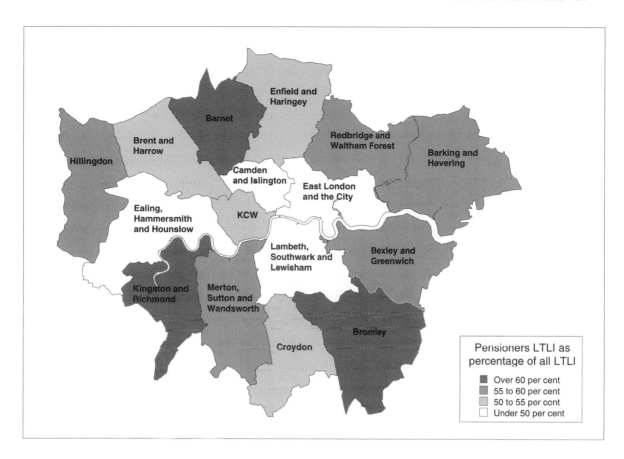

Map 8: Proportion of all-age long-term limiting illness reported by people of pensionable age, London, 1991

Health of the Nation mortality targets

Targets for reducing mortality rates were set in the *'Health of the Nation'* (DoH, 1991) for a number of the main causes of death in England. These included coronary heart disease (CHD), stroke, lung cancer and suicide. In this section we consider performance against these targets, comparing types of socio-economic area in London with similar areas outside the capital.

Coronary heart disease and stroke

This section considers mortality rates from CHD and stroke for people aged under 65 years and those between 65 and 74. Figure 13 shows the mortality rate from CHD for the under 65 age-group; Figure 14 shows the rate for the 65-74 age-group. In both cases London has a lower mortality rate than the rest of the country. This confirms the findings shown in Figure 10 above. In both London and the rest of the country, there is a gradient across types of socio-economic area, mortality rates increasing with level of deprivation. However, this gradient is less steep in London. Inner-deprived areas of the capital have a CHD mortality rate for those aged under 65 years which is 16 per cent lower than comparable areas in the rest of the country; the difference when high-status areas are compared is just five per cent.

Furthermore, the mortality rate in London for those aged under 65 years is only five per cent less than that of the rest of England, whereas the difference for the 65-74 age-group is 13 per cent.

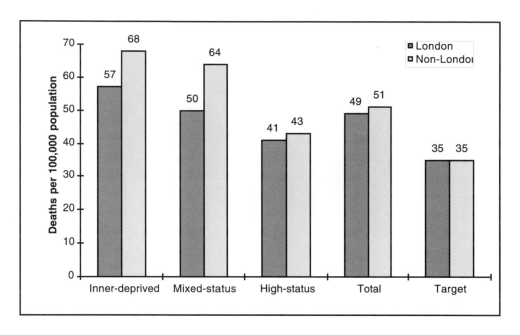

Figure 13: Mortality rate from CHD, for people aged under 65 years, London and England, 1993 (target = 35 per 100,000 by the year 2000)

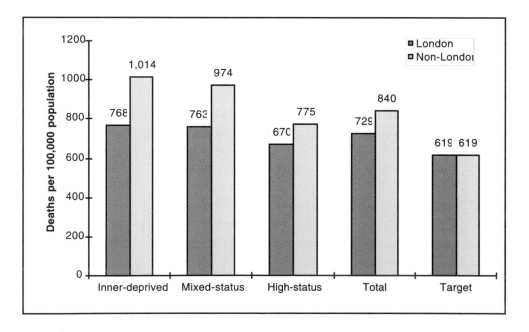

Figure 14: Mortality rate from CHD, for the 65-74 age-group, London and England, 1993 (target = 619 per 100,000 by the year 2000)

Figure 15 shows the mortality rate from stroke for those aged under 65; Figure 16 shows the same rate for those in the 65-74 age-group. Again, the greatest mortality rates tend to be in inner-deprived areas, both in London and the rest of England. An exception is stroke for those in the 65-74 age-group where there are seven more deaths per 100,000 population in high-status London than in inner-deprived areas of the capital – 206 compared with 199 deaths. London has a slightly greater mortality rate than other parts of the country for those aged under 65 years – 12.3 compared with 11.2 deaths per 100,000 population. However, the mortality rate in London is still less for the older age-groups when compared with the rest of England. For example, for those in the 65-74 age-group London has a mortality rate of 199 deaths per 100,000 compared with 222 in the rest of England.

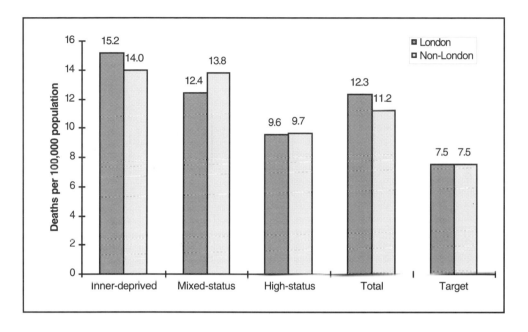

Figure 15: Mortality rate from stroke, for people aged under 65 years, London and England, 1993 (target = 7.5 per 100,000 by the year 2000)

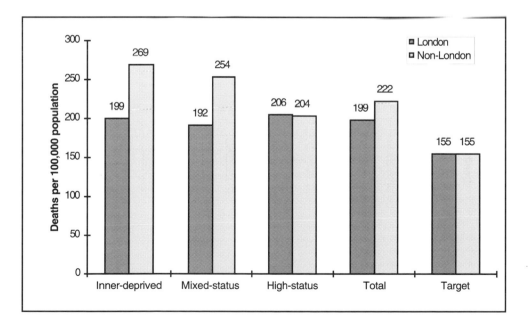

Figure 16: Mortality rate from stroke, for the 65-74 age-group, London and England, 1993 (target = 155 per 100,000 by the year 2000)

Lung cancer

As Figure 17 shows, the target mortality rate for lung cancer, in contrast to those for CHD and stroke, has been achieved by both London and the rest of England as a whole. Both high- and mixed-status London areas have reached the target. London as a whole has approximately the same mortality rate as the rest of the country – 38 compared with 37 deaths per 100,000 population – but has lower rates in both inner-deprived and mixed-status areas.

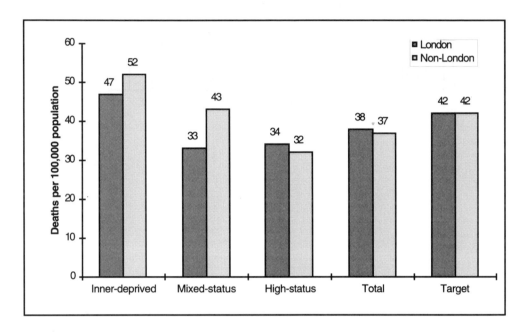

Figure 17: Mortality rate from lung cancer, for those aged 75 years and over, London and England, 1993 (target = 42 per 100,000 by the year 2000)

Suicide

Figure 18 shows a lower mortality rate from suicide in London when compared with the rest of the country, for all types of socio-economic area except inner-deprived. Moreover, only inner-deprived areas of London fail to meet the Health of the Nation target of 9.4 deaths per 100,000 population.

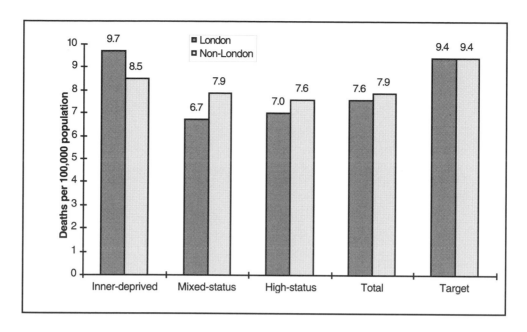

Figure 18: Mortality rate from suicide, London and England, 1993
(target = 9.4 per 100,000 by the year 2000)

5 Socio-economic indicators

We conclude this chapter by considering a number of socio-economic indicators of London's
population which are commonly related to the use of health services. These include the
UPA8 score and the York acute and psychiatric needs indices.

Under Privileged Area (UPA8) score

One measure of the level of socio-economic deprivation in London is the Under Privileged
Area (UPA8) score. This measure, constructed by the Department of General Practice at
St Mary's Medical School, reflects the following:

• Older people living alone;

• Lone parent households;

• Children aged under five;

• Proportion of workforce unskilled;

• Unemployment;

• Overcrowding;

• Proportion of the population that moved recently;

• Proportion of the population belonging to minority ethnic groups.

Data are based on the 1991 Census, and hence reflect the DHAs and local authority wards
at that time.

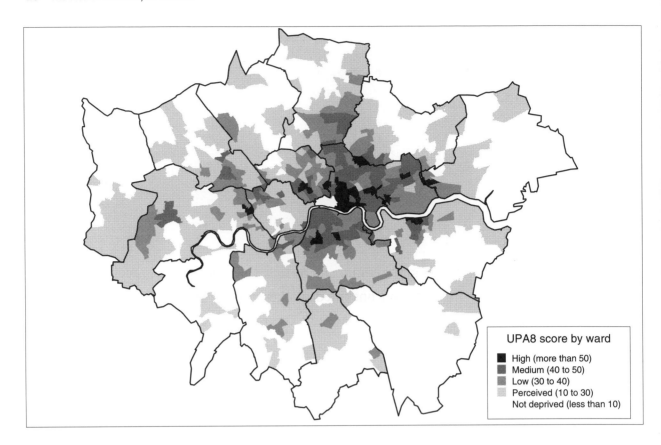

UPA8 score by ward

■ High (more than 50)
■ Medium (40 to 50)
■ Low (30 to 40)
■ Perceived (10 to 30)
  Not deprived (less than 10)

Map 9: Underprivileged Area Score (UPA8), by London LA ward, 1991

Map 9 shows the range of UPA8 scores in London. UPA8 scores of more than 30, 40 and 50 attract three bands of deprivation payment for GPs. These are shown by the three deeper shades on the map. The most deprived areas in London are concentrated in a crescent in the east of the capital. This stretches from the north of Lambeth and Southwark, through Tower Hamlets, Newham and Hackney, and reaches the eastern part of Haringey. A particular pocket of deprivation is found in the west of Tower Hamlets and the south of Hackney, just east of the city. This is centred on Spitalfields which is the most deprived ward in the capital using the UPA8 score.

Apart from this area, the most deprived wards tend to appear singly, although usually surrounded by comparatively deprived areas. Other areas of deprivation are in Greenwich, in the north of Hammersmith and Kensington, stretching into Brent, and in the south of Camden and Islington, around King's Cross.

However, research by the Department of General Practice at St. Mary's suggests that GPs perceive they are working in a deprived area if the UPA8 score is 10 or above. These are also indicated on the map. Although 220 of London's 786 wards have UPA8 scores of over 30, a further 305 have scores of between 10 and 30: GPs perceive these wards as deprived, but they do not attract payments. The map shows that deprivation on this definition is more widespread across London, though deprivation attracting payments is concentrated in the east. For example, only 13 out of 67 wards in Ealing, Hammersmith and Hounslow are deprived enough to attract deprivation payments, yet a further 47 wards have UPA8 scores of over 10. Likewise, in Merton, Sutton and Wandsworth, only seven out of 68 wards attract payments, but a further 34 are deprived on this different definition.

Components of deprivation

Socio-economic conditions are not identical in areas with similar UPA8 scores. Table 4 shows the components of deprivation of the ten wards with the highest UPA8 scores in London vary considerably. Thus, Spitalfields has very high scores on proportion of minority ethnic population, unemployment and overcrowding, while its elderly alone and lone parent household scores are lower than the national average. By contrast, Liddle with a similar UPA8 score has lower minority ethnic and overcrowding scores but much higher scores for lone parent households and unskilled workers. Similarly, Weavers ward in Tower Hamlets and Gascoigne ward in Barking have almost identical UPA8 scores but a different composition of factors.

This analysis shows that socio-economic deprivation is not a single phenomenon, but a combination of a number of factors which may differ in importance and impact. All deprived areas are not the same.

Table 4: UPA8 scores and component variables, ten most deprived wards in London, 1991

Local Authority	Ward	Elderly Alone	Under 5	Lone Parent	Unskilled	Unem- ployed	Over- crowded	Moved	Minority Ethnic	UPA8
T.Hamlets	Spitalfields	4.03	11.93	2.81	2.94	33.12	56.99	9.74	72.90	68.40
Southwark	Liddle	3.37	12.01	17.70	8.19	31.03	22.21	9.60	37.74	64.31
T.Hamlets	St Dunstan's	6.34	11.55	6.84	4.54	27.28	38.28	6.93	44.69	63.71
Camden	King's Cross	8.17	8.54	6.03	7.24	21.96	22.38	25.21	24.81	62.32
T.Hamlets	Holy Trinity	6.81	9.78	7.29	6.92	24.58	29.23	8.96	31.54	57.80
Greenwich	St Mary's	8.41	10.99	16.43	5.03	23.84	10.04	12.53	9.76	57.37
T.Hamlets	St Mary's	6.38	9.44	2.71	3.84	19.38	37.99	14.73	50.74	56.36
T.Hamlets	Weavers	7.27	9.43	6.71	4.00	24.89	30.81	8.03	34.16	55.15
Barking	Gascoigne	6.35	14.77	15.63	7.29	17.91	8.01	12.51	4.94	55.07
T.Hamlets	Shadwell	4.24	10.77	5.57	3.30	22.15	36.20	14.85	43.12	54.59
England and Wales	Mean	6.04	6.35	3.36	2.61	8.11	3.63	9.52	3.33	0.00

(Table 4 is ordered by UPA8 score.)

National comparisons

This section compares UPA8 scores and their component variables for different types of socio-economic area in London with similar areas in the rest of the country. These are presented as weighted mean scores of 1991 DHAs in each type of area. We would expect, and find, a clear gradient in the UPA8 score across types of socio-economic area. Figure 19 shows that London as a whole has a higher level of deprivation, on the basis of UPA8 score, than similar areas in the rest of England. However, there is some variation across type of area, with mixed-status and high-status areas in London appearing more deprived than their counterparts elsewhere, and inner-deprived areas less so. This analysis is based on a set of socio-economic groupings which were derived for the first London Commission (King's Fund, 1992). These are given in Appendix 3.

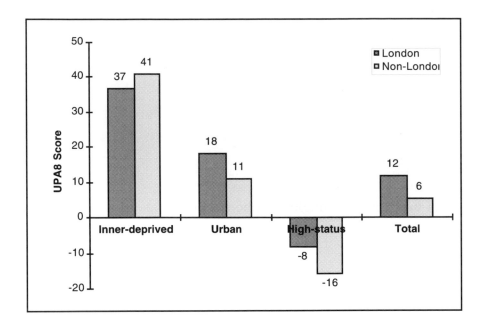

Figure 19: Mean UPA8 score, London and England, 1991

Table 5 compares average values for the components of the UPA8 score, by type of area in London and England. London tends to record higher scores on minority ethnic, recent change of address and overcrowding, but lower on unemployment, unskilled workers, lone parent households and children under five.

Table 5: Mean score for UPA8 component variables, London and England, 1991

Component	London				Non-London			
	Inner-deprived	Mixed-status	High-status	Total	Inner-deprived	Mixed-status	High-status	Total
Elderly living alone	6.2	5.7	6.0	6.0	6.5	6.3	5.7	6.1
Under 5	7.3	7.3	6.5	6.9	8.2	7.1	6.5	7.0
Lone parent households	7.7	5.5	3.1	5.1	8.5	5.1	3.1	4.8
Unskilled	3.5	3.3	1.9	2.7	3.8	3.3	2.0	2.9
Unemployed	16.3	11.1	7.1	11.1	18.8	11.1	6.9	10.6
Overcrowded	12.5	8.7	4.5	8.0	9.9	5.5	3.2	5.2
Moved	13.3	10.6	10.0	11.3	10.2	9.3	9.0	9.3
Minority ethnic	21.7	18.9	9.8	15.4	15.0	5.4	3.7	5.9

Acute and psychiatric needs indices

We conclude this section by considering the acute and psychiatric needs indices which are used as a basis of the Department of Health's allocation formula for the distribution of funding to DHAs for Hospital and Community Health Services. These needs indices were developed by a group of researchers at the University of York and are discussed more fully in *'A Formula for Distributing NHS Revenues Based on Small Area Use of Hospital Beds'*

(Carr-Hill *et al*, 1994). We consider variation in the indices and their component variables across local authority wards in London.

Acute needs index

The following variables are included in the acute needs index:

- Standardised Mortality Ratio (SMR) aged 0-74 years;

- Standardised Illness Ratio (SIR) aged 0-74 years;

- proportion of those of pensionable age living alone;

- proportion of dependants in single carer households;

- proportion of economically active unemployed.

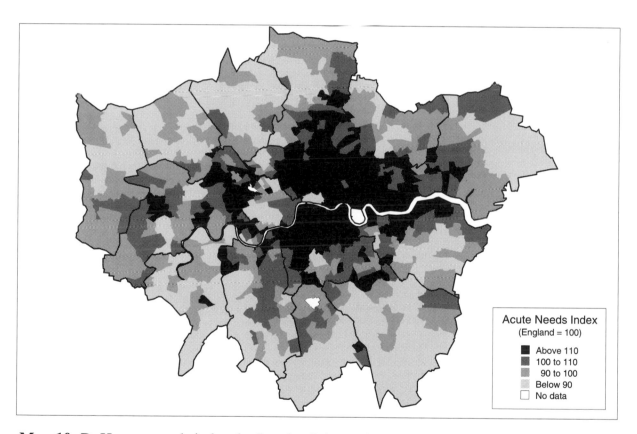

Acute Needs Index
(England = 100)

- ■ Above 110
- ▨ 100 to 110
- ▦ 90 to 100
- ░ Below 90
- □ No data

Map 10: DoH acute needs index, by London LA ward, 1991

Map 10 shows the acute needs index, by ward of London, where England equals 100. Perhaps unsurprisingly, this reveals a similar pattern to that of the UPA8 score in Map 9. Northern parts of Lambeth, Southwark and Lewisham, the whole of the boroughs of Hackney, Tower Hamlets and Newham and the eastern half of Haringey form a 'crescent of deprivation'. However, higher levels of need are also present in almost all of Islington and much of Camden. Other areas of need are revealed in west London – in the north of Kensington and Hammersmith and in Brent – and in Greenwich, particularly on the south bank of the Thames. However, it is clear that East London and the City, and Lambeth, Southwark and Lewisham DHAs have the greatest need for acute services on the basis of this indicator: twenty of the thirty wards recording the highest value in the capital are in these districts.

In comparison with the rest of England, London as a whole appears close to the national average – indexed to 100 in our analysis. There are 381 wards with an index greater than 100, and 380 with an index less than 100. This, however, masks great variation within London. The ward with the greatest level of acute need, St Mary's in Greenwich, has an index of 132 whereas that with the smallest level, Cheam South in Sutton, has an index of just 71.

■ Components of acute need

We noted in the section above on the UPA8 score that wards with similar scores do not necessarily have a similar composition of the component indicators of need. Table 6 shows this is true also of the acute needs index. For example, the four Hackney wards that feature in the ten London wards with the greatest acute needs index have greater standardised illness ratios, but their SMRs tend to be less than in the other wards.

This variation confirms that need depends on a combination of factors which may differ in importance and impact from area to area. However, there is less variation in these component measures of acute need than was the case with the UPA8 score. Thus, none of the ten wards has a score for any component variable which is less than the national average.

Table 6: Acute needs index and component variables, ten most deprived wards in London, 1994/95

Local Authority	Ward	Index	SMR 0-74	SIR 0-74	Old Alone %	Single carer %	Unem-ployed %
Greenwich	St Mary's	132	171	157	47	34	24
Brent	Carlton	131	161	156	47	41	22
Hackney	Queensbridge	130	158	164	41	32	27
Newham	Ordnance	130	137	163	48	37	28
Kensington & Chelsea	Golborne	130	153	156	50	32	24
Hackney	King's Park	129	138	160	49	36	27
Hackney	Eastdown	128	127	174	43	31	28
Southwark	Consort	128	138	159	44	35	25
Hackney	Haggerston	127	140	160	42	32	26
Lambeth	Vassall	127	164	139	44	39	23
England		100	100	100	33	20	9

(Table 6 is ordered by acute needs index.)

Psychiatric needs index

The following variables are included in the psychiatric needs index:

• Standardised Mortality Ratio (SMR) aged 0-74 years;

• proportion of population in households headed by a lone parent;

• proportion of dependants with no carer;

• proportion of those of pensionable age living alone;

• proportion of population born in the New Commonwealth;

• proportion of adult population who are permanently sick.

Map 11 shows the psychiatric needs index, by ward of London, where England equals 100. The distribution of areas in London with greatest psychiatric needs is similar to that for the acute index. Again, the 'crescent of deprivation' to the east of the City of London is apparent, as is the Kensington, Hammersmith and Brent cluster. However, at the individual ward level there is much greater variation from the England average than was the case for the acute index. Whereas no London ward has an acute needs index greater than 132, there are 250 wards which have a psychiatric index greater than this value. Overall there are 450 wards in London where the psychiatric needs index is above the national average.

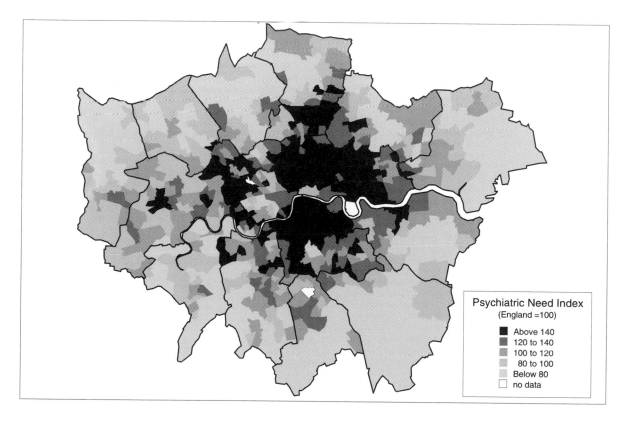

Map 11: DoH psychiatric needs index, by London LA ward, 1991

■ Components of psychiatric need

Table 7 shows there is some variation in the composition of the component indicators of need for wards which attain similar levels on the psychiatric needs index. The variable where there is greatest variation, even when just the ten most deprived wards in London are considered, is the proportion of residents born in the New Commonwealth. This takes a value in St. Mary's in Greenwich which is less than a third of that in King's Park, Hackney.

Table 7: Psychiatric needs index and component variables, ten most deprived wards in London, 1994/95

Local Authority	Ward	Index	SMR 0-74	Old Alone %	Lone Parent %	New Common-wealth %	No Carer %	Perm-anently Sick %
Brent	Carlton	242	161	47	37	18	22	7
Kensington & Chelsea	Golborne	207	153	50	25	12	17	7
Westminster	Queen's Park	203	131	44	26	16	18	7
Southwark	Consort	201	138	44	28	15	22	6
Hackney	King's Park	200	138	49	27	20	16	6
Newham	Ordnance	200	137	48	30	10	18	7
Hammersmith & Fulham	White City & Shepherds Bush	198	148	47	30	16	16	6
Hackney	Chatham	198	133	41	31	15	21	6
Greenwich	St Mary's	197	171	47	31	6	22	6
Lambeth	Vassall	196	164	44	30	15	15	5

(Table 7 is ordered by psychiatric needs index.)

The psychiatric need index in Carlton ward in Brent is a full 35 points higher than any other London ward. Only 11 points separate the next nine wards. This high score in Carlton ward reflects consistently high scores in each variable.

There are seven wards which feature in the ten most deprived, measured in terms of either the psychiatric or acute needs indices. However, only one, St. Mary's in Greenwich, is among the ten wards with the highest UPA8 score as well. This analysis of needs at a highly disaggregated geographic level reveals both similarities and differences when some of the more commonly used indicators of need are considered.

Chapter 2

Hospital Admissions

Summary

Hospital provision

- Although just 14 per cent of the population of England live in London, 16 per cent of hospital activity nationally, as measured by FCEs, is produced in the capital's hospitals.

- London provides a greater proportion of elective compared to emergency care than elsewhere in the country: 54 per cent of activity is elective compared with 51 per cent in the rest of England. Hospitals in inner-deprived areas, whether in London or outside, provide proportionately more elective care: 58 per cent in the case of London and 55 per cent in similar areas elsewhere in England.

- The proportion of total activity provided as day cases is higher in London than elsewhere in the country: 31 compared to 26 per cent. The higher day case rate in London is driven by two factors: a higher proportion of elective cases (54:51) and a higher day case rate among these elective cases (57:51).

- The proportion of elective activity varies across London: in north-west London 59 per cent of total activity is elective; in the east just 50 per cent is.

- On the other hand, hospitals in inner-deprived areas of London perform more elective procedures, but a lower proportion of these are treated as day cases than in London as a whole.

- There has been a significant increase in the proportion of day case activity in England since 1989/90, from 18 to 26 per cent. However, in 1989/90 London had a similar rate to England, whereas the rate is now substantially more in the capital, particularly in north-west London where it is 36 per cent.

- There is a degree of concentration on certain specialties in London hospitals, both as a whole and by sector of the capital. Thus, 22 per cent of all national haematology FCEs occur in London, and 18 per cent of anaesthetics and medicine. By contrast, the proportions are 13 per cent for orthopaedics and geriatrics and 14 per cent for ENT and psychiatric.

- The proportion, by specialty, of elective FCEs in London is fairly similar to that of the rest of England except for: medicine where the ratios to total activity are 45 and 34 per cent respectively; paediatrics with ratios of 17 and 12 per cent; and, geriatrics where London has just five per cent elective admissions compared to 12 per cent in the rest of the county.

- 59 per cent of psychiatric episodes in London are emergency compared with 55 per cent in England as a whole. Moreover, London has a higher proportion of transfers between hospitals in the psychiatric specialty.

- The north-west sector of London has a higher proportion of day cases than London as a whole in most specialties: in medicine 40 per cent are day cases compared with 30 per cent in London as a whole.

- London has a higher proportion of day cases than the rest of England in all specialties except orthopaedics and geriatrics. The difference in medicine episodes is substantial – 30 compared to 21 per cent are performed as day cases.

- On the other hand, hospitals in inner-deprived areas of London have a lower day case rate than that of comparable parts of England, especially in the surgical specialties and paediatrics.

- There are differences in the age distribution of patients treated, both between sectors of London, and between London and the rest of England: overall, London hospitals treat a younger group of patients even when viewed on a specialty-by-specialty basis.

- In London only 46 per cent of ophthalmology FCEs are for those aged over 65 years, compared with 56 per cent in the rest of England. Similarly, in London just 17 per cent of psychiatric episodes are for those aged over 65 years compared with 26 per cent in the rest of England.

- An exception is medicine for older people. In London, 69 per cent of episodes in this specialty are for those aged 75 and over compared with 59 per cent outside the capital. A younger sub-group of the population appears to be treated by geriatricians outside the capital.

- London has a higher proportion of elective admissions than the rest of the country for almost every age-group. The exception is those aged 75 years and over, and especially those over 85 years where the London elective proportion of 17 per cent compares with an England figure of 21 per cent.

Other issues

- The FCE measures periods under the care of a consultant in one trust provider, and not the number of admissions to hospitals. On average there are eight per cent more episodes than admissions in England as a whole. However, data recording practices may vary both over time and between trusts.

- London as a whole has a lower rate of episode inflation than the rest of the country, six compared with eight per cent. However, the ratio in inner-deprived areas of London is greater than that in comparable areas elsewhere in the country, whereas that in mixed-status and high-status areas is significantly lower.

- The episode-to-admission ratio tends to be very low for elective admissions, but higher for emergencies: emergency episode inflation for England as a whole is 14 per cent.

- Similarly, the inflation rate for day cases is virtually negligible whereas the in-patient rate is approximately ten per cent for England as a whole.

- There is some variation in episode inflation across sectors of London with the figure for emergency admissions ranging from eight per cent in the south east to 16 per cent in the east, and for in-patient cases, from six per cent in the south east to 11 per cent in the east.

- In London, the proportion of episodes which are transfers between hospitals, in most specialties, is relatively small and similar to that in the rest of England.

- However, significant differences occur for two specialties: seven per cent of psychiatric episodes are transfers in the rest of England compared with 11 per cent in London; the position is reversed for geriatric episodes where four per cent of episodes are transfers in London compared with seven per cent in England as a whole.

- The destination of patients on discharge from hospital is similar across sectors of London and between London and England. However, differences emerge when the hospital population is considered by age-group. Throughout the country, the proportion of discharges home falls with age.

- There are more deaths per hospital admission among those aged 85 years and over in London when compared with the rest of England: 19 compared to 16 per cent. The figures for other age-groups are broadly comparable.

- A greater proportion of episodes in London involve an operative procedure compared with the rest of England: 56 compared with 54 per cent. This holds for emergency FCEs, but London has a slightly smaller proportion of elective episodes involving an operative procedure than the rest of the country.

- Sixty per cent of operative elective FCEs are performed as day cases in London: the rate varies from 57 per cent in the east and north-central sectors to 66 per cent in the south. This compares with just 53 per cent in the rest of England.

Key Facts

Hospital provision	*London*	*Rest of England*
Total hospital provision:	1,468,000 FCEs	7,922,000 FCEs
Expressed as a proportion of the national total:	16%	84%
Proportion of elective FCEs:	54%	51%
Day case rate:	31%	26%
Day case rate for elective FCEs:	57%	51%

Specialties

The largest specialty groups:

• Medicine	415,000 (28%)	23%
• Surgery and urology	324,000 (22%)	23%
• Obstetrics and Gynaecology	212,000 (14%)	13%
• Orthopaedics	106,000 (7%)	9%
• Paediatrics	79,000 (5%)	6%
• Geriatrics	74,000 (5%)	6%

Age-groups

Total FCEs provided, by age-group:

• 0-14	218,000 (15%)	15%
• 15-64	906,000 (62%)	58%
• 65+	344,000 (23%)	27%

Diagnoses

Most common broad diagnoses of FCEs:

• Cancer	11%	10%
• Urinary diseases	9%	9%
• Digestive diseases	9%	10%

Other issues

Episode-to-admission ratio

The episode-to-admission ratio:

• All admissions	1.06	1.08
• Emergency admissions	1.12	1.15
• Elective admissions	1.01	1.03

Operative procedures

Proportion of FCEs involving an operative procedure:	56%	54%
Proportion of elective operative FCEs:	77%	78%
Day case rate for operative FCEs:	46%	42%

Specialties with the greatest number of FCEs involving an operative procedure (percentage of specialty total in parenthesis):

• Surgery and urology	253,000 (78%)	78%
• Medicine	172,000 (41%)	36%
• Obstetrics and Gynaecology	128,000 (61%)	56%
• Orthopaedics	78,000 (73%)	74%
• Ophthalmology	46,000 (91%)	91%
• ENT	43,000 (80%)	87%

1 Introduction

This chapter provides a detailed analysis of admissions to London hospitals. Sections are included on:

- in-patient and day case activity;

- the distinction between FCEs and hospital admissions;

- transfer admissions and discharge destination; and,

- operative procedures carried out in London.

Activity is measured in finished consultant episodes (FCEs) and classified by type of admission (emergency or elective), the specialty the patient was admitted into, the diagnosis of patient (according to broad diagnosis groups), and the age of the patient.

2 Data sources

Hospital admission data are taken from the Department of Health (DoH) Hospital Episode System (HES) database. Data refer to 1994/95 and both acute hospital and community trusts are included.

3 Hospital provision

This section compares the provision of FCEs in London hospitals, both across sectors of London and with similar areas in the rest of England. A provider perspective is adopted indicating what London supplies in terms of FCEs, and considering in various ways the composition of this supply. This is related to services provided to London's resident population in Chapter 3, '*Hospital Utilisation Rates*'. The following basic analyses are presented: the total number of FCEs in London and elsewhere; the proportion of in-patients and day cases; and, the proportion by admission method (i.e. whether emergency, elective, maternity or other). We also consider the proportion of elective work that is day case, and the effect of this on the overall day case rate.

FCEs are considered at three further levels. First, by the specialty group of the episode, e.g. general surgery or ophthalmology. Specialties are analysed both in terms of the absolute number of FCEs and as two proportions: the specialty as a proportion of the total work in each geographic area, and the quantity of FCEs in the specialty as a proportion of the England total. Proportions of each specialty by admission method and by day case are also presented.

These analyses by specialty group are repeated at two other levels of analysis: the provision of FCEs by age-group and by diagnosis group.

Total FCEs in London and England

As Table 1 shows, there are more FCEs provided in the northern sectors of London than those south of the Thames. This is unsurprising as there are more trusts in north London than south of the river. The highest total of FCEs are produced in the north-west sector which has both the greatest population and the most trusts (19) including some with the largest number of FCEs in the capital, e.g. St. Mary's or the Hammersmith. By contrast, the south sector has the smallest population and only five major acute hospital trusts.

Table 1: Total FCEs in London, 1994/95

Sector	North West	North Central	East	South East	South	London
Total FCEs	397,621	276,225	291,666	284,693	217,764	1,467,969

Comparisons with the rest of the country reveal little at this very aggregated level, but as Figure 1 shows, London hospitals produce around 16 per cent of the national total of FCEs. This compares with just over 14 per cent of the population of England living in London. This may be due to a number of factors: the location of more hospitals per capita in London than elsewhere; the lower provision of other forms of health and social care; a greater need for hospital care among London's population; and the fact that London is a net exporter of care to the rest of the country. For example, hospitals in inner-deprived London, home to a number of major teaching hospitals, provide six per cent of all FCEs in England. In the case of some clinical specialties, the proportion is even higher.

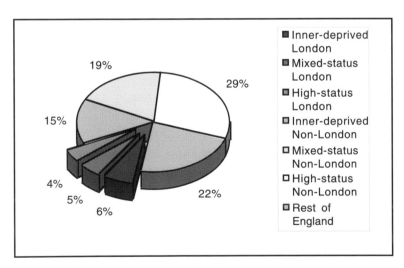

(Percentages may not sum exactly due to rounding.)

Figure 1: Proportion of total England FCEs, by type of area, 1994/95

FCEs by admission method

(Technical note: this section considers the method by which patients were admitted for an FCE. The HES database has a number of codes for admission method which can be grouped as Emergency, Elective, Maternity and Other (transfers from other hospitals). There is also a code for unknown, but this is a very

small percentage of FCEs and has been ignored for the purposes of this chapter. Our particular interest in this section is with emergency and elective admissions. Transfers are dealt with in the section on transfers below. Maternity admission data are complex but those referred to here do <u>not</u> include birth and delivery episodes. This is considered further in Box 1.)

Table 2 shows the proportion of FCEs by admission method in each sector of London. Emergency and elective admissions account for over 90 per cent of all FCEs in London hospitals. There is some variation between sectors: the north west has a high proportion of elective admissions and an unusually low proportion of emergencies. This higher level of elective admission in the north west may reflect the combination of major teaching hospitals and three former SHAs (the Hammersmith, the Royal Brompton and the Royal Marsden), which by their nature are likely to carry out more elective procedures, often of a complex nature, and have fewer emergency admissions than the typical local district general hospital (DGH).

Table 2: Proportion of FCEs, by admission method, by sector of London, 1994/95

Admission Method	North West	North Central	East	South East	South	London
	%	%	%	%	%	%
Elective	59	53	50	52	51	54
Emergency	35	38	43	40	39	39
Maternity	4	6	5	5	6	5
Other	2	3	1	3	3	2

(Tables 2 and 3 are ordered by admission method in London with greatest proportion of FCEs.)

Box 1: Maternity admissions

It is important to understand what is meant by maternity admissions in this report. The HES system contains four basic types of episode: general episodes; delivery episodes; birth episodes and formally detained mental health episodes which can only be used for unfinished episodes. Only general episodes are included in this chapter; thus delivery and birth episodes are excluded. Essentially, each time a birth occurs two episodes are recorded, one for the birth (well babies) and one for the delivery. Birth and delivery episodes add an additional 180,000 episodes in London and 980,000 in the rest of the country. The maternity admissions therefore only include activity involving pregnant women which does not involve delivery or birth. 95 per cent of these episodes are in the childbirth, V-code or ill-defined diagnosis groups. Examples of common diagnoses are complications of pregnancy, early threatened labour and perineal trauma. Therefore, the fact that these episodes are recorded as maternity admissions does not imply that they refer to a delivery or birth episode. They are a mixture of episodes, some of which may be similar to emergencies. For simplicity of analysis we have chosen to exclude them from detailed discussion.

Considering the proportion of admissions by type of socio-economic area, in both London and the rest of England, the highest rates of elective admission are in inner-deprived areas where major teaching and single specialty hospitals tend to be located. London as a whole has a higher proportion of elective FCEs when compared with the rest of England. This results from the higher relative rate in both inner-deprived and mixed-status areas. There is a higher rate of maternity admissions in mixed-status London (seven per cent) than elsewhere (four to five per cent).

Table 3: Proportion of FCEs by admission method, London and England, 1994/95

Admission Method	London				Non-London				England
	Inner-deprived	Mixed-status	High-status	Total	Inner-deprived	Mixed-status	High-status	Total	
	%	%	%	%	%	%	%	%	%
Elective	58	52	50	54	55	48	50	51	51
Emergency	35	39	43	39	36	45	43	42	42
Maternity	4	7	5	5	4	5	4	4	4
Other	3	2	2	2	3	2	3	3	3

The day case rate

(Technical note: as well as in-patient and day case, HES provides a code 5 – other maternity. HES documentation notes that this should no longer be used, and the number of records with this code are indeed tiny. Therefore, we have excluded 'other maternity' from this analysis.)

In recent years there has been a drive to increase the proportion of activity performed as day cases. A number of factors have contributed including the Audit Commission report, *'All in a day's work'* (Audit Commission, 1992), the Royal College of Surgeon's recommendation that 50 per cent of elective surgery could be carried out as day cases, and a belief that day cases are often more cost-effective than in-patient treatment.

As Figure 2 indicates, the highest rate for day cases in London is in the north-west sector – 36 per cent: in London as whole the rate is 31 per cent. This high proportion of day cases is linked to the higher proportion of elective admissions in this sector. In fact every emergency admission should be recorded as an in-patient case although in practice there are a few which are recorded incorrectly. It is therefore unsurprising that the north-west sector, with the highest proportion of elective admissions in London, also has the highest proportion of day cases. This link is illustrated clearly below.

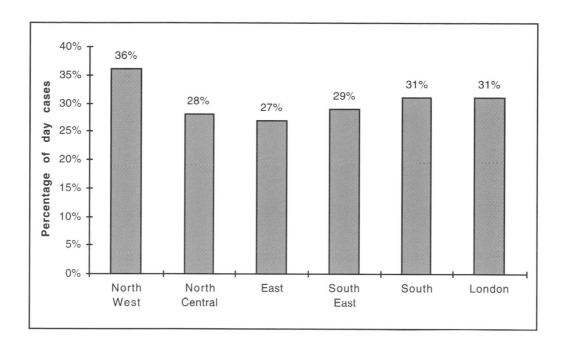

Figure 2: Proportion of day cases, by sector of London, 1994/95

In comparison with the rest of England, Figure 3 shows London has a higher proportion of activity carried out as day cases – 31 to 26 per cent. This is a significant change from the situation in 1989/90, reported by the previous London Commission, when London as a whole had a similar proportion of day case activity, and inner-deprived and mixed-status London had lower rates than comparable areas in the rest of the country. While across the country there has been an increase in the proportion of FCEs carried out as day cases, the more rapid increase has been in London. Recent concerns about the provision of emergency care in London's hospitals may reflect an over-concentration on increasing elective care, and particularly elective day cases, at the expense of the availability of emergency care in the capital. To assess this requires further detailed investigation.

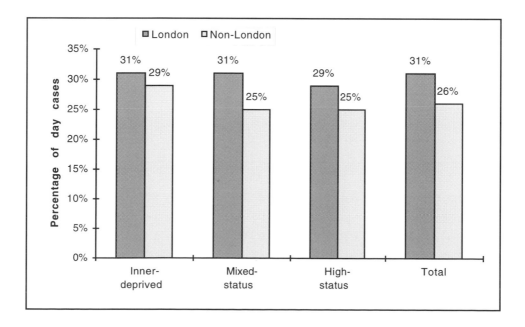

Figure 3: Proportion of day cases, London and England, 1994/95

Furthermore, in London, as in the rest of England, there is a higher proportion of day case activity in more deprived areas. This is more likely to reflect the nature of the hospitals in these areas rather than the deprivation present among the population. We would expect that to mitigate in the opposite direction. Nevertheless, the situation has changed since 1989/90 when high-status areas in London had the greatest day case rates, and the rest of England had the same rate regardless of the socio-economic status of the area.

The relation between elective admissions and day case rate

The proportion of total work carried out as day cases (and this is the figure most often quoted in national reports) depends on two factors: the proportion of elective work, which gives the proportion of total episodes that effectively *can* be carried out as day cases; and the day case rate for these elective episodes. Figure 4 shows that the proportion of elective FCEs in London which are carried out as day cases is over 50 per cent in all sectors.

The north-west sector has both the highest proportion of elective admissions, 59 per cent against 54 per cent for London as a whole, and the highest day case rate for these elective admissions, 61 per cent against 57 per cent for the whole of London. It is therefore unsurprising that the north west has the highest proportion of day cases – 36 per cent compared with 31 per cent in London as a whole.

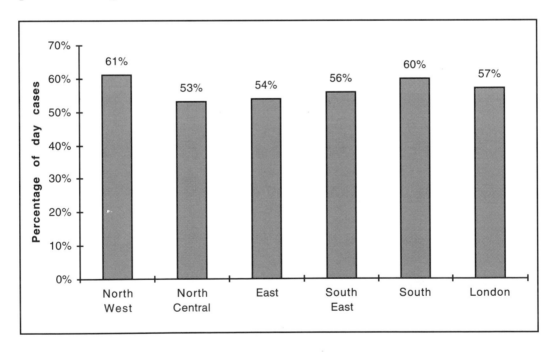

Figure 4: Proportion of elective FCEs that are day cases, by sector of London, 1994/95

On the other hand, a mixed picture emerges when the high day case rate in inner-deprived areas of London is examined in more detail. The high rate is due to a high proportion of elective activity (as Table 3 makes clear) and not the proportion of elective activity carried out as day cases. In fact, Figure 5 shows inner-deprived London has the lowest proportion of elective work carried out as day cases in London. The high day case rate is due entirely to a higher total proportion of elective work, which compensates for the lower proportion of this carried out as day cases. This is consistent with the more specialised nature of hospitals in central London. These are more likely to carry out specialist treatments less suited to be performed as day cases than the more routine treatments at DGHs. Nevertheless, as Figure 5 also shows, in London as a whole, a higher proportion of elective work is carried out as day cases than in comparable parts of the country: this reflects primarily the effect of hospitals in mixed- and high-status areas.

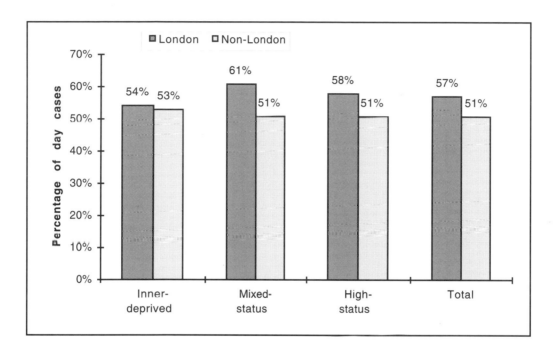

Figure 5: Proportion of elective FCEs that are day cases, London and England, 1994/95

The specialty composition of FCEs

This section takes a more detailed perspective on activity, considering the position with respect to key specialty groups. These have been constructed following classifications used for the Health Service Indicators (DoH, 1995a). For further information on these see Appendix 4.

Total activity

Table 4 shows the composition of activity in London for each of the specialty groups. Over 75 per cent of activity is in five specialty groups: medicine, surgery and urology, obstetrics and gynaecology, orthopaedics and paediatrics. It was noted above that north-west London provides the largest number of FCEs. At the specialty level the effect of individual specialist hospitals can be seen. For example, the north west has over 135,000 FCEs in the largest specialty group, medicine, nearly twice that of any other sector. This is partially explained by the location of a number of specialist hospitals for medical sub-specialties in this sector – the Royal Marsden (medical oncology), the Royal Brompton (thoracic medicine) and Harefield (cardiology). In a similar way the north-central sector has a large number of FCEs in ENT (the RNTNE) and haematology (UCLH and the Royal Free Hampstead). The east has over twice as many ophthalmology FCEs as any other sector: this is due to Moorfields.

Table 4: FCEs by specialty, by sector of London, 1994/95

Specialty Group	North West	North Central	East	South East	South	London
Medicine	136,209	66,842	78,237	77,564	56,031	414,882
Surgery/Urology	81,681	61,633	58,515	68,735	53,558	324,123
Obs. and Gynae.	51,595	42,049	46,620	38,183	33,102	211,550
Orthopaedics	33,153	18,824	20,123	20,195	13,764	106,060
Paediatrics	17,383	14,806	12,180	19,328	15,017	78,714
Geriatrics	16,668	16,586	14,987	13,793	11,607	73,642
ENT	11,484	15,096	10,052	9,579	7,469	53,679
Ophthalmology	9,483	5,231	21,704	7,806	6,970	51,194
Psychiatric	8,713	6,486	7,321	8,499	9,100	40,120
Haematology	6,194	12,840	11,023	5,665	2,417	38,140
Dental	8,101	4,208	6,188	8,550	6,568	33,615
Other non-acute	12,463	9,717	2,239	1,061	780	26,260
Anaesthetics	2,754	1,845	2,474	5,671	1,380	14,125
Total	397,621	276,225	291,666	284,693	217,764	1,467,969

(Tables 4-7 are ordered by size of specialty in London.)

(Technical note: the 'Other non-acute' group consists of GP beds; the '800' series of non-acute specialties such as clinical oncology, radiology, general pathology etc.; and community and occupational medicine. These are all defined by the HSI handbook as non-acute.)

Proportion of total FCEs by specialty

The proportion of total activity due to a particular specialty varies across sectors of London, and between London and the rest of the country. Thus, as Table 5 shows, medicine is a higher proportion of total activity in the north-west sector – 34 per cent of all activity compared with 28 per cent in London as a whole. A similar situation is shown for ENT and haematology in the north-central sector and ophthalmology in east London. Again, this reflects the effect of specialist hospitals.

Table 5: Proportion of FCEs in specialty groups, by sector of London, 1994/95

Specialty Group	North West %	North Central %	East %	South East %	South %	London %
Medicine	34	24	27	27	26	28
Surgery/Urology	21	22	20	24	25	22
Obs. and Gynae.	13	15	16	13	15	14
Orthopaedics	8	7	7	7	6	7
Paediatrics	4	5	4	7	7	5
Geriatrics	4	6	5	5	5	5
ENT	3	5	3	3	3	4
Ophthalmology	2	2	7	3	3	3
Psychiatric	2	2	3	3	4	3
Haematology	2	5	4	2	1	3
Dental	2	2	2	3	3	2
Other non-acute	3	4	1	0	0	2
Anaesthetics	1	1	1	2	1	1
Total	100	100	100	100	100	100

Table 6 compares London with the rest of England and reveals that 28 per cent of total activity in London as a whole is in the medical group whereas the figure for England is just 24 per cent. There is considerable variation across types of socio-economic area. In inner-deprived London, medicine accounts for 35 per cent of total activity, compared with 27 per cent in comparable areas outside of London. Medicine for older people (geriatrics) is a smaller proportion of total activity in London, particularly in inner-deprived London, than it is in the rest of the country. There are several possible explanations: London has a younger population; the medicine specialty may incorporate cases which, outside London, would be in medicine for older people; there is less provision for older people in London hospitals. Further detailed analysis at a hospital level would be required to test these hypotheses.

It is also noticeable that orthopaedics is a lower proportion of total activity in London than in the rest of England. This again may reflect a younger population, with less demand, for example, for routine joint replacement which is most commonly carried out on people aged 65 and above. Again, this hypothesis could be tested with more detailed analysis, going beyond the HES dataset.

Table 6: Proportion of FCEs in specialty groups, London and England, 1994/95

Specialty group	London				Non-London				England
	Inner-deprived	Mixed-status	High-status	Total	Inner-deprived	Mixed-status	High-status	Total	
	%	%	%	%	%	%	%	%	%
Medicine	35	24	23	28	27	23	23	23	24
Surgery/Urology	20	22	26	22	24	23	23	23	23
Obs. and Gynae.	12	17	15	14	12	14	13	13	13
Orthopaedics	6	9	8	7	8	9	9	9	9
Paediatrics	5	5	6	5	6	7	6	6	6
Geriatrics	3	5	7	5	4	6	6	6	6
ENT	4	4	3	4	4	5	4	4	4
Ophthalmology	5	2	3	3	3	3	3	3	3
Psychiatric	2	4	2	3	2	3	3	3	3
Haematology	3	3	1	3	2	1	2	2	2
Dental	2	2	2	2	2	2	2	2	2
Other non-acute	1	2	3	2	4	2	3	3	3
Anaesthetics	1	1	1	1	1	1	1	1	1
Total	100	100	100	100	100	100	100	100	100

Proportion of England activity provided in London, by specialty

We observed that 16 per cent of all hospital activity in England takes place in London. Table 7 shows this proportion varies across specialties. London provides an even greater proportion of the total England provision for some specialties, but less for others. This is particularly true of hospitals in inner-deprived London.

Thus, for example, 12 per cent of all haematology FCEs in England is provided by hospitals in inner-deprived London. Similarly nine per cent of all medicine and ophthalmology occurs there. The specialities where London provides less than 16 per cent of the national total tend to be those with a large proportion of 'routine' elective work such as orthopaedics and ENT. Interestingly, only 14 per cent of England's psychiatric FCEs are provided in London.

Table 7: Proportion of England activity provided in London, by specialty, 1994/95

Specialty Group	London				Non-London				England
	Inner-deprived	Mixed-status	High-status	Total	Inner-deprived	Mixed-status	High-status	Total	
	%	%	%	%	%	%	%	%	%
Medicine	9	5	4	18	17	18	27	82	100
Surgery/Urology	5	5	5	15	15	19	29	85	100
Obs. and Gynae.	6	6	5	17	13	21	29	83	100
Orthopaedics	4	5	4	13	12	20	30	87	100
Paediatrics	6	5	4	15	15	22	29	85	100
Geriatrics	3	4	5	13	10	21	29	87	100
ENT	6	4	3	14	14	22	30	86	100
Ophthalmology	9	3	4	16	15	19	28	84	100
Psychiatric	5	6	3	14	10	18	31	86	100
Haematology	12	7	3	22	17	16	26	78	100
Dental	6	5	5	17	15	14	32	83	100
Other non-acute	2	3	4	9	20	12	30	91	100
Anaesthetics	10	4	4	18	13	17	34	82	100
Total	6	5	4	16	15	19	29	84	100

FCEs by admission method, by specialty

This section contrasts the proportion of FCEs which were emergency or elective admissions in each specialty. Table 8 shows, by sector of London, the proportion of elective admissions in each specialty group. In general, most of the balance will be emergency admissions: just two per cent are transfers from other hospitals. Two exceptions to this are psychiatry where London has a significant proportion of transfers, and obstetrics and gynaecology where maternity admissions are significant. These two specialties are shown separately in Tables 9 and 10. There is a high proportion of emergencies in the psychiatric specialty. However, the south sector of London, where 49 per cent of psychiatric episodes are elective, reveals a different pattern from the rest of London. Transfers are almost negligible in this sector.

In the obstetrics and gynaecology specialty, elective episodes form by far the largest proportion of just elective and emergency admissions, consistently across the sectors of London. However, maternity episodes are a substantial proportion in each sector – between 30 and 39 per cent. These were discussed in more detail in Box 1. It may be that such episodes are more like emergencies than elective cases.

Not surprisingly, the highest elective rates are in surgical specialties with the exception of orthopaedics, where the trauma function of the specialty ensures that the split between emergency and elective is more even. Conversely, the medical specialty and paediatrics tend to have a higher proportion of emergency FCEs. There are interesting differences between sectors of London. For example, the east sector generally has a higher proportion of emergencies and a lower proportion of elective admissions than the rest of London, reflecting the overall position observed in Table 2. Why this should be is not revealed by the data. It may reflect a less healthy population in this sector, or differences in the management of care. Further analysis would be required to investigate this.

Table 8: Proportion of total FCEs that are elective, by specialty, by sector of London, 1994/95

Specialty Group	North West	North Central	East	South East	South	London
	%	%	%	%	%	%
Anaesthetics	98	98	87	96	98	95
Dental	90	93	90	94	94	92
Ophthalmology	93	94	90	89	94	92
ENT	83	91	87	80	84	85
Haematology	78	85	80	78	72	80
Other non-acute	90	81	21	53	57	79
Surgery/Urology	71	70	64	71	69	69
All specialty average	**59**	**53**	**50**	**52**	**51**	**54**
Orthopaedics	62	52	45	48	57	54
Medicine	56	42	37	45	36	45
Paediatrics	19	20	7	16	23	17
Geriatrics	7	4	3	5	7	5

(Tables 8 and 11 are ordered by specialty with the highest proportion of elective admissions in London.)

Table 9: Proportion of psychiatric FCEs, by admission method, by sector of London, 1994/95

Admission Method	North West	North Central	East	South East	South	London
	%	%	%	%	%	%
Elective	19	9	27	15	49	25
Emergency	63	77	68	50	45	59
Transfers	16	14	5	20	1	11

(Technical Note: fifteen per cent of psychiatric FCEs in the south-east sector are recorded as maternity admissions. These are almost all at one hospital. Unfortunately these records contain little information: all bar one has a 799 diagnosis code indicating an ill-defined or unknown cause of morbidity. It is difficult therefore to gain any further understanding about these peculiar admissions. The most probable explanation is a mistake in coding.)

Table 10: Proportion of obstetrics and gynaecology FCEs, by admission method, by sector of London, 1994/95

Admission Method	North West	North Central	East	South East	South	London
	%	%	%	%	%	%
Elective	55	43	48	46	46	48
Emergency	15	18	18	20	15	17
Maternity	30	39	34	34	38	34

Table 11 compares the proportion of elective FCEs in London with that in the rest of the country. As before, psychiatry and obstetrics and gynaecology are shown separately in Tables 12 and 13.

Table 11: Proportion of total FCEs that are elective, by specialty, London and England, 1994/95

Specialty Group	London				Non-London				England
	Inner-deprived %	Mixed-status %	High-status %	Total %	Inner-deprived %	Mixed-status %	High-status %	Total %	%
Anaesthetics	96	90	99	95	88	92	92	91	92
Dental	92	93	91	92	90	90	92	91	91
Ophthalmology	90	91	96	92	91	92	92	92	92
ENT	87	83	85	85	84	86	85	85	85
Haematology	81	82	70	80	74	80	77	78	78
Other non-acute	68	81	83	79	91	57	45	56	58
Surgery/Urology	69	70	69	69	69	67	67	68	68
All specialty average	**58**	**52**	**50**	**54**	**55**	**48**	**50**	**51**	**52**
Orthopaedics	49	53	58	54	49	52	51	52	52
Medicine	56	38	31	45	41	31	34	34	36
Paediatrics	21	19	12	17	22	7	10	12	12
Geriatrics	5	5	5	5	14	8	12	12	11

In most cases the proportion of elective FCEs in London is similar to that in the rest of England. The major exception is medicine, where 45 per cent of FCEs in London are elective compared to 36 per cent in England as a whole. This is primarily due to the high level of medical elective admissions in inner-deprived London. In Table 11 the only specialty with a smaller proportion of elective admissions in London is geriatrics where just five per cent of episodes are elective, compared with 12 per cent outside the capital.

Table 12: Psychiatric FCEs, by admission method, London and England, 1994/95

Admission Method	London				Non-London				England
	Inner-deprived %	Mixed-status %	High-status %	Total %	Inner-deprived %	Mixed-status %	High-status %	Total %	%
Elective	11	38	23	25	34	35	33	37	36
Emergency	64	52	66	59	53	57	57	54	55
Transfers	16	9	7	11	9	7	8	7	7

Table 13: Obstetrics and gynaecology FCEs, by admission method, London and England, 1994/95

Admission Method	London				Non-London				England
	Inner-deprived %	Mixed-status %	High-status %	Total %	Inner-deprived %	Mixed-status %	High-status %	Total %	%
Elective	50	47	48	48	52	48	50	51	50
Emergency	20	15	17	17	17	20	21	20	19
Maternity	30	38	35	34	29	32	28	29	30

Table 12 shows psychiatric FCEs are more likely to be emergencies in London: just 25 per cent are elective and 59 per cent are emergencies. Indeed, in inner-deprived London only 11 per cent of psychiatric FCEs are elective. In the rest of the country, regardless of the type of area, a third of psychiatric FCEs are elective. The greater proportion of emergencies in London would seem to confirm that the demand for emergency psychiatric care in London is greater than elsewhere in the country. Moreover, London has a greater proportion of transfers than other parts of England. It may be more common in London for patients in need of mental health services to be admitted first to general acute hospitals and then transferred on to specialist hospitals. Further analysis of the dataset would be required to test this hypothesis.

Day case rate, by specialty

Finally in this section we consider the proportions of day cases in each specialty group, comparing differences across sectors of London, and between London and the rest of England.

Confirming the overall sectoral position, Table 14 shows that the north west has a high proportion of day cases in most specialties, compared with other parts of London. For example, 40 per cent of all medical episodes are day cases compared with only 30 per cent in the capital as a whole.

Virtually all psychiatric and geriatric episodes are in-patients: the exception is the east sector where 13 per cent of psychiatric episodes are day cases. This is due to the pattern of treatment at one trust where nearly 40 per cent of psychiatric episodes are day cases. Ironically, the east sector has one of the lowest day case rates in the capital for most other specialties, which is unsurprising given the lower proportion of elective episodes noted above.

Table 14: Proportion of FCEs that are day cases, by specialty, by sector of London, 1994/95

Specialty Group	North West %	North Central %	East %	South East %	South %	London %
Anaesthetics	90	81	81	83	94	85
Dental	73	51	59	67	73	66
Haematology	62	68	57	56	38	60
Other non-acute	70	64	3	3	6	58
Ophthalmology	58	49	40	48	76	50
Surgery/Urology	35	34	32	37	40	36
Obs. and Gynae.	38	26	32	29	31	32
All specialty average	**36**	**28**	**27**	**29**	**31**	**31**
Medicine	40	23	22	28	26	30
ENT	27	23	26	23	49	28
Orthopaedics	23	22	14	21	25	21
Paediatrics	11	8	4	5	11	8
Psychiatric	0	0	13	0	2	3
Geriatrics	3	0	0	3	0	1

(Tables 14 and 15 are ordered by the specialty with the highest day case rate in London.)

Table 15 shows London as a whole, in comparison with the rest of England, has a higher day case rate in 11 of the 13 specialty groups. There are some significant differences. For example, in medicine 30 per cent of episodes are day cases in London compared with just 21 per cent in the rest of the country. However, this masks differences between types of socio-economic area. For example, inner-deprived London has a lower day case rate than comparable areas in the rest of the country for the majority of specialties. Nevertheless, the overall day case rate in inner-deprived London is greater than inner-deprived areas elsewhere: this is primarily due to medicine.

Table 15: Proportion of FCEs that are day cases, by specialty, London and England, 1994/95

Specialty Group	London Inner-deprived %	London Mixed-status %	London High-status %	London Total %	Non-London Inner-deprived %	Non-London Mixed-status %	Non-London High-status %	Non-London Total %	England %
Anaesthetics	85	84	85	85	74	77	79	77	78
Dental	63	75	61	66	63	59	63	60	61
Haematology	57	71	42	60	56	60	56	58	59
Other non-acute	41	71	57	58	68	36	20	33	35
Ophthalmology	45	50	64	50	50	41	45	44	45
Surgery/Urology	29	40	39	36	33	35	34	34	34
Obs. and Gynae.	31	32	32	32	33	28	29	30	30
All specialty average	**31**	**31**	**29**	**31**	**29**	**25**	**25**	**26**	**26**
Medicine	35	28	20	30	22	19	21	21	22
ENT	26	31	27	28	26	26	28	27	27
Orthopaedics	16	20	28	21	20	23	21	22	21
Paediatrics	7	10	6	8	13	2	4	5	5
Geriatrics	1	1	1	1	2	1	1	2	2
Psychiatric	0	7	0	3	0	1	0	0	1

Figure 6 shows the variation between London and England in the proportion of FCEs which are day cases, for seven key specialty groups. The pattern of more day case activity in London is maintained across almost all specialties and areas of the capital.

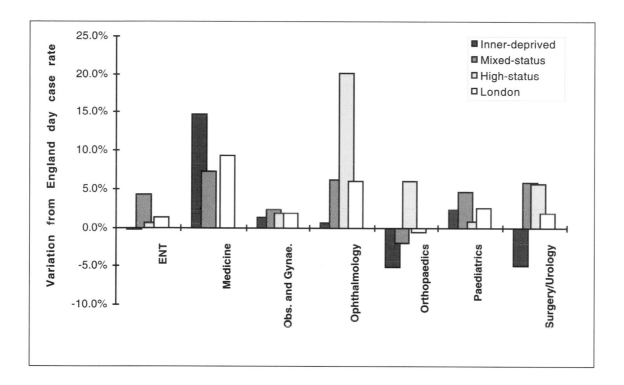

Figure 6: Variation between London and England day case rates, by specialty, 1994/95

The age composition of FCEs

This section considers activity by age-group using the following groupings: 0-14, 15-44, 45-64, 65-74, 75-84, 85+. The HES dataset also includes an 'invalid' code for episodes without an age recorded. These are considerably less than one per cent of total FCEs and are not shown as a separate group. However, for consistency with previous tables, the 'Total' row in Tables 16 and 19 shows absolute totals including records with no age recorded.

Total activity

Tables 16 – 18 show the breakdown of total activity in each sector of London by age-group, the proportion of activity in each age-group, for all sectors, and the proportion of London's activity in each sector, for all age-groups. There is a degree of sectoral concentration on particular age-groups. A higher proportion of FCEs is provided to older people, those aged 65 and over, in south London – 27 per cent compared to a London average of 24 per cent. A particularly high proportion of children aged under 15 are treated in north-central London – 19 per cent compared to a London average of 15 per cent. As Table 18 shows, nearly a quarter of all FCEs in London for this age-group were in this sector. This is not surprising since Great Ormond Street Hospital for Sick Children is located in this sector.

The north-west sector treats the highest proportion of patients in the 45-64 age-group – over 30 per cent of all London FCEs for this age-group were performed in this sector. Differences between sectors are picked up in the previous section on specialties, although we indicate later that there are sectoral differences in the age distribution of patients, even within specialties.

Table 16: FCEs by age-group, by sector of London, 1994/95

Age-group	North West	North Central	East	South East	South	London
0-14	46,736	51,917	42,394	43,178	33,934	218,160
15-44	153,041	106,398	105,184	107,406	79,027	551,055
45-64	109,070	57,701	70,960	69,365	47,415	354,511
65-74	51,434	32,068	41,689	37,504	30,249	192,944
75-84	31,720	23,561	26,865	22,937	23,086	128,168
85+	5,449	4,464	4,424	3,981	4,034	22,352
Total	397,621	276,225	291,666	284,693	217,764	1,467,969

Table 17: Proportion of FCEs in each age-group, by sector of London, 1994/95

Age-group	North West %	North Central %	East %	South East %	South %	London %
0-14	12	19	15	15	16	15
15-44	38	39	36	38	36	38
45-64	27	21	24	24	22	24
65-74	13	12	14	13	14	13
75-84	8	9	9	8	11	9
85+	1	2	2	1	2	2
Total	100	100	100	100	100	100

Table 18: Proportion of London's FCEs in each sector, by age-group, 1994/95

Age-group	North West %	North Central %	East %	South East %	South %	London %
0-14	21	24	19	20	16	100
15-44	28	19	19	19	14	100
45-64	31	16	20	20	13	100
65-74	27	17	22	19	16	100
75-84	25	18	21	18	18	100
85+	24	20	20	18	18	100
Total	27	19	20	19	15	100

Tables 19 and 20 compare the age distribution of activity in London with the rest of England. London hospitals treat proportionately more patients in the 15-44 age-group and proportionately less of those aged 65 and over, compared to England as a whole. In inner-deprived areas of London only 19 per cent of FCEs are provided to people aged 65 years and over compared to 24 per cent in inner-deprived areas outside of London, and 27 per cent in the rest of England as a whole. By contrast, high-status areas in London have a higher proportion of FCEs among older people than comparable areas elsewhere.

Table 19: FCEs by age-group, London and England, 1994/95

| Age-group | London | | | | Non-London | | | | England |
	Inner-deprived	Mixed-status	High-status	Total	Inner-deprived	Mixed-status	High-status	Total	
0-14	103,299	60,798	54,063	218,160	224,770	287,277	409,391	1,204,833	1,422,993
15-44	228,917	180,218	141,920	551,055	474,702	632,257	928,655	2,689,126	3,240,182
45-64	153,902	107,075	93,533	354,511	361,142	428,746	630,109	1,904,332	2,258,842
65-74	70,988	59,822	62134	192,944	192,262	260,748	405,089	1,199,314	1,392,258
75-84	38,684	43065	46,419	128,168	109,112	160,030	277,904	794,454	922,623
85+	6,796	7,464	8,092	22,352	16,302	24,208	46,759	127,344	149,696
Total	603,061	458,564	406,344	1,467,969	1,378,686	1,794,367	2,698,771	7,922,285	9,390,254

Table 20: Proportion of FCEs in each age-group, London and England, 1994/95

| Age-group | London | | | | Non-London | | | | England |
	Inner-deprived %	Mixed-status %	High-status %	Total %	Inner-deprived %	Mixed-status %	High-status %	Total %	%
0-14	17	13	13	15	16	16	15	15	15
15-44	38	39	35	38	34	35	34	34	35
45-64	26	23	23	24	26	24	23	24	24
65-74	12	13	15	13	14	15	15	15	15
75-84	6	9	11	9	8	9	10	10	10
85+	1	2	2	2	1	1	2	2	2
Total	100	100	100	100	100	100	100	100	100

Day case rate, by age-group

Table 21 shows the proportion of day cases in each age-group, by sector of London. The highest day case rates in London are in the 15-44 and 45-64 age-groups. Confirming the general pattern for day cases, the north-west sector has the highest day case rates in London for both these age-groups – 41 compared with 35 per cent for the whole of London in the 15-44 age-group, and 43 compared with 36 per cent in the 45-64 age-group.

Table 21: Proportion of FCEs as day cases, by age-group, by sector of London, 1994/95

Age-group	North West %	North Central %	East %	South East %	South %	London %
0-14	27	26	24	22	29	26
15-44	41	31	32	34	36	35
45-64	43	34	30	34	35	36
65-74	31	23	23	25	26	26
75-84	16	14	15	16	18	16
85+	7	5	7	7	9	7

Table 22 shows London has a higher day case rate in all age-groups than the rest of England. This is also true when types of socio-economic area are compared. Unlike the sectors of London, there is no one type of socio-economic area in London with a clearly higher proportion of day cases than the others. In fact around 18 per cent of total England day cases are performed in London, whatever age-group is considered. By contrast, London hospitals perform between 13 and 16 per cent of England's in-patient FCEs, depending on which age-group is considered.

Table 22: Proportion of FCEs as day cases, by age-group, London and England, 1994/95

| Age-group | London | | | | Non-London | | | | England |
	Inner-deprived %	Mixed-status %	High-status %	Total %	Inner-deprived %	Mixed-status %	High-status %	Total %	%
0-14	27	26	21	26	25	17	21	20	21
15-44	35	35	36	35	35	31	31	32	33
45-64	36	38	35	36	33	30	31	31	32
65-74	28	27	24	26	23	19	20	20	21
75-84	16	16	15	16	14	11	11	11	12
85+	7	6	7	7	6	5	5	5	5

Proportion of elective FCEs, by age-group

Table 23 shows the proportion of elective FCEs in each age-group, by sector of London. There are significant sectoral differences. Hospitals in the south tend to treat a higher proportion of patients aged 75 years and over as elective admissions when compared with those in other sectors. On the other hand, hospitals in the north-west sector treat significantly more people aged between 15 and 74 years as elective admissions. For individual trusts, up to 75 per cent of all admissions are elective in these age-groups.

The highest proportion of elective cases for the 0-14 age-group is in the north-central sector where Great Ormond Street Hospital for Sick Children is located. In the case of one trust in the east sector, 44 per cent of FCEs in the 15-44 age-group are emergency admissions compared with a London average of just 30 per cent and an England figure of 33 per cent. This may reflect the fact that some DGHs in the east sector serve mainly local populations in very deprived areas of London. Further analysis using the HES database and additional local data sources might shed some light on these findings.

Table 23: Proportion of elective FCEs, by age-group, by sector of London, 1994/95

Age-group	North West	North Central	East	South East	South	London
	%	%	%	%	%	%
0-14	49	58	46	43	48	49
15-44	61	53	52	54	54	55
45-64	70	64	60	65	59	65
65-74	56	48	48	52	50	51
75-84	33	30	32	33	37	33
85+	16	15	17	17	22	17

Table 24 shows that London hospitals have a higher proportion of elective cases in all age-groups up to 74 years when compared with the rest of England. This is particularly true for the 0-14 age-group where 49 per cent of FCEs in London are elective compared with 42 per cent in England as a whole. In London, the proportion of elective episodes increases with the level of deprivation in an area, from high-status to inner-deprived, for most age-groups. For example, inner-deprived London is the only part of the country where, for the 0-14 age-group, over 50 per cent of FCEs are elective.

Table 24: Proportion of elective FCEs, by age-group, London and England, 1994/95

Age-group	London				Non-London				England
	Inner-deprived	Mixed-status	High-status	Total	Inner-deprived	Mixed-status	High-status	Total	
	%	%	%	%	%	%	%	%	%
0-14	56	47	39	49	47	35	41	41	42
15-44	58	53	54	55	58	53	53	54	54
45-64	68	62	62	65	65	59	61	61	62
65-74	56	50	48	51	53	46	49	49	49
75-84	36	33	31	33	37	31	33	34	34
85+	19	17	16	17	21	19	22	22	21

The specialty composition of FCEs, by age-group

London hospitals have a higher proportion of FCEs in the younger age-groups. By analysing the age profiles of each specialty group this result can be examined in more detail. Results are reported briefly here. Detailed tables are available on request. For most specialties the proportion of total FCEs in age-groups over 64 years is less than in the rest of England. This is generally quite a small difference. For example, 28 per cent of medicine FCEs in London are provided to those aged 65 and over, whereas in the rest of England the figure is 31 per cent. The pattern is repeated for surgery and urology, 25 compared with 27 per cent, and orthopaedics, 23 compared with 24 per cent.

There are bigger differences in some specialties: for example, in ophthalmology only 46 per cent of FCEs in London are provided to people aged 65 years and over compared with 56 per cent elsewhere. This is due to a large difference between inner-deprived London and comparable areas in the rest of the country – 38 compared with 49 per cent. In mixed-

and high-status areas London has a *higher* proportion of patients aged 65 and over. A similar situation exists in psychiatry. Only 17 per cent of psychiatric FCEs in London are provided to people aged 65 and over compared with 26 per cent in the rest of England. In London 60 per cent of all psychiatric FCEs are provided to the 15-44 age-group compared with 47 per cent in the rest of England.

A significant difference arises in medicine for older people (geriatrics). As this specialty has an older age structure, the interesting comparison is between the 65-74 age-group and those aged 75 years and over. Sixty-nine per cent of all FCEs in this specialty in London are provided to people aged 75 years and over compared with just 59 per cent outside of the capital. The reason for this is unclear: it may be that there are different protocols for admitting patients under geriatricians in London. It is often claimed that distinctions between medicine and medicine for older people can be rather blurred, and may differ from trust to trust. Further analysis using both the HES database and local data and knowledge would be necessary in order to examine these findings further.

The diagnostic composition of FCEs

(Technical note: the diagnosis groups used in this section are based on the groupings of ICD 9 classifications used in 'Analysing Changes in Emergency Medical Admissions' (Harrison et al, 1995). A fuller description of these can be found in Appendix 5.)

This section provides an analysis, by diagnosis, of the provision of FCEs in London. There are approximately 5,800 separate diagnoses recorded. We have aggregated these into 21 diagnosis groups. The six most common groups account for over 50 per cent of activity in London.

Total activity

(Technical note: there is a high proportion of childbirth diagnoses which may seem surprising as the HES dataset queried excluded delivery and birth episodes. However, this reflects 'childbirth' episodes which refer to diagnoses that, although associated with pregnancy, are not deliveries in a completely normal case (code 650), which are excluded from the general episode set. Typical 'childbirth' diagnoses represented here include abortion, complications of pregnancy and perineal trauma as a result of delivery. V-code diagnoses are where the primary diagnosis recorded is a diagnosis contained in the 'Supplementary classification (V code)' chapter of ICD 9. Ill-defined diagnoses are ICD9 codes 780 to 799, the chapter referred to as 'Symptoms, signs and ill-defined conditions'.)

Table 25 shows for each sector of London, the proportion of FCEs by diagnosis group. Individual providers in a sector may have considerable influence on the pattern of diseases treated there. For example, the high proportion of cancer FCEs in the north-west sector is largely due to the Royal Marsden hospital. Similarly, the higher proportion of FCEs for nervous diagnoses (which include ophthalmic problems) in the east is due to Moorfields.

Table 25: Proportion of total FCEs, by diagnosis group, by sector of London, 1994/95

Diagnosis Group	North West %	North Central %	East %	South East %	South %	London %
Cancer	16	9	10	8	8	11
Urinary	9	9	10	10	10	9
Digestive	9	8	9	9	11	9
V code	8	11	6	9	6	8
Ill-defined	7	8	7	8	9	8
Childbirth	6	8	9	6	7	7
Respiratory/Thoracic	7	7	7	7	6	7
Cardiac	7	6	8	8	6	7
Trauma	6	5	5	7	6	6
Nervous	4	5	8	5	6	6
Musculo-Skeletal	6	5	5	5	5	5
Mental	3	3	2	3	4	3
Skin	2	2	2	3	3	2
Vascular	2	2	2	2	2	2
Oral	2	1	2	3	3	2
Blood	1	3	2	2	1	2
Endocrine	2	2	2	2	1	2
Cerebrovascular	1	2	1	1	1	1
Infectious Diseases	1	2	1	1	1	1
Congenital	1	1	1	1	1	1
Perinatal	0	0	0	0	1	0

(Tables 25-28 are ordered by the proportion of FCEs in each diagnosis group for London.)

Table 26 shows that the proportions of total FCEs in each diagnosis group in London are similar to those in England. In only one of 21 groups is there a difference of more than one per cent in the proportion of total FCEs. This is the trauma group which is responsible for six per cent of FCEs in London compared with eight per cent in the rest of England. Diagnostic composition is also similar when types of socio-economic area in London are compared with equivalent areas in the rest of the country.

Table 26: Proportion of total FCEs, by diagnosis group, London and England, 1994/95

| Diagnosis Group | London | | | | Non-London | | | | England |
	Inner-deprived %	Mixed-status %	High-status %	Total %	Inner-deprived %	Mixed-status %	High-status %	Total %	%
Cancer	11	10	11	11	11	9	9	10	10
Urinary	8	11	10	9	9	10	10	9	9
Digestive	8	9	11	9	9	9	10	10	10
V code	9	9	5	8	5	5	8	7	7
Ill-defined	7	8	9	8	9	9	8	9	9
Childbirth	7	8	6	7	6	7	6	6	6
Respiratory/Thor.	6	7	8	7	7	8	7	7	7
Cardiac	8	6	7	7	7	6	5	6	6
Trauma	5	6	7	6	8	8	8	8	7
Nervous	7	5	5	6	6	6	6	6	6
Musculo-Skeletal	5	6	6	5	6	6	6	6	6
Mental	3	4	3	3	3	4	3	3	3
Skin	2	2	3	2	2	2	2	2	2
Vascular	2	2	2	2	2	2	2	2	2
Oral	2	2	2	2	2	2	2	2	2
Blood	2	2	1	2	1	1	1	1	1
Endocrine	2	1	1	2	2	1	1	1	1
Cerebrovascular	1	1	2	1	2	2	1	2	2
Infectious Diseases	1	1	1	1	2	2	1	1	1
Congenital	1	1	1	1	2	1	1	1	1
Perinatal	0	1	0	0	0	0	0	0	0

Day case rate, by diagnosis group

Table 27 shows, by sector of London, the proportion of day cases for each diagnosis group. The north-west sector has the greatest proportion of day cases for four of the six largest diagnosis groups, which between them account for over 50 per cent of total activity in the capital. The east sector has the smallest proportion of day cases in half of the groups. London has a day case rate of over 50 per cent in only four diagnosis groups: skin, oral, blood and v-code. We show in Table 29 that in each of these groups over 60 per cent of FCEs in London are elective admissions.

Table 27: Proportion of FCEs that are day cases, by diagnosis group, by sector of London, 1994/95

Diagnosis Group	North West	North Central	East	South East	South	London
	%	%	%	%	%	%
Cancer	53	41	33	34	45	44
Urinary	47	42	38	43	38	42
Digestive	38	32	37	35	41	37
V code	73	51	52	60	22	55
Ill-defined	26	23	22	22	32	25
Childbirth	25	20	23	25	18	23
Respiratory/Thoracic	10	3	5	4	14	7
Cardiac	14	5	7	11	13	10
Trauma	7	4	5	5	5	5
Nervous	46	30	39	38	61	36
Musculo-Skeletal	41	31	26	41	33	42
Mental	1	0	0	1	3	1
Skin	53	49	49	51	60	53
Vascular	24	30	22	26	33	27
Oral	74	60	63	71	77	70
Blood	39	60	35	33	34	57
Endocrine	37	27	17	41	29	30
Cerebrovascular	1	0	0	0	1	0
Infectious Diseases	15	12	16	11	16	14
Congenital	24	24	17	27	30	24
Perinatal	4	3	0	4	7	4

Table 28 compares the capital with the rest of the country, showing that London has a greater proportion of day cases in each diagnosis group, with the exception of the congenital and cerebrovascular groups (both of which have comparatively small numbers of FCEs). This confirms the position for day cases as a whole shown earlier in Figure 3.

Table 28: Proportion of FCEs that are day cases, by diagnosis group, London and England, 1994/95

Diagnosis Group	London				Non-London				England
	Inner-deprived %	Mixed-status %	High-status %	Total %	Inner-deprived %	Mixed-status %	High-status %	Total %	%
Cancer	36	51	48	44	37	43	39	40	40
Urinary	35	45	47	42	38	37	42	39	40
Digestive	37	39	35	37	36	34	36	34	35
V code	69	45	40	55	53	45	37	40	43
Ill-defined	25	27	23	25	22	18	17	17	19
Childbirth	28	18	20	23	25	13	14	17	18
Respiratory/Thor.	9	8	4	7	4	4	5	4	5
Cardiac	15	9	3	10	8	4	2	4	5
Trauma	5	6	4	5	6	5	4	4	4
Nervous	38	44	49	42	37	33	37	36	37
Musculo-Skeletal	38	33	35	36	30	33	32	32	32
Mental	1	2	1	1	1	1	1	1	1
Skin	43	55	60	53	44	47	39	42	44
Vascular	22	32	26	27	20	22	24	22	22
Oral	70	75	65	70	61	60	65	61	63
Blood	48	46	26	43	40	35	34	34	36
Endocrine	34	27	25	30	24	27	27	26	27
Cerebrovascular	0	1	0	0	2	0	0	1	1
Infectious Diseases	12	17	13	14	11	7	9	9	10
Congenital	21	31	28	24	23	28	29	28	27
Perinatal	2	2	12	4	10	3	3	3	3

Proportion of elective FCEs, by diagnosis group

This section considers the proportion of FCEs that are elective, for each diagnosis group. For most groups, the remaining FCEs are almost all emergencies, with four exceptions: cerebrovascular, cardiac and mental which have a large proportion of transfers; and childbirth which has a large proportion of maternity admissions (see previous technical note). These four groups are shown separately: all admission methods which account for one per cent or more of activity are included.

Table 29 shows the proportion of elective admissions, by diagnosis group, for the sectors of London. The pattern is similar to the equivalent analysis by specialty group or by total FCEs. Typically, the north west has a greater proportion of elective admissions in each diagnosis group than London as a whole and the east sector has a lower proportion of elective admissions.

Comparison with Table 27 above shows that the diagnoses with large proportions of elective admissions tend also to be those with large proportions of day cases. For example, 95 per cent of oral diagnoses are elective admissions in London: 70 per cent of oral diagnoses are day cases. The day case rate is dependent on the proportion of elective admissions.

Table 29: Proportion of elective FCEs, by diagnosis group, by sector of London, 1994/95

Diagnosis Group	North West	North Central	East	South East	South	London
	%	%	%	%	%	%
Cancer	81	78	65	74	78	76
Urinary	78	76	76	75	66	75
Digestive	58	54	54	57	57	56
V code	86	73	82	79	48	76
Ill-defined	41	39	32	36	41	38
Respiratory/Thoracic	32	33	29	25	27	29
Trauma	16	9	9	14	13	13
Nervous	78	78	83	75	81	79
Musculo-Skeletal	84	74	68	77	75	77
Skin	66	61	62	65	73	66
Vascular	68	69	62	69	72	68
Oral	92	95	95	96	97	95
Blood	56	74	55	51	54	60
Endocrine	56	50	60	57	50	55
Infectious Diseases	25	26	23	21	22	24
Congenital	81	86	80	80	79	81
Perinatal	16	6	2	8	13	10

(Tables 29 and 32 are ordered by the proportion of FCEs in each diagnosis group for London, excluding childbirth, cardiac, cerebrovascular and mental groups.)

Table 30 shows childbirth FCEs in London in more detail. In all sectors except the southeast, over 50 per cent of childbirth episodes are recorded as maternity episodes. It is unclear whether variation between sectors represents a real difference in the management of these episodes, or whether this is merely a result of differences in recording practice by individual trusts.

Table 30: Childbirth FCEs, by admission method, by sector of London, 1994/95

Admission Method	North West	North Central	East	South East	South	London
	%	%	%	%	%	%
Elective	29	26	26	31	23	27
Emergency	20	22	21	31	22	23
Maternity	51	51	54	37	54	50

Table 31 shows cerebrovascular, cardiac and mental diagnosis group FCEs in London in more detail. In each case transfers account for five to eight per cent of such FCEs. However, in individual sectors the proportion can be higher often resulting from the position at one trust.

Table 31: Cardiac, cerebrovascular and mental FCEs, by admission method, by sector of London, 1994/95

Diagnosis Group	Admission Method	North West %	North Central %	East %	South East %	South %	London %
Cardiac	Elective	40	18	28	42	30	33
	Emergency	56	77	69	50	62	61
	Transfer	4	5	3	8	9	5
Cerebrovascular	Elective	10	9	6	9	9	9
	Emergency	85	80	89	87	76	84
	Transfer	5	11	5	3	13	7
Mental	Elective	23	10	9	14	43	21
	Emergency	68	78	85	68	52	69
	Transfer	7	13	6	15	1	8

Table 32 compares the proportion of FCEs that are elective for each diagnosis group, between types of socio-economic area in London and England. No consistent pattern emerges. For the four largest diagnosis groups, cancer, urinary, digestive and v code, the proportion of FCEs that are elective is fairly similar, both between London and England as a whole, and between similar areas inside and outside of the capital. However, there are larger proportions of elective FCEs in London in the cardiac, infectious diseases and ill-defined groups, whereas the mental group has a smaller proportion of elective admissions.

Table 32: Proportion of elective admissions, by diagnosis group, London and England, 1994/95

Diagnosis Group	London Inner-deprived %	London Mixed-status %	London High-status %	London Total %	Non-London Inner-deprived %	Non-London Mixed-status %	Non-London High-status %	Non-London Total %	England %
Cancer	73	77	79	76	76	77	76	76	76
Urinary	74	73	77	75	71	78	77	76	76
Digestive	58	58	52	56	60	55	57	56	56
V code	87	64	73	76	82	74	68	72	73
Ill-defined	43	37	33	38	37	27	28	29	30
Respiratory/Thor.	35	28	24	29	30	29	32	30	30
Trauma	14	13	11	13	15	12	11	12	12
Nervous	82	75	78	79	77	77	79	78	79
Musculo-Skeletal	77	77	76	77	75	76	76	75	75
Skin	59	65	72	66	62	65	59	61	62
Vascular	69	70	66	68	67	68	66	67	67
Oral	95	94	96	95	92	95	96	95	95
Blood	66	60	44	60	59	55	55	56	57
Endocrine	63	48	42	55	52	48	49	48	50
Infectious Diseases	28	23	18	24	19	11	15	14	16
Congenital	81	81	82	81	74	81	79	79	79
Perinatal	5	11	15	10	16	6	4	5	6

Table 33 shows that London has a slightly smaller proportion of childbirth FCEs that are maternity admissions than similar areas in the rest of England. As already noted, it is unclear whether this variation reflects differences in practice or recording.

Table 33: Childbirth FCEs, by admission method, London and England, 1994/95

| Admission Method | London | | | | Non-London | | | | England |
| | Inner-deprived | Mixed-status | High-status | Total | Inner-deprived | Mixed-status | High-status | Total | |
	%	%	%	%	%	%	%	%	%
Elective	33	22	24	27	31	18	16	20	21
Emergency	22	21	25	23	21	25	24	25	24
Maternity	45	56	50	50	46	57	57	54	53

Table 34 shows the position for the cerebrovascular, cardiac and mental diagnoses. This is often driven by one or two providers. For example, in the case of the cardiac diagnosis group the large proportion of elective FCEs in inner-deprived London, 49 compared with 28 per cent in inner-deprived areas in the rest of England, is largely driven by the high proportions of elective FCEs at the Royal Hospitals Trust and Guy's and St. Thomas's. Table 34 also shows a similar proportion of transfers in the rest of England to that in London as a whole, although there are often differences between comparable types of area.

Table 34: Cardiac, cerebrovascular and mental FCEs, by admission method, London and England, 1994/95

| Diagnosis Group | Admission Method | London | | | | Non-London | | | | England |
| | | Inner-deprived | Mixed-status | High-status | Total | Inner-deprived | Mixed-status | High-status | Total | |
		%	%	%	%	%	%	%	%	%
Cardiac	Elective	49	21	18	33	28	16	17	17	21
	Emergency	45	73	78	61	64	79	77	78	74
	Transfer	6	5	4	5	6	4	5	5	5
Cerebrovascular	Elective	15	7	5	9	16	9	10	10	10
	Emergency	79	84	88	84	72	81	81	80	81
	Transfer	6	9	7	7	9	10	10	9	9
Mental	Elective	12	31	18	21	26	37	29	32	31
	Emergency	73	62	74	69	63	56	61	60	61
	Transfer	13	5	5	8	7	7	8	7	7

4 Other issues

We turn now to consider other issues related to hospital admissions. First, we analyse the relation between admissions and FCEs. We then compare the number of episodes resulting from a transfer of a patient between hospitals, and analyse the discharge destination of patients once a hospital episode is complete. Finally, we provide a detailed analysis of operative procedures in London.

Episodes and admissions

This chapter has focused on finished consultant episodes (FCEs) as a measure of hospital activity. However, there has been considerable discussion of the appropriateness of this measure (Clarke, 1992; Seng *et al*, 1993). Although 94 per cent of admissions to hospital result in just one episode, it is possible that several episodes may be associated with one patient stay. This is because an episode is defined as '*a period of care under a consultant in one health care provider*'. If there is consistency in the application of this definition, between trusts and over time, then the choice of episodes or admissions for analysis should have little impact. Even then, it is true that some forms of activity are more likely to result in multiple episodes within admissions than others, e.g. emergency compared to elective admissions.

Greater problems arise if there is considerable variation in the practical definition of episodes, either between hospitals, or over time. For example, how dialysis is treated, or the use of emergency admission wards. Evidence from the Department of Health shows that there has been a gradual increase in episode-admission 'inflation' since 1991/92, and considerable variation between hospitals (Health Committee, 1996). For our purpose it is important to consider if there are systematic differences within London, or between London and the rest of England.

Therefore, we now consider the ratio of episodes to admissions. This gives the average number of FCEs that result from each admission to hospital. It may highlight differences in the pattern of care with, for example, patients being frequently transferred between consultants (and, usually, specialties) while remaining in the same trust. On the other hand, where there are substantial or unusual differences in practice, it may reflect inappropriate definitional decisions.

We consider the breakdown of the episode-to-admission ratio, first, according to whether admission was elective or emergency, and second, whether in-patient or day case. Considerable differences arise which can be broken down further, by age and by specialty.

Episode-to-admission ratio, by admission method

Table 35 shows the ratio of episodes to admissions across sectors of London according to admission method. On average there are more episodes per emergency admission than other types of admission. This is unsurprising as emergencies, by their nature unexpected, may have to be admitted as a general patient before being transferred to more specialist care. In contrast, elective admissions are planned and therefore should be managed more straightforwardly.

The elective episode-to-admission ratio is low: for every 100 elective admissions, only one or two result in more than one episode. This holds across all sectors of London. By contrast, there are 12 per cent more emergency FCEs than emergency admissions in London overall, with considerable variation across the capital. The south sector has the highest ratio of episodes to admissions, and in particular, a ratio of maternity episodes to admissions which is far greater than elsewhere in London. However, this is due to the position at one trust, where there are a number of admissions comprising a very large number of episodes. This is considered further in Box 2. For the moment we illustrate the potential for distortion by providing two tables – Tables 35 and 36, the first with data from that trust removed from the analysis, the second including it. Thereafter in this section we exclude the aberrant trust from the analysis.

Table 35: Episode-to-admission ratio, by admission method, by sector of London, excluding aberrant trust, 1994/95

Admission Method	North West	North Central	East	South East	South	London
Elective	1.01	1.01	1.01	1.01	1.01	1.01
Emergency	1.12	1.11	1.16	1.08	1.12	1.12
Maternity	1.01	1.02	1.02	1.03	1.00	1.02
Total	1.05	1.05	1.07	1.04	1.06	1.06

(Tables 35-37 exclude 'other' and 'not known' admissions as these are comparatively small in number and may give rise to misleading ratios.)

Table 36: Episode-to-admission ratio, by admission method, by sector of London, all trusts included, 1994/95

Admission Method	North West	North Central	East	South East	South	London
Elective	1.01	1.01	1.01	1.01	1.02	1.01
Emergency	1.12	1.11	1.16	1.08	1.21	1.13
Maternity	1.01	1.02	1.02	1.03	1.21	1.05
Total	1.05	1.05	1.07	1.04	1.11	1.06

This analysis shows the potentially distorting effect of just one trust. For example, the ratio for maternity admissions in the south sector is reduced from 1.21 to 1.00, the lowest ratio of the five sectors, rather than by far the highest.

Table 37 compares the episode-to-admission ratio in London with that of similar areas of the rest of the country. London in general has a smaller ratio than the rest of England. This result is somewhat surprising as the increased sub-specialisation in London hospitals, particularly for medical specialties, might make it likely that London would have a greater ratio. The greater episode-to-admission ratio in the rest of the country reflects the position in high-status areas outside of the capital where there is an overall ratio of 1.12 episodes per admission, far greater than anywhere else in England, and a ratio of 1.2 for emergency admissions. Thus, while in London the highest ratios tend to be found in more deprived areas, the reverse is true outside of the capital.

Box 2: Episode Orders

This box considers the relationship between episodes and admissions within London and compares London with the rest of the country, using the proportion of episodes by episode number (that is first, second, third, etc., episode of a hospital spell).

Table 38 shows, by sector of London, the proportion of episodes which were the first, second, third, fourth, or fifth or later episode of a hospital spell. In this context, spell and admission are synonymous. With the exception of the south sector, less than two per cent of episodes are later than the third in a hospital spell. In the south, the relatively high proportion of fourth or later episodes results from one trust. No other trust in London has a spell comprising more than 20 episodes whereas this trust has <u>five</u> spells that reached the 87th episode. Furthermore, 80 per cent of all fifth or later episodes in London take place at this trust.

Detailed analysis of the HES dataset reveals that multi-episode spells at this trust are the result of long-stay patients with chronic renal failure who are transferred to the trust's renal unit every two or three days for dialysis. Each incidence of dialysis is counted as a separate FCE, and each stay on a normal ward between dialyses is also counted as a separate FCE. Thus, the trust has many spells comprising more than 50 FCEs. In this it is unique in London. The trust therefore has a distorting effect on the proportion of FCEs by episode number.

Table 38: Proportion of FCEs, by episode number, London, 1994/95

Episode Number	North West %	North Central %	East %	South East %	South %	London %
1	95	95	93	96	90	94
2	3	4	5	3	5	4
3	1	1	1	1	2	1
4	0	0	0	0	1	0
5+	0	0	0	0	3	1

Table 39 compares the position in London with that of the rest of England. Proportions of FCEs by episode number are very similar. London has a slightly higher proportion of fifth or later episodes, but as noted above, this results from an unusual pattern at just one London trust. Multi-episode spells are slightly more common in high-status areas outside of London. However, there is little substantial difference between London and other areas of England. In London and England as a whole, approximately 94 per cent of FCEs are admission episodes.

Table 39: Proportion of FCEs, by episode number, London and England, 1994/95

	London				Non-London				
Episode Number	Inner-deprived %	Mixed-status %	High-status %	Total %	Inner-deprived %	Mixed-status %	High-status %	Total %	England %
1	94	93	95	94	95	95	93	94	94
2	5	4	3	4	4	4	5	5	5
3	1	1	1	1	1	1	1	1	1
4	0	0	0	0	0	0	0	0	0
5+	0	1	0	1	0	0	0	0	0

Table 37: Episode-to-admission ratio, by admission method, London and England, 1994/95

Admission Method	London				Non-London				England
	Inner-deprived	Mixed-status	High-status	Total	Inner-deprived	Mixed-status	High-status	Total	
Elective	1.01	1.01	1.01	1.01	1.01	1.03	1.05	1.03	1.03
Emergency	1.14	1.10	1.10	1.12	1.10	1.13	1.20	1.15	1.14
Maternity	1.03	1.01	1.00	1.02	1.02	1.03	1.12	1.05	1.05
Total	1.06	1.05	1.05	1.06	1.05	1.07	1.12	1.08	1.08

Episode-to-admission ratio, by in-patient and day case

This section considers the episode-to-admission ratios for in-patients and day cases separately. The ratio for day cases should be very close to one as it is unlikely that trusts plan to admit a patient for a day and during that day transfer the patient from one consultant to another. A day case episode-to-admission ratio greater than one may reflect inaccurate recording of day cases rather than the genuine position. For example, if a planned day case results in an overnight stay it should be recorded as an in-patient not a day case.

Table 40 shows that for each sector of London the episode-to-admission ratio for day cases is approximately one – in fact less than one-tenth of one per cent of day cases require a transfer to another consultant. On the other hand, the in-patient episode-to-admission ratio varies between 1.06 in the south east and 1.11 in the east. Thus, any comparison between areas, of episode-to-admission inflation, must take account of variations in the proportion of day case admissions. Other things being equal, an area with a higher proportion of day cases is likely to have less episode inflation.

Table 40: Episode-to-admission ratio, by in-patient and day case, by sector of London, 1994/95

Patient Type	North West	North Central	East	South East	South	London
In-patient	1.08	1.08	1.11	1.06	1.09	1.08
Day case	1.00	1.00	1.00	1.00	1.00	1.00
Total	1.05	1.05	1.07	1.04	1.06	1.06

(Tables 40 and 41 exclude 'other maternity' admissions as these are comparatively small in number and may give rise to misleading ratios.)

Table 41 compares London with the rest of England showing a higher ratio of episodes to admissions nationally, mainly due to high-status areas outside of the capital. Mixed-status and high-status areas outside London reveal an unusual level of episode inflation among day cases – in high-status areas the number of day case episodes is five per cent greater than the number of day case admissions. This implies that trusts are managing their workload so that two episodes are planned and performed on a single patient in one day. This is somewhat unlikely. However, whether this represents inaccurate recording or a high proportion of patients requiring a further episode after a day case needs further analysis of the HES database as well as discussion with individual providers.

Table 41: Episode-to-admission ratio, by in-patient and day case, London and England, 1994/95

Patient Type	London				Non-London				
	Inner-deprived	Mixed-status	High-status	Total	Inner-deprived	Mixed-status	High-status	Total	England
In-patient	1.10	1.07	1.07	1.09	1.06	1.09	1.15	1.11	1.10
Day case	1.00	1.00	1.00	1.00	1.00	1.02	1.05	1.02	1.02
Total	1.06	1.05	1.05	1.06	1.05	1.07	1.12	1.08	1.08

Nevertheless, considering in-patient cases alone, London has a lower inflation rate than the rest of England although, as previously noted, inner-deprived London trusts show a higher episode-to-admission ratio whereas those in mixed- and high-status areas have a ratio substantially lower than comparable areas elsewhere. These differences between London and England in episode-to-admission ratio may reflect differences in the age and specialty composition of hospital episodes rather than different care management practices. This is examined in more detail in the next section.

The effect of age composition on episode-to-admission ratio

One potential explanation for differences between London and the rest of England is the different age composition of their workloads: a smaller proportion of FCEs in London are for older age-groups. These tend to have a higher episode-to-admission ratio. Table 42 shows that episode-to-admission ratios are indeed greater for the older age-groups. However, this is not the primary cause of the higher all-age ratio outside of London since, for each age-group, London has a lower inflation rate than the rest of England.

Table 42: Episode-to-admission ratio, by age-group, London and England, 1994/95

Age-group	London				Non-London				
	Inner-deprived	Mixed-status	High-status	Total	Inner-deprived	Mixed-status	High-status	Total	England
0-14	1.05	1.04	1.02	1.04	1.02	1.07	1.09	1.06	1.06
15-44	1.04	1.02	1.02	1.03	1.01	1.04	1.09	1.05	1.05
45-64	1.06	1.05	1.05	1.06	1.06	1.09	1.12	1.08	1.08
65-74	1.10	1.08	1.08	1.09	1.09	1.11	1.16	1.12	1.12
75-84	1.14	1.11	1.12	1.12	1.13	1.12	1.21	1.15	1.15
85+	1.17	1.15	1.13	1.16	1.17	1.10	1.24	1.16	1.16
Total	1.06	1.05	1.05	1.06	1.05	1.07	1.12	1.08	1.08

This is demonstrated in Table 43 which standardises for the proportion of admissions in each age-group. The difference between the standardised and unstandardised ratios shows the effect on the all-age ratio if actual age-group ratios are applied to the total admissions in each area, standardised according to the proportion of admissions in each age-group in

England. Differences in the proportion of total admissions in each age-group do not in themselves explain differences between London and the rest of the country although there is a slight increase in the standardised ratio for London.

Table 43: Standardised all-age episode-to-admission ratio, London and England, 1994/95

Ratio	London				Non-London				England
	Inner-deprived	Mixed-status	High-status	Total	Inner-deprived	Mixed-status	High-status	Total	
Unstandardised	1.063	1.049	1.050	1.055	1.047	1.073	1.121	1.082	1.079
Standardised	1.068	1.052	1.047	1.059	1.050	1.074	1.120	1.082	1.079

(Figures shown to three decimal places as there are only small changes to the ratio.)

The effect of specialty composition on episode-to-admission ratio

Table 44 provides a comparison between London and England of the episode-to-admission ratio for different specialty groups. There is considerable variation between specialties. The ratio for geriatrics is by far the greatest, both in London and the rest of the country, with that of medicine also relatively high throughout. For most specialties – the exception is the paediatric group – the episode-to-admission ratio is lower in London than in the rest of England. Thus, differences in the specialty composition of the workload do not appear to be significant in explaining the overall higher episode-to-admission ratio outside of the capital.

Table 44: Episode-to-admission ratio, by specialty group, London and England, 1994/95

Specialty Group	London				Non-London				England
	Inner-deprived	Mixed-status	High-status	Total	Inner-deprived	Mixed-status	High-status	Total	
Geriatrics	1.29	1.16	1.18	1.20	1.28	1.22	1.26	1.23	1.23
Paediatrics	1.11	1.09	1.04	1.09	1.02	1.05	1.15	1.08	1.08
Medicine	1.07	1.08	1.11	1.08	1.16	1.12	1.17	1.14	1.13
Psychiatric	1.18	1.04	1.07	1.08	1.10	1.11	1.10	1.08	1.08
Unknown	1.10	1.01	1.13	1.06	1.04	1.05	1.04	1.11	1.09
All specialty average	**1.06**	**1.05**	**1.05**	**1.06**	**1.05**	**1.07**	**1.12**	**1.08**	**1.08**
Surgery/Urology	1.08	1.05	1.03	1.05	1.06	1.06	1.08	1.06	1.06
Haematology	1.04	1.05	1.04	1.04	1.05	1.03	1.08	1.05	1.05
Other non-acute	1.03	1.02	1.01	1.02	1.01	1.19	1.11	1.09	1.09
Orthopaedics	1.04	1.02	1.01	1.02	1.04	1.03	1.06	1.04	1.04
Obs. and Gynae.	1.02	1.01	1.01	1.01	1.01	1.03	1.05	1.03	1.03
Anaesthetics	1.01	1.01	1.01	1.01	1.11	1.08	1.08	1.09	1.08
ENT	1.01	1.01	1.00	1.01	1.08	1.03	1.05	1.04	1.03
Dental	1.01	1.00	1.00	1.01	1.01	1.03	1.07	1.04	1.03
Ophthalmology	1.00	1.01	1.00	1.00	1.01	1.02	1.04	1.02	1.02

(Table 44 is ordered by the London ratio.)

Transfer admissions

Transfers of patients between hospitals occur quite frequently in some areas of London for certain specialties. This section considers transfer episodes in more detail, analysing by specialty and by age-group. These are transfers into hospitals. Transfers out are dealt with in the next section on discharge destination.

The specialty composition of transfers

Table 45 shows the number and proportion of transfer FCEs, by specialty group, for each sector of London. The greatest proportion of transfers occurs in the psychiatric specialty, although in absolute terms there are more transfers of medicine and surgery patients. There is wide variation between sectors. In the south east, 20 per cent of psychiatric FCEs are transfers from other hospitals, but just one per cent are transfers in the south. The high proportion of transfers in the south east is due to the Bethlem and Maudsley trust where over a quarter of all FCEs are transfers. Similarly in the geriatrics specialty there is considerable variation between sectors: from one per cent in the south east to 11 per cent in the north-central sector. The south-east and north-central sectors have a greater proportion of transfers across all specialties, three times more than that in the east or north west.

Table 45: Inter-hospital transfers, by specialty, by sector of London, 1994/95

Specialty Group	North West		North Central		East		South East		South		London	
		%		%		%		%		%		%
Psychiatric	1,358	16	891	14	360	5	1,738	20	102	1	4,450	11
Geriatrics	357	2	1,798	11	229	2	178	1	388	3	2,950	4
Paediatrics	243	1	578	4	132	1	1,100	6	424	3	2,478	3
Medicine	1,872	1	1,927	3	878	1	2,446	3	1,970	4	9,093	2
Surgery/Urology	1,573	2	1,838	3	1,049	2	1,492	2	2,005	4	7,957	2
Other non-acute	167	1	180	2	4	0	72	7	37	5	460	2
Orthopaedics	186	1	117	1	113	1	96	0	137	1	649	1
ENT	56	0	63	0	16	0	231	2	23	0	390	1
Anaesthetics	16	1	22	1	30	1	112	2	4	0	185	1
Unknown	11	1	0	0	0	0	0	0	0	0	11	1
Obs. and Gynae.	41	0	56	0	9	0	52	0	149	0	307	0
Haematology	16	0	43	0	20	0	16	0	29	1	124	0
Ophthalmology	5	0	13	0	13	0	9	0	63	1	103	0
Dental	31	0	5	0	5	0	40	0	17	0	98	0
Total	5,931	1	7,532	3	2,860	1	7,584	3	5,347	2	29,254	2

(Tables 45 and 46 are ordered by specialty in London with the greatest proportion of transfers.)

Table 46 compares the proportion of transfers in London with similar areas in the rest of the country. Most noticeable differences occur in the psychiatric and geriatric specialties. Just seven per cent of psychiatric episodes are transfers in the rest of England compared to 11 per cent in London. The situation is reversed for geriatric episodes where just four per cent are transfers in London compared with seven per cent for the rest of the country.

The other significant difference occurs for 'other non-acute' episodes but this heterogeneous group is a relatively small proportion of total activity. The average proportion of transfers for activity as a whole is similar throughout the country. Specialty differences suggest different management of patients or the existence of more specialised facilities. For example, the effect of Bethlem and Maudsley is clear: 16 per cent of psychiatric FCEs in inner-deprived London are transfers.

Table 46: Inter-hospital transfers as a proportion of total FCEs, by specialty, London and England, 1994/95

Specialty Group	London				Non-London				England
	Inner-deprived	Mixed-status	High-status	Total	Inner-deprived	Mixed-status	High-status	Total	
	%	%	%	%	%	%	%	%	%
Psychiatric	16	9	7	11	9	7	8	7	7
Geriatrics	4	3	5	4	6	8	8	7	7
Paediatrics	5	3	1	3	4	1	4	3	3
Medicine	2	2	2	2	4	2	2	3	3
Surgery/Urology	3	2	2	2	3	1	2	2	2
Other non-acute	3	2	1	2	1	3	8	7	6
All specialty average	**2**	**2**	**2**	**2**	**3**	**2**	**2**	**2**	**2**
Orthopaedics	1	1	1	1	1	1	1	1	1
ENT	1	1	0	1	1	0	0	0	0
Anaesthetics	2	1	0	1	5	1	0	1	1
Unknown	0	0	1	1	0	2	0	1	1
Obs. and Gynae.	0	0	0	0	0	0	0	0	0
Haematology	0	0	0	0	1	0	1	1	1
Ophthalmology	0	1	0	0	0	0	0	0	0
Dental	0	0	0	0	1	1	0	1	1

The age composition of transfers

In this section we look briefly at the age composition of transfers. Table 47 indicates that the highest proportions of transfers occur in the 0-14, 75-84 and 85+ age-groups. In the north-central sector in particular, eight per cent of episodes for people aged 85 years and over are transfers. This reflects a high proportion of transfers to community trusts in this sector.

Table 47: Inter-hospital transfers, by age-group, by sector of London, 1994/95

Age-group	North West		North		East Central		South		South East		London	
		%		%		%		%		%		%
0-14	724	2	2,043	4	582	1	1,426	3	978	3	5,753	3
15-44	1,927	1	1,212	1	579	1	2,578	2	1,063	1	7,359	1
45-64	1,629	1	1,259	2	769	1	2,119	3	1,782	4	7,559	2
65-74	898	2	1,055	3	542	1	1,068	3	860	3	4,423	2
75-84	624	2	1,246	5	350	1	602	3	552	2	3,376	3
85+	124	2	335	8	38	1	131	3	112	3	740	3
Total	5,931	1	7,156	3	2,860	1	7,960	3	5,347	2	29,254	2

Table 48 compares London with similar areas in the rest of the country, showing that London has comparatively smaller proportions of transfers among older age-groups. For example, in the 85+ age-group five per cent of FCEs outside of London are transfers compared with only three per cent in London. In the north-central sector of London, where the proportion is of a similar magnitude, nearly all the transfers admissions are to community hospitals. The smaller proportion of transfers in older age-groups in London may represent a difference in the pattern of care for older people between London and the rest of the country, with fewer patients in London being transferred into community hospitals than is the case in the rest of the country.

Table 48: Inter-hospital transfers as a proportion of total FCEs, by age-group, London and England, 1994/95

| Age-group | London | | | | Non-London | | | | England |
	Inner-deprived %	Mixed-status %	High-status %	Total %	Inner-deprived %	Mixed-status %	High-status %	Total %	%
0-14	4	2	1	3	4	1	2	2	2
15-44	2	1	1	1	2	1	1	1	1
45-64	2	2	2	2	3	2	2	2	2
65-74	3	2	2	2	3	3	3	3	3
75-84	3	2	3	3	3	5	5	4	4
85+	4	3	3	3	4	5	6	5	4
Total	2	2	2	2	3	2	2	2	2

Discharge destination

In this section we consider where patients are discharged on completion of their hospital spell. The effect of age on discharge destination is also analysed. This section differs from the rest of the analysis in that only discharges are considered: episodes where the patient is transferred to the care of another consultant are excluded. Such multi-episode spells are considered in the previous section, *'Episodes and admissions'*. There are 13 discharge destination codes which have been combined into four groups: home (usual or temporary residence, and penal institutions), other hospital (transfers to other hospitals), residential care (local authority or NHS), and death. A very small proportion of cases where destination on discharge is not recorded have been excluded from the analysis.

Table 49 shows a similar pattern of discharge destination across sectors of London. There is a slightly lower proportion of deaths in the north-west sector; only the south sector shows a positive proportion of discharges to residential care.

Table 49: Proportion of admissions, by discharge destination, by sector of London, 1994/95

Discharge Destination	North West %	North Central %	East %	South East %	South %	London %
Home	95	94	94	94	94	95
Other hospital	2	3	2	3	2	2
Residential care	0	0	0	0	1	0
Died	2	3	3	3	3	3

Table 50 compares London with England and again there is a similar pattern of discharge destination. It is only when a more detailed age breakdown is considered that differences emerge.

Table 50: Proportion of admissions, by discharge destination, London and England, 1994/95

| Discharge Destination | London | | | | Non-London | | | | England |
	Inner-deprived %	Mixed-status %	High-status %	Total %	Inner-deprived %	Mixed-status %	High-status %	Total %	%
Home	95	95	93	95	95	94	93	94	94
Other hospital	2	2	3	2	2	3	3	3	3
Residential care	0	1	0	0	0	0	0	0	0
Died	2	3	3	3	2	3	3	3	3

The effect of age composition on discharge destination

Age is an important determinant of discharge destination. For older age-groups a larger proportion of admissions result in discharge to residential establishments. This is of particular interest in London because, as is noted in Chapter 8, there is a relative shortage of residential care places in the capital. Table 51 shows the breakdown by age-group, across sectors of London.

Table 51: Proportion of admissions, by discharge destination, by age-group, by sector of London, 1994/95

Age-group	Discharge Destination	North West %	North Central %	East %	South East %	South %	London %
0-64	Home	97	97	97	97	97	97
	Other hospital	2	2	2	2	2	2
	Residential care	0	0	0	0	1	0
	Died	1	1	1	1	1	1
65-74	Home	91	89	89	89	89	90
	Other hospital	4	5	3	4	4	4
	Residential care	0	1	0	1	1	1
	Died	5	6	7	6	6	6
75-84	Home	82	80	80	81	81	81
	Other hospital	6	7	6	5	5	6
	Residential care	1	1	1	1	2	1
	Died	11	11	12	12	12	11
85+	Home	73	67	68	69	71	70
	Other hospital	8	10	9	8	8	9
	Residential care	2	3	2	2	3	2
	Died	17	19	20	21	19	19

The proportion of deaths also increases with age. Thus, 19 per cent of hospital admissions in London for those aged 85 years and over result in death. Similarly, transfers to other hospitals and residential care are a greater proportion of discharges among older age-groups, representing 11 per cent of all discharges in the 85+ age-group, compared with two per cent in the 0-64 age-group. There is a clear gradient with the proportion of discharges to the patient's home falling as the age of the patient increases. Comparatively little variation is revealed between sectors: the proportion of deaths tends to be slightly above average in the east sector, and below average in the north-west. This may be due to variations in the proportion of emergency FCEs between sectors.

Table 52 provides a similar comparison between London and the rest of England. For all age-groups, there are less deaths as a proportion of admissions in inner-deprived areas, both in London and the rest of the country, when compared with other types of socio-economic area. This may be linked to the fact that there are comparatively fewer emergency admissions in inner-deprived areas.

Table 52: Proportion of admissions, by discharge destination, by age-group, London and England, 1994/95

| Age-group | Discharge Destination | London | | | | Non-London | | | | England |
		Inner-deprived %	Mixed-status %	High-status %	Total %	Inner-deprived %	Mixed-status %	High-status %	Total %	%
0-64	Home	97	97	97	97	97	97	97	97	97
	Other hospital	2	2	2	2	2	1	2	2	2
	Residential care	0	0	0	0	0	0	0	0	0
	Died	1	1	1	1	1	1	1	1	1
65-74	Home	90	90	89	90	90	88	88	88	88
	Other hospital	4	3	4	4	4	4	5	5	5
	Residential care	1	1	0	1	0	0	1	1	1
	Died	5	6	7	6	6	7	6	6	6
75-84	Home	82	83	79	81	82	79	78	79	79
	Other hospital	7	4	8	6	7	8	9	9	9
	Residential care	2	2	1	1	1	1	2	1	1
	Died	10	12	12	11	10	11	11	11	11
85+	Home	70	73	66	70	72	69	68	69	69
	Other hospital	9	5	12	9	10	12	12	13	12
	Residential care	3	3	2	2	2	2	3	2	2
	Died	17	20	20	19	16	17	17	16	17

Figure 7 compares London and the rest of England, for the 85+ age-group, showing that London has a greater proportion of deaths and a smaller proportion of transfers to other hospitals.

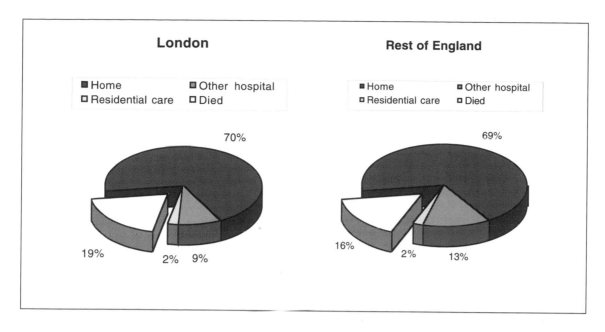

Figure 7: Proportion of discharges by destination, 85+ age-group, London and England, 1994/95

Operative procedures

(Technical note: 'Operative procedures' are treatments which are recorded with an OPCS 4 code. These include 'operations' in non-surgical specialties: for example, blood transfusions (X32-33) in haematology and endoscopic investigations in medicine. As the term 'operation' is commonly associated with surgical procedures only, this section will use the term 'operative procedure'.)

Total operative FCEs

So far we have considered episodes of hospital care. Over 50 per cent of these involve some form of operative procedure. This section considers the provision of operative procedures in hospitals. 'Operative' FCEs may include procedures which are not considered surgical, e.g. blood transfusion.

Table 53 shows the absolute total and proportion of FCEs with at least one operative procedure, by sector of London. The highest proportion of operative FCEs, 59 per cent, is in the south sector while the north-west and north-central sectors record just 53 per cent.

Table 53: The proportion of operative FCEs, by sector of London, 1994/95

Sector	North West	North Central	East	South East	South	London
Operative FCEs	212,781	147,784	163,194	163,975	129,079	816,813
Proportion of total FCEs	53%	53%	55%	58%	59%	56%

Table 54 shows that, in comparison with the rest of the country, London as a whole has a slightly higher proportion of FCEs where there was an operative procedure. The difference is most apparent in mixed-status areas. This may reflect differences in the pattern of care with fewer episodes involving an operative procedure, or differences in recording practices with minor procedures being recorded in some hospitals but not in others.

Table 54: The proportion of operative FCEs, London and England, 1994/95

Type of Area	London				Non-London				England
	Inner-deprived	Mixed-status	High-status	Total	Inner-deprived	Mixed-status	High-status	Total	
Operative FCEs	333,582	256,378	226,853	816,813	758,089	915,999	1,451,687	4,244,344	5,061,157
Proportion of total FCEs	55%	56%	56%	56%	55%	51%	54%	54%	54%

Operative FCEs, by admission method

We consider two aspects of the emergency/elective composition of operative procedures: first, the division of operative procedures as a whole between emergency and elective work; and second, the proportion of elective and emergency admissions respectively where an operative procedure was performed. Table 55 shows the proportion of total operative procedures, by admission method, for each sector of London. Although there is some variation across sectors, the great majority of operative FCEs are elective. The small proportion which are neither emergency nor elective are mainly maternity. Although 47 per cent of total FCEs in London are elective, 77 per cent of operative FCEs are elective. These operative FCEs are largely surgical operations.

Table 55: Operative FCEs, by admission method, by sector of London, 1994/95

Admission Method	North West %	North Central %	East %	South East %	South %	London %
Elective	81	77	74	78	74	77
Emergency	17	19	21	19	21	19
Other	1	5	5	2	4	3
Total	100	100	100	100	100	100

Table 56 compares London with the rest of England showing a similar lower proportion of emergency operative FCEs. There is no significant difference between types of socio-economic area in the capital, or between London and the rest of the country.

Table 56: Operative FCEs, by admission method, London and England, 1994/95

Admission Method	London				Non-London				England
	Inner-deprived %	Mixed-status %	High-status %	Total %	Inner-deprived %	Mixed-status %	High-status %	Total %	%
Elective	78	77	77	77	78	80	77	78	78
Emergency	18	19	21	19	18	19	21	20	20
Other	4	4	2	3	4	1	2	2	2
Total	100	100	100	100	100	100	100	100	100

Table 57 shows, for each sector of London, the proportion of emergency and elective admissions where at least one operative procedure was performed. A lower proportion of elective FCEs were operative in the north-west sector compared with other sectors. In over one-quarter of elective FCEs in that sector there was no associated operative procedure. Various factors may be involved: a higher proportion of total FCEs are elective in the north-west sector (see Table 2); there may be differences in the pattern of care, or a high proportion of cancellations of operations after the patient has been admitted, i.e. after the episode has started. There is less difference in the proportion of emergencies where an operative procedure was carried out: in between 69 and 74 per cent of cases no operative procedure was required.

Table 57: Operative FCEs as a proportion of total FCEs, by admission method, by sector of London, 1994/95

Admission Method	North West	North Central	East	South East	South	London
	%	%	%	%	%	%
Elective	74	77	83	87	86	80
Emergency	26	27	28	28	31	28

Differences emerge when London is compared with England. Table 58 shows that operative FCEs are a smaller proportion of total FCEs in the case of elective admissions, but a greater proportion of emergency admissions, when London is compared with other parts of England. A greater proportion of emergency operative FCEs is apparent in inner-deprived and mixed-status areas, 29 and 27 per cent respectively compared with 26 and 21 per cent.

Table 58: Operative FCEs as a proportion of total FCEs, by admission method, London and England, 1994/95

Admission Method	London				Non-London				England
	Inner-deprived	Mixed-status	High-status	Total	Inner-deprived	Mixed-status	High-status	Total	
	%	%	%	%	%	%	%	%	%
Elective	75	83	86	80	77	85	82	82	82
Emergency	29	27	28	28	26	21	27	26	26

The day case rate for operative FCEs

We have concentrated on the proportion of total FCEs that are operative. We now analyse operative FCEs themselves in more detail, considering the division between day cases and in-patients. The small number of 'other maternity' admissions are ignored.

Figure 8 shows, by sector of London, the proportion of operative FCEs that are day cases. The highest proportion of day cases is in the north-west sector where 50 per cent of operative FCEs are day cases. This contrasts with just 42 per cent in the east sector and is consistent with the variation between sectors in the proportion of all FCEs which are day cases (see Figure 2). It is also clear that FCEs which involve an operative procedure are more likely to be day cases than those which do not.

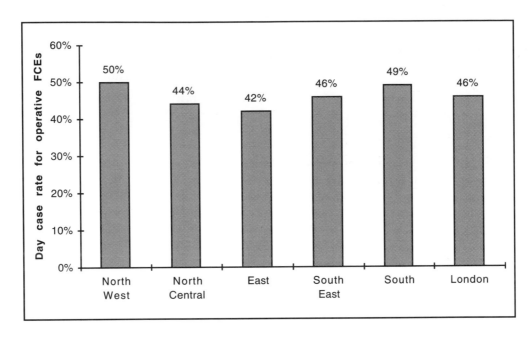

Figure 8: Proportion of day case operative FCEs, by sector of London, 1994/95

Figure 9 compares types of socio-economic area in London with similar areas in the rest of England. London has a higher proportion of day case operative FCEs than the rest of England, regardless of type of socio-economic area. Inner-deprived London, with the smallest proportion of day cases in the capital, 44 per cent, still approximates to the greatest proportion found outside of the capital – in mixed-status areas.

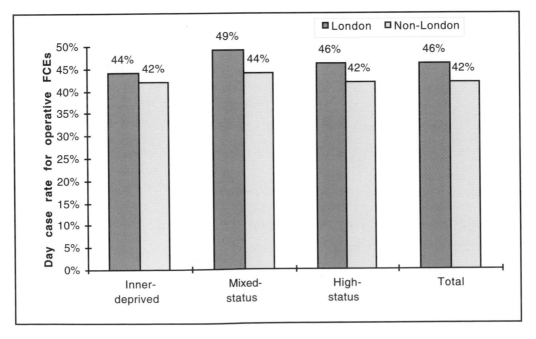

Figure 9: Proportion of day case operative FCEs, London and England, 1994/95

The day case rate for elective operative FCEs

This section considers emergency and elective operative FCEs separately. Day cases are almost always elective admissions. Hence, separate consideration of elective cases affords a more appropriate comparison of day case rates, as a trust with a high proportion of elective admissions will tend to have a higher day case rate than one with a high proportion of emergency admissions, other things being equal.

Figure 10 shows, by sector of London, the proportion of elective operative FCEs that are day cases. It becomes clear that the high proportion of day-case operative FCEs in the north-west sector is due to the high proportion of FCEs that are elective there. In fact, the day case rate for elective admissions alone is five per cent lower in this sector than in the south, and is only slightly higher than the London average. This contrasts with the pattern observed for total FCEs. The north-west sector has the highest proportion of elective work and also the highest day case rate for that elective work (see Table 2 and Figure 4).

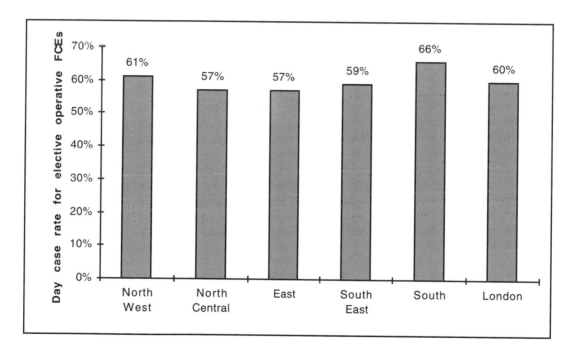

Figure 10: Proportion of elective operative FCEs that are day cases, by sector of London, 1994/95

Figure 11 compares London with the rest of England, showing a higher proportion of day cases among elective operative FCEs in London – 60 compared with 53 per cent. This reflects mainly the position in mixed- and high-status areas. Hospitals in inner-deprived areas of London have day case rates more similar to those in the rest of the country.

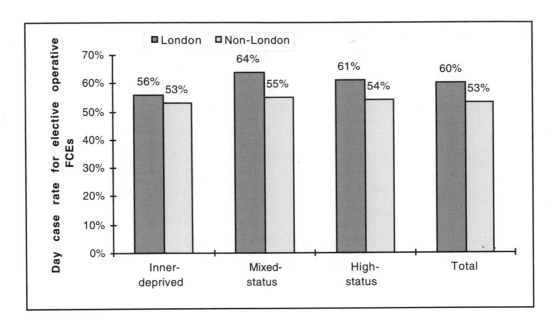

Figure 11: Proportion of elective operative FCEs that are day cases, London and England, 1994/95

The specialty composition of operative FCEs

Finally, we consider the specialty composition of operative FCEs. Table 59 shows, not unexpectedly, that surgical specialty groups have more operative FCEs in absolute terms than medical. At this level the effect of individual providers is apparent. For example, the large number of medical operative FCEs in the north west reflects the location of the Royal Marsden, the Royal Brompton and Harefield hospitals in this sector.

Table 59: Operative FCEs, by specialty group, by sector of London, 1994/95

Specialty Group	North West	North Central	East	South East	South	London
Surgery/Urology	65,069	45,216	43,218	54,846	44,449	252,797
Medicine	54,684	24,334	29,079	36,953	26,953	172,003
Obs. and Gynae.	30,782	25,124	30,236	21,364	20,925	128,431
Orthopaedics	23,515	13,600	14,362	14,669	11,806	77,952
Ophthalmology	8,777	4,455	19,670	7,000	6,564	46,466
ENT	9,665	11,089	8,025	7,875	6,509	43,163
Dental	7,681	3,739	5,740	8,040	6,366	31,566
Haematology	4,244	10,067	6,691	4,710	1,969	27,681
Anaesthetics	2,265	1,457	2,356	3,928	1,305	11,311
Other non-acute	1,644	5,793	1,160	141	98	8,836
Geriatrics	2,231	1,369	1,848	1,812	931	8,190
Paediatrics	1,295	1,532	802	2,594	1,202	7,424
Psychiatric	8	9	8	13	2	40
Total	212,781	147,784	163,194	163,975	129,079	816,813

(Tables 59 and 60 are ordered by specialty with the greatest number of operative FCEs in London.)

Table 60 contrasts the position in London with the rest of England. It is only in inner-deprived London that the medical specialties group has the greatest absolute number of operative FCEs, in contrast with other parts of the capital, and the rest of the country.

Table 60: Operative FCEs, by specialty group, London and England, 1994/95

Specialty Group	London Inner-deprived	Mixed-status	High-status	Total	Non-London Inner-deprived	Mixed-status	High-status	Total	England
Surgery/Uro.	87,631	79,195	85,971	252,797	265,962	317,647	480,710	1,436,611	1,689,408
Medicine	91,878	43,599	36,526	172,003	150,207	126,112	221,623	660,174	832,177
Obs. & Gynae.	44,441	48,574	35,416	128,431	89,934	137,764	202,269	582,319	710,750
Orthopaedics	23,792	27,185	26,974	77,952	75,941	122,044	186,590	546,437	624,389
Ophthalmology	26,665	9,133	10,668	46,466	45,025	54,888	81,320	250,740	297,206
ENT	19,016	13,661	10,486	43,163	48,391	73,679	101,157	295,984	339,147
Dental	11,982	10,712	8,872	31,566	30,150	27,128	60,173	159,647	191,213
Haematology	14,099	10,066	3,516	27,681	15,827	15,770	33,158	87,719	115,400
Anaesthetics	5,380	3,209	2,722	11,311	8,848	11,500	22,846	55,400	66,711
Other non-acute	2,280	5,234	1,322	8,836	10,270	12,397	27,436	68,737	77,573
Geriatrics	2,750	2,310	3,130	8,190	8,414	11,532	19,949	62,170	70,360
Paediatrics	3,624	2,634	1,167	7,424	8,761	4,944	12,484	33,628	41,052
Psychiatric	17	6	17	40	346	550	1,220	3,243	3,283
Total	333,582	256,378	226,853	816,813	758,089	915,999	1,451,687	4,244,344	5,061,157

Table 61 compares, by sector of London, the proportion of operative procedures for each specialty group, showing clearly a high proportion in most surgical specialties. In dental surgery and ophthalmology, for example, over 90 per cent of FCEs involve an operative procedure. Over 73 per cent of FCEs in most surgical specialties – obstetrics and gynaecology is the exception – include an operative procedure. This contrasts with 41 per cent in medicine. Just 11 per cent of geriatric FCEs in London involve an operative procedure, and the figure for psychiatric FCEs is less than one per cent.

Table 61: Proportion of total FCEs that are operative, by specialty, by sector of London, 1994/95

Specialty Group	North West %	North Central %	East %	South East %	South %	London %
Dental	95	89	93	94	97	94
Ophthalmology	93	85	91	90	94	91
ENT	84	73	80	82	87	80
Anaesthetics	82	79	95	69	95	80
Surgery/Urology	80	73	74	80	83	78
Orthopaedics	71	72	71	73	86	73
Haematology	69	78	61	83	81	73
Obs. and Gynae.	60	60	65	56	63	61
All specialty average	**54**	**54**	**56**	**58**	**59**	**56**
Medicine	40	36	37	48	48	41
Other non-acute	13	60	52	13	13	34
Geriatrics	13	8	12	13	8	11
Paediatrics	7	10	7	13	8	9
Psychiatric	0	0	0	0	0	0

(Tables 61-63 and 65-67 are ordered by specialty with the greatest proportion of operative FCEs in London.)

Table 62, which compares types of socio-economic area in London with similar areas in the rest of the country, shows a slightly higher proportion of operative FCEs in the capital: 56 to 54 per cent. The relative position varies across specialties with a higher proportion of operative FCEs in London in the medicine, obstetrics and gynaecology and haematology specialties, and a lower proportion in ENT and anaesthetics.

Table 62: Proportion of total FCEs that are operative FCEs, by specialty, London and England, 1994/95

Specialty Group	London				Non-London				England
	Inner-deprived	Mixed-status	High-status	Total	Inner-deprived	Mixed-status	High-status	Total	
	%	%	%	%	%	%	%	%	%
Dental	92	96	95	94	96	93	93	94	94
Ophthalmology	89	92	93	91	91	90	91	91	91
ENT	75	85	87	80	86	86	88	87	86
Anaesthetics	69	93	95	80	75	85	89	84	83
Surgery/Urology	73	80	81	78	78	76	79	78	78
Orthopaedics	70	68	84	73	71	74	74	74	74
Haematology	67	79	81	73	54	59	76	66	68
Obs. and Gynae.	62	62	58	61	52	53	57	56	57
All specialty average	**55**	**56**	**56**	**56**	**55**	**51**	**54**	**54**	**54**
Medicine	44	39	39	41	39	31	37	36	37
Other non-acute	34	59	12	34	17	33	30	25	26
Geriatrics	14	9	11	11	14	10	12	13	13
Paediatrics	12	11	5	9	11	4	8	7	7
Psychiatric	0	0	0	0	1	1	1	1	1

The specialty composition of elective operative FCEs

Table 63 shows, by sector of London, the proportion of operative FCEs in each specialty that are elective. Operative FCEs are more likely to be elective than others. In London, for all specialty groups, the proportion of operative FCEs that are elective is greater by at least ten per cent than the proportion of total FCEs that are. In the case of paediatrics, 48 per cent of operative FCEs are elective compared with 17 per cent of total FCEs, and in medicine, 73 per cent against 45 per cent.

Table 63: Proportion of operative FCEs that are elective, by specialty, by sector of London, 1994/95

Specialty Group	North West	North Central	East	South East	South	London
	%	%	%	%	%	%
Anaesthetics	99	100	87	98	99	96
Ophthalmology	95	96	92	93	97	94
Dental	91	94	92	95	95	93
ENT	90	95	94	90	92	92
Haematology	88	92	87	85	80	88
Surgery/Urology	81	81	78	81	78	80
Medicine	80	69	70	75	64	73
Orthopaedics	72	60	57	61	62	64
Paediatrics	64	49	22	46	50	48
Geriatrics	29	5	2	24	8	15

For the specialties in Table 63, almost all other FCEs are emergency admissions. Psychiatry is not considered as there were only 40 operative FCEs in the whole of the capital in 1994/95. Gynaecology is considered in more detail in Table 64.

Table 64: Obstetrics and gynaecology operative FCEs, by admission method, by sector of London, 1994/95

Admission Method	North West %	North Central %	East %	South East %	South %	London %
Elective	83	66	66	77	70	73
Emergency	14	16	15	20	15	16
Maternity	2	17	19	2	15	11

Maternity admissions in Table 64 refer to obstetric admissions where no birth occurs (see Box 1): nationally there are 30 to 40 per cent more obstetric episodes than there are births. Maternity admissions are a significant proportion of obstetric and gynaecology operative FCEs in the north-central, east and south sectors. In the south and north-central sectors this is due to a large proportion of maternity admissions at just a few trusts.

Table 65 compares the proportion of operative FCEs in London that are elective with the proportion in the rest of England. Elective proportions are similar for the surgical specialties, but in non-surgical specialties – medicine, haematology and paediatrics – the proportion of elective admissions tends to be higher in London.

Table 65: Proportion of operative FCEs that are elective, by specialty, London and England, 1994/95

Specialty Group	London Inner-deprived %	Mixed-status %	High-status %	Total %	Non-London Inner-deprived %	Mixed-status %	High-status %	Total %	England %
Anaesthetics	98	91	99	96	93	97	96	94	94
Ophthalmology	92	95	98	94	93	96	95	96	96
Dental	93	93	93	93	91	92	93	93	93
ENT	93	90	93	92	91	94	92	92	92
Haematology	89	91	75	88	83	86	82	83	84
Other non-acute	74	94	45	81	85	93	83	88	87
Surgery/Urology	79	81	80	80	79	82	80	81	81
Medicine	78	70	66	73	73	73	66	65	67
Orthopaedics	61	65	65	64	64	65	64	67	67
Paediatrics	46	61	25	48	50	40	39	36	38

The day case rate for operative FCEs, by specialty

Finally, we consider the proportion of operative FCEs performed as day cases, by specialty. Psychiatry has been excluded as the number of operative FCEs in London is so small. A comparison of Table 66 with Table 14 shows, for all specialties, the day case rate for operative FCEs is higher than that for all FCEs, in some cases quite significantly: for example, in medicine.

Table 66: Proportion of operative FCEs that are day cases, by specialty, by sector of London, 1994/95

Specialty Group	North West	North Central	East	South East	South	London
	%	%	%	%	%	%
Anaesthetics	91	94	81	87	95	89
Haematology	74	76	73	63	44	71
Dental	74	54	61	69	74	68
Medicine	61	46	51	51	50	54
Ophthalmology	59	50	41	51	79	52
Obs. and Gynae.	57	40	43	50	49	48
Surgery/Urology	41	42	40	44	46	42
ENT	30	25	27	26	54	31
Orthopaedics	30	25	18	27	28	26
Paediatrics	21	14	11	12	33	17
Geriatrics	23	1	1	19	0	11

There are relatively high day case rates in geriatrics in the north-west and south-east sectors, and a low day case rate in orthopaedics in the east sector. This low day case rate in orthopaedics in the east results from a day case rate of less than ten per cent at one trust.

Table 67 compares types of socio-economic area in London with similar areas in the rest of the country. For most specialties London trusts have a higher proportion of day cases than the rest of the country. Exceptions are paediatrics, geriatrics and orthopaedics: in the latter case, a low day case rate in inner-deprived London results in a slightly lower overall London day case rate for operative FCEs – 26 compared with 28 per cent.

Table 67: Proportion of operative FCEs that are day cases, by specialty, London and England, 1994/95

Specialty Group	London				Non-London				England
	Inner-deprived	Mixed-status	High-status	Total	Inner-deprived	Mixed-status	High-status	Total	
	%	%	%	%	%	%	%	%	%
Anaesthetics	92	85	86	89	81	85	85	83	84
Haematology	70	81	45	71	64	65	63	63	65
Dental	66	75	63	68	64	60	63	61	62
Medicine	54	56	49	54	44	54	49	49	50
Ophthalmology	47	53	66	52	51	43	46	45	46
Obs. and Gynae.	43	49	52	48	48	48	43	46	46
Surgery/Urology	35	46	47	42	40	44	40	41	41
ENT	29	35	30	31	29	29	31	29	29
Orthopaedics	20	27	31	26	26	29	26	28	28
Paediatrics	9	29	16	17	27	11	24	22	21
Geriatrics	6	13	14	11	13	11	10	12	12

Chapter 3

Hospital Utilisation Rates

Summary

The use of hospitals

- London hospitals produce 14 per cent more FCEs, 1.44 million in total, than are used by the residents of London, 1.24 million. The remainder are provided chiefly to residents of south-east England though some 29,000 come from the rest of England and further afield.

- However, when account is taken of the use made by local residents, there are sectors of London which are net exporters of care, the north west for example, and others which are net importers of care, the south for example.

- London has a lower overall actual hospitalisation rate than England as a whole, 184 compared with 192. Although age-sex standardisation increases London's hospitalisation rate relative to the national figure, at 188, it remains less than that of England.

- The actual rate is less in London than in England for three broad specialty groups: acute, geriatric and psychiatric. However standardisation reduces the difference substantially: to almost the same in acute, eight per cent less in psychiatric, and in the case of the geriatric specialty, London has a three per cent higher standardised hospitalisation rate.

- There is considerable variation in actual geriatric and psychiatric hospitalisation rates across the London DHAs, but much less in the acute group of specialties. This holds when rates are standardised for age and sex.

- There is comparatively little variation in the acute hospitalisation rate across the five sectors of London, whether actual or standardised figures are considered. However, there are pronounced differences in both geriatric and psychiatric specialties.

- Inner-deprived areas of London have a considerably lower acute hospitalisation rate than their counterparts elsewhere in England – a standardised rate of 170 compared with 207. The England average is 168. The same is true to a lesser extent of mixed-status areas and it is only when high-status areas are compared that London has a higher hospitalisation rate.

- London as a whole has a lower psychiatric hospitalisation rate than the rest of England, primarily due to the extremely low rate in high-status areas, 70 per cent of the England average. The psychiatric hospitalisation rate in inner-deprived London is 12 per cent higher than the England average. On the other hand, inner-deprived areas of London use substantially less geriatric services than similar areas in other parts of the country.

- Since 1989/90 there have been significant changes in the use of acute hospital services by residents of London. In particular, inner-deprived areas of the capital, which in 1989/90 had hospitalisation rates close to those of similar areas elsewhere in England, in 1994/95 use significantly less acute services – some 20 per cent less. There has been an equalisation of rates across London DHAs resulting in much less variation between types of socio-economic area.

The impact of patient flows

- In total, London hospitals export approximately 200,000 FCEs to the rest of the country. On the other hand, residents of London receive 37,000 FCEs from hospitals outside the capital. This implies a net export of 162,000 FCEs, or 11 per cent of total activity. Net export as a proportion of total activity is greatest for acute FCEs, which form the overwhelming majority of total activity.

- Since 1988/89, net export of acute activity has increased from 9.5 per cent of FCEs to 12 per cent. This is surprising since the introduction of the internal market was expected to limit exports of care from London to the rest of the country.

- The export of acute care by London providers is greatest from the former SHAs and other single specialty hospitals. Nearly half of acute FCEs at these hospitals are provided to non-Londoners.

- Central London teaching hospitals and those close to the border of London both export approximately 15 per cent of acute FCEs produced to the rest of the country. However, while the teaching group exports care to all areas of the country, and even abroad, export of care by the border group is more local – almost entirely to residents of the DHAs bordering London.

Key Facts

The use of hospitals	*London*	*Rest of England*
Total utilisation of hospital services:	1,280,000 FCEs	8,050,000 FCEs
Unstandardised hospitalisation rate per 1,000 resident population:	183.5	192.9
Standardised hospitalisation rate per 1,000 resident population:	188.1	192.1
Standardised hospitalisation rate per 1,000 resident population, by broad specialty group:		
• Acute	167.7	167.9
• Geriatric	11.8	11.4
• Psychiatric	5.6	6.1
Standardised hospitalisation index:		
• Acute	100	100
• Geriatric	103	100
• Psychiatric	92	101

The impact of patient flows

Patient flows

	London	*Rest of England*
Net export of FCEs by London providers to the rest of the country:	162,000 FCEs	–
Net export, by broad specialty group ('minus' denotes a net import):		
• Acute	155,000 FCEs	–
• Geriatric	-300 FCEs	–
• Psychiatric	1,100 FCEs	–

The market in London

	London	*Rest of England*
Proportion of acute FCEs provided to non-London Thames residents, by provider type:		
• Specialist	26%	–
• Teaching	10%	–
• Border	14%	–
• Other acute	4%	–
• Other non-acute	2%	–
• Total	10%	–
• Total excluding SHAs	9%	–
Proportion of acute FCEs provided to non-Thames residents, by provider type:		
• Specialist	21%	–
• Teaching	5%	–
• Border	2%	–
• Other acute	1%	–
• Other non-acute	0%	–
• Total	4%	–
• Total excluding SHAs	3%	–

1 Introduction

The previous chapter concentrated on a provider or supply-side perspective, considering the provision of health care in London regardless of where the patient resided. We turn now to the demand side, analysing the use of hospitals in England by London residents regardless of where the hospital is located. We then consider the use which non-residents of London make of the capital's hospitals by analysing flows of patients into London hospitals.

2 Data sources

As before, hospital admission data are taken from the Department of Health (DoH) Hospital Episode System (HES) database. Data refer to 1994/95 and both acute hospital and community trusts are included.

3 The use of hospitals

To understand the relationship between services provided by London's hospitals and the services received by London residents, the term, 'London FCEs', is used to indicate activity which takes place in London's hospitals and, 'Londoner FCEs', to indicate activity provided to people living in London. We present the absolute number of FCEs by district of residence of patient, before going on to compare unstandardised and standardised hospitalisation rates between London and the rest of the country. Some further analysis by diagnosis group is also provided.

Total FCEs

(Technical note: in this section we aggregate specialty groups into four larger groups: acute, geriatric, psychiatric and other non-acute. Geriatric and psychiatric are self-explanatory, containing these specialties only. Acute includes, medicine, surgery/urology, obstetrics and gynaecology, ophthalmology, orthopaedics, haematology, ENT, paediatrics, dental surgery and anaesthetics. Other non-acute consists of GP beds; the '800' series of non-acute specialties such as clinical oncology, radiology, general pathology etc.; and community and occupational medicine.)

Table 1 shows, by broad specialty group, the total number of FCEs provided to London DHA residents. Although most of this activity takes place in London hospitals, we shall see that there are flows of London patients to hospitals outside the capital. In 1994/95, Londoners used a total of 1,280,000 FCEs; this contrasts with 1,468,000 FCEs provided by London hospitals. The difference confirms our earlier suggestion that London is exporting care to the rest of the country. More detailed consideration of the flow of patients between areas is provided in a later section. In absolute terms, residents of Lambeth, Southwark and Lewisham receive the greatest number of FCEs, followed by Ealing, Hammersmith and Hounslow, Merton, Sutton and Wandsworth, and East London and the City.

Table 1: Total FCEs, by London DHA, 1994/95

DHA	Acute	Geriatric	Psychiatric	Other non-acute	Total
Kensington, Chelsea and Westminster	55,254	2,593	1,981	999	60,827
East London and the City	95,842	5,052	3,440	546	104,881
Camden and Islington	60,432	4,356	3,104	759	68,652
Lambeth, Southwark and Lewisham	124,130	5,822	5,308	1,132	136,391
Brent and Harrow	78,585	5,721	2,151	1,908	88,365
Ealing, Hammersmith and Hounslow	107,776	5,638	2,367	2,293	118,075
Enfield and Haringey	80,284	4,497	2,046	3,720	90,546
Redbridge and Waltham Forest	75,360	5,443	3,605	1,693	86,101
Merton, Sutton and Wandsworth	105,783	6,512	5,324	284	117,903
Hillingdon	37,923	2,333	1,180	2,126	43,562
Barnet	47,439	5,024	1,059	1,486	55,008
Barking and Havering	65,025	4,918	1,283	1,038	72,264
Bexley and Greenwich	65,283	4,708	1,242	207	71,439
Bromley	46,904	3,557	1,368	144	51,973
Croydon	51,379	2,964	1,938	306	56,588
Kingston and Richmond	50,269	3,086	1,669	1,280	56,303
London	1,147,668	72,224	39,063	19,923	1,278,879
England	8,175,250	555,784	295,135	304,574	9,330,744

Table 2 provides a breakdown by sector of London. Although the greatest number of FCEs are provided to residents of north-west London – 24 per cent of total Londoner FCEs – 28 per cent of London FCEs are produced in this sector. By contrast, the proportion of total Londoner FCEs in the south sector is 18 per cent while only 14 per cent of London FCEs are produced there. This clearly indicates there are flows between sectors. Flows are looked at in more detail in the next section.

Table 2: Total FCEs, by sector of London, 1994/95

Specialty Group	North West	North Central	East	South East	South	London
Acute	279,538	188,154	236,227	236,317	207,431	1,147,668
Psychiatric	7,679	6,209	8,328	7,917	8,930	39,063
Geriatrics	16,285	13,877	15,414	14,086	12,562	72,224
Other non-acute	7,327	5,965	3,278	1,483	1,870	19,923
Total	310,829	214,206	263,246	259,803	230,794	1,278,879

Table 3 compares London with England. Fourteen per cent of both total and acute FCEs are provided to the residents of London, a similar percentage to London as a proportion of the England population, and in contrast to the 16 per cent of all England activity that takes place in London.

Table 3: Total FCEs, London and England, 1994/95

Specialty Group	London				Non London				England
	Inner-deprived	Mixed status	High status	Total	Inner deprived	Mixed status	High status	Total	
Acute	335,659	447,788	364,222	1,147,668	988,084	1,740,386	2,603,904	7,027,582	8,175,250
Psychiatric	17,822	27,812	26,590	72,224	56,698	116,942	174,590	483,560	555,784
Geriatrics	13,834	15,492	9,738	39,063	32,050	56,091	93,761	256,072	295,135
Other non-acute	3,436	9,899	6,588	19,923	19,579	57,874	112,727	284,651	304,574
Total	370,751	500,991	407,137	1,278,879	1,096,411	1,971,293	2,984,981	8,051,865	9,330,744

We present pure activity figures to give some indication of the size and location of overall demand for hospital care thereby providing a perspective on what level of local provision might be required. However, for comparisons between areas it is more interesting to consider utilisation per capita resident population, known as the hospitalisation rate. An analysis of hospitalisation rates is presented below.

Unstandardised hospitalisation rate

This section presents London DHA hospitalisation rates, by three main specialty groups – acute, geriatric and psychiatric. The distinction between acute and geriatric is not always useful as it may reflect differences in practice, between trusts where older people are cared for by a consultant in the geriatric specialty, and others where the tendency is to treat older people in the medicine specialty. However, findings can be refined by considering hospitalisation by age-group across the combined geriatric and acute specialties, and by diagnosis group.

Hospitalisation rates are expressed as FCEs per 1,000 resident population, first unstandardised for the age and sex distribution of DHA areas, and then taking account of age-sex standardisation. The first allows consideration of the actual local demand faced by London's hospital services in terms of resident population. The age distribution of an area of course has an impact on these demands (but so will other factors affecting health status). Hospitalisation rates standardised for age and sex are provided in the next section.

Table 4 shows unstandardised hospitalisation rates, by London DHA, for total FCEs, and three broad specialty groups: acute, psychiatric and geriatric. The 'other non-acute' group is excluded as it is small and heterogeneous. An England figure is added for ease of comparison. London has lower unstandardised hospitalisation rates than the country as a whole. For total activity, the hospitalisation rate per 1,000 London residents is four per cent less than that of the rest of England. For acute specialties, the difference is smaller: the London rate is just two per cent less than that of England. There is of course variation across London with residents of Merton, Sutton and Wandsworth, for example, using more acute and psychiatric hospital services than the England average, but less geriatric.

Table 4: Unstandardised hospitalisation rate, by London DHA, 1994/95 (FCEs per 1,000 resident population)

DHA	Acute	Geriatric	Psychiatric	Total
Kensington, Chelsea and Westminster	162.2	7.6	5.8	178.6
East London and the City	161.0	8.5	5.8	176.2
Camden and Islington	168.7	12.2	8.7	191.6
Lambeth, Southwark and Lewisham	169.7	8.0	7.3	186.4
Brent and Harrow	170.9	12.4	4.7	192.2
Ealing, Hammersmith and Hounslow	166.0	8.7	3.6	181.9
Enfield and Haringey	169.9	9.5	4.3	191.6
Redbridge and Waltham Forest	165.5	12.0	7.9	189.0
Merton, Sutton and Wandsworth	171.5	10.6	8.6	191.1
Hillingdon	156.0	9.6	4.9	179.2
Barnet	153.9	16.3	3.4	178.4
Barking and Havering	172.3	13.0	3.4	191.5
Bexley and Greenwich	150.4	10.8	2.9	164.6
Bromley	160.5	12.2	4.7	177.9
Croydon	157.1	9.1	5.9	173.0
Kingston and Richmond	163.4	10.0	5.4	183.1
London	164.7	10.4	5.6	183.5
England	167.8	11.4	6.1	191.6

In comparison with 1989/90, there has been an increase in the unstandardised hospitalisation rate for acute specialties. In 1989/90 the rate was 145 in 'Inner' London and 126 in 'Outer' London, compared with a total London figure in 1994/95 of 165, as shown above (Boyle and Smaje, 1992). These figures are not quite comparable as the 1994/95 definition of acute specialties (based on DoH usage) includes anaesthetics whereas the previous DoH definition (which was used by the first London Commission) excluded that specialty. However, this has comparatively little effect as anaesthetics accounts for less than two FCEs per 1,000 population in both London and England.

The unstandardised acute hospitalisation rate has increased in London but less quickly than in England, where it has risen from 125 in 1989/90 to 168 in 1994/95. London had a higher hospitalisation rate than the rest of the country in 1989/90. The position is now reversed.

Comparing individual DHAs in London with their position in 1989/90 is complicated by the many changes in DHA boundaries which have occurred. Taking DHAs with minimal changes – Barnet, Hillingdon, Croydon and Bromley – acute hospitalisation rates have increased by between 20 and 45 FCEs per 1,000 population. However, these were among those with the lowest rates in 1989/90. Such increases have not been repeated in other areas. There was wide variation in hospitalisation rates across London in 1989/90, from a low of just 113, in both Bromley and Redbridge, to a high of 203 in Bloomsbury. By contrast, in 1994/95 the highest rate is 172 in Barking and Havering, whereas the lowest rate is 150 in Bexley and Greenwich. The aggregation of London into larger DHAs may be masking more pronounced variation at a lower level. This is examined in more detail in the section on local authority ward-level hospitalisation rates.

Table 5 shows unstandardised hospitalisation rates for each sector of London. There is comparatively little variation in the acute hospitalisation rate between the five sectors. By contrast, there are pronounced differences in psychiatric and geriatric hospitalisation rates. For example, residents in the south have a psychiatric hospitalisation rate almost 60 per cent higher than those in the north west.

Table 5: Unstandardised hospitalisation rate, by sector of London, 1994/95 (FCEs per 1,000 resident population)

Specialty Group	North West	North Central	East	South East	South	London
Acute	165.2	165.2	165.4	162.1	165.7	164.7
Psychiatric	4.5	5.5	5.8	5.4	7.1	5.6
Geriatric	9.6	12.2	10.8	9.7	10.0	10.4
Total	183.6	188.0	184.3	178.2	184.4	183.5

Table 6 compares London with England, showing that, with the exception of high-status areas, London has lower acute and geriatric hospitalisation rates than comparable areas in the rest of the country. This is particularly true of inner-deprived areas where the difference for the acute specialties is 40 FCEs per 1,000 population, almost 25 per cent of the inner-deprived London rate. By contrast, London has an equivalent psychiatric hospitalisation rate in inner-deprived and mixed-status areas but a lower rate in high-status areas. For each specialty group, London as a whole has a lower hospitalisation rate than the rest of England.

Table 6: Unstandardised hospitalisation rate, London and England, 1994/95 (FCEs per 1,000 resident population)

Specialty Group	London				Non-London				England
	Inner-deprived	Mixed-status	High-status	Total	Inner-deprived	Mixed-status	High-status	Total	
Acute	165.7	168.7	159.1	164.7	205.6	180.2	154.5	168.4	167.8
Psychiatric	6.8	5.8	4.3	5.6	6.7	5.8	5.6	6.1	6.1
Geriatric	8.8	10.5	11.6	10.4	11.8	12.1	10.4	11.6	11.4
Total	183.0	188.8	177.8	183.5	228.2	204.1	177.1	192.9	191.6

The evidence on changes in acute hospitalisation rates is surprising. In 1989/90, comparisons across types of socio-economic area, between London and the rest of the country, revealed similar hospitalisation rates. For example, inner-deprived areas outside the capital had a hospitalisation rate just two FCEs per 1,000 resident population greater than that of similar areas in London. This analysis of unstandardised hospitalisation rates suggests that the rate has increased more slowly in London than the rest of England over the last five years, with the result that the London rate is now less than the crude England average. It is considerably less when inner-deprived areas of the capital are compared with similar areas in the rest of the country such as Manchester or Liverpool. Moreover, there appears to have been an equalisation of rates across the capital.

Age-sex standardised hospitalisation rates

Hospitalisation rates are affected by the age and sex composition of areas. We present hospitalisation rates standardised for age and sex, both as a rate per 1,000 resident population, and against an index of 100 for England as a whole to facilitate comparison.

Table 7 and Figure 1 show the standardised hospitalisation rate for London DHAs, for the main specialty groups. Since the capital has a somewhat younger population structure than average, the London age-sex standardised hospitalisation rate is greater than the unstandardised version. The difference between London and England for acute specialties falls from over three FCEs per 1,000 population to approximate equality. Londoners make greater than average use of the geriatric specialty once population structure is taken into account but still use less psychiatric care.

The standardised total hospitalisation rate in London is 3.5 FCEs per 1,000 less than England. This reflects the relatively high use of other non-acute services such as GP maternity and community medicine in the rest of the country.

Table 7: Standardised hospitalisation rate, by London DHA, 1994/95 (FCEs per 1,000 resident population, age-sex standardised on England rates)

DHA Code	DHA	Acute	Geriatric	Psychiatric	Total
1	Kensington, Chelsea and Westminster	164.9	8.7	5.7	182.5
2	East London and the City	167.0	11.9	5.9	186.1
3	Camden and Islington	172.2	14.5	8.6	197.4
4	Lambeth, Southwark and Lewisham	174.3	10.0	7.2	193.9
5	Brent and Harrow	174.5	14.8	4.7	198.1
6	Ealing, Hammersmith and Hounslow	170.2	10.7	3.6	188.5
7	Enfield and Haringey	174.0	11.1	4.3	197.8
8	Redbridge and Waltham Forest	168.2	12.8	7.9	192.8
9	Merton, Sutton and Wandsworth	175.2	11.7	8.5	196.0
10	Hillingdon	158.3	10.5	4.8	182.7
11	Barnet	155.7	16.4	3.4	180.4
12	Barking and Havering	171.3	12.9	3.4	190.4
13	Bexley and Greenwich	151.7	11.6	2.9	166.6
14	Bromley	159.0	11.2	4.6	175.3
15	Croydon	159.7	10.8	6.0	177.6
16	Kingston and Richmond	164.4	9.8	5.3	183.6
	London	167.7	11.8	5.6	188.1
	England	167.8	11.4	6.1	191.6

(The DHA code is provided for ease of presentation in Figure 1.)

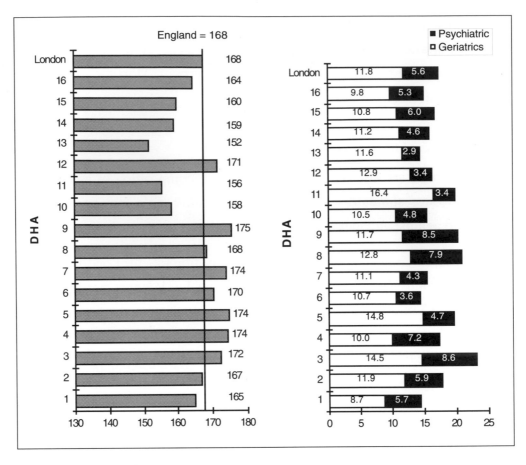

(See Table 7 for DHA codes.)

Figure 1: Acute, geriatric and psychiatric standardised hospitalisation rates, by London DHA, 1994/95

Table 8 and Figure 2 provide an index of hospitalisation rates in London, taking the England rate as 100. There is significant variation across London DHAs in the psychiatric and geriatric specialties. The standardised psychiatric hospitalisation index in London as a whole is eight per cent less than that of England, but varies from 140 in Camden and Islington and Merton, Sutton and Wandsworth to under 50 in Bexley and Greenwich. There is also considerable variation across London in the use of geriatric services, from 75 per cent of the England rate in Kensington, Chelsea and Westminster to over 40 per cent above the England average in Barnet. It is clear from Figure 2 that there are very few examples of London DHAs with significantly higher hospitalisation rates than the England average: in fact the only examples are in the geriatric and psychiatric specialties.

Table 8: Standardised hospitalisation index, by London DHA, 1994/95 (England = 100)

DHA Code	DHA	Acute	Geriatric	Psychiatric	Total
1	Kensington, Chelsea and Westminster	98	76	93	95
2	East London and the City	99	104	98	97
3	Camden and Islington	103	127	141	103
4	Lambeth, Southwark and Lewisham	104	88	119	101
5	Brent and Harrow	104	130	78	103
6	Ealing, Hammersmith and Hounslow	101	94	60	98
7	Enfield and Haringey	104	98	72	103
8	Redbridge and Waltham Forest	100	112	131	101
9	Merton, Sutton and Wandsworth	104	102	140	102
10	Hillingdon	94	92	80	95
11	Barnet	93	143	56	94
12	Barking and Havering	102	113	56	99
13	Bexley and Greenwich	90	102	47	87
14	Bromley	95	98	77	91
15	Croydon	95	94	99	93
16	Kingston and Richmond	98	86	88	96
	London	100	103	92	98

(The DHA code is provided for ease of presentation in Figure 2 below.)

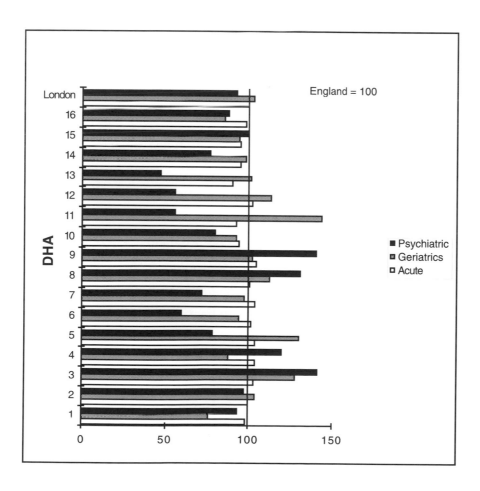

(See Table 8 for DHA codes.)

Figure 2: Standardised hospitalisation index, by London DHA, 1994/95 (England = 100)

Tables 9 and 10 show the standardised hospitalisation rate and index by sector of London. There is little variation in the acute index across sectors but the psychiatric index ranges from 75 in the north west to 117 in the south, whereas the geriatric index has a range of 95 to 120.

Table 9: Standardised hospitalisation rate, by sector of London, 1994/95 (FCEs per 1,000 resident population, age-sex standardised on England rates)

Specialty Group	North West	North Central	East	South East	South	London	England
Acute	168.6	168.4	168.5	164.4	168.5	167.7	167.8
Psychiatric	4.5	5.4	5.9	5.4	7.1	5.6	6.1
Geriatric	11.4	13.7	12.5	10.8	10.9	11.8	11.4
Total	189.0	192.9	189.5	181.9	188.1	188.1	191.6

Table 10: Standardised hospitalisation index, by sector of London, 1994/95 (England =100)

Specialty Group	North West	North Central	East	South East	South	London	England
Acute	100	100	100	98	100	100	100
Psychiatric	75	89	97	89	117	92	100
Geriatric	100	120	110	95	96	103	100
Total	99	101	99	95	98	98	100

Tables 11 and 12 compare hospitalisation rates between types of socio-economic area in London and England. There remains a comparatively low acute hospitalisation rate in inner-deprived London when compared with similar areas in the rest of England, even when age and sex are taken into account. The acute hospitalisation rate in inner-deprived areas outside of London is 23 per cent more than the England average, but only one per cent more in comparable parts of the capital. However, there is a high psychiatric hospitalisation rate in inner-deprived areas of London – 12 per cent above the England rate. On the other hand, the psychiatric hospitalisation rate in high-status areas is considerably below the England average.

Table 11: Standardised hospitalisation rate, London and England, 1994/95 (FCEs per 1,000 resident population, age-sex standardised on England rates)

| Specialty Group | London | | | | Non-London | | | | England |
	Inner-deprived	Mixed-status	High-status	Total	Inner-deprived	Mixed-status	High-status	Total	
Acute	170.2	172.4	160.0	167.7	207.1	180.3	154.1	167.9	167.8
Psychiatric	6.8	5.8	4.2	5.6	6.7	5.9	5.6	6.1	6.1
Geriatric	11.1	12.1	12.0	11.8	12.2	12.8	10.6	11.4	11.4
Total	190.3	194.3	179.1	188.1	230.1	205.0	177.0	192.1	191.6

The contrast between acute and psychiatric hospitalisation rates is interesting. Mixed-status London has a slightly higher acute hospitalisation rate than inner-deprived London, but the psychiatric hospitalisation rate is considerably more in the inner-deprived areas of the capital. One interpretation is that hospitalisation for psychiatric reasons in London is more dependent on the relative deprivation of the area of residence than is the case for acute specialties. A number of factors might be involved. For example, there may be a greater relative need for psychiatric than acute services in more deprived areas; or it may reflect differences in the management of psychiatric patients depending on the type of area in which they live. Further analysis using both the HES dataset and local knowledge and data may shed more light on these findings.

Table 12: Standardised hospitalisation index, London and England, 1994/95 (England=100)

Specialty Group	London				Non-London				England
	Inner-deprived	Mixed-status	High-status	Total	Inner-deprived	Mixed-status	High-status	Total	
Acute	101	103	95	100	123	107	92	100	100
Psychiatric	112	96	70	92	110	97	92	101	100
Geriatric	97	106	105	103	107	112	93	100	100
Total	99	101	93	98	120	107	92	100	100

Hospitalisation rate by diagnosis group

This section compares hospitalisation rates using the diagnosis groups discussed in Chapter 2, both across sectors of London, and between London and the rest of the country. Table 13 shows unstandardised rates for each sector of London.

Table 13: Unstandardised hospitalisation rate, by diagnosis group, by sector of London, 1994/95 (FCEs per 1,000 resident population)

Diagnosis Group	North West	North Central	East	South East	South	London
Cancer	19	17	17	14	21	18
Urinary	17	18	19	16	18	17
Digestive	17	16	17	17	19	17
Ill-defined	14	14	13	15	16	14
Childbirth	12	18	19	11	12	14
V code	14	18	13	15	11	14
Respiratory/Thoracic	12	13	14	14	12	13
Trauma	11	10	10	12	11	11
Cardiac	10	11	12	11	10	11
Nervous	11	10	9	10	11	10
Musculo-Skeletal	10	9	9	9	9	9
Mental	6	6	5	5	7	6
Skin	5	4	4	4	5	5
Oral	4	3	4	5	5	4
Vascular	4	4	3	4	4	4
Blood	3	5	4	4	3	4
Endocrine	3	3	3	3	2	3
Cerebrovascular	2	3	3	3	2	3
Infectious Diseases	2	3	2	2	2	2
Congenital	1	2	1	1	2	2
Perinatal	1	1	1	1	2	1
Total	184	188	184	178	184	184

(Tables 13 and 14 are ordered by diagnosis group with the highest hospitalisation rate in London. Figures may not sum due to rounding.)

The diagnosis group with the highest hospitalisation rate in London as a whole is the cancer group. However, for individual diagnosis groups there is variation across the capital: for example, in the north-central sector there is a higher hospitalisation rate for childbirth and v codes. For most diagnosis groups there is a close correspondence between the hospitalisation rate in a sector and the amount of such activity provided in that sector: see Table 25 in Chapter 2 on page 57 for a comparison. A better understanding of this relationship between diagnostic hospitalisation rates and levels of activity in a sector, within a given diagnosis group, would be afforded by the construction of a patient flow matrix, by diagnosis group.

Table 14 compares hospitalisation rates, by diagnosis group, between London and the rest of the country. London residents generally have a lower hospitalisation rate, particularly in inner-deprived areas. London as a whole has a lower hospitalisation rate than the rest of England in six diagnosis groups, a similar rate in 12 and a higher rate in only three: skin complaints, blood disorders and conditions associated with childbirth.

Table 14: Unstandardised hospitalisation rate, by diagnosis group, London and England, 1994/95 (FCEs per 1,000 resident population)

| Diagnosis Group | London | | | | Non-London | | | | England |
	Inner-deprived	Mixed-status	High-status	Total	Inner-deprived	Mixed-status	High-status	Total	
Cancer	15	18	19	18	21	18	17	18	18
Urinary	16	18	18	17	19	18	16	17	17
Digestive	17	17	18	17	22	18	17	18	18
Ill-defined	14	15	15	14	27	22	15	19	18
Childbirth	18	14	11	14	15	12	11	11	11
V code	13	17	12	14	13	12	14	14	14
Respiratory/Thoracic	13	13	13	13	17	15	11	13	13
Trauma	12	11	11	11	18	15	13	14	14
Cardiac	10	11	11	11	14	12	10	11	11
Nervous	9	10	10	10	13	12	11	12	11
Musculo-Skeletal	9	9	10	9	12	12	11	12	12
Mental	7	6	5	6	7	7	6	6	6
Skin	4	5	5	5	5	5	4	4	4
Oral	4	4	3	4	4	3	4	4	4
Vascular	4	4	4	4	5	5	4	5	5
Blood	4	4	3	4	3	3	2	3	3
Endocrine	4	3	2	3	3	3	2	3	3
Cerebrovascular	2	2	3	3	4	3	2	3	3
Infectious Diseases	3	2	2	2	3	3	2	2	2
Congenital	2	2	1	2	2	2	2	2	2
Perinatal	1	1	1	1	0	1	1	1	1
Total	183	189	178	184	228	204	177	193	192

Inner-deprived Londoners have a lower hospitalisation rate in 12 diagnosis groups. The inner-deprived London hospitalisation rate for ill-defined conditions is just half that of similar areas in the rest of the country. This may reflect better diagnosis or recording in London, but there are other groups with significant, if less spectacular differences. For example, the hospitalisation rate for trauma for residents of inner-deprived areas outside London is 50 per cent higher than for Londoners, while the rates for cancer, digestive and respiratory diagnoses are over 25 per cent higher.

These tables reflect hospital activity. They do not purport to be the relative incidence of these diagnoses in the London population compared with the rest of the country. The lower hospitalisation rate in London may reflect a healthier population in the capital, or it may reflect a higher threshold for access to hospital care for Londoners than for residents of the rest of England. Furthermore, even a breakdown of hospitalisation rate by diagnosis may not accurately reflect differences in the breakdown of the various diseases. For example, the higher hospitalisation rate for conditions related to childbirth in London may reflect differences in recording. Similarly, the presence of a specialist hospital may increase the hospitalisation rate for local residents.

Local authority ward-level hospitalisation rate

In this section we look briefly at the hospitalisation rate for all specialties, by London local authority electoral ward. Map 1 shows the age-sex standardised hospitalisation rate across London wards. There are 784 electoral wards in London, but for this analysis, the 25 small wards in the City of London have been combined, to produce a total of 760. Of these, 340 have a hospitalisation rate above the England average of 192 FCEs, one is at the national average and 419 have a rate below. Excluding one very low outlier in Greenwich, both the ward with the greatest and with the lowest hospitalisation rate in London are located in the borough of Kensington and Chelsea.

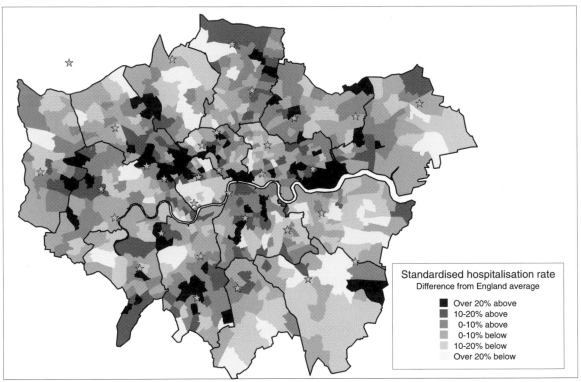

Standardised hospitalisation rate
Difference from England average

■ Over 20% above
■ 10-20% above
■ 0-10% above
■ 0-10% below
□ 10-20% below
□ Over 20% below

* indicates acute trust headquarters

Map 1: Standardised hospitalisation rate, all specialites, by London LA ward, 1994/95

There is great variation in ward-level hospitalisation rates in Kensington, Chelsea and Westminster DHA: the north of the district has very high rates; the south has the lowest in the capital. Of the 15 wards in London with the greatest hospitalisation rates, six are in Kensington, Chelsea and Westminster; on the other hand, nine of the 15 wards with the lowest rates are also in this DHA. The north-south divide in this DHA is clearly shown by the map. The variation would appear to reflect socio-economic differences across the DHA, with much greater deprivation in the north of the district.

The map demonstrates where clusters of high and low hospitalisation are located. The following areas are clusters of high hospitalisation:

- north Kensington, north Westminster and south Brent;

- south Merton and north Sutton;

- on the border between Brent and Barnet around Edgware;

- south Kingston; and,

- the City and the south of Camden and Islington.

These areas with high hospitalisation rates are not uniformly in inner-deprived DHAs. Indeed, only the first and last of these clusters are classified as inner-deprived. Kingston is classified as high-status, Merton and Sutton is part of a mixed-status area, Brent and Harrow is mixed-status and Barnet is high-status.

By contrast, the following areas have a lower than average hospitalisation rate:

- the south of Kensington, Chelsea and Westminster;

- north Ealing;

- the centre of Barnet;

- some parts of Hackney;

- north-west Merton;

- most of southern Croydon and the majority of Bromley; and,

- most of Bexley.

The map also shows the location of acute trust headquarters. In most cases, wards where hospitals are located have above average hospitalisation rates. There are exceptions: Chelsea and Westminster is in the heart of a low hospitalisation area of Kensington and Chelsea, as is the Homerton in Hackney. Seventeen of the 40 wards with the highest hospitalisation rates in London contain, or are adjacent to, an acute trust headquarters.

Wards with very high and very low hospitalisation rates exist side-by-side in London. The classification of London DHAs between higher and lower levels of deprivation does not preclude the location of some wards with low hospitalisation rates in inner-deprived London, while others with very high rates can be found in high-status areas. However, a word of warning is appropriate. At this highly disaggregated geographic level, the data may not be robust enough to allow definite conclusions. If the postcode of the patient is inaccurate or missing on the records of one or more trusts, this may have an enormous impact at the electoral ward level. Hence, these variations in hospitalisation rate, point to interesting areas for further research and analysis, but too much reliance can not be placed upon them.

4 The impact of patient flows

In considering the supply of hospital services in London on the one hand, and the use which Londoners make of hospitals on the other, it is already clear that more is produced in London than Londoners themselves use; comparing sectors of London, some are net exporters of care and others are net importers. In this section we consider the market for hospital care in England in terms of sources of demand and supply, by providing a *'patient flow'* analysis for the three main specialty groups: acute, psychiatric and geriatric.

Patient flows

London produces a total of 1.47 million FCEs but residents of the capital consume just 1.28 million episodes. Of these, 1.24 million episodes are provided by London hospitals, or 84 per cent of total production in London. The remainder, some 37,000 FCEs, are provided to London residents by hospitals outside the capital. Thus, the net export of care by London is 203,000 or 14 per cent of total production. Care provided to non-residents of England (mainly from Scotland and Wales) is included in this figure. Data on care provided outside of England for English residents are not available. London exports approximately 12,000 FCEs to non-English residents: inward flows are likely to be small.

These figures, however, include Mount Vernon and Watford Hospitals trust. This consists of two main sites, Mount Vernon hospital which is in London, and Watford General which is not. These two hospitals cannot be separated on the HES database. However, the treatment of activity from this trust is likely to be important for any analysis of London patient flows. Therefore, using estimates of patient flows to these two hospitals made in 1994 by Hillingdon Health Agency (Hillingdon Health Agency, 1994), we have calculated flows taking account of the location of hospitals in this trust. Our estimates suggest that, excluding Watford General Hospital, London hospitals produce a total 1.44 million episodes, of which 1.24 million were consumed by London residents. Residents of London still consume 37,000 FCEs outside the capital, resulting in a net export of 162,000 FCEs from London hospitals to the rest of the country. These figures, which probably reflect patient flows more accurately – especially if comparisons are made over time – are presented in Table 15 and Figure 3.

Table 15: Patient flows in FCEs, between London and the rest of the world, by specialty group, 1994/95

Specialty Group	Column A *Number of FCEs provided in London*	Column B *Total & % of Col. A (London provision) used by Londoners*		Column C *London imports from rest of England*	Column D *Total used by Londoners, Col. B plus Col. C*	Column E *Net London exports, Col. A minus Col. D*	
Acute	1,302,765	1,117,643	86%	30,025	1,147,668	155,097	12%
Psychiatric	40,120	37,740	94%	1,323	39,063	1,057	3%
Geriatric	71,938	68,995	96%	3,229	72,224	-286	-0.4%
Total	1,441,176	1,241,972	86%	36,907	1,278,879	162,297	11%

(Technical note: the small heterogeneous group, 'other non-acute', is excluded: hence the total figure is slightly more than the sum of acute, psychiatric and geriatric.)

Figure 3 provides an aggregate view of patient flows broken down by acute, geriatric and psychiatric specialties. Taking acute first, London produces 1.3 million FCEs but residents of London consume just 1.1 million of these episodes, or 86 per cent. However, residents of London also consume approximately 30,000 FCEs in hospitals outside the capital. Thus, the net export of acute care by London is 155,000 FCEs or 12 per cent of total production. London exports approximately 12,000 acute FCEs to non-English residents.

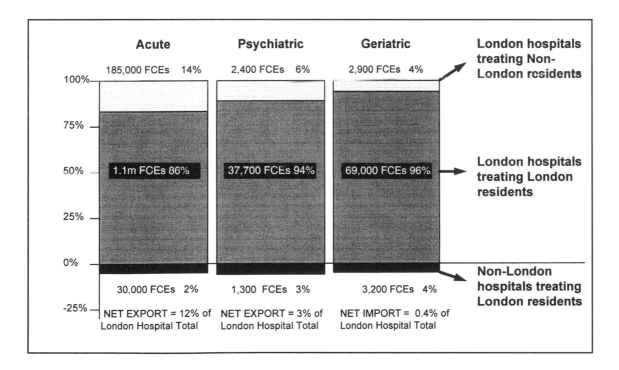

Figure 3: Patient flows in FCEs, between London and the rest of the world, by specialty group, 1994/95

London produces 40,100 psychiatric FCEs. Residents of London consume approximately 37,700 of these episodes, or 94 per cent. However, residents of London also consume approximately 1,300 FCEs in hospitals outside the capital. Thus, there is a net export of psychiatric care by London of 1,100 episodes or three per cent of total production. London provides about 150 psychiatric FCEs to non-English residents. The picture here is complicated by the probability that patterns differ between long- and short-stay patients, and emergency and elective admissions and transfers.

Finally, considering the geriatric specialty, London produces 72,000 FCEs of which residents of London consume 69,000, or 96 per cent. However, residents of London also consume approximately 3,200 FCEs in hospitals outside the capital. Thus, there is a net import of geriatric care by London of 286 episodes or 0.4 per cent of total London production.

Changes to patient flows

The analysis provided by the first London Commission, using data for 1988/89, concentrated on flows of acute hospital services, and a distinction was drawn between the activity of hospitals managed by Special Health Authorities (SHAs) and that of other London hospitals (King's Fund, 1992). The SHAs were then independent of local health authorities.

By combining SHA and other London hospitals it is possible to provide comparable figures for 1988/89, at least for the acute specialties. Unfortunately, data are not available for the other specialty groups. Thus, London as a whole produced 1.05 million episodes of acute care in 1988/89. Six years later London hospitals produced 24 per cent more activity, measured in FCEs. London residents consumed 925,000 episodes of London's hospital activity in 1988/89, exporting 11.5 per cent to non-London residents. At the same time London residents were provided with approximately 19,700 FCEs in hospitals outside the capital. Thus, the net export of hospital activity from London hospitals in 1988/89 was approximately 101,000 FCEs or 9.6 per cent of total London production.

This compares with a net export of 12 per cent from London in 1994/95, representing some 155,000 FCEs, over 50 per cent greater than the earlier figure. This is unexpected given the common assumption that the internal NHS market would result in a withdrawal of activity from London hospitals as purchasers choose to use their local hospitals for reasons of both cost and access.

London appears to have increased acute production by over 250,000 FCEs in just six years, but almost 25 per cent of this has been delivered to non-London residents. This is in line with earlier findings which showed that, although London is producing more activity, and more efficiently, hospitalisation rates in London have not risen as quickly as those nationally, particularly when comparisons are made with similar areas elsewhere in England. We now provide a detailed analysis of flows to establish more accurately their nature.

The market for hospital services in London

This section considers flows of patients into London hospitals in greater detail. Acute, geriatric and psychiatric FCEs are considered separately. A more detailed analysis of acute specialties is provided. London's trusts are divided between five groups: the first three are likely to attract a significant proportion of activity from outside London, albeit for different reasons; the fourth and fifth would be expected to serve a more local population. These groups are:

- specialist hospitals, i.e. the former SHAs (except the Hammersmith) and other single specialty hospitals such as the Royal National Orthopaedic and the Harefield hospital;

- central London teaching hospitals;

- hospitals which are located on the border of London, such as the Wellhouse in Barnet, or St. Helier in Sutton;

- other acute trusts; and,

- other non-acute trusts.

A full list of the trusts belonging to these groups is provided in Appendix 6. Specialist and central teaching hospitals are likely to attract non-London residents by virtue of the specialist treatment available and the reputation of clinical staff. On the other hand, border trusts are likely to attract patients from outside London because of their proximity. We provide a breakdown of the use of acute, psychiatric and geriatric services by region of residence for these five groups of London trust hospitals.

Region of residence is defined as follows: the Thames NHS Executive Regional Offices are re-classified as London and 'rest of Thames'; other Regional Offices – North and Yorkshire, Trent, Oxford and Anglia, South and West, West Midlands and North West – are presented as they stand; and the rest of the world, including other parts of Britain, is recorded as 'other'. For most trusts, there is a proportion of FCEs where the district of residence of the patient is not known. These have been redistributed to the nine regions in proportion to known usage. This may lead to under-estimation of flows, as it is less likely that local patients have an unknown district of residence.

Acute flows

Table 16 provides a breakdown, by region of residence, of the utilisation of acute FCEs produced by London hospitals. Fourteen per cent of all acute activity in London hospitals is provided to non-London residents, a significant increase on the position in 1988/89, as we have seen.

Greatest inflows are to specialist hospitals, where nearly half of all FCEs are provided to non-London residents. Twenty-six per cent of FCEs in these hospitals are provided to residents of other parts of the Thames regions – equivalent to over 26,000 FCEs – and 13 per cent to Oxford and Anglia and South and West combined. In five of the 11 specialist hospitals, more than half of total acute FCEs are provided to non-London residents.

Table 16: Proportion of acute FCEs provided by London hospitals, by region of residence, by provider type, 1994/95

Provider Type	London %	Rest of Thames %	Northern & York- shire %	Trent %	Oxford & Anglia %	South & West %	West Mid- lands %	North West %	Other %	Total %
Specialist	53	26	1	1	9	4	1	1	6	100
Teaching	85	10	0	0	2	1	0	0	1	100
Border	84	14	0	0	1	0	0	0	0	100
Other acute	95	4	0	0	0	0	0	0	0	100
Other non-acute	98	2	0	0	0	0	0	0	0	100
Total	86	10	0	0	2	1	0	0	1	100
Total ex. SHAs	88	9	0	0	1	1	0	0	1	100

The border and teaching groups also provide a significant proportion of activity to non-London residents. In certain trusts in the teaching group over 20 per cent of FCEs are provided to non-Londoners. Teaching hospitals provide care to residents across the south and south east of England – Thames, South and West and Oxford and Anglia regions. By contrast, the border group provides almost all FCEs either to residents of London or the rest of the Thames region. These border hospitals act more as local providers to residents on the boundaries of the capital. There is very little export of care by other providers. Only two per cent of activity in non-acute trusts is provided to non-Londoners.

■ Acute elective flows

Acute FCEs provided in London hospitals are more likely to be elective than is the case in the rest of the country, especially in inner-deprived areas of the capital. We now compare the proportion of acute elective FCEs that London trusts export with total episodes produced in the capital.

Table 17 compares, for each group of London hospitals, the proportion of total acute FCEs which are elective, provided to each region. Specialist and teaching hospitals provide a greater proportion of elective FCEs to other regions than to London residents. This is particularly true of teaching hospitals. For specialist hospitals, the elective proportion of total activity provided to London and the rest of the Thames region is similar – this accounts for three-quarters of activity at these providers – whereas the proportion of elective FCEs for residents elsewhere is up to ten per cent greater. For teaching hospitals, all areas outside London receive a greater proportion of elective work. This suggests these trusts attract patients for elective work from the rest of the country.

Table 17: Elective FCEs as a proportion of total acute FCEs provided by London hospitals, by region of residence, by provider type, 1994/95

Provider Type	London	Rest of Thames	Northern & York- shire	Trent	Oxford & Anglia	South & West	West Mid- lands	North West	Other	Total
	%	%	%	%	%	%	%	%	%	%
Specialist	76	79	87	87	84	84	87	87	83	79
Teaching	59	74	71	70	74	70	73	66	65	61
Border	50	53	14	13	46	28	4	17	6	51
Other acute	50	66	42	54	63	66	35	28	40	51
Other non-acute	18	17	0	0	100	-	-	0	0	18
Total	55	68	70	74	75	72	72	67	70	57
Total ex. SHAs	54	66	64	66	72	66	65	59	61	56

By contrast, the elective proportion of total FCEs in border providers tends to be lower for non-residents than for residents of London, with the exception of the rest of the Thames regions and Oxford and Anglia where the proportion is similar. Non-residents from farther afield treated in these hospitals tend to be emergencies. However, it should be borne in mind that, with the exception of the specialist group, and to a lesser extent the teaching group, the number of FCEs provided to regions outside the Thames is very small, and so it would be unwise to draw firm conclusions on this evidence alone.

Table 18 takes a slightly different perspective, considering the proportion of total elective FCEs provided to each region by London provider groups. There is a slightly higher proportion of elective FCEs provided in London for non-Londoners than is the case for all FCEs, 17 per cent compared with 14 per cent. In particular, teaching hospitals and specialist hospitals provide a higher proportion to non-residents. In contrast, the proportion of elective FCEs provided to non-Londoners by the border trusts is no different to the proportion of total FCEs.

Table 18: Proportion of acute elective FCEs provided by London hospitals, by region of residence, by provider type, 1994/95

Provider Type	London	Rest of Thames	Northern & York shire	Trent	Oxford & Anglia	South & West	West Mid- lands	North West	Other	Total
	%	%	%	%	%	%	%	%	%	%
Specialist	51	26	1	1	9	4	1	1	6	100
Teaching	82	12	0	0	2	1	0	0	1	100
Border	84	15	0	0	0	0	0	0	0	100
Other acute	94	6	0	0	0	0	0	0	0	100
Other non-acute	98	2	0	0	0	0	0	0	0	100
Total	83	12	0	0	2	1	0	0	1	100
Total ex. SHAs	86	11	0	0	1	1	0	0	1	100

■ Acute day case flows

Table 19 shows day cases as a proportion of total acute activity provided, disaggregated by region of residence. SHAs and other specialist hospitals are shown separately as these have quite different day case rates. SHAs and teaching hospitals provide the greatest proportion of day cases. In almost every case the proportion of day cases provided for Thames residents is greater than for other parts of England, and of these the greatest proportion is for Londoners. There seems to be a distance effect operating here. The only exception is the 'other acute' group.

Table 19: Day cases as a proportion of acute FCEs, by region of residence, by provider type, 1994/95

Provider Type	London	Rest of Thames	Northern & York- shire	Trent	Oxford & Anglia	South & West	West Mid- lands	North West	Other	Total
	%	%	%	%	%	%	%	%	%	%
SHAs	37	36	23	22	30	27	4	3	29	35
Other specialist	21	17	9	14	15	15	2	4	8	19
Teaching	36	31	20	20	32	20	17	18	16	35
Border	32	32	2	3	25	6	3	7	4	31
Other acute	32	33	5	16	26	33	9	6	5	32
Other non-acute	8	1	0	0	0	-	-	0	0	7
Total	31	25	11	10	17	13	9	9	8	30
Total ex. SHAs	32	28	14	15	22	17	12	10	12	31

Table 20 shows a regional breakdown of the utilisation of acute day case FCEs, by London provider type. A slightly greater proportion of day cases is provided for London residents than is observed for all FCEs, particularly in specialist and teaching hospitals. This would suggest that London providers are not increasing their day case rate by providing more day cases to non-London residents.

Table 20: Proportion of total acute day cases provided by London hospitals, by region of residence, by provider type, 1994/95

Provider Type	London	Rest of Thames	Northern & York- shire	Trent	Oxford & Anglia	South & West	West Mid- lands	North West	Other	Total
	%	%	%	%	%	%	%	%	%	%
SHAs	54	27	0	1	7	4	1	0	6	100
Other specialist	65	24	0	0	7	2	0	0	1	100
Teaching	88	9	0	0	2	1	0	0	1	100
Border	85	15	0	0	0	0	0	0	0	100
Other acute	95	4	0	0	0	0	0	0	0	100
Other non-acute	100	0	0	0	0	0	0	0	0	100
Total	87	10	0	0	1	1	0	0	1	100
Total ex. SHAs	88	10	0	0	1	1	0	0	1	100

Table 21 shows day cases as a proportion of elective FCEs provided, broken down by region of residence. We have noted previously that most day cases occur among elective admissions. Once again, the highest day case rates are for London residents, followed by residents of the rest of the Thames region. SHAs, which have the highest day case rates as a proportion of total FCEs, have a lower day case rate as a proportion of elective activity than most other acute London providers. The high day case rate at SHA hospitals clearly results from a high proportion of elective FCEs. This is consistent with these hospitals doing more complex procedures.

Table 21: Day cases as a proportion of acute elective FCEs, by region of residence, by provider type, 1994/95

Provider Type	London	Rest of Thames	Northern & York-shire	Trent	Oxford & Anglia	South & West	West Mid-lands	North West	Other	Total
	%	%	%	%	%	%	%	%	%	%
SHA	48	46	27	23	36	32	30	28	35	44
Other specialist	29	20	11	21	17	18	13	19	10	24
Teaching	60	43	28	29	43	29	24	27	24	57
Border	63	60	11	26	54	21	69	42	67	62
Other acute	63	49	13	30	41	50	25	23	13	62
Other non-acute	41	7	-	-	0	-	-	-	-	40
Total	62	49	26	29	44	32	24	27	24	60
Total ex. SHA	59	42	22	21	38	29	5	10	19	56

Geriatric flows

There is a smaller proportional inflow of patients to London in the geriatric (medicine for older people) specialty, with only four per cent of FCEs in London provided to non-London residents. Table 22 shows that, with the exception of the border group, virtually all FCEs are provided to Londoners. Ten per cent of FCEs in the border group are provided to residents of the rest of the Thames region, indicating that these hospitals are probably acting more as local providers to non-London residents. There are no geriatric FCEs provided by the group of specialist hospitals.

Table 22: Proportion of geriatric FCEs provided by London hospitals, by region of residence, by provider type, 1994/95

Provider Type	London	Rest of Thames	Northern & York-shire	Trent	Oxford & Anglia	South & West	West Mid-lands	North West	Other	Total
	%	%	%	%	%	%	%	%	%	%
Teaching	99	0	0	0	0	0	0	0	0	100
Border	90	10	0	0	0	0	0	0	0	100
Other acute	98	2	0	0	0	0	0	0	0	100
Other non-acute	99	0	0	0	0	0	0	0	0	100
Total	96	4	0	0	0	0	0	0	0	100

Psychiatric flows

Approximately six per cent of London psychiatric FCEs are provided for non-London residents. Table 23 shows that the specialist group and the border group are the greatest exporters of care, though much less than is the case for the acute specialties. For example, only ten per cent of psychiatric FCEs at the Bethlem and Maudsley are provided to non-

Londoners, unlike the pattern at other former SHA hospitals. However, of these, there is a significant flow of patients from the rest of the country. Only the specialist group has such a flow from outside the Thames regions. For border providers, nearly all flows are from the rest of the Thames regions.

Table 23: Proportion of psychiatric FCEs provided by London hospitals, by region of residence, by provider type, 1994/95

Provider Type	London %	Rest of Thames %	Northern & York- shire %	Trent %	Oxford & Anglia %	South & West %	West Mid- lands %	North West %	Other %	Total %
Specialist	88	7	0	0	2	1	1	1	1	100
Teaching	97	1	0	0	0	0	0	0	1	100
Border	88	10	0	0	0	0	0	0	1	100
Other acute	94	6	0	0	0	0	0	0	0	100
Other non-acute	97	2	0	0	0	0	0	0	0	100
Total	94	4	0	0	0	0	0	0	0	100
Total ex. SHAs	94	4	0	0	0	0	0	0	0	100

■Psychiatric elective flows

Table 24 shows the proportion of elective psychiatric FCEs, produced in London, which are provided to each region. In London as a whole, a slightly greater proportion of elective FCEs are provided to non-Londoners than was the case for total psychiatric FCEs. For example, 35 per cent of elective FCEs provided by London's specialist providers – in this case mainly the Bethlem and Maudsley with some activity at Great Ormond Street and the National Hospital for Neurology and Neurosurgery– are provided to non-Londoners, compared with only 12 per cent of total FCEs.

Table 24: Proportion of psychiatric elective FCEs provided by London hospitals, by region of residence, by provider type, 1994/95

Provider Type	London %	Rest of Thames %	Northern & York- shire %	Trent %	Oxford & Anglia %	South & West %	West Mid- lands %	North West %	Other %	Total %
Specialist	65	21	0	0	5	4	2	1	2	100
Teaching	96	3	0	0	0	1	0	0	0	100
Border	84	15	0	0	0	0	0	0	0	100
Other acute	99	1	0	0	0	0	0	0	0	100
Other non-acute	95	4	0	0	0	1	0	0	0	100
Total	92	6	0	0	0	1	0	0	0	100
Total ex. SHAs	93	6	0	0	0	0	0	0	0	100

Table 25 shows a regional breakdown of the elective proportion of total psychiatric FCEs provided by London trusts. A greater proportion of non-elective FCEs produced at London hospitals are provided to residents of the capital than to non-London residents; the only exception is the other acute group. In particular, only 11 per cent of FCEs involving Londoners are elective in specialist hospitals, compared with 44 per cent of those involving residents of the rest of the Thames regions.

Table 25: Elective FCEs as a proportion of total psychiatric FCEs, by region of residence, by provider type, 1994/95

Provider Type	London	Rest of Thames	Northern & York- shire	Trent	Oxford & Anglia	South & West	West Mid- lands	North West	Other	Total
	%	%	%	%	%	%	%	%	%	%
Specialist	11	44	49	100	37	35	53	14	47	15
Teaching	13	35	14	0	0	20	0	0	0	13
Border	28	44	26	0	14	73	49	75	2	29
Other acute	45	7	34	98	25	38	-	0	78	43
Other non-acute	22	51	13	22	16	45	23	22	19	22
Total	25	37	18	23	23	41	34	25	17	25
Total ex. SHAs	26	37	17	20	15	44	24	33	13	26

The findings presented in this section show the considerable potential for further analysis of the market for London's hospital services, particularly as more data become available. This can most usefully take place in conjunction with detailed analysis at the local level to provide both confirmation and a better understanding of the results.

Chapter 4

Other Hospital-related Issues

Summary

Other hospital activity

- If A&E attendance rates are calculated in terms of local resident population, London as a whole has a significantly higher rate than the rest of the country: the London rate is 32 per cent greater than that of the rest of England; comparing inner-deprived areas, the difference is 29 per cent, and 22 per cent for high-status areas.

- To some extent this may reflect the use of services by the large commuting and tourist population in London. However, other major urban areas also have large commuting populations. Moreover, the difference between high-status areas is probably the most significant indicator of a different pattern of use since such areas are less likely to have significant transient populations.

- Whether these differences represent substantial local use or not, there is clearly a greater burden on A&E services in the capital. There is little variation across sectors except in the south where the rate is rather lower but still above the England average.

- Annual attendances per A&E department in London vary from 48,000 in the north-central sector to 63,000 in the south, compared with an average England figure of approximately 45,000.

- Twenty per cent of total out-patient attendances in England take place in London hospitals: this compares with 16 per cent of FCEs and 14 per cent of the population.

- There is significant variation across London with the north-central sector recording some 58 per cent more out-patient attendances per capita than the south.

- London provides 42 per cent more out-patient attendances per capita resident population than the England average. Inner-deprived areas both inside and outside the capital have substantially higher rates, in the case of London over twice the national average.

- However, as with A&E attendances, there is a significant proportion of non-local attenders.

- A proportion of patients with out-patient appointments fails to turn up. The average non-attendance rate in London is 14 per cent, compared with an England figure of 11 per cent. Inner-deprived areas in general have a high non-attendance rate, 16 per cent in London and 15 per cent outside the capital. There is also some variation across sectors of London, from 12 per cent in the south to 16 per cent in the east.

- Day care facilities are non-residential facilities for people with learning disabilities and mental health problems, and for older people. London has a low attendance rate at day care facilities when compared with the rest of England.

Ambulance services

- Demand for ambulance services in London is 60 per cent greater than in the rest of the country. However, this is based on emergency calls per capita resident population. It is likely that a larger proportion of emergency calls served by the LAS are for non-residents than would be the case in other parts of England, but not so much as to account for the substantial difference in demand which is observed.

- Although the LAS has in the past performed worse against response targets for emergency calls than services in the rest of England, a substantial improvement has occurred very recently.

- Thus, in 1994/95, the LAS achieved just 68 per cent compliance with a target response time of 14 minutes. This compares with an expected standard of 95 per cent which most other services either achieved or came close to.

- However, the latest evidence shows a substantial improvement in LAS performance so that in March 1996 compliance with the 14 minute target had reached 89 per cent. When performance is considered on a DHA basis, all areas achieved over 80 per cent and most were approaching 90 per cent or more.

Physical resources

- Since 1982 there has been a rapid reduction in the number of acute beds in London hospitals, from 4.1 per 1,000 resident population to 2.4 in 1994/95.

- Bed availability has fallen less quickly in England: hence, the excess of acute beds in London over the rest of England has fallen from 40 per cent in 1982 to seven per cent in 1994/95.

- When acute and geriatric beds are considered together the excess in London over England is just three per cent in 1994/95.

- Such comparisons based on the location of beds and hence hospitals take no account of who uses the facilities. Fourteen per cent of acute FCEs in London hospitals are provided to non-London residents. In inner-deprived London hospitals, which have substantially more beds in terms of local population than the England average, 44 per cent of FCEs are provided to non-residents; although a large proportion are residents of other parts of the capital.

- Between 1991/92 and 1993/94, overall provision of theatre sessions in London fell by two per cent whereas the number of sessions in England as a whole grew by two per cent. Nevertheless, in 1993/94, London has more theatre sessions available in terms of resident population than is the case in England as a whole – 20.7 per 1,000 compared to 17.6.

- London has comparatively more specialist surgery theatre sessions than the rest of the country and fewer sessions for general surgery and orthopaedics. This reflects particularly the position in hospitals in inner-deprived areas of London.

Human resources

- There is some variation in the average number of staff employed by trusts, both between sectors of London, and between London and the rest of the country. In London, this tends to reflect the location of single specialty hospitals, or of some of the larger merged trusts. The average size of non-acute trusts, in terms of staff numbers, is ten per cent less in London compared with England as a whole. The average size of acute trusts is similar.

- However, there is variation in staff-mix. Trusts in London, whether acute or non-acute, tend to employ more doctors and administrative and clerical staff as a proportion of total staff, and commensurably less nurses. This is particularly true of acute trusts in inner-deprived London where, in some cases, the ratio of nurse to doctor is closer to three rather than the national average of over five.

- Finally, non-acute trusts, whether in London or outside, employ approximately 50 per cent less staff than acute trusts. Of these, proportionately less are doctors and more are nurses.

Key Facts

Other hospital activity	*London*	*Rest of England*
A&E activity		
Total A&E first attendances:	2,090,000	9,510,000
Attendance rate per 1,000 resident population:	300	228
Average capacity of A&E departments:	53,800	44,800
Out-patient activity		
Total attendances:	7,751,000	31,555,000
Attendance rate per 1,000 resident population:	1,112	756
Follow-up per first attendance:	2.8	2.8
Day care activity		
Attendance rate per 1,000 resident population (1993/94):	132	147

Ambulance services

	London	*Rest of England*
Total emergency calls:	542,500	1,974,000
Emergency call rate per 1,000 resident population:	78	49
Performance against lower response target (1994/95):	68%	96%
Performance against lower response target (March 1996):	89%	–

Physical resources

	London	*Rest of England*
Acute beds per 1,000 resident population (1994/95):	2.4	2.2
Acute beds per 1,000 resident population (1982):	4.1	2.9
Geriatric specialty beds per 1,000 resident population (1994/95):	0.7	0.7
Geriatric specialty beds per 1,000 resident population (1982):	1.2	1.2
Available theatre sessions per 1,000 resident population:	21	18
Specialty composition of theatre sessions:		
• General surgery	21%	25%
• Specialist surgery	17%	10%
• Orthopaedics	14%	19%
• Gynaecology	12%	13%
• ENT	7%	8%

Human resources

	London	*Rest of England*
Average number of employees per acute trust:	2,154	2,110
Average number of employees per non-acute trust:	1,116	1,252

1 Introduction

This chapter considers a number of issues relating to hospital activity. Sections are included on:

- Accident and Emergency (A&E) and out-patient departments;

- NHS day care;

- ambulance services in London;

- physical resources available to London's hospitals; and,

- human resources in London's hospitals.

2 Data sources

A&E and out-patient data are taken from the Department of Health (DoH) publication, *'Out-patients and ward attenders, England 1994/95'*, (DoH, 1995b). The analysis of ambulance services is based on the DoH return, KA34, and local data from the London Ambulance Service. The analysis of day care services is based on the data underlying the DoH publication, *'NHS day care facilities, England 1993/94'*, (DoH, 1995c). Bed availability data are taken from the DoH publication, *'Bed Availability for England, 1994/95'* (DoH, 1995d). The analysis of theatre resources is based on the data underlying the DoH publication, *'NHS operating theatres availability and use, England 1993/94'* (DoH, 1994a). Finally, data on human resources are from an Audit Commission analysis based on the DoH return, TFR3.

3 Other hospital activity

In this section we consider several types of ambulatory care offered within hospital settings. The nature of these services are quite different. Included are A&E services, out-patient departments and day care.

A&E activity

We first consider the use of A&E departments. The data do not identify the district of residence of A&E attenders. In some parts of London there may be a significant proportion of non-local attenders. Indeed, if A&E attendances were related to admissions, the information on district of residence of those admitted to London hospitals clearly indicates a substantial non-local element. Nevertheless, for the purposes of providing simple comparisons, we relate total attendances to local resident population.

A&E data are presented as first and total attendances. First attendances are those which involve a patient attending an A&E department for the first time: presumably in urgent need of medical attention. On the other hand, total attendances include non-urgent attendances at a later date. We analyse first attendances as these give a better indication of urgent need for A&E services.

First attendance rate

Figure 1 shows considerable variation between sectors of London in the number of first attendances per 1,000 resident population. In particular, the south and north-west sectors have a much lower attendance rate than the others. Highest rates are in the north-central and east sectors.

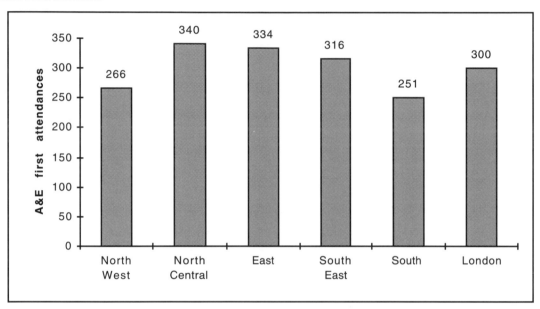

Figure 1: A&E first attendances per 1,000 resident population, by sector of London, 1994/95

Figure 2 compares London with England showing a higher A&E attendance rate in London than in the rest of England, for all types of socio-economic area. This may indicate a greater use of A&E services by London residents. This would be consistent with the hypothesis that Londoners use hospital A&E departments inappropriately, as their first point of contact with health services, rather than GPs. On the other hand, it may reflect the use of London A&E departments by non-residents. The population of the capital is swelled considerably by commuters and tourists. However, the fact that even high-status areas, which are not particularly associated with inflows of tourists or commuters, also show greater than average attendance – 25 per cent greater than the non-London average – may point to a local effect. Further analysis using other local datasets would be required to test this adequately.

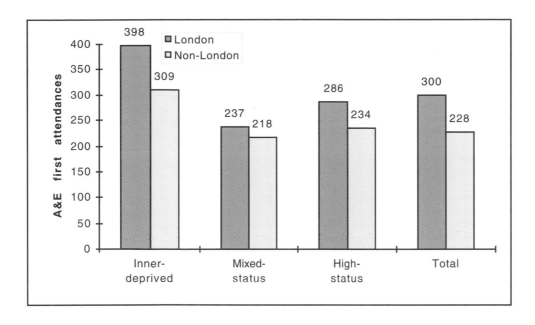

Figure 2: A&E first attendances per 1,000 resident population, London and England, 1994/95

A&E capacity

We turn now to the capacity of A&E departments. Individual trusts may have more than one A&E department. For example, in the south-east sector both Guy's and St. Thomas's hospitals have A&E departments as did Greenwich and Brook hospitals in 1994/95. However, the number of A&E departments at each trust are not routinely recorded in the data set used for this analysis. Only through more detailed knowledge of health services in an area can the precise configuration of A&E departments be presented. Thus, we present data here for first attendances per A&E department for London only. Other complications arise concerning what should be regarded as an A&E department. We adopted the following rule. A&E departments at single specialty hospitals such as Great Ormond Street have been included, but A&E departments at single specialty units which are part of general acute trusts have not. Also Bart's A&E which closed in January 1995 has been counted only for the time it was open.

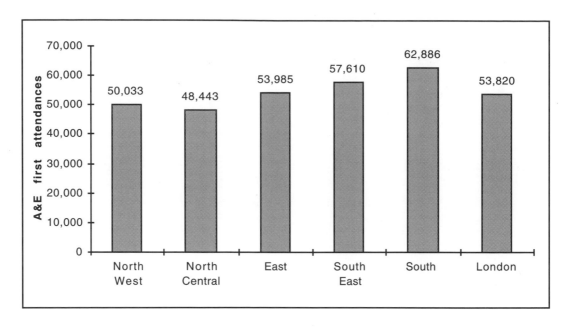

Figure 3: A&E first attendances per A&E department, by sector of London, 1994/95

Figure 3 shows the average number of first attendances per A&E department, by sector of London. There is variation across sectors with the highest average in the south where there are just five A&E departments. As shown above, this sector has the lowest A&E attendance rate. Average sectoral attendance per A&E department varies from 48,000 to 63,000.

Figure 4 compares London with an estimate for England as a whole. The England figure is approximate, based on the number of trusts rather than A&E departments. This provides an upper limit on the number of first attendances per A&E department in England: the actual figure may be lower. Nevertheless, it is interesting that the number of first attendances per department in England as a whole is 17 per cent (9,000) less than that of London.

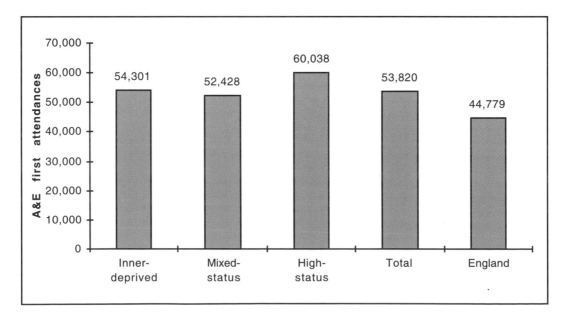

Figure 4: A&E first attendances per A&E department, London and England, 1994/95

Out-patient activity

We now consider the use of out-patient services. Data are presented on:

- total attendances;

- first and follow-up attendances; and,

- non-attendance rates;

Private out-patient activity is discussed in Chapter 5.

Total attendances

Table 1 shows the total number of out patient attendances, by sector of London. Of approaching eight million out-patient attendances in London, 26 per cent were first attendances. The ratio of follow-up attendances to first attendances is 2.8 in London as a whole with little variation except in the north west where the follow-up ratio is 3.1.

Table 1: Out-patient attendances, by sector of London, 1994/95

	North West '000	North Central '000	East '000	South East '000	South '000	London '000
Total attendances	2,016	1,533	1,597	1,541	1,065	7,751
First attendances	493	403	418	422	279	2,016
Follow-up attendances	1,523	1,129	1,179	1,119	785	5,735
Ratio of follow-up to first	3.1	2.8	2.8	2.7	2.8	2.8

Table 2 compares the provision of out-patient attendances in London with that in the rest of the country. Around 20 per cent of all out-patient attendances in England take place in London hospitals. This compares with 16 per cent of England's FCEs and the 14 per cent of England's population living in London. The ratio of follow-up attendances to first attendances is very similar when London is compared with the rest of the country. There is, however, variation in the rest of England across types of socio-economic area with a higher ratio in more deprived areas. This gradient is absent in London.

Table 2: Out-patient attendances, London and England, 1994/95

	London				Non-London				
	Inner-deprived '000	Mixed-status '000	High-status '000	Total '000	Inner-deprived '000	Mixed-status '000	High-status '000	Total '000	England '000
Total attendances	3,666	1,910	2,176	7,751	5,523	7,528	11,662	31,555	39,306
First attendances	961	502	554	2,016	1,298	1,929	3,240	8,347	10,363
Follow-up attendances	2,705	1,408	1,622	5,735	4,225	5,598	8,421	23,208	28,943
Ratio of follow-up to first	2.8	2.8	2.7	2.8	3.2	2.9	2.6	2.8	2.8

Attendance rate

Figure 5 relates the total number of out-patient attendances in London hospitals to the local resident population. As with A&E attendances, the data do not identify the district of residence of out-patient attenders; there will be a significant proportion of non-local attenders. Nevertheless, the rate of out-patient attendance per capita local resident population gives an indication of local use and capacity. There is significant variation across London with the north-central sector recording some 58 per cent more per capita than the south.

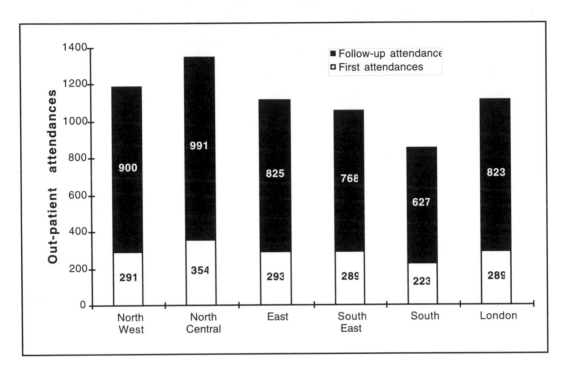

Figure 5: Out-patient attendances per 1,000 resident population, by sector of London, 1994/95

Figure 6 shows London as a whole provides substantially more out-patient services per capita resident population than the rest of England, some 47 per cent. Inner-deprived areas both inside and outside the capital have much higher rates, in the case of London over twice the national average. Again, the higher rate in London reflects the use of services by non-local residents. However, the scale of the difference is greater than that for in-patient services, indicating either genuinely more use of out-patient services by Londoners or a greater inflow of non-residents. If there were greater inflows of non-residents, then the data suggest there are less in-patient cases associated with these out-patient attendances. This could be the case given that people may travel for an expert opinion but still have their in-patient care provided locally. Further detailed research using locally available data is required to test these findings more fully.

However, 44 per cent of in-patient activity in inner-deprived London hospitals is provided to non-residents. If an equivalent rate applied to out-patient attendances, the local resident out-patient attendance rate in inner-deprived London would remain 30 per cent above the England average.

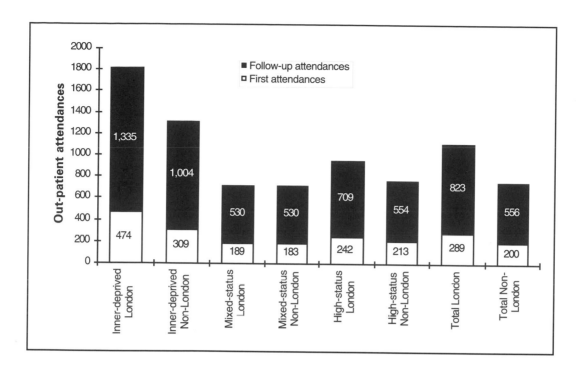

Figure 6: Out-patient attendances per 1,000 resident population, London and England, 1994/95

Non-attendance rate

Thus far we have considered out-patient attendances. However, on many occasions the individual patient has an appointment but fails to attend. Figure 7 shows non-attenders as a proportion of total appointments offered, i.e. total out-patient attendances plus non-attenders, by sector of London. Non-attendance rates vary between 12 and 16 per cent across sectors of London. The rate of 16 per cent in the east sector reflects non-attendance rates of 20 per cent and over at a small number of trusts.

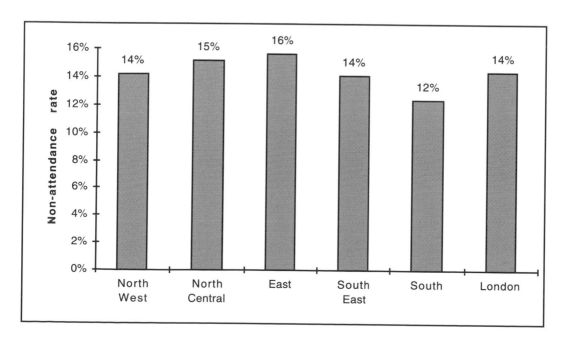

Figure 7: Out-patient non-attendance rate, by sector of London, 1994/95

Figure 8 compares out-patient non-attendance rates in London with those in the rest of the country: there is a higher rate in the capital than elsewhere. Throughout the country there tend to be greater non-attendance rates in more deprived areas. In inner-deprived London, for example, there are trusts with non-attendance rates of 25 per cent or more.

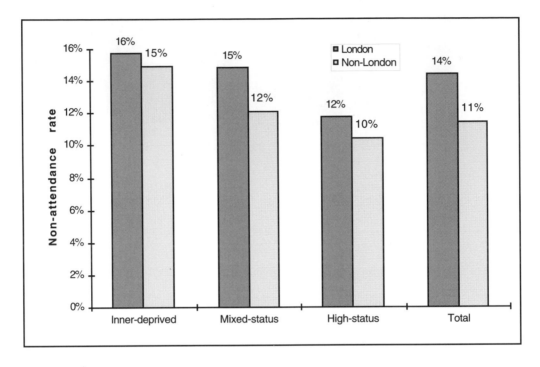

Figure 8: Out-patient non-attendance rate, London and England, 1994/95

Day care activity

This section considers the use of NHS day care facilities. These are non-residential facilities for people with learning disabilities and mental health problems, and for older people. They should not be confused with day cases. Data are presented for the number of attendances per 1,000 resident population and the number of attendances per first attendance. A first attendance is the first in a series of attendances at day care facilities, in the same specialty and at the same provider.

Attendance rate

Figure 9 shows that the number of attendances per 1,000 resident population ranges from 76 in the east sector of London to 232 in the south sector. The high attendance rate in the south is driven by one DHA with by far the greatest attendance rate in London – 458 attendances per 1,000 population.

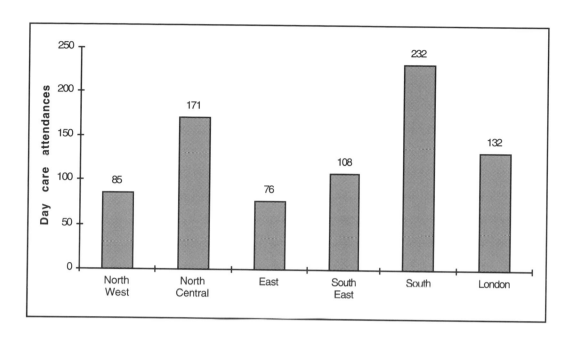

Figure 9: Day care attendance rate per 1,000 resident population, by sector of London, 1993/94

Figure 10 shows that London a whole has a low attendance rate when compared with the rest of England, particularly in inner-deprived and mixed-status areas. In high-status London areas, the attendance rate is greater than similar areas in the rest of the country, 180 per 1,000 resident population compared with 145. However, this is due entirely to the effect of one DHA. Excluding this DHA from the calculation, high-status areas of London would show a lower attendance rate than similar areas in the rest of the country – 127 compared with 145.

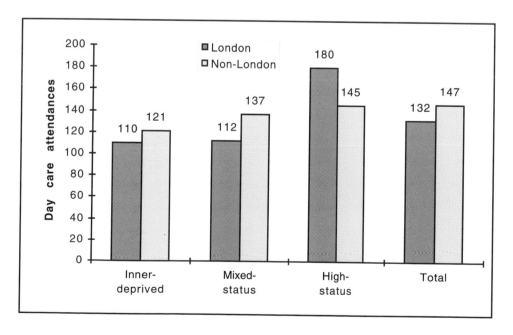

Figure 10: Day care attendance rate per 1,000 resident population, London and England, 1993/94

Attendances per first attendance

The attendance rate is useful for understanding the *level* of provision of NHS day care services. However, the ratio of total attendances to first attendance is valuable for understanding the *pattern* of care. It reveals whether a high attendance rate is the result of a few patients being seen many times, or comparatively more patients being seen less often.

Figure 11 shows that attendances per first attendance range from 17 in the north-central sector to 70 in the south sector. Once again, the higher rate in the south is the result of an unusual pattern of care in one DHA, which has an average of 134 attendances per first attendance. By contrast, the average for London as a whole is 32. The high ratio of total to first attendances explains the overall high attendance rate in this DHA: the rate of first attendances per 1,000 resident population is unremarkable.

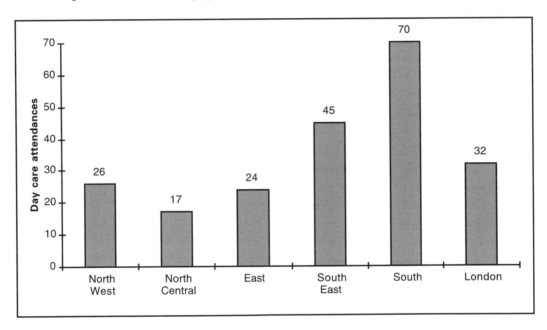

Figure 11: Total day care attendances per first attendance, by sector of London, 1993/94

Figure 12 shows that both inner-deprived and mixed-status areas of London have fewer attendances per first attendance than comparable areas in the rest of England. High-status areas have more as a result of the very high ratio in one DHA noted above. If this were excluded, then London as a whole would have a lower ratio of total to first attendances than the rest of the country.

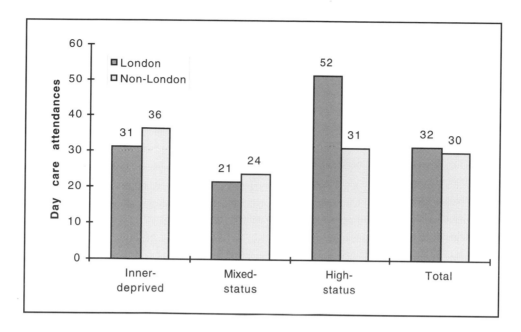

Figure 12: Total day care attendances per first attendance, London and England, 1993/94

4 Ambulance services

The performance of the London Ambulance Service (LAS) is a crucial factor in the delivery of emergency services in London. We analyse performance using DoH data on ambulance services together with more recent data from the LAS which allows analysis by individual DHA and by LAS division. The data do not allow our usual sectoral and socio-economic group analyses.

Emergency call rate

This section compares the demand for ambulance services in London with that in the rest of England. Figure 13 shows London has a 58 per cent greater annual rate of use of ambulance services, in terms of emergency calls per 1,000 resident population, compared with the rest of England – 78 against 49 calls. Users of ambulance services are not necessarily local residents but data are not available which allow identification of district of residence. Some of the extra use in London undoubtedly pertains to visitors to the capital, though this is unlikely to explain the great discrepancy between London and national usage.

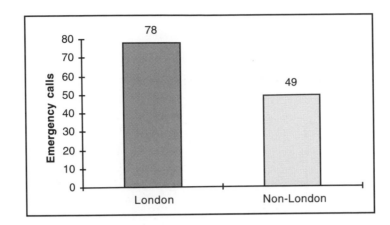

Figure 13: Emergency calls per 1,000 resident population, London and England, 1994/95

Performance against response targets

For some time the LAS has performed less well against response targets than any other ambulance service in the country. Figure 14 confirms this for 1994/95. The LAS's compliance with the lower target in 1994/95 is 68 per cent, whereas only one other ambulance service has a percentage under 90 per cent. The standard required in the Patient's Charter is 95 per cent. Other metropolitan services, such as Greater Manchester and the West Midlands, matched the England average.

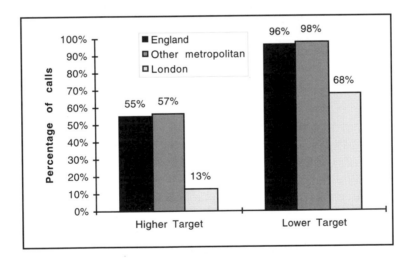

(Higher and lower response targets: the higher is eight minutes, the lower, 14 minutes in urban areas and 19 minutes in rural areas.)

Figure 14: Proportion of calls meeting higher and lower response targets, London, other metropolitan areas and England, 1994/95

The history of the LAS's problems is well documented (Health Committee, 1995). A review of LAS performance against the 14-minute target over the last seven years shows that performance against the target declined from the late 1980s until 1992/93, the date of the infamous LAS computer crash: see Figure 15. Since then there has been a steady improvement against the standard. Indeed, in the last quarter of 1995/96 the LAS's performance against this target reached over 80 per cent, and by April 1996 approached 90 per cent.

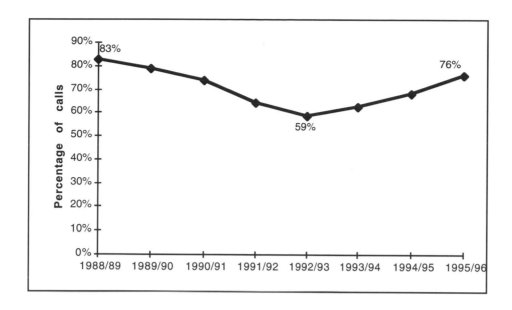

Figure 15: Proportion of calls meeting the 14-minute response target, London, 1988/89 to 1995/96

Local LAS performance

We now consider the performance of the LAS against the 14-minute response time target using 1995/96 LAS data. The LAS is divided into four divisions: north west, north east, south and central. The north-west division consists of Hillingdon, Brent and Harrow, Ealing, Hammersmith and Hounslow and Barnet health authorities; the north-east consists of Enfield and Haringey, Redbridge and Waltham Forest and Barking and Havering; the south consists of all health authorities south of the Thames with the exception of Lambeth, Southwark and Lewisham; the central division is coterminous with our 'inner-deprived' area of London, consisting of Kensington, Chelsea and Westminster, Camden and Islington, East London and the City and Lambeth, Southwark and Lewisham.

Table 3: Change in LAS performance against the 14-minute target, by division, 1995/96

Division	April 1995 %	March 1996 %	Change %
North west	75	90	+15
North east	74	88	+14
LAS	**77**	**89**	**+12**
South	79	90	+11
Central	78	87	+9

(Tables 3 and 4 are ordered by percentage change in compliance with response target.)

Table 3 shows the change in performance in each of the ambulance divisions. All LAS divisions had reached or were approaching 90 per cent compliance with the 14-minute response target. Improvement has been most rapid in the north-west and north-east divisions.

Table 4: Change in LAS performance against the 14 minute target, by DHA, 1995/96

DHA	May 1995 %	March 1996 %	change %
Enfield and Haringey	69	91	+22
Barnet	67	85	+18
Brent and Harrow	74	90	+16
Hillingdon	75	91	+16
Bromley	74	89	+15
Croydon	73	88	+15
Camden and Islington	70	84	+14
Ealing, Hammersmith and Hounslow	76	90	+14
Kensington, Chelsea and Westminster	76	90	+14
Redbridge and Waltham Forest	74	88	+14
Merton, Sutton and Wandsworth	79	92	+13
Barking and Havering	75	87	+12
Lambeth, Southwark and Lewisham	79	91	+12
Bexley and Greenwich	79	89	+10
East London and the City	73	82	+9
Kingston and Richmond	85	93	+8

Table 4 provides a more detailed analysis, by London DHA. Unfortunately, as data are available only as percentage performance against response target, it is not possible to aggregate these into figures for the sectors and socio-economic areas of London used elsewhere in this chapter. Data are only available from May 1995 onwards. Compliance improved by between eight and 22 per cent for the London DHA areas. By March 1996 the performance of the LAS had improved to greater than 80 per cent compliance in every DHA in London: in only two was it less than 85 per cent, Camden and Islington and East London and the City.

5 Physical resources

This section considers the level of hospital provision in London in terms of location of hospitals and hence availability of in-patient bed resources. A brief discussion of operating theatre sessions is also included.

Hospitals

There are over 40 acute hospital trusts and 20 community or mental health trusts in London. All may be responsible for the management of hospital sites, and in some cases, trusts have responsibility for several sites. Over two-thirds of the acute trusts are in north London; 18 are in inner-deprived London. Map 1 shows the configuration of acute trusts in London; Map 2 shows the position in central London.

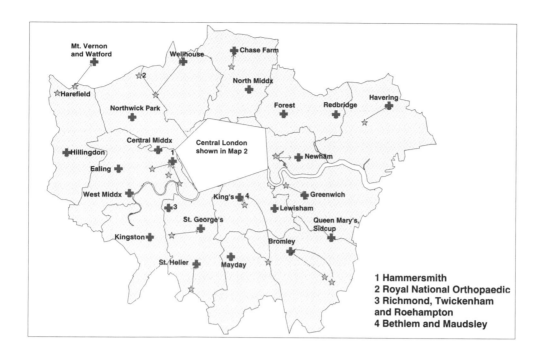

'Crosses' show acute trust headquarters; 'stars' show satellite units and single specialty hospitals.

Map 1: Acute hospitals in London, 1997

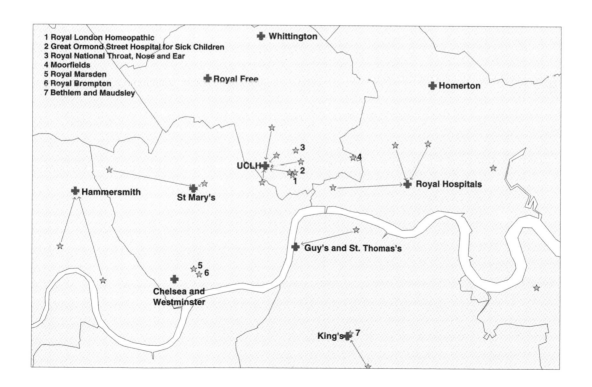

'Crosses' show acute trust headquarters; 'stars' show satellite units and single-specialty hospitals.

Map 2: Acute hospitals in central London, 1997

Beds

This section compares the availability of acute and geriatric hospital beds per 1,000 resident population in London with that of the rest of England over the last decade. The location of SHA beds in London complicates the analysis of bed availability. Based on previous patient flows, we include two-thirds of the SHA beds as London hospital beds.

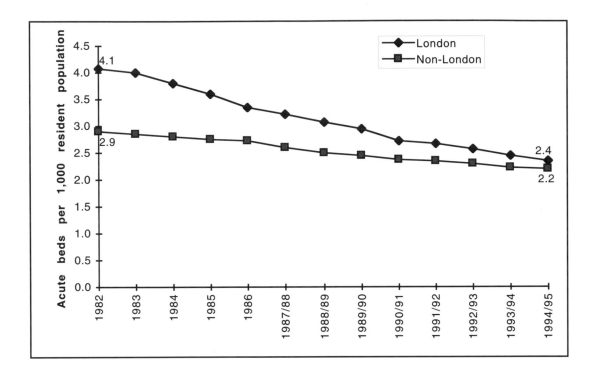

Figure 16: Acute bed availability, London and England, 1982 to 1994/95

Figure 16 shows two features of the provision of acute beds in London since 1982: a reduction in the number of beds in London, and at a faster pace than in the rest of England as a whole. The reduction from 4.1 per 1,000 resident population in 1982 to 2.4 in 1994/95 in part reflects adjustments that have taken place nationally as changes in medical practice have reduced the need for patients to occupy a hospital bed for long periods.

However, it is clear from Figure 16 that changes have taken place faster in London than in the rest of England. Since 1982 London has lost 40 per cent of its acute beds compared with a non-London reduction of just 24 per cent. London's *over-provision* of acute beds compared with the rest of England has fallen from 40 per cent in 1982 to just seven per cent in 1994/95. This reduction in beds to a figure comparable with England must be set alongside the relative under-provision of other parts of the health care system in London such as the lack of residential care places which is noted in Chapter 8.

Figure 17 shows a similar situation if geriatric beds, which are used for care of older people, are added to the provision of acute beds. There has been a reduction in the number of beds per capita nationally, but again, the reduction has been more rapid in London, to the extent that there is now little over-provision in the capital. It is clear that the argument that London is *over-bedded* in comparison with the rest of the country is no longer relevant.

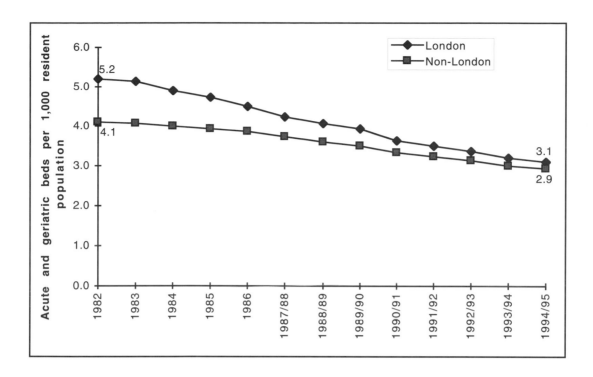

Figure 17: Acute plus geriatric bed availability, London and England, 1982 to 1994/95

Bed provision in London

Figure 18 shows that the greatest provision of acute beds per 1,000 resident population is in the north-central and north-west sectors of London. This is not surprising as over half of London's acute trusts are located in these two sectors: these include almost all London's single specialty hospitals, and six out of eight former SHAs. This comparatively great provision of acute beds is the result of a large number of providers: the providers themselves are not unusually large. In London there are five trusts with over 1,000 beds: three in the east sector, one in the south east, and one in the north west.

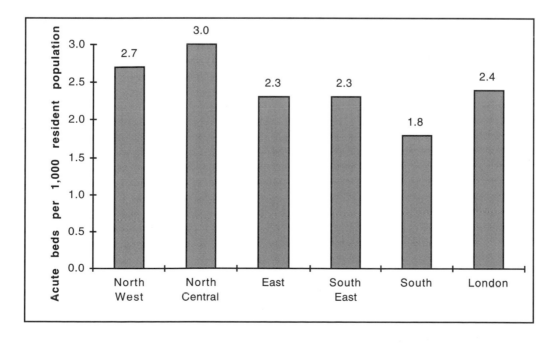

Figure 18: Acute bed availability, by sector of London, 1994/95

Provision of acute beds south of the Thames is less than that north of the river. In particular, the south sector has just 1.8 acute beds per 1,000 resident population, which is considerably less than the England average. In Chapter 7 we note that the provision of primary care south of the river is better than in north London. If the balance of health services in the capital is skewed towards the hospital sector this would seem to apply more obviously to north rather than south London.

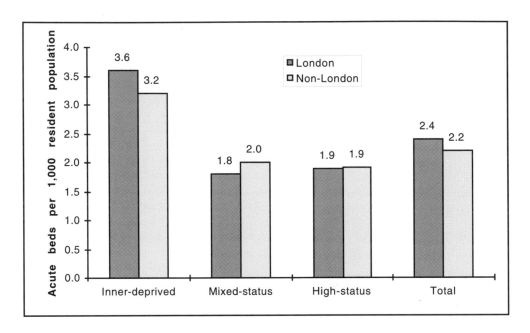

Figure 19: Acute bed availability, London and England, 1994/95

Figure 19 compares the provision of beds, by type of socio-economic area, between London and the rest of England. In both London and the rest of England there are more acute beds per resident population in inner-deprived areas than in other areas. This reflects the location of 27 trusts and directly managed units in inner-deprived London. There are just 38 in the rest of the capital, despite having a population two-and-a half times as great.

London has proportionately more acute beds than the rest of England but fewer beds in high- and mixed-status areas. However, this discussion of the location of beds takes no account of who uses them. Fourteen per cent of acute FCEs in London hospitals are provided to non-London residents. In inner-deprived London hospitals, 44 per cent of FCEs are provided to non-residents: a large proportion of these are residents of other parts of the capital. The equivalent figures are 25 and 23 per cent for mixed- and high-status areas respectively.

Pay-beds

The analysis in this section follows the tradition when discussing bed availability of including all beds in NHS hospitals. However, a proportion of these are NHS pay-beds used by patients who are privately funded. There is an argument for excluding these from any analysis of beds available for NHS patients, although this has not usually been done.

Partially this reflects the fact that the distinction has been rather unclear in the past, and partially that there are no data available which differentiate 'private' and 'public' NHS beds.

However, the analysis in Chapter 5 shows that a proportion of activity in NHS hospitals is paid for privately, and that there are clear differences between London and elsewhere in this respect – one per cent nationally but two per cent in the capital. It is possible to use fairly weak assumptions to determine the level of bed availability once pay-beds are removed. Assuming that beds occupied by private FCEs are not available at that time for use by NHS patients, bed availability figures can be reduced accordingly. The results are shown in Figure 20 which compares London with England.

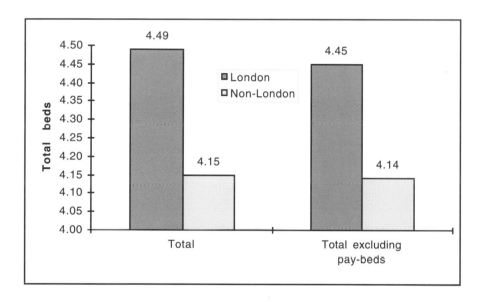

Figure 20: Total beds per 1,000 resident population, including and excluding NHS pay-beds, London and England, 1994/95

The provision of total hospital beds per 1,000 resident population falls by just 0.04 in London and by 0.01 in the rest of the country. Thus, although including pay-beds has an effect that is greater in London than England, the impact is minimal. The assumption used here sets a maximum level of bed availability, in effect assuming that all unoccupied beds are potentially available to NHS patients.

Theatre sessions

(Technical note: this section uses theatre sessions rather than number of theatres to measure the provision of theatres in London. This makes the measurement of theatre availability by specialty easier. Data were not available for Barking and Havering DHA prior to the foundation of the Havering Hospitals Trust in 1993/94. Thus, the time series analysis excludes this DHA. Analyses which use only 1993/94 data include figures for Havering Hospitals Trust.)

This section outlines how provision has changed in London compared with the rest of England; considers provision of theatre sessions, by sector of London; compares provision between types of socio-economic area in London and similar areas in the rest of the country; and, considers availability of sessions by specialty.

Change in theatre session availability

Figure 21 compares changes, between 1991/92 and 1993/94, in total theatre session availability in London and the rest of England: provision in 1991/92 is indexed at 100. There were 151,277 sessions in London in 1993/94, approximately 98 per cent of the 1991/92 level. By contrast, there were 882,015 sessions in England, two per cent more than the 1991/92 level.

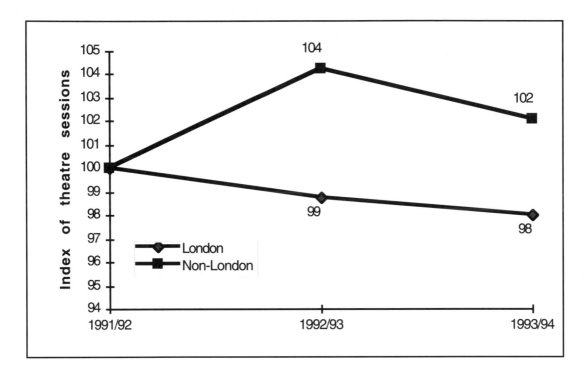

Figure 21: Change in theatre session availability, 1991/92 to 1993/94, London and England (1991/92 = 100)

The reduction in the number of theatre sessions in London has been driven by changes in the south and east sectors. In the south there was a reduction of around 500 sessions, or two per cent of the total. Calculations in the east are complicated by the lack of data for Barking and Havering DHA, as noted above. However, there were 4,200 fewer sessions in hospitals located in the remainder of the east sector in 1993/94 in comparison with 1991/92, a reduction of 16 per cent.

In contrast, there was an increase of almost seven per cent in the number of theatre sessions available in the north-central sector, Map 3 shows the availability of theatre sessions by London DHA; Map 4 shows the change in available sessions since 1991/92.

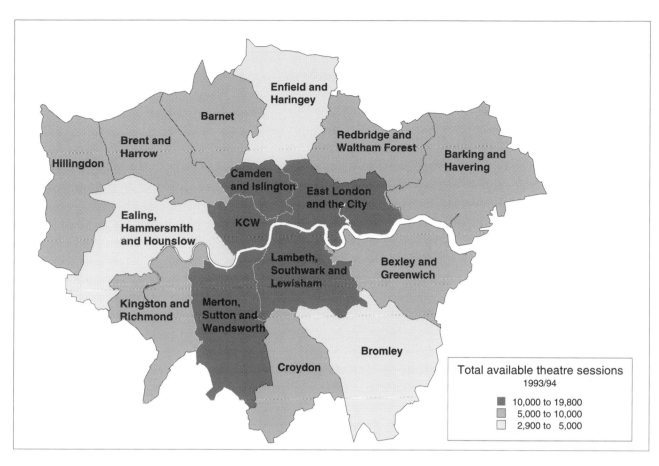

Map 3: Available theatre sessions in London, 1993/94

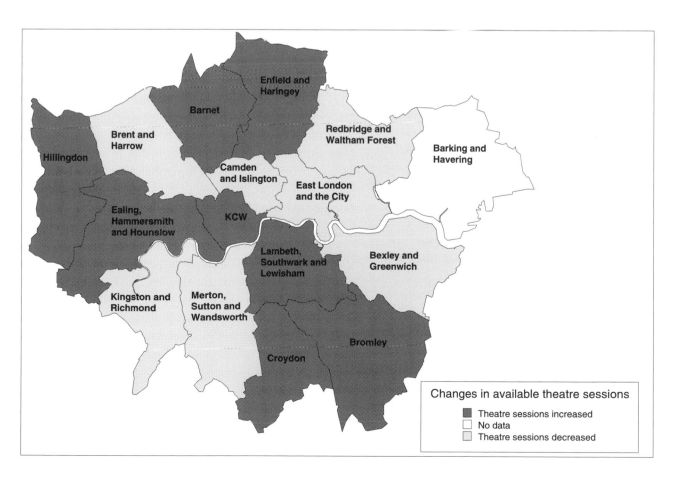

Map 4: Change in available theatre sessions in London, 1991/92 to 1993/94

National comparisons

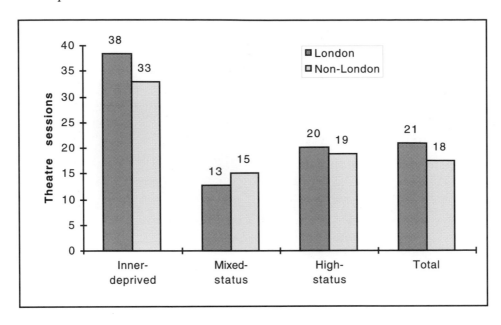

Figure 22: Theatre sessions per 1,000 resident population, London and England, 1993/94

Figure 22 shows that inner-deprived areas, both in London and the rest of England, have more theatre sessions available per 1,000 resident population than other types of socio-economic area. There are 38 sessions per 1,000 resident population in inner-deprived London compared with 21 in the capital as a whole. This concentration of theatre sessions mirrors that of hospitals and beds in inner-deprived areas. However, these hospitals provide services to other areas of London, and indeed to other parts of the country. This high level of provision is further strengthened by the greater level of specialist surgery sessions, e.g. neurosurgery, paediatric surgery, in these areas. This is discussed below.

The specialty composition of theatre sessions

This section considers in detail the specialty composition of theatre sessions. Table 5 compares the proportion of theatre sessions, by specialty, between London and the rest of England. In this table, neurosurgery, plastic surgery, cardiothoracic surgery and paediatric surgery are grouped together as 'specialist' surgery.

Table 5: Proportion of theatre sessions, by specialty, London and England, 1993/94

	London				Non-London				England
	Inner-deprived %	Mixed-status %	High-status %	Total %	Inner-deprived %	Mixed-status %	High-status %	Total %	%
General surgery	19	25	23	21	19	25	26	25	24
Specialist surgery	22	10	10	17	19	8	9	10	11
Orthopaedics	9	22	16	14	13	21	19	19	18
Gynaecology	11	15	12	12	10	14	14	13	13
Urology	7	9	6	7	7	6	6	7	7
ENT	8	6	5	7	8	8	8	8	8
Ophthalmology	10	5	5	7	7	7	6	7	7
Dental surgery	5	5	5	5	5	4	4	5	5

(Table 5 is ordered by specialty with the greatest proportion of theatre sessions in London.)

London as a whole has comparatively more specialist surgery theatre sessions than the rest of the country and fewer sessions for general surgery and orthopaedics. Hospitals located in inner-deprived areas, both in London and the rest of the country, have more specialist theatre sessions and fewer general surgery and orthopaedic theatre sessions. This is not surprising as, in London, specialist surgery sessions are often in single specialty hospitals. These are almost all located in inner-deprived areas.

6 Human resources

(Technical note: data presented are for total trust staff only, based on trust accounts. Data for staff in directly managed units were not available. However, total DMUs in England in 1994/95 comprised some ten per cent of all provider units. In London there were eight DMUs. These units tended to be smaller, and were less likely to be acute.)

This section considers the availability of human resources, comparing trusts in London with those in the rest of the country. The total number of staff in NHS trusts in England in 1994/95 was 685,000 of which 110,000 were in London trusts. We compare the average number of staff in acute and non-acute trusts, by staff group, and the proportions of total staff in each group. Eight groups are identified: Medical & Dental (M&D); Nursing & Midwifery (N&M); Professions Allied to Medicine (PAM); Ancillary; Administration & Clerical (A&C); Works; Other Professional & Technical (P&T); and, all other.

Acute trusts

In this section 'acute' is defined as acute hospitals, combined acute and community hospitals (as staff involved in acute and community health care cannot be separated from each other in the data available), and single specialty hospitals (excluding mental health trusts). In each case, data refer to number of staff, not whole time equivalents (WTEs).

Table 6 compares the average number of employees at each acute trust, by staff group, across sectors of London. Acute trusts in the north-west and north-central sectors employ considerably fewer staff on average than trusts in other sectors, reflecting the number of smaller single specialty trusts in these sectors. The south-east and east sectors are home to Guy's and St. Thomas's, with 6,400 employees, the largest NHS trust employer in the country, the Royal Hospitals with 5,400, the third largest, and King's with 4,500 employees.

Table 6: Average number of acute trust employees, by staff group, by sector of London, 1994/95

Staff Group	North West	North Central	East	South East	South	London
M&D	187	175	279	307	252	224
N&M	708	730	1,147	1,386	972	914
PAM	99	84	105	151	151	110
Ancillary	86	171	281	384	170	192
A&C	367	348	492	588	431	422
Works	31	23	56	69	41	40
P&T	159	182	267	297	215	209
All other	30	36	89	65	9	43
Total	1,668	1,748	2,715	3,246	2,240	2,154

Table 7 compares the proportion of total staff in each staff group. Proportions are similar for both the M&D and N&M group. Greatest variation occurs in three groups: ancillary, A&C, and PAM. The proportion of ancillary staff is lowest in the north west. This may reflect variations in the contracting-out of catering and domestic services implying that staff working in these services are no longer counted as trust employees.

The greatest proportion of A&C staff is in the north west, some 22 per cent. Other sectors range between 18 and 20 per cent. However, variation within London is generally less than that between London and the rest of the country, as is shown in Table 9. This also holds for the M&D and N&M groups.

Table 7: Average proportion of acute trust employees, by staff group, by sector of London, 1994/95

Staff Group	North West	North Central	East	South East	South	London
	%	%	%	%	%	%
M&D	11	10	10	9	11	10
N&M	42	42	42	43	43	42
PAM	6	5	4	5	7	5
Ancillary	5	10	10	12	8	9
A&C	22	20	18	18	19	20
Works	2	1	2	2	2	2
P&T	10	10	10	9	10	10
All other	2	2	3	2	0	2

Table 8 compares the position in London with that in the rest of the country. London trusts as a whole have a slightly greater average number of employees than those in the rest of the country. However, comparisons between trusts in similar types of socio-economic area reveal that London trusts employ fewer staff than non-London trusts in comparable areas. The overall London average is higher because a greater proportion of trusts in London are in inner-deprived areas where trusts tend to be larger.

Table 8: Average number of acute trust employees, by staff group, London and England, 1994/95

Staff Group	London				Non-London				England
	Inner-deprived	Mixed-status	High-status	Total	Inner-deprived	Mixed-status	High-status	Total	
M&D	259	204	197	224	217	164	172	169	179
N&M	952	895	883	914	1,121	1,078	936	970	960
PAM	105	120	108	110	139	137	111	120	119
Ancillary	261	134	157	192	337	280	218	250	240
A&C	472	413	365	422	443	375	361	361	372
Works	41	39	38	40	51	46	33	38	39
P&T	260	180	168	209	250	155	161	164	172
All other	56	23	47	43	32	44	36	36	37
Total	2,405	2,008	1,965	2,154	2,590	2,279	2,028	2,110	2,117

Table 9 shows acute trusts in London as a whole have proportionately more staff in the M&D and A&C groups and proportionately fewer nurses, midwives and ancillary workers. The N&M group is just 42 per cent of the total in London compared with 46 per cent in the rest of the country: this proportion falls to 40 per cent in inner-deprived areas of the capital. Some large teaching hospitals and single specialty hospitals in inner-deprived London, have uniquely high proportions of doctors and low proportions of nurses. In the most extreme cases there are just two or three nursing staff for each doctor compared with the national average of well over five. The different staff-mix in London hospitals is reflected in the variations in staff costs which are discussed in Chapter 9. However, this chapter also shows that London trusts spend more on agency staff. As a high proportion of these are likely to be nursing staff, this may mean that Table 9 underestimates the true proportion of staff in the N&M group in London trusts, particularly when compared with the rest of the country.

Table 9: Average proportion of acute trust employees, by staff group, London and England, 1994/95

Staff Group	London				Non-London				England
	Inner-deprived	Mixed-status	High-status	Total	Inner-deprived	Mixed-status	High-status	Total	
	%	%	%	%	%	%	%	%	%
M&D	11	10	10	10	8	7	8	8	8
N&M	40	45	45	42	43	47	46	46	45
PAM	4	6	6	5	5	6	5	6	6
Ancillary	11	7	8	9	13	12	11	12	11
A&C	20	21	19	20	17	16	18	17	18
Works	2	2	2	2	2	2	2	2	2
P&T	11	9	9	10	10	7	8	8	8
All other	2	1	2	2	1	2	2	2	2

Non-acute trusts

Table 10 compares the average number of employees at each non-acute trust, by staff group, across sectors of London. Non-acute trusts are either community, mental health or learning disabilities trusts: ambulance trusts have been excluded. Clear differences emerge in the staffing of non-acute and acute trusts in London. Non-acute trusts employ fewer staff on average than acute trusts: in London as a whole approximately fifty per cent less.

Table 10: Average number of non-acute trust employees, by staff group, by sector of London, 1994/95

Staff Group	North West	North Central	East	South East	South	London
M&D	63	82	n/a	73	27	61
N&M	659	837	n/a	613	429	625
PAM	70	127	n/a	67	62	78
Ancillary	40	113	n/a	51	49	59
A&C	201	289	n/a	220	154	212
Works	14	17	n/a	11	8	12
P&T	55	78	n/a	38	18	46
All other	15	39	n/a	32	8	22
Total	1,118	1,581	n/a	1,105	757	1,116

(Tables 10 and 11 reflect the fact that in 1994/95 there were no wholly non-acute trusts in the east sector. Community services in East London and the City were provided by a DMU, in Redbridge and Waltham Forest by combined trusts, and in Barking and Havering by a community trust with a headquarters outside London.)

Non-acute trusts employ proportionately fewer doctors and more nurses than acute trusts. Table 11 shows that the proportion of doctors in non-acute London trusts as a whole, at five per cent, is half the proportion in acute trusts: see Table 7. By contrast, the proportion of nurses is 56 per cent compared with 42 per cent in acute trusts. Differences are also observed in professions allied to medicine, e.g. physiotherapy and occupational therapy, where the proportion is seven per cent in non-acute trusts against five per cent in acute.

Table 11: Average proportion of non-acute trust employees, by staff group, by sector of London, 1994/95

Staff Group	North West %	North Central %	East %	South East %	South %	London %
M&D	6	5	n/a	7	4	5
N&M	59	53	n/a	55	57	56
PAM	6	8	n/a	6	8	7
Ancillary	4	7	n/a	5	6	5
A&C	18	18	n/a	20	20	19
Works	1	1	n/a	1	1	1
P&T	5	5	n/a	3	2	4
All other	1	2	n/a	3	1	2

Table 12 compares the average number of employees in non-acute trusts, by staff group, between London and the rest of England. The average number of employees in non-acute trusts in London is over ten per cent less than in the rest of England.

Table 12: Average number of non-acute trust employees, by staff group, London and England, 1994/95

Staff Group	London				Non-London				England
	Inner-deprived	Mixed-status	High-status	Total	Inner-deprived	Mixed-status	High-status	Total	
M&D	85	56	39	61	77	46	39	42	44
N&M	678	611	581	625	1,067	760	670	736	721
PAM	90	77	65	78	130	92	82	92	90
Ancillary	59	54	65	59	202	121	97	114	107
A&C	254	196	185	212	311	185	172	183	187
Works	11	14	11	12	24	20	18	19	18
P&T	55	49	30	46	68	40	35	37	38
All other	46	11	11	22	53	36	21	27	27
Total	1,281	1,067	990	1,116	1,931	1,300	1,134	1,252	1,234

Finally, Table 13 shows that, as with acute trusts, non-acute trusts in London employ comparatively more staff in the M&D and A&C groups and comparatively fewer nurses and ancillary workers. The difference is greatest in inner-deprived London where seven per cent of staff are classified as belonging to the M&D group and 20 per cent to the A&C group compared with three and 15 per cent respectively in the rest of England as a whole. On the other hand, nurses are 53 per cent of the workforce in inner-deprived London compared with 59 per cent in the rest of England.

Table 13: Average proportion of non-acute trust employees, by staff group, London and England, 1994/95

Staff Group	London				Non-London				England
	Inner-deprived	Mixed-status	High-status	Total	Inner-deprived	Mixed-status	High-status	Total	
	%	%	%	%	%	%	%	%	%
M&D	7	5	4	5	4	4	3	3	4
N&M	53	57	59	56	55	58	59	59	58
PAM	7	7	7	7	7	7	7	7	7
Ancillary	5	5	7	5	10	9	9	9	9
A&C	20	18	19	19	16	14	15	15	15
Works	1	1	1	1	1	2	2	2	1
P&T	4	5	3	4	4	3	3	3	3
All other	4	1	1	2	3	3	2	2	2
Total	100	100	100	100	100	100	100	100	100

Chapter 5

Independent Hospital Provision

Summary

Provision of private care

- A higher proportion of activity in NHS hospitals in London is paid for privately compared with the rest of England: approximately two compared with one per cent.

- There is considerable variation in London with the east, south-east and south sectors close to the England average whereas over three per cent of activity in the north-west and north-central sectors is private.

- In London as elsewhere a high proportion of private FCEs are elective: 86 per cent compared with just 54 per cent of total activity.

- The day case rate for private FCEs in London, at 28 per cent, is low compared with the rest of England figure of 39 per cent – and less than the 31 per cent recorded for all activity. This difference may reflect two facets of private activity in London: a concentration on more complex procedures where an overnight stay is desirable; or a different pattern of care with a greater likelihood of overnight stay for a given condition.

- A small proportion of out-patient attendances are paid for privately. The position is very similar to that for in-patient care with a higher volume of private activity in London than elsewhere.

- The majority of independent hospitals in London are located in inner-deprived areas with 35 per cent in one DHA alone, Kensington, Chelsea and Westminster. This contrasts with the position outside the capital where most such hospitals are located in high-status areas.

- London has substantially more independent beds than the rest of England – 45 per 100,000 resident population compared with 20. However, there are substantial flows of patients to these independent hospitals from the rest of England, as well as other countries.

- The independent sector in London employs around 29 per cent of all private nurses in England, which corresponds to the preponderance of independent hospitals in the capital.

- It is estimated that 25 per cent of total independent sector acute episodes of care in England were provided in hospitals in London in 1992/93.

- The north-west sector provides by far the greatest proportion of London's independent sector activity: nearly 82,000 private patient episodes or 49 per cent of the London total.

- Just 55 per cent of activity in the north-west sector is provided to residents of London, 27 per cent to patients from the rest of England and 17 per cent to people from outside of the country. A similar proportion of activity in the south-east and south sectors is provided to residents of London, though there is a much smaller proportion of activity provided to non-English residents. By contrast, 78 per cent of independent sector activity in the east sector is provided to London residents, whereas in the north-central sector the figure is just 21 per cent.

- The proportion of day cases in independent hospitals in London is 33 per cent compared with a day case rate for elective patients in London NHS hospitals of 57 per cent. The day case rate for elective NHS patients is even higher in the north-west sector, at 61 per cent. However, this sector has the lowest day case rate across London for independent hospital activity, at 27 per cent.

Use of private care

- London residents as a whole make greater use of pay-beds in NHS hospitals, though this amounts to only one per cent of activity for Londoners in NHS hospitals.

- There is considerable variation in the use of NHS pay-beds across London with residents of Kensington, Chelsea and Westminster, Barnet and, to a lesser extent, Camden and Islington, making more use of such facilities. Over five per cent of FCEs in NHS hospitals for residents of Kensington, Chelsea and Westminster is paid for privately. Residents of Lambeth, Southwark and Lewisham, on the other hand, have a proportion similar to that of inner-deprived areas in the rest of the country – approximately 0.5 per cent of FCEs – and East London and the City is rather lower at 0.37 per cent.

- Estimated hospitalisation rates for London DHAs in independent sector hospitals, for 1992/93, range widely, from 3.5 per 1,000 resident population in Redbridge to over 40 in Hampstead. Higher levels of deprivation are to some extent correlated with a lower independent sector hospitalisation rate.

- Where independent sector hospitalisation rates are particularly high – such as in Hampstead or Barnet – this adds substantially to overall hospitalisation rates in these areas.

Key Facts

Provision of private care	London	Rest of England
NHS hospitals		
FCEs provided in NHS pay-beds:	30,100	71,000
Proportion of total FCEs in NHS hospitals:	2%	1%
Proportion of total FCEs that are elective:	86%	87%
Day case rate:	28%	39%
The largest specialty groups:		
• Medicine	35%	20%
• Surgery and Urology	25%	24%
• Obstetrics and Gynaecology	10%	9%
• Ophthalmology	8%	10%
• Orthopaedics	6%	12%
Total private out-patient attendances in NHS hospitals:	65,000	82,000
Proportion of total out-patient attendances in NHS hospitals:	0.8%	0.3%
The independent sector		
Independent hospitals:	74	264
Independent beds:	3,162	8,187
Independent beds per 100,000 residents:	45	20
Total patients in independent hospitals (1992/93):	165,000	485,000
Total patients by area of residence:		
• London	91,000	–
• The rest of England	56,000	–
• The rest of the world	19,000	–
Day case rate in independent hospitals:	33%	–
Use of private care		
Proportion of privately funded FCEs in NHS hospitals:	1.3%	1.0%
Independent hospitalisation rate per 1,000 resident population:	14.7	11.4

1 Introduction

This chapter outlines briefly what is known about the provision of private hospital care in London in comparison with the rest of the country. A provider-based analysis of private activity in NHS pay-beds and in independent hospitals is included. We also consider the human and physical resources available to the independent sector in London. This is followed by a section on the utilisation of private facilities, both NHS pay-beds and independent sector hospitals.

2 Data sources

Activity data for NHS pay-beds are based on analysis of the HES dataset. Activity data from the independent sector are provided by Jonathan Nicholl, University of Sheffield Medical School, based on a survey of activity in independent sector hospitals in 1992/93 (Williams and Nicholl, 1995). Data on independent sector human and physical resources are taken from the Department of Health publication, *'Private hospitals, homes and clinics registered under Section 23 of the Registered Homes Act 1984, Vol. 2, 1994/95'* (DoH, 1995e).

3 Provision of private care

Most of the analysis in previous chapters considers activity in NHS hospitals irrespective of who pays for it. This reflects the usual way in which data on NHS activity are presented at a national level. However, there are substantial differences between London and the rest of England in respect of the importance of privately-funded activity, both within the NHS provider sector, and in the independent hospital sector. Therefore, in this section we present a provider-based perspective on 'private' activity.

NHS hospitals

(Technical note: in this section all patients that are recorded as category 20-23 (private patients) or category 30-33 (amenity patients, where a charge is made for accommodation but not for treatment) are counted as being <u>private</u> patients. Only five per cent of these are amenity. These categories of patient are defined in the NHS Act of 1977 (DHSS, 1977).)

Total FCEs

Figure 1 shows, by sector, the absolute number and proportion of private FCEs in NHS hospitals in London. Figure 2 shows the proportion of total FCEs in each sector which are private. Most private FCEs occur in the north-west and north-central sectors of the capital – around 75 per cent of the total. In both sectors private FCEs account for over three per cent of total activity, compared with just under one per cent in the other London sectors.

Table 1 shows the ten trusts in London with the greatest number of private FCEs together with four others where there is a high proportion of private activity. Of these 14 trusts, seven are in the north-west sector and five in the north-central sector. Three hospitals in London have over ten per cent private activity: the Royal Marsden, Harefield and Great Ormond Street, all of which are in the north-central or north-west sector. Indeed, 16 of the 20 London NHS hospitals with the greatest proportions of private activity are in these sectors.

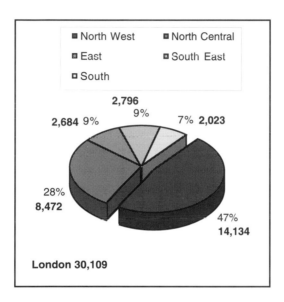

Figure 1: Private FCEs, by sector of London, 1994/95

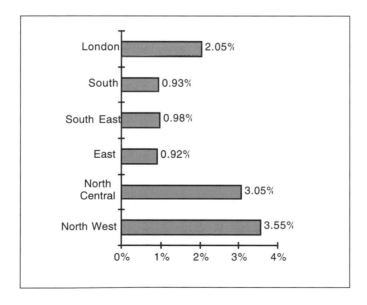

Figure 2: Proportion of FCEs that are private, by sector of London, 1994/95

Table 1: The ten trusts with the greatest number of private FCEs in London, 1994/95

Trust	Total Private FCEs	Private FCEs as proportion of total %
Hammersmith Hospitals	3,342	5
The Royal Marsden	2,918	17
The Royal Free Hampstead	2,631	6
University College London Hospitals	2,627	7
St. Mary's	2,406	5
Great Ormond Street Hospital for Sick Children	2,061	10
Guy's and St. Thomas's	1,713	2
Northwick Park and St. Mark's	1,345	4
Moorfields Eye Hospital	1,316	8
Royal Brompton	1,017	8
Harefield Hospital	983	12
Royal National Orthopaedic Hospital	600	8
National Hospital for Neurology	401	7
Royal National Throat, Nose and Ear	376	5

(Table 1 is ordered by the total number of private FCEs.)

Figures 3 and 4 compare London with the rest of the country. Thirty per cent of all private patients in NHS pay-beds are in London, and nearly 20 per cent in inner-deprived London. In London, the proportion of total FCEs that are private is over twice that of the rest of England. In inner-deprived London, over 3 per cent of all FCEs are private.

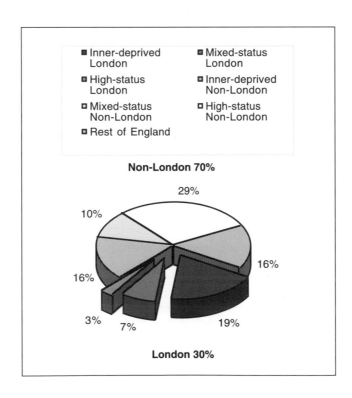

Figure 3: Private FCEs, London and England, 1994/95

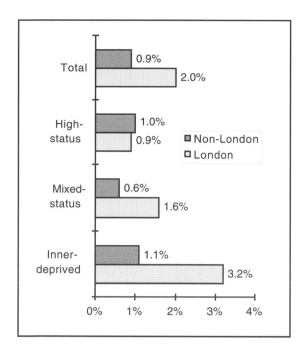

Figure 4: Proportion of FCEs that are private, London and England, 1994/95

■ Proportion of elective FCEs

Private FCEs are more likely to be elective than total FCEs produced in NHS hospitals. Figure 5 shows that 86 per cent of private FCEs in London are elective: this compares with 54 per cent of total FCEs. However, there is considerable variation across London, with 94 per cent of private FCEs elective in the north-central sector, compared with only 70 per cent in the south sector. This is largely due to higher emergency rates at the two major providers of private FCEs in this sector.

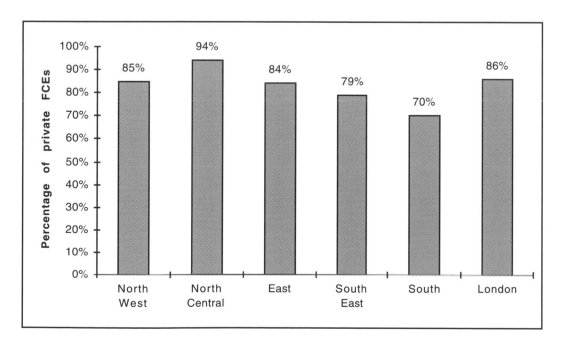

Figure 5: Proportion of private FCEs that are elective, by sector of London, 1994/95

Figure 6 shows that a slightly greater proportion of private FCEs are elective in the rest of the country than is the case in London. This is true of inner-deprived and mixed-status areas: high-status areas in London have a slightly higher proportion of elective private FCEs than comparable areas in the rest of the country.

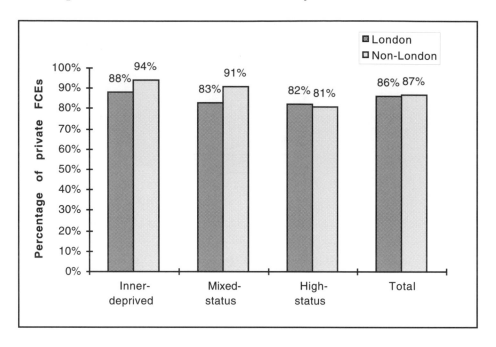

Figure 6: Proportion of private FCEs that are elective, London and England, 1994/95

■ Day case rate

The overall day case rate tends to increase with the proportion of elective FCEs. However, as Figure 7 shows, the day case rate for private FCEs in London is 28 per cent, which is less than the rate for all FCEs, 31 per cent, as shown in Figure 2 of Chapter 2 on page 41: this is despite a much greater proportion of elective private FCEs. The north-central and south sectors have higher day case rates for private FCEs than for non-private, but the rates for the east and south-east sectors are significantly lower.

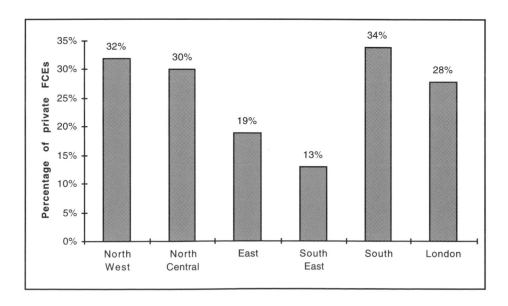

Figure 7: Day case rates for private FCEs, by sector of London, 1994/95

Figure 8 shows there is a lower day case rate in London compared with the rest of the country. In particular, the rate in inner-deprived London is only half that of inner-deprived areas in the rest of the country. This difference is only partly explained by the higher proportion of elective FCEs in the rest of the country. Moreover, even the day case rate outside London is low given the high proportion of elective activity. Further analysis of the HES dataset is required to understand these differences in the pattern of private activity.

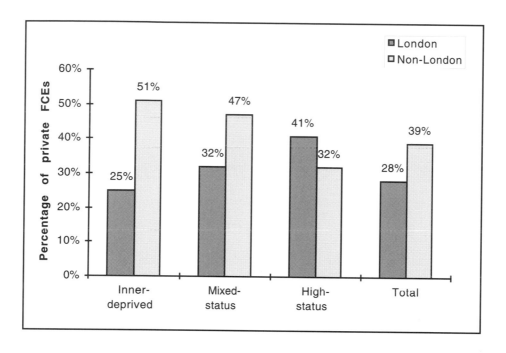

Figure 8: Day case rates for private FCEs, London and England, 1994/95

■ The specialty composition of private FCEs

Table 2 shows that almost 85 per cent of private activity in London occurs in just five specialty groups: medicine, surgery and urology, obstetrics and gynaecology, ophthalmology and orthopaedics. Individual trusts have a considerable impact on the specialty composition of private FCEs in any given sector.

Table 2: Proportion of private FCEs, by specialty group, by sector of London, 1994/95

Specialty Group	North West %	North Central %	East %	South East %	South %	London %
Medicine	45	26	20	26	34	35
Surgery/Urology	24	27	13	34	31	25
Obs. and Gynae.	10	8	4	17	10	10
Ophthalmology	2	2	55	8	8	8
Orthopaedics	7	6	1	5	6	6
Haematology	1	13	2	1	4	5
ENT	2	7	2	1	1	3
Other non-acute	4	4	1	1	1	3
Paediatrics	1	4	0	4	2	2
Dental	1	2	0	2	1	1
Anaesthetics	1	1	0	0	0	1
Geriatrics	0	0	0	0	1	0
Unknown	0	0	0	0	0	0
Psychiatric	0	0	0	0	0	0
Total	100	100	100	100	100	100

(Tables 2 and 3 are ordered by specialty with the greatest proportion of FCEs in London.)

Table 3 compares the proportions of private FCEs in each specialty group in London with those in the rest of England. The major difference is a smaller proportion of private medical activity in the rest of the country which is compensated by a greater proportion of orthopaedic, ENT and psychiatric FCEs. The difference is particularly influenced by the relative provision of private medical FCEs in inner-deprived areas. In inner-deprived London, 40 per cent of private FCEs are medicine, twice the proportion in similar areas in the rest of the country.

Table 3: Proportion of private FCEs, by specialty group, London and England, 1994/95

Specialty group	London Inner-deprived %	London Mixed-status %	London High-status %	London Total %	Non-London Inner-deprived %	Non-London Mixed-status %	Non-London High-status %	Non-London Total %	England %
Medicine	40	25	29	35	20	21	22	20	24
Surgery/Urology	24	30	26	25	20	27	25	24	25
Obs. and Gynae.	7	15	14	10	12	13	8	9	9
Ophthalmology	10	3	7	8	8	13	8	10	9
Orthopaedics	3	13	3	6	6	9	14	12	10
Haematology	6	3	1	5	1	0	1	1	2
ENT	4	3	2	3	3	6	5	5	5
Other non-acute	2	2	13	3	27	4	3	9	7
Paediatrics	2	3	1	2	0	0	1	0	1
Dental	2	1	1	1	1	2	2	2	2
Anaesthetics	0	1	1	1	1	1	1	1	1
Geriatrics	0	0	0	0	0	1	1	1	1
Unknown	0	1	0	0	0	0	1	0	0
Psychiatric	0	0	0	0	0	3	9	5	3
Total	100	100	100	100	100	100	100	100	100

■ Out-patient attendances

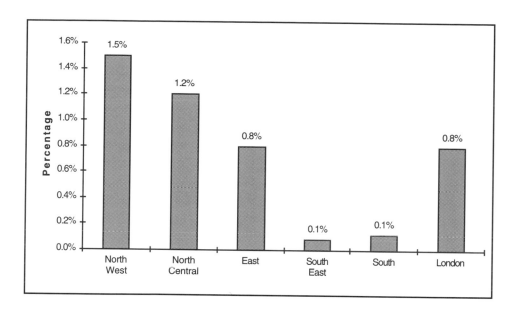

Figure 9: Proportion of private out-patient attendances, by sector of London, 1994/95

Out-patient attendances were discussed in Chapter 4. A proportion of these are funded privately. Figure 9 shows the considerable variation across London with the greatest proportion of private attendances in the north-west sector, and virtually none in the south and south-east sectors.

Figure 10 shows that the proportion of private out-patient attendances is higher in London than elsewhere in the country. Inner-deprived London has a higher proportion of private attendances than any other type of area. This probably reflects the nature of hospitals in inner-deprived London rather than the nature of the local population as this would be expected to mitigate in the opposite direction. In the rest of the country, the greatest proportion of private out-patient attendances is in high-status areas.

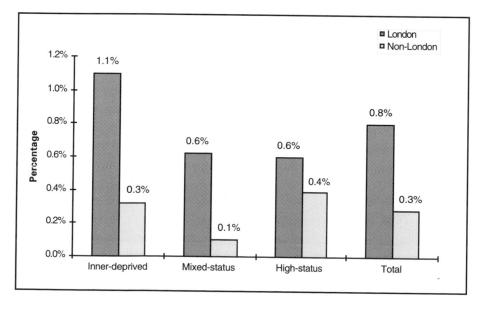

Figure 10: Proportion of private out-patient attendances, London and England, 1994/95

The independent sector

This section compares the provision of independent hospitals and beds in London with that in the rest of England. The independent sector consists of private and voluntary providers. Data are also presented on independent sector nursing. We conclude this section by considering the level of independent hospital activity in London.

Independent hospitals

Map 1 shows the number of independent hospitals in each DHA in London. There are 26 of London's 74 independent hospitals in Kensington, Chelsea and Westminster. Barnet with eight has the next greatest number. There are no independent hospitals in two DHAs: Barking and Havering in the east, and Bexley and Greenwich in the south east.

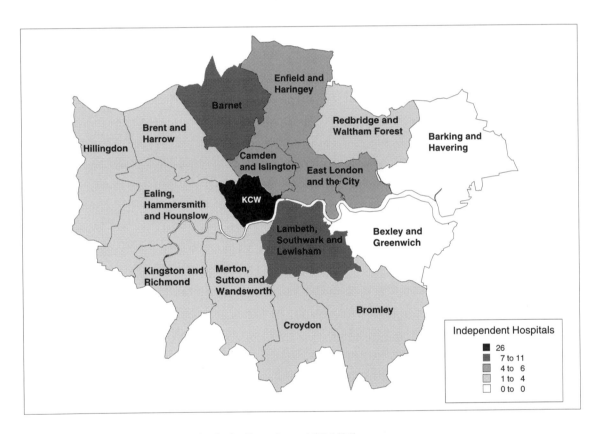

Map 1: Independent hospitals in London, 1994/95

Figure 11 compares London with the rest of England. The majority of independent hospitals in London are located in inner-deprived areas whereas the majority in the rest of the country are in high-status areas. This seems to reflect more the prestige of central London locations than a desire to locate close to probable users. We show below that London's independent hospitals are less dependent on local patients. Only 55 per cent of patients in London's independent hospitals are from London. By contrast, independent hospitals outside of London are likely to be more dependent on the local population: most are located in high-status areas where a greater proportion of the population may use private health care.

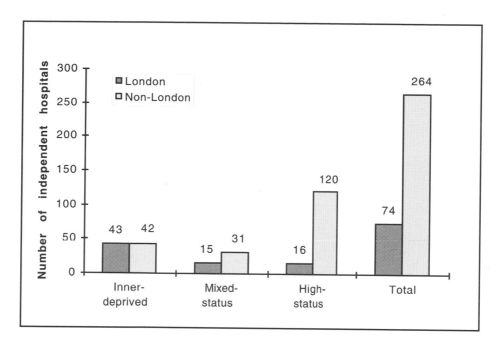

Figure 11: Independent hospitals, London and England, 1994/95

Independent bed availability

Map 2 shows that the number of independent beds available in individual London DHAs varies considerably. Forty-two per cent of independent beds in London – 1,336 – are located in Kensington, Chelsea and Westminster. No other DHA has more than 300 beds. There are only 36 beds in neighbouring Camden and Islington.

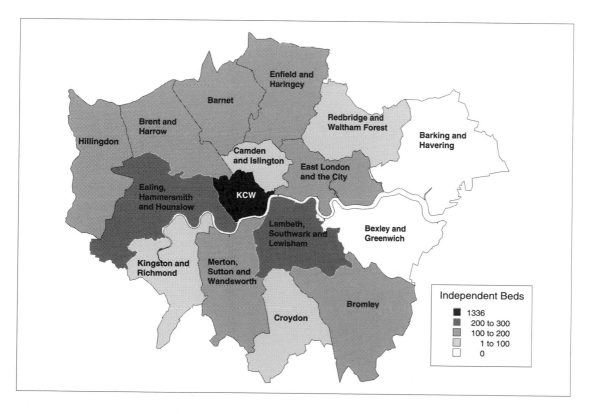

Map 2: Independent hospital beds in London, 1994/95

Figure 12 compares the provision of independent beds in London with that of the rest of the country. Unsurprisingly, there is a similar pattern to the provision of independent hospitals. The majority of independent beds in London are located in inner-deprived areas: the majority of independent beds outside the capital are located in high-status areas. London has 28 per cent of all independent beds in the country.

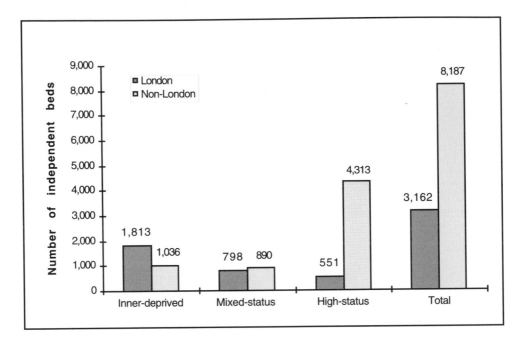

Figure 12: Independent hospital beds, London and England, 1994/95

Map 3 relates the availability of independent beds to resident population, showing the number of beds per 100,000 population in London DHAs. Provision in Kensington, Chelsea and Westminster stands out dramatically, with 392 beds per 100,000 residents compared with a London average of 45. By contrast, there are no beds in Barking and Havering and Bexley and Greenwich, and only 10 beds per 100,000 residents in Camden and Islington.

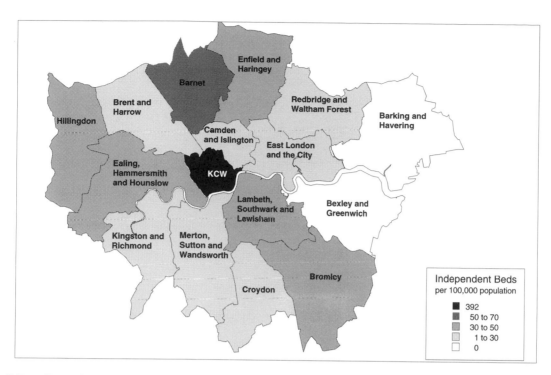

Map 3: Independent hospital beds in London per 100,000 resident population, 1994/95

Figure 13 shows London has over twice as many independent beds per resident population as the rest of England: in inner-deprived London there are 90 beds per 100,000 residents, over four times as many. However, this is largely due to the concentration of hospitals in Kensington, Chelsea and Westminster. If this DHA area were excluded from the analysis, the number of independent beds per 100,000 population in London falls from 45 to 28.

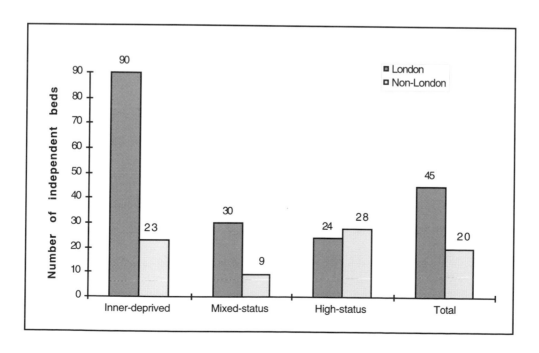

Figure 13: Independent hospital beds per 100,000 residents, London and England, 1994/95

Independent sector nursing

This section compares the provision of independent sector nursing, both across London and between London and the rest of the country. Figure 14 shows that 60 per cent of independent sector nurses in London are employed in the north-west sector. Nearly 1,400 of these are employed in hospitals in Kensington, Chelsea and Westminster. Indeed, 14 per cent of all independent sector nurses in England are employed in this DHA.

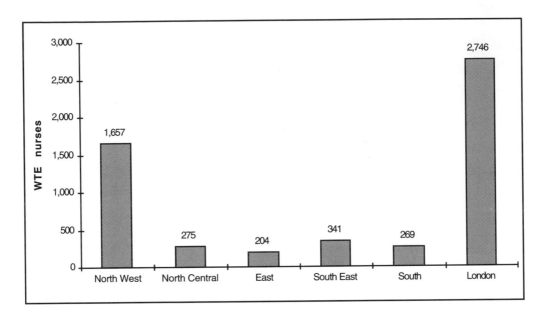

Figure 14: Provision of independent sector nurses, by sector of London, 1994/95

Figure 15 compares the number of WTE independent nurses across types of socio-economic area, between London and the rest of England. The capital has more such nurses in both inner-deprived and mixed-status areas than comparable areas elsewhere. London as a whole has around 29 per cent of all independent sector nurses in the country.

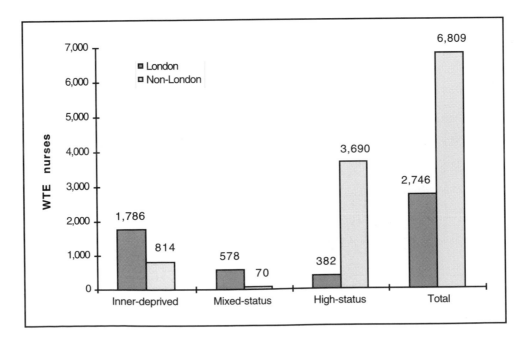

Figure 15: Provision of independent sector nurses, London and England, 1994/95

Activity

We complete the picture by considering the provision of private health care in independent sector hospitals in London. Data were provided by Jonathan Nicholl, University of Sheffield Medical School, based on a survey of activity in independent sector hospitals in 1992/93. Hence, the data refer to a rather earlier period than most of the material considered here. Also, data are aggregated into sectors of London by health authority as these were constituted in 1989/90.

In London as a whole there were over 165,000 private patient episodes in independent hospitals in 1992/93 out of a total of 650,000 in England. This is some 11 per cent of the total number of FCEs produced in NHS hospitals in London in 1994/95. As Figure 16 shows, the north-west sector provided by far the greatest proportion of London's independent sector activity: nearly 82,000 private patient episodes or 49 per cent of the London total. This is not surprising as this sector has the largest number of independent hospitals, most of which are in Kensington, Chelsea and Westminster. By contrast, activity in other sectors of London ranged between 16,000 and 25,000 private patients.

Figure 16 also shows that just 55 per cent of activity in the north-west sector is provided to residents of London, 27 per cent to people from the rest of England and 17 per cent to people from outside the country. A similar proportion of activity in the south-east and south sectors is provided to residents of London, though there is a much smaller proportion of activity provided to non-English residents. By contrast, 78 per cent of independent sector activity in the east sector is provided to London residents, whereas in the north-central sector the figure is just 21 per cent.

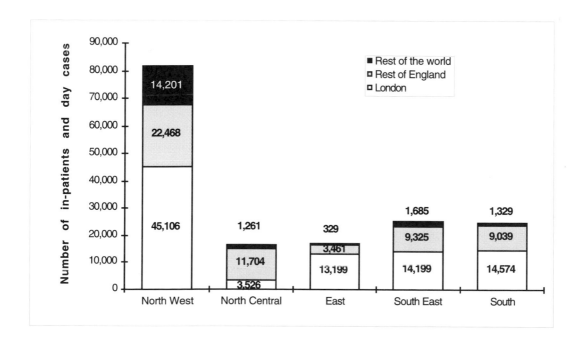

Figure 16: Independent hospital in-patients and day cases, by sector of London, 1992/93

■ Day case rate

The proportion of day cases in independent hospitals in London is 33 per cent compared with a day case rate for elective patients in London NHS hospitals of 57 per cent. Activity in independent hospitals is mainly elective surgery. The day case rate for elective NHS patients is even higher in the north-west sector, at 61 per cent. However, this sector has the lowest day case rate across London for independent hospital activity, at 27 per cent.

Day case rates vary depending on the area of residence of the patient. As Figure 17 shows, throughout London the lowest day case rates are associated with patients from outside England. However, with the exception of the east sector, non-Londoners have a higher day case rate than residents of the capital. This is somewhat surprising. In NHS hospitals the day case rate for non-residents tends to be less than that for Londoners, which may imply that people are more likely to travel to London for specialised treatment, not available on a day case basis. This seems not to be the case for people using independent hospitals, but conclusions remain tentative without further investigation of these findings.

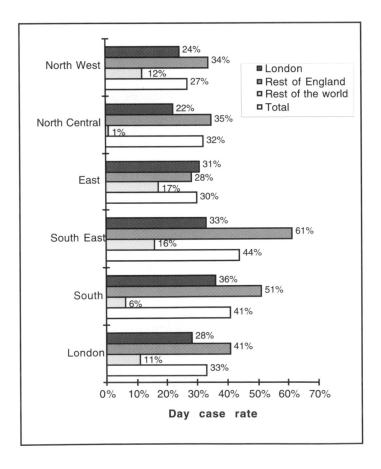

Figure 17: Independent hospital day case rate, by sector of London, 1992/93

4 Use of private care

We now consider the hospitalisation rate for those patients funding their own care whether in NHS or independent sector hospitals. Hospitalisation rates reported previously have included care in NHS beds which has been paid for privately.

NHS pay-beds

Table 4 shows, by DHA of residence, the proportion of FCEs performed in NHS hospitals categorised as for private or amenity patients – which we have termed privately-funded care in NHS hospitals. Kensington, Chelsea and Westminster has by far the highest proportion of such patients – over five times the England average. A higher proportion of private FCEs might be expected in the least deprived areas; yet Kensington, Chelsea and Westminster is categorised as an inner-deprived area. This gives some further insight into the diverse nature of London even within geographic aggregates which are designated as deprived. As the analysis of needs indices in Chapter 1 showed, pockets of affluence and deprivation exist alongside each other in London.

Table 4: Proportion of total FCEs in NHS hospitals, categorised as private or amenity, by London DHA of residence, 1994/95

DHA	Private or Amenity %
Kensington, Chelsea and Westminster	5.24
Barnet	2.83
Camden and Islington	1.91
Kingston and Richmond	1.87
Ealing, Hammersmith and Hounslow	1.72
Brent and Harrow	1.69
Hillingdon	1.40
Bromley	1.25
Merton, Sutton and Wandsworth	1.19
Croydon	0.91
Enfield and Haringey	0.82
Barking and Havering	0.56
Lambeth, Southwark and Lewisham	0.52
Redbridge and Waltham Forest	0.51
Bexley and Greenwich	0.39
East London and the City	0.37

(Table 4 is ordered by the DHA with the greatest proportion of private or amenity FCEs.)

Figure 18 compares the proportion of private NHS patients in London with that in the rest of the country. In the rest of England there is a gradient, the proportion of private FCEs increasing as the level of deprivation declines. However, in London the greatest proportion of private FCEs is in inner-deprived areas. This is due to the impact of Kensington, Chelsea and Westminster and, to a lesser extent, Camden and Islington. Residents of Lambeth, Southwark and Lewisham have a similar proportion to that of inner-deprived areas in the rest of the country: approximately 0.5 per cent of FCEs are private or amenity. The proportion in East London and the City is rather lower at 0.37 per cent.

However, London as a whole has a higher proportion of private FCEs than is the case in the rest of the country. Indeed, the proportion in the mixed-status group in London – the lowest in the capital – is as great as that in high-status areas in the rest of the country. London residents make greater use of pay-beds in NHS hospitals, though this still amounts only to just over one per cent of activity for Londoners in NHS hospitals.

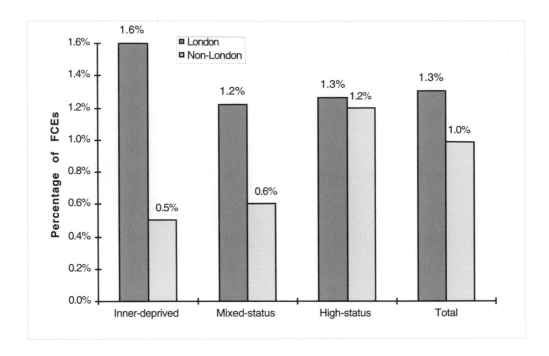

Figure 18: Proportion of total FCEs in NHS hospitals, categorised as private or amenity, by DHA of residence, London and England, 1994/95

Table 5 shows the ten DHAs in England with the greatest proportion of privately-funded NHS activity. Three are in London. With the exception of Somerset, the other six are in the south east of England. London DHAs are also in eleventh, fifteenth and sixteenth positions. It is likely that much of the private activity in south-east England is provided in London hospitals.

Table 5: The ten DHAs with the greatest proportion of total FCEs in NHS hospitals, categorised as private or amenity, by DHA of residence, England, 1994/95

DHA	Private or Amenity %
Kensington, Chelsea and Westminster	**5.24**
Mid Surrey	3.79
South West Surrey	3.59
Barnet	**2.83**
North West Surrey	2.51
Oxfordshire	2.21
North West Hertfordshire	2.11
East Sussex	1.99
Camden and Islington	**1.91**
Somerset	1.91

The independent sector

We now consider hospitalisation rates in independent hospitals using the 1992/93 data set referred to previously. Hospitalisation rates are calculated on the basis of former London health authorities, using 1992 mid-year population estimates. Table 6 reveals that the highest independent hospitalisation rate per 1,000 resident population was in Hampstead (this is now part of Camden and Islington DHA), followed by Barnet and Riverside (much of which is now Kensington, Chelsea and Westminster DHA).

Socio-economic groupings for these former London health authorities were provided for the first King's Fund London Commission. The constitution of these groups is given in Appendix 3. As might be expected, the level of deprivation associated with these former health authority areas is to some extent negatively correlated with the independent hospitalisation rate. With the exception of Hampstead and Riverside, both of which contain more affluent areas alongside deprived localities, health authorities in inner-deprived areas tend to have lower independent hospitalisation rates, of 12 per 1,000 population, or less. By contrast, with the exception of Redbridge, independent hospitalisation rates in high-status areas are among the highest in the capital.

Table 6: Independent hospitalisation rate, by London DHA, 1992/93

DHA	Independent hospitalisation rate per 1,000 resident population
Hampstead	41.6
Barnet	38.2
Riverside	34.4
Harrow	25.9
Barking Havering and Brentwood	25.7
Merton and Sutton	23.2
Kingston and Esher	20.7
Bromley	19.2
Waltham Forest	18.1
Enfield	16.2
Richmond, Twickenham and Roehampton	15.4
Bexley	15.0
Bloomsbury and Islington	14.7
West Lambeth	14.0
Croydon	13.0
Haringey	12.1
Hounslow and Spelthorne	12.0
Parkside	9.9
Hillingdon	9.0
City and Hackney	5.1
Newham	4.8
Wandsworth	4.8
Greenwich	4.6
Ealing	4.5
Tower Hamlets	4.4
Lewisham	3.8
Camberwell	3.7
Redbridge	3.5

(Table 6 is based on former London health authorities.)

Chapter 6

Community Health Services

Summary

Provision of services

Contact rates

- There is wide variation across London in the contact rate for all elements of CHS. In general, for any given community health service, there is one sector of London with a higher contact rate than the average across the capital. These greater rates are driven by one or two providers with high levels of activity, rather than a consistent pattern across the sector.

- There is frequently great disparity between the contact rates of neighbouring sectors, suggesting the possibility of some cross-sectoral provision of care.

- For all services with the exception of specialist nursing, inner-deprived London has a greater contact rate than other types of socio-economic area in the capital.

- Contact rates are similar in London as a whole to those in the rest of the country for all services except community nurses for learning disabilities. The lower rate for this service may be linked to the lower provision of residential care for this group by local authority social services, shown in Chapter 8.

Measuring contacts

- An **initial contact** is the first in an episode of care with a service provider. The ratio of total contacts to initial contacts (CIC) is a measure of the number of contacts in any given episode.

- The ratio of total to initial contacts varies greatly across London. High contact rates in London seem to reflect patients being seen more frequently rather than a greater relative number of individual patients.

- With the exception of speech therapy, chiropody and community nursing for learning disabilities, CIC ratios are generally higher in inner-deprived London than in other parts of the capital.

- London has higher CIC ratios than the rest of the country for all services except community nursing for learning disabilities and chiropody, indicating that there are more contacts per patient episode in London than is the case in the rest of the country.

- A **first contact** is the first time a patient is seen in the financial year by a community health care professional. The ratio of total to first contacts (CFC) is a measure of the total number of contacts per patient per year.

- In both London and the rest of England, CFC ratios tend to be less than CIC ratios, implying fewer initial contacts then first contacts, and hence that many episodes of care last over a year.

- CFC ratios are higher in London than in the rest of England for district nurses, lower for community nurses for learning disabilities, and similar for other services.

Location of community contacts

- Consistently throughout London and England, approximately 80 per cent of community contacts take place in the patient's home.

Key Facts

	London	*Rest of England*
Total community contacts (1994/95 unless stated):	10,321,000	64,530,000
• District nurse contacts	5,023,000	33,013,000
• Health visitor contacts	2,616,000	15,295,000
• Community learning disability and mental health nurse contacts	698,000	4,774,000
• Specialist nurse contacts	31,000	217,000
• Speech therapist contacts (1993/94)	490,000	2,606,000
• Chiropodist contacts (1993/94)	1,084,000	6,921,000
• Dietician contacts (1993/94)	379,000	1,703,000
Contact rate per 1,000 resident population (1994/95 unless stated):		
• District nurse contacts	765	784
• Health visitor contacts	515	485
• Community learning disability and mental health nurse contacts	106	113
• Specialist nurse contacts	4.9	5.1
• Speech therapist contacts (1993/94)	70	62
• Chiropodist contacts (1993/94)	164	164
• Dietician contacts (1993/94)	52	41
Proportion of contacts in the client's home:	81%	81%

1 Introduction

This chapter considers the provision of Community Health Services (CHS) in London. These comprise contacts between health professionals and patients in community-based settings. The following services are considered:

- district nurses;

- community nurses for learning disabilities and mental health;

- health visitors;

- specialist nurses;

- speech therapists;

- chiropodists; and,

- dieticians.

Availability of data is a constraint on the analysis. For example, community activity by physiotherapists and occupational therapists is not discussed as data were not available. CHS activity in London is considered in three ways. First, we present contact rate per capita resident population. Then the pattern of care provided is considered in terms of contacts per initial contact (CIC), and contacts per first contact (CFC). The distinction between these two measures is rather involved: a full explanation using DoH definitions is given. Finally, we consider where community contacts take place. An analysis of community trust human resources is presented in Chapter 4, *'Other Hospital-Related Activity'*.

2 Data sources

This chapter uses the data underlying DoH publications concerning CHS, for the financial year, 1994/95, unless otherwise stated (DoH, 1995f; DoH, 1995g; DoH, 1995h; DoH, 1995i; DoH, 1995j; DoH, 1995k; DoH, 1996b; DoH, 1996c). These data are from the DoH returns: KT23, 25, 29 and KC55-59. Since data for community contacts are given by provider, the analysis is aggregated according to where the provider of the service is located, not where the patient resides. To allow comparison with other areas of the country, activity is expressed as a contact rate per capita resident population of the DHA in which the provider is located. Both activity and resident population are aggregated according to sector of London or type of socio-economic area.

3 Provision of services

We consider now the provision of services, first in terms of contact rates per capita resident population, and then by discussing more closely the pattern of care provided, including briefly where contacts occur.

Contact rates

This section considers the level of provision of community care in London in terms of total contacts per capita resident population. Since the data available do not allow differentiation of contacts by age, contact rates are not expressed in terms of one or more age-groups, although in some cases this would enhance the analysis.

District nurses

Figure 1 shows a similar contact rate for district nurses across sectors of London, except in the south east where the rate is 825 contacts per 1,000 resident population compared with a London average of 765. There are five providers of this service in the south-east sector, all providing over 175,000 contacts per year, and in one case 400,000 contacts per year.

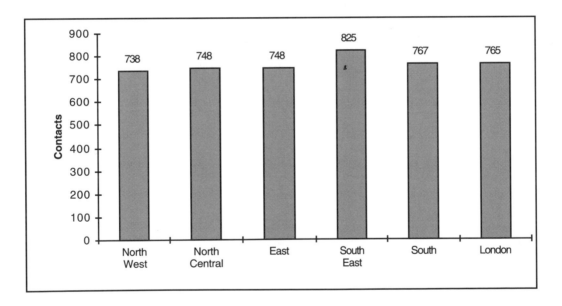

Figure 1: District nurse contacts per 1,000 resident population, by sector of London, 1994/95

Figure 2 shows London as a whole has a slightly lower contact rate than the rest of the country. However, this may be explained by the somewhat younger age-structure in the capital: most district nurse contacts are with people aged 75 years and over. There is variation across types of socio-economic area: in inner-deprived areas of London the contact rate is 38 per cent more than in similar areas in the rest of the country. The four biggest providers of district nursing services in London are in inner-deprived areas: hence the contact rate is considerably more than twice that in mixed-status London, suggesting the possibility that inner-deprived London providers may supply this service to residents of mixed-status areas. To test this finding would require more detailed local data.

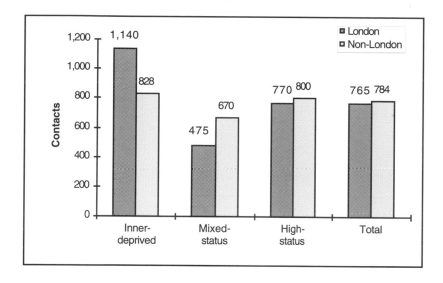

Figure 2: District nurse contacts per 1,000 resident population, London and England, 1994/95

Community nurses for learning disabilities

Figure 3 reveals considerable variation in the contact rate across sectors of London: the east sector has a contact rate nearly four times that of the south east, reflecting a large number of contacts by one provider. Figure 4 shows provision in London is very low in comparison with the rest of England. Part of the reason for this, as Figure 20 demonstrates, is that London has fewer contacts per initial contact than the rest of England. However, this in itself is not enough to explain the difference. Further analysis, using data on the provision of residential care for people with learning disabilities by social services, as well as CHS data, might help to shed some light on these findings.

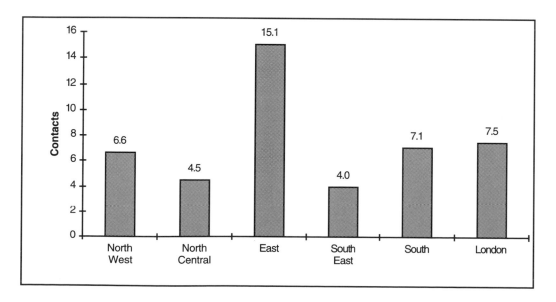

Figure 3: Community nurses for learning disabilities, contacts per 10,000 resident population, by sector of London, 1994/95

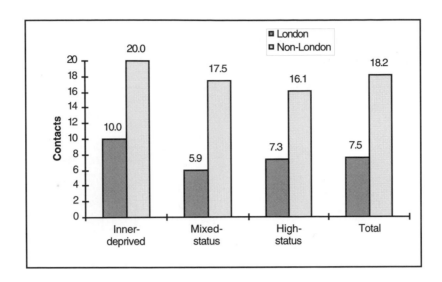

Figure 4: Community nurses for learning disabilities, contacts per 10,000 resident population, London and England, 1994/95

Community nurses for mental health

Figure 5 shows that the north-west sector has 127 contacts per 10,000 resident population compared with between 82 to 94 in other sectors of the capital. The two largest providers of this service are in the north-west sector. As is shown in Figure 2, this sector also has a high ratio of contacts to initial contacts.

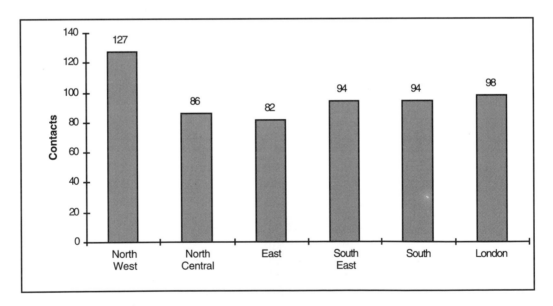

Figure 5: Community nurses for mental health, contacts per 10,000 resident population, by sector of London, 1994/95

Figure 6 shows that, compared to the rest of England, London has a slightly higher contact rate for community mental health nurses.

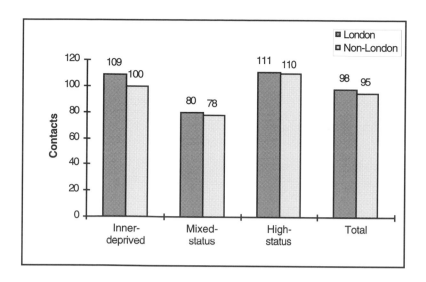

Figure 6: Community nurses for mental health, contacts per 10,000 resident population, London and England, 1994/95

Health visitors

(Technical note: the data supporting this section are based on a DoH report, 'Professional Advice and Support Programmes' (DoH, 1996c), which primarily, though not entirely, reflects health visitor activity. The data cover health visitors and 'other groups'. These are aggregated under the title, health visitors.)

Once again, as Figure 7 shows, there is considerable variation in contact rates across the capital, ranging from a high rate in the south east of 664 per 1,000 resident population to a low rate of 363 in the south. The south-east sector has more large providers than the south. As these are neighbouring sectors, it may be that trusts in the south-east sector provide this service for some residents of the south sector. Further investigation would be required to confirm this, using locally-based knowledge and data.

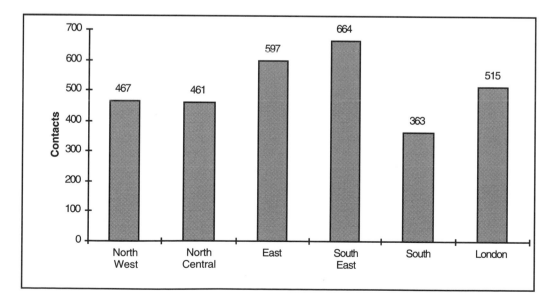

Figure 7: Health visitor contacts per 1,000 resident population, by sector of London, 1994/95

Figure 8 demonstrates that London has a slightly higher health visitor contact rate than the rest of the country. This is due to a higher rate in inner-deprived areas – approximately 790 contacts per 1,000 residents compared with 490. The contact rate in mixed- and high-status areas in London is less than that of similar areas elsewhere in England. As with district nurse services, the contact rate for inner-deprived providers is over twice that of mixed-status providers.

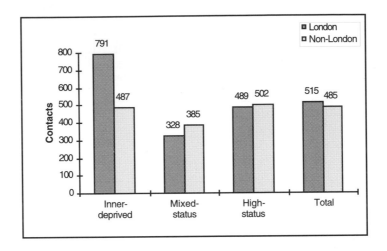

Figure 8: Health visitor contacts per 1,000 resident population, London and England, 1994/95

Specialist Nurses

(Technical note: 'Specialist nurse' is a generic term used to cover Macmillan, Hospice, Marie Curie, Stoma Therapy, Continence, Diabetes, Premature Baby, Oncology, Terminal Care, Catheter, Breast Care and Community Paediatric Nurses.)

The contact rate for specialist nurses is generally lower than for other types of community-based care. Figure 9 shows significant variation across sectors. Contact rates in the north-central and east sectors are twice those in the south and south east. This reflects differences in individual specialties. For example, in the east sector there is a higher contact rate for continence nurses than elsewhere: nearly half of all continence nurse contacts are provided in this sector.

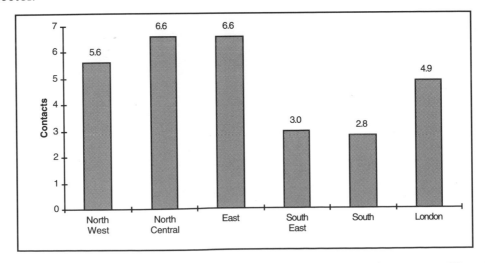

Figure 9: Specialist nurse contacts per 1,000 resident population, by sector of London, 1994/95

Figure 10 shows that the rate in London as a whole is slightly less than that of the rest of England; though it is greater in inner-deprived and high-status areas of the capital. In London and England, highest contact rates for specialist nurses are in high-status areas. At an individual specialty level, London has comparatively higher rates for continence, terminal care and community paediatrics and lower rates for Macmillan, stoma therapy and breast care.

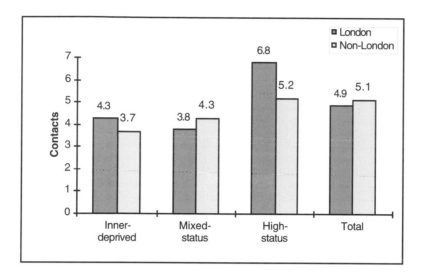

Figure 10: Specialist nurse contacts per 1,000 resident population, London and England, 1994/95

We now consider contact rates for three other clinical professional services: speech therapy, chiropody and dietetics. The data available for these services refer to 1993/94.

Speech therapists

As Figure 11 shows, the contact rate for speech therapists varies between 60 contacts per 1,000 resident population in the north west and over 80 in the east. By far the biggest individual provider is in the east sector.

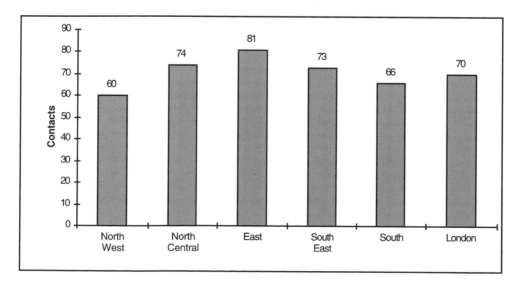

Figure 11: Speech therapist contacts per 1,000 resident population, by sector of London, 1993/94

As Figure 12 shows, the highest contact rate is in inner-deprived areas of London. Four of the five largest London providers of these services are in this area, providing nearly 30 per cent of all contacts in the capital. That London has a higher contact rate than the rest of England – 70 contacts per 1,000 resident population compared with 62 – is due to this much higher contact rate in inner-deprived areas.

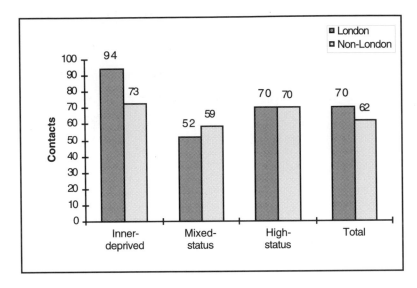

Figure 12: Speech therapist contacts per 1,000 resident population, London and England, 1993/94

Chiropodists

Figure 13 shows considerable variation in chiropodist contact rates across sectors of London, with the highest rate of 200 per 1,000 resident population in the south. There are four large providers of chiropody in the south whereas other sectors have one or, at most, two significant providers.

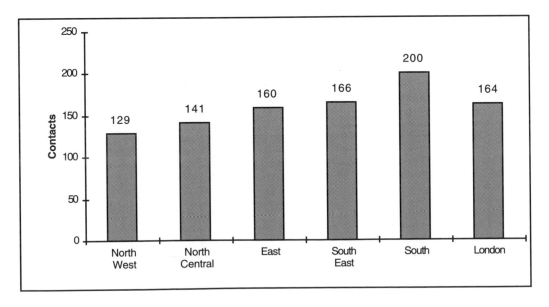

Figure 13: Chiropodist contacts per 1,000 resident population, by sector of London, 1993/94

Figure 14 shows a similar contact rate in London as a whole to that of the rest of England. There is variation between types of socio-economic area: mixed-status areas of London have lower rates than comparable areas in the rest of England; high-status areas of London have relatively greater contact rates.

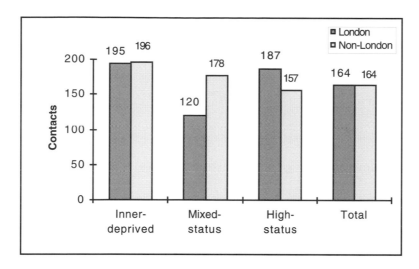

Figure 14: Chiropodist contacts per 1,000 resident population, London and England, 1993/94

Dieticians

Figure 15 shows significantly higher dietician contact rates in the north-central sector, 82 per 1,000 resident population, and the north west, 65 per 1,000 population, when compared with the rest of London. Unlike other community services, dietetic services are often provided by acute hospitals rather than community trusts. Thus, these higher contact rates are driven by activity provided by a small number of acute trusts in the north-central and north-west sectors.

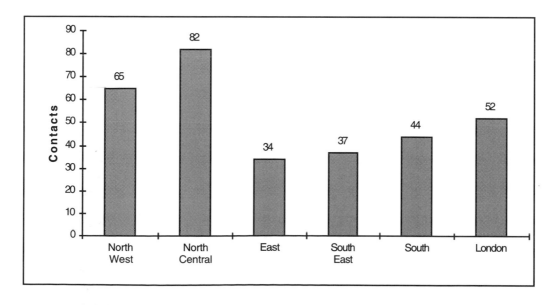

Figure 15: Dietician contacts per 1,000 resident population, by sector of London, 1993/94

Figure 16 shows that inner-deprived areas, both in London and the rest of England, have dietician contact rates over twice those of other types of socio-economic area. London as a whole has a higher contact rate than that nationally, with 52 contacts per 1,000 resident population compared with 41 in the rest of England.

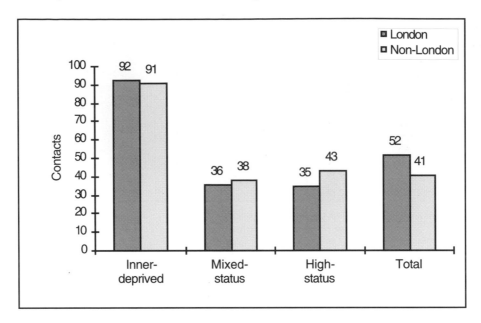

Figure 16: Dietician contacts per 1,000 resident population, London and England, 1993/94

Measuring Contacts

Total contact rates are useful for understanding the *level* of provision of community services. However, the ratio of total contacts to both initial contact and first contact is valuable for understanding the *pattern* of care. The terminology is explained in Box 1, which outlines the difference between total, first and initial contacts.

Contact-to-initial-contact (CIC) ratio

In this section we consider the contact-to-initial-contact (CIC) ratio for district nurses, community nurses for learning disabilities, community nurses for mental health, speech therapists, chiropodists and dieticians. This indicates the number of times a patient is seen within any particular episode of care. There may be a degree of over-estimation if a number of episodes of care go across financial years and hence, for some episodes, the initial contact associated with a series of contacts in that year is not recorded.

■ District nurses

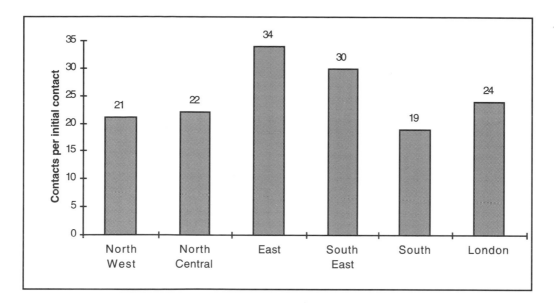

Figure 17: Contacts per initial contact by district nurse, by sector of London, 1994/95

Figure 17 reveals some variation across sectors of London. The north west, north central and south have around 20 contacts per initial contact compared with 30 or more in the east and south east. As Figure 18 shows, London has a higher CIC ratio than the rest of the country, 24 compared with 17: there is a particularly high ratio among providers in inner-deprived areas of London.

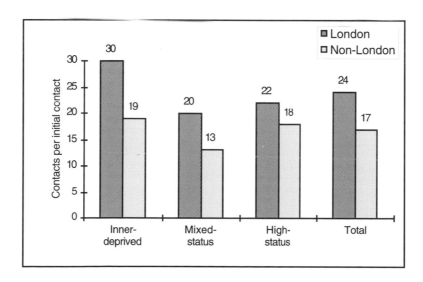

Figure 18: Contacts per initial contact by district nurse, London and England, 1994/95

■ Community nurses for learning disabilities

Figure 19 shows that the east sector of London has an extremely high CIC ratio of 74, nearly three times that of any other sector. In part this is due to an unusually high ratio in one provider. However, all four providers in this sector have ratios of over 60 contacts per initial contact. Consideration of contact-to-first-contact ratio in the next section shows these findings require careful examination.

Box 1: Contacts: First or Initial?

In considering CHS activity a distinction is drawn between total, first and initial contacts. First and initial contacts give an indication of the number of individual patients with whom a contact has been made rather than just the total number of contacts. This is useful in determining differences in the pattern of care between providers: for example, whether many patients are seen just a few times, or fewer patients are seen more often.

The following definitions are taken from the DoH report, '*Patient Care in the Community – District Nursing 1994/95*', (paragraphs 3.2 – 3.3) (DoH, 1995g). They apply equally to other community services.

A **first contact** is the first time a patient is seen in the financial year by a district nurse. A subsequent contact with a different nurse employed by the same service provider does not count as a first contact, so each patient is recorded only once in any year by any trust or district.

An **initial contact** is the first in an episode of care with a service provider. An episode of care may be initiated by a referral to the service from a hospital, GP or other health service professional. Where a previous episode of care for the same patient did not end with a positive discharge from care, a new episode is recorded only if more than six months have elapsed since the last contact.

In other words, the contact-to-first contact ratio (CFC) shows the number of contacts per individual patient in the financial year, and the contact-to-initial contact ratio (CIC) will tend to indicate the number of contacts per patient episode in the financial year.

However, the situation is quite complex. A contact could be: a first contact, i.e. the first time the patient has been seen in the year, but part of an ongoing episode of care; an initial contact, i.e. the first contact in a new episode of care, but for a patient who had already been seen that year; both, i.e. the first contact in a new episode *and* the first time the patient has been seen in the year; or neither.

Using these data is further complicated as reports on different services provide different information. The number of initial contacts and first contacts at each provider are given for district nurses, community nurses for mental health and learning disabilities and chiropody services. Only the number of initial contacts are available for speech therapy and dietetic services. The number of first contacts only are available for health visitors. There are no data on either for specialist care nursing.

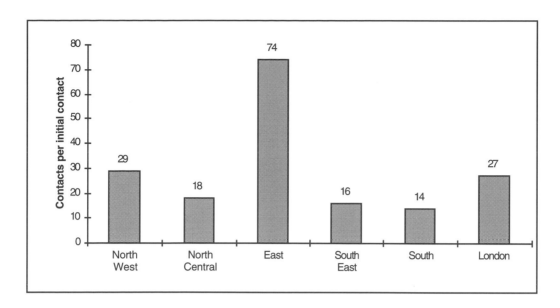

Figure 19: Contacts per initial contact by community nurse for learning disabilities, by sector of London, 1994/95

Figure 20 shows little variation between different types of socio-economic area in London: in each case the CIC ratio lies between 26 and 28. However, for each type of socio-economic area, and for London as a whole, the ratio is less than that of comparable areas elsewhere, implying that an individual episode of care comprises fewer contacts in London than elsewhere.

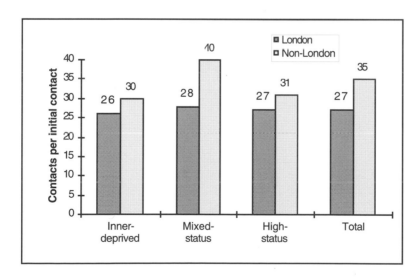

Figure 20: Contacts per initial contact by community nurse for learning disabilities, London and England, 1994/95

■ Community nurses for mental health

Figure 21 shows some variation in the CIC ratio for mental health nurses across sectors of London, from 13 in the south to 22 in the north west. This is largely due to two north-west London providers that have both a large number of contacts and high CIC ratios.

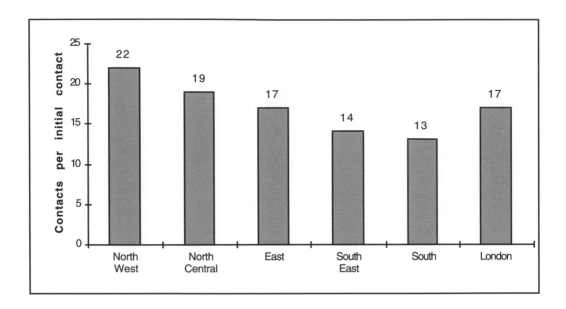

Figure 21: Contacts per initial contact by community nurse for mental health, by sector of London, 1994/95

Figure 22 shows London as a whole has a larger CIC ratio compared with the rest of England. Thus, each episode of nursing care for people with mental health problems involves more individual contacts in London than is the case in the rest of the country.

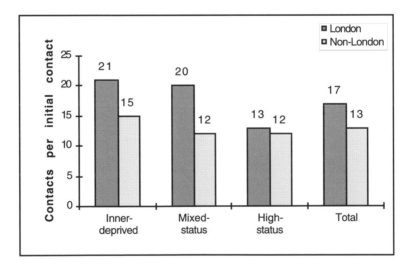

Figure 22: Contacts per initial contact by community nurse for mental health, London and England, 1994/95

■ Speech therapists

Figure 23 shows, across sectors of London, considerable variation in the CIC ratio for speech therapists, ranging from eight in the north-central sector to 14 in the east. Figure 24 reveals that London has a slightly greater ratio than the rest of England, as have all types of socio-economic area in London when compared with similar areas outside the capital.

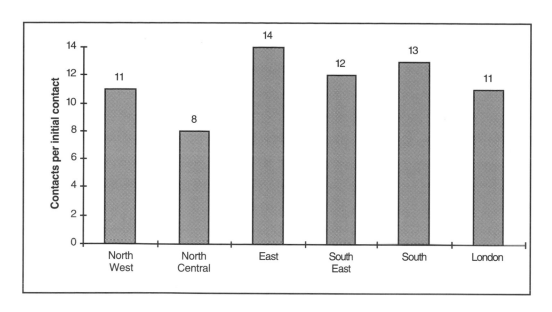

Figure 23: Contacts per initial contact by speech therapist, by sector of London, 1993/94

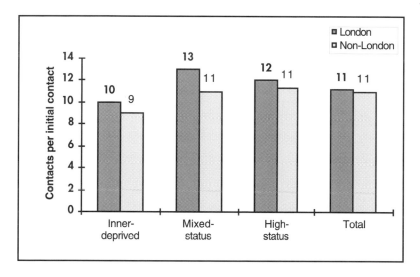

Figure 24: Contacts per initial contact by speech therapist, London and England, 1993/94

■ Chiropodists

As Figure 25 shows, there is considerable variation in the chiropody CIC ratio across sectors of London, from under six in the north-west sector to over 11 in the east. Figure 26 shows that, for both London and the rest of England, the ratio is greatest in mixed-status areas. London as a whole has a slightly lower ratio than that of the rest of England.

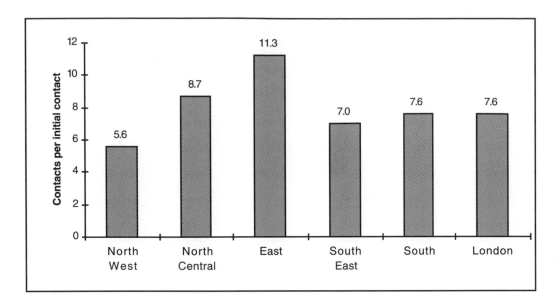

Figure 25: Contacts per initial contact by chiropodist, by sector of London, 1993/94

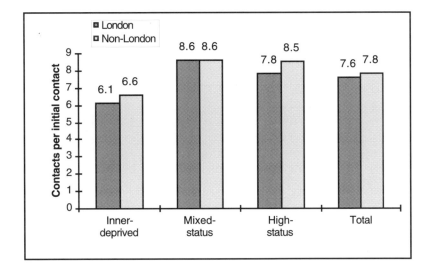

Figure 26: Contacts per initial contact by chiropodist, London and England, 1993/94

■ Dieticians

Figure 27 shows some variation across London in the CIC ratio for dieticians, from approximately three in the east, south east and south to over four in the north-central sector: reflecting the position at one provider where the ratio of 16 contacts per initial contact is twice that of any other in London and the third highest in the country. Figure 28 shows that, in both London and the rest of the country, the greatest CIC ratios are in inner-deprived areas. London as a whole has a slightly greater ratio than the rest of England.

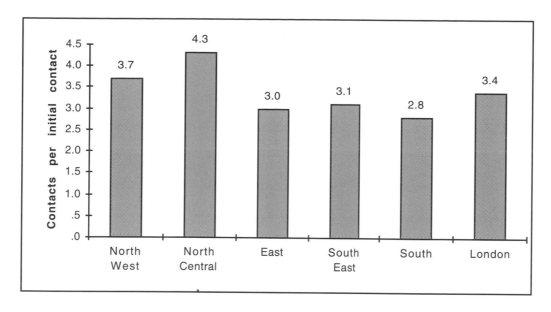

Figure 27: Contacts per initial contact by dietician, by sector of London, 1993/94

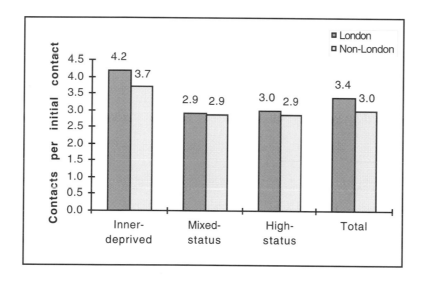

Figure 28: Contacts per initial contact by dietician, London and England, 1993/94

Contact-to-first-contact ratio (CFC)

We continue by considering the contact-to-first-contact ratio, providing comparisons between sectors of London, and between London and the rest of England. This provides a measure of the number of contacts per patient in a financial year. There may be more than one episode of care involved. The CFC can be more than the CIC, indicating several episodes within the same year. On the other hand, the CIC can exceed the CFC if episodes go across financial years, and hence no actual initial contact occurs in that particular year. We compare CFC with CIC for any given service where the data allow.

■ District nurses

Figure 29 shows the variation in the CFC ratio across sectors of London: between 16 in the south to 24 in the south east. Comparing Figure 29 with Figure 17, we see that the CFC ratio is lower in every sector – except north-central – indicating there are more first than initial contacts and, thus, episodes of more than one year in duration are common. In the north-central sector, on the other hand, the data suggest that trusts may provide more than one episode of care in the same financial year to the same patient.

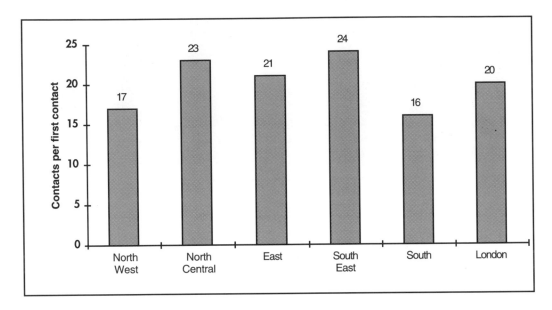

Figure 29: Contacts per first contact by district nurse, by sector of London, 1994/95

Figure 30 shows that London as a whole has a greater CFC ratio than that of the rest of England. This holds when comparisons are made across types of socio-economic area. On average there are more district nurse contacts per individual patient in London than in the rest of the country.

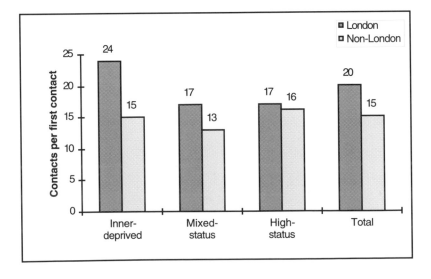

Figure 30: Contacts per first contact by district nurse, London and England, 1994/95

■ Community nurses for learning disabilities

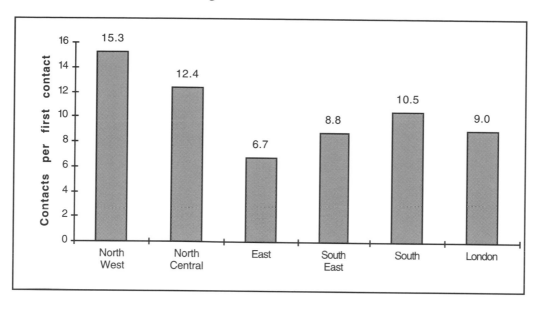

Figure 31: Contacts per first contact by community nurse for learning disabilities, by sector of London, 1994/95

Figure 31 shows considerable variation in CFC ratios across sectors of London. Comparing Figure 31 with Figure 19, the CFC ratio in four of the five sectors is between 50 and 75 per cent of the CIC ratio. However, the east sector has a very high CIC ratio of 74 and a CFC ratio of just 6.7. This is mainly due to one provider that has a CFC ratio of just four, suggesting a large number of patients seen infrequently over the year. Other providers in the east also have a high CIC ratio, but have CFC ratios of around 20, closer to the average elsewhere in London. The implication is that very different patterns of care may exist across London even though total contact rates are similar. Figure 32 shows that London as a whole has a considerably lower CFC ratio than the rest of England.

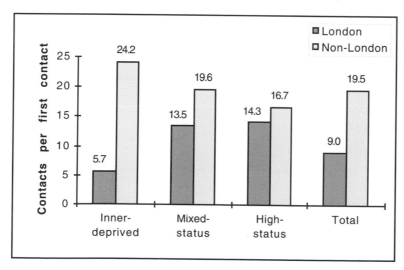

Figure 32: Contacts per first contact by community nurse for learning disabilities, London and England, 1994/95

■ Community nurses for mental health

Figure 33 shows similar CFC ratios across sectors of London. In each case these are less than the CIC ratios shown in Figure 21: the biggest difference is in the north-west sector – 22 compared with 9.7. In one north-west trust there are nearly seven times as many first contacts as initial contacts, suggesting a large number of patients with long episodes of care that commenced in previous financial years. Figure 34 shows that the CFC ratio for London as a whole is slightly higher than that of the rest of England: there is more variation when types of socio-economic area are compared.

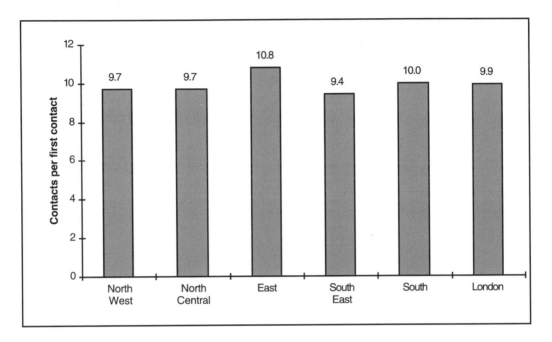

Figure 33: Contacts per first contact by community nurse for mental health, by sector of London, 1994/95

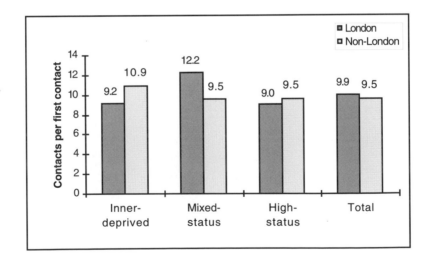

Figure 34: Contacts per first contact by community nurse for mental health, London and England, 1994/95

■ Health visitors

Figure 35 shows considerable variation, across sectors of London, in the CFC ratio for health visitors, with a maximum of 8.8 in the south east and a minimum of 3.8 in the south. Thus, although the total contact rate in the south east is nearly twice that of the south, this is due mainly to more contacts per patient in that sector rather than more patients. Data on initial contacts are not available for health visitors.

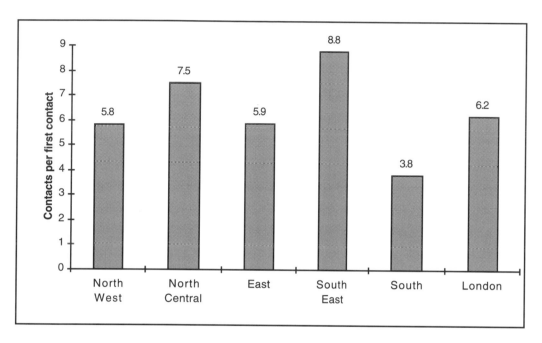

Figure 35: Contacts per first contact by health visitor, by sector of London, 1994/95

Figure 36 shows that the CFC ratio in London as a whole for health visitors is slightly less than that of the rest of England. Whereas the ratio is similar in the rest of England across types of socio-economic area, in London the ratio is highest in inner-deprived areas.

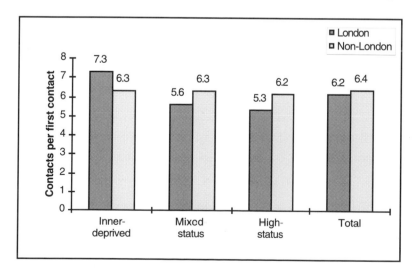

Figure 36: Contacts per first contact by health visitor, London and England, 1994/95

The location of community contacts

Finally, we consider where community contacts take place. Contact location is recorded as the patient home, NHS property (a combination of GP practices and acute and community hospitals), residential homes, or a catch-all 'other'. These data combine information on district nurses, community nurses for learning disabilities and community nurses for mental health.

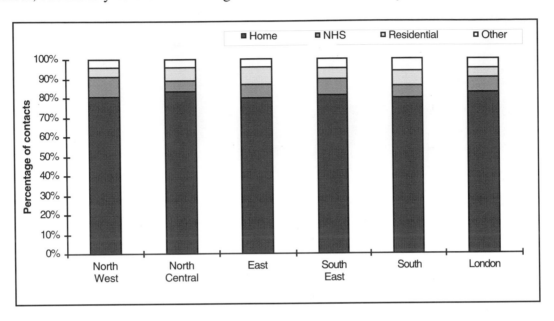

Figure 37: Proportion of district and community nurse contacts by location, by sector of London, 1994/95

As Figure 37 shows, the proportion of contacts occurring in each location is similar across sectors of London. Approximately 80 per cent of contacts take place in the patient's home. The north-west sector has the highest level of contacts on NHS property, but this is still only ten per cent of all contacts in the sector. Figure 38 shows a similar pattern when London is compared with the rest of England: around 80 per cent of all contacts take place in the patient's home.

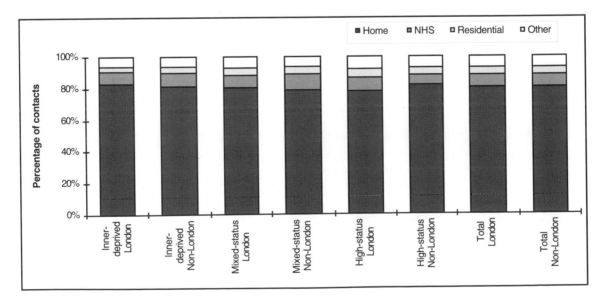

Figure 38: Proportion of district and community nurse contacts by location, London and England, 1994/95

Chapter 7

Family Health Services

Summary

General Medical Services

Provision of services

- Based on national survey data, the GP contact rate per resident population is 17 per cent higher in inner London than outer London, and some 12 per cent higher than the England average.

- GPs in London, particularly those in inner-deprived areas, perform less well against national targets for immunisation and screening than those in the rest of England.

- The proportion of children aged under five years provided with child health surveillance in London is 58 per cent compared with 76 per cent in the rest of the country. Geographic location within London, for example whether the GP is north or south of the river, is more of a factor than level of deprivation.

- There are more new registrations and registration check-ups with GPs per 1,000 resident population in London than in the rest of the country, particularly in inner-deprived areas of the capital. This reflects a more mobile population in London.

Physical resources

- The condition of London GP premises remains poor with a quarter below minimum standard. There is considerable variation across London with just 14 per cent below standard in the south compared with 45 per cent in the east.

- There has been an improvement since 1992/93 but the position has deteriorated since 1990/91 when just 20 per cent of GP premises in London were considered to be below minimum standard.

- London has substantially more GP premises below minimum standard than the rest of England where the average is just two per cent.

- There remains considerable variation in the proportion of GP practices in London without a practice nurse, ranging from ten per cent in the south east to 21 per cent in the east.

- Although London as a whole has improved, from 25 per cent of GPs without a practice nurse in 1991/92 to 14 per cent in 1994/95, the position remains substantially worse than England as a whole where just four per cent have no practice nurse. In 1991/92 the England figure was eight per cent.

Human resources

- London as a whole has a similar number of GPs per capita resident population as the rest of England; however, there are more GPs per capita in inner-deprived London than in comparable areas in the rest of the country.

- List inflation in London is ten per cent compared with just two per cent in the rest of England; however, list inflation has fallen substantially in the capital since 1990/91 when it was 19 per cent.

- There is considerable variation across London in the number of GPs who practice single-handedly, from 13 per cent in the south to 25 per cent in the east.

- London as a whole has twice the number of single-handed GPs as the rest of England – 20 compared with nine per cent. This position has not changed radically since 1990/91.

- London as a whole has a higher proportion of GPs aged 65 years and over than the rest of the country – 4.6 compared with 2.7 per cent.

- The proportion of GPs providing minor surgery varies across London from 46 per cent in the east to 62 per cent in the south and south-east sectors.

- In London as a whole a much lower proportion of GPs provide minor surgery than is the case in the rest of England – 56 compared with 85 per cent.

- In London as a whole 39 per cent of GPs are aged 50 years and over compared with 29 per cent elsewhere, and just 27 per cent are aged under 40 years compared with 35 per cent. Future provision of GPs is to some extent affected by the age profile of the current cohort.

- The provision of practice nurses per GP in London as a whole is similar to that in the rest of the country. However, a higher proportion of GPs are without a nurse indicating that the distribution of practice nurses between GPs is somewhat different in London. This is likely to reflect the higher proportion of GPs in the capital that practice single-handedly.

- 'Other practice staff' employed by GPs include chiropodists, counsellors, physiotherapists, clerical and managerial staff. There is considerable variation across London in the number of 'other practice staff' per GP, from 1.6 in the north-central sector to 2.6 in the south east.

- London as a whole has more practice staff per GP than other areas of the country. This is a significant change from 1990/91 when there was slightly less provision in the capital than in England as a whole.

Pharmaceutical Services

- London as a whole has more pharmacies relative to resident population than the rest of England, but these dispense fewer prescriptions on average than those outside the capital.

- There is considerable variation across London in the number of prescriptions dispensed per capita resident population, from 7.6 in the south to 9.5 in the east sector.

- In London as a whole approximately four per cent less prescriptions are dispensed per capita resident population than is the case in the rest of England. The difference is even greater, at 24 per cent, when inner-deprived areas of London are compared with similar areas outside of the capital.

- The relative position of London and England has changed since 1990/91: the number of prescriptions dispensed has increased by 18 per cent in London but just eight per cent nationally, over the intervening four years.

General Ophthalmic Services

- There is considerable variation across London in the number of sight tests per capita resident population funded by health authorities, from approximately 11 per 100 in the south to 16 per 100 in the east.

- However, London as a whole has a similar number of funded sight tests per capita as the rest of the country.

- London as a whole has 50 per cent more ophthalmic opticians and twice as many ophthalmic medical practitioners as the rest of the country.

Key Facts

General Medical Services	*London*	*Rest of England*
Provision of services		
Proportion of resident population consulting a GP:	16.0%	15.7%
Proportion of GPs achieving higher childhood immunisation target:	56%	86%
Proportion of GPs achieving higher booster target:	53%	86%
Proportion of GPs achieving cervical cytology target:	56%	94%
Proportion of children provided with child health surveillance:	58%	76%
Registration check-ups per 1,000 resident population:	95	59
Physical resources		
Proportion of practices below minimum standard:	26%	2%
Proportion of practices with no practice nurse:	14%	4%
Human resources		
Resident population per GP:	1,805	1,827
List inflation:	10%	2%
Proportion of single-handed GPs:	20%	9%
Proportion of GPs on minor surgery list:	56%	85%
Pharmaceutical Services		
Total community pharmacies:	1,850	7,920
Prescriptions per month by community pharmacies:	4.9 million	30.3 million
Average prescriptions per capita per annum:	8.4	8.7
General Ophthalmic Services		
Total funded sight tests:	911,000	5,472,000
Total ophthalmic professionals:	2,750	10,100

1 Introduction

This chapter considers the delivery of Family Health Services (FHS) in London. Sections are included on General Medical Services (GMS), Pharmaceutical Services (PS), and General Ophthalmic Services (GOS). General Dental Services (GDS) are not discussed due to the unavailability of comparative data. Activity is analysed across sectors of London and comparisons are made with similar areas outside the capital. Physical and human resources available for the delivery of services are also discussed.

2 Data sources

Most of the GMS analysis is based on data derived from the DoH Health Service Indicators for 1994/95, (DoH, 1996d). Other sources are the DoH report, *'GMS Base Statistics for October 1995'* (DoH, 1996e), and the General Household Survey (GHS) for 1992/93 and 1993/94 (OPCS, 1994; OPCS, 1995). Analysis of GOS and PS activity and resources is based on the data underlying the DoH Statistical Bulletins, *'Ophthalmic Statistics for England 1984/85 to 1994/95'* (DoH, 1995m) and *'General Pharmaceutical Services in England 1994/95'* (DoH, 1995n). Data for GMS, PS and GOS refer to Family Health Services Authorities (FHSAs). As these are now coterminous with DHAs, these data are referred to as 'by DHA' in the text.

3 General Medical Services

Perhaps the key element of General Medical Services is the General Practitioner (GP). It is notoriously difficult to measure adequately the range and quality of service provision in this sector. Nevertheless, this section considers a number of indicators of services provided, and also compares the human and physical resources available for the delivery of health care.

Provision of services

First, we consider some general indicators of levels of GMS activity. These include GP contact rates, provision of immunisation and cervical cytology screening, child health surveillance and registration check-ups.

GP contact rates

Data on GP contacts per capita resident population are not routinely available. However, the General Household Survey (GHS) asks a question – of private households only – concerning consultation with an NHS GP in the previous two weeks. Combining data from the GHS for 1992/93 and 1993/94 to increase sample size, it is possible to estimate GP utilisation rates for broad aggregate areas. However, individuals may have multiple visits to a GP within the sample period and so these rates could underestimate total activity. Comparisons remain valid if the probability of multiple visits does not vary between areas.

Table 1: Proportion of sample population consulting an NHS GP, London and England, 1992/93 and 1993/94

Area	%
Inner London	17.6
Outer London	15.1
Other Metropolitan	16.7
Other Non-metropolitan	15.3
London	16.0
Non-London	15.7
England	15.7

Table 1 indicates higher GP utilisation in inner London and other metropolitan areas, which equate approximately to inner-deprived and mixed-status areas in the Midlands and the North of England. Residents of inner London appear to use GP services more frequently than those in outer London – by some 17 per cent. Inner London has the highest utilisation of any of the standard regions used by the GHS, whereas outer London is among the lowest.

GP performance targets

Data are available for GP performance against nationally agreed DoH targets for childhood immunisation, school-age boosters and cervical cytology screening. Higher and lower targets are set for each. Table 2 shows the proportion of GPs in each London DHA achieving the targets in 1994/95. Data for Kensington, Chelsea and Westminster are unavailable.

Table 2: Performance of GPs against DoH targets, 1994/95

DHA	Proportion of GPs achieving specific targets					
	Childhood immun. 70%	Childhood immun. 90%	Booster 70%	Booster 90%	Cervical cytology 70%	Cervical cytology 90%
Camden and Islington	61	44	61	43	84	34
East London and the City	47	24	47	31	93	50
Kensington, Chelsea & Westminster	No data	No data	No data	No data	No data	No data
Lambeth, Southwark & Lewisham	60	51	26	18	72	32
Brent and Harrow	83	60	79	64	93	49
Ealing, Hammersmith and Harrow	84	54	85	55	92	41
Enfield and Haringey	89	58	89	67	92	55
Merton, Sutton and Wandsworth	87	67	86	57	92	59
Redbridge and Waltham Forest	74	52	77	58	98	67
Barking and Havering	89	52	98	70	99	80
Barnet	82	57	81	57	97	52
Bromley	94	75	95	75	99	96
Croydon	97	75	92	73	99	77
Bexley and Greenwich	86	60	87	64	98	83
Hillingdon	93	72	89	70	99	76
Kingston and Richmond	99	89	99	74	100	98

It is clear from Table 2 that no DHA does very badly against one target and notably well against another. Furthermore, as Figures 1, 2 and 3 show, there is a gradient of performance against these targets, both in London and the rest of England, with GPs in inner-deprived areas doing worse than those in high-status areas. This gradient is less steep outside of London.

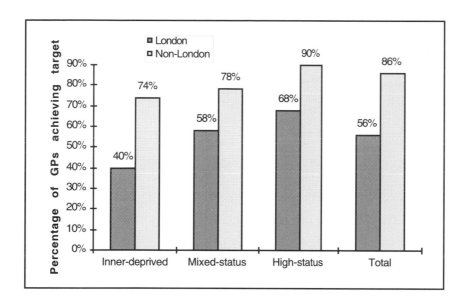

Figure 1: Performance against the higher target for childhood immunisation, London and England, 1994/95

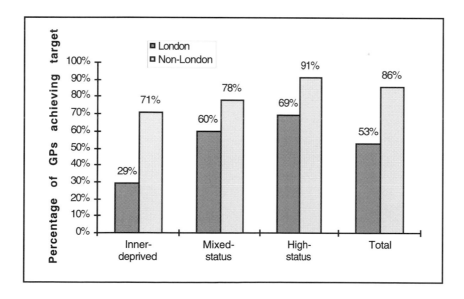

Figure 2: Performance against the higher target for school-age boosters, London and England, 1994/95

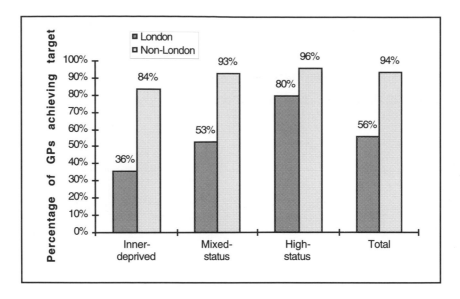

Figure 3: Performance against the higher target for cervical cytology, London and England, 1994/95

London performs less well than the rest of the country against each target, especially in inner-deprived areas. Even high-status areas of London perform less well than inner-deprived areas outside the capital. However, it is arguable that these targets, particularly for cervical cytology, are not appropriate for inner-deprived London with its highly mobile population.

Child health surveillance

Figure 4 shows that the proportion of children aged under five years receiving child health surveillance is greatest in the south sector. In the north-central and east sectors, no DHA provides child health surveillance services to more than 52 per cent of the local population aged under five. By contrast, all DHAs in the south sector provide the service to at least 70 per cent of children: in Kingston and Richmond the figure is 79 per cent.

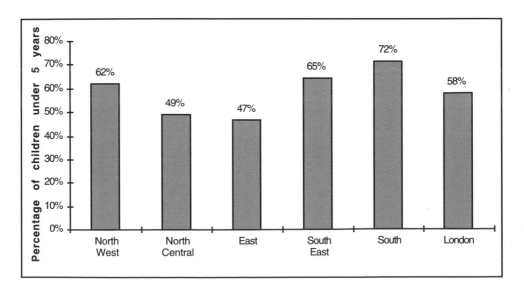

Figure 4: Provision of child health surveillance, by sector of London, 1994/95

Geographical sector rather than the type of socio-economic area within which a GP practices seems to be a better indicator of the likely level of provision of this service. For example, inner-deprived Lambeth, Southwark and Lewisham in the south east has a higher proportion of children provided with child health surveillance than high-status Barnet in the north-central sector. Figure 5 shows a range of provision of child health surveillance from 52 to 65 per cent, between inner-deprived and high-status areas in London: the range across sectors is from 47 to 72 per cent, between the east and south sectors.

A number of factors may affect the ability of GPs to deliver this service. A more mobile population in inner London makes long-term surveillance of individual residents less tenable. Moreover, GPs in deprived areas may have to spend more time 'crisis managing' very sick patients, with less time, therefore, to offer a longer-term, preventative service such as this. However, that the link between level of provision and type of socio-economic area is not as strong as that with geographical location indicates other factors may be at work. For example, more practices in the south and south-east sectors have a practice nurse. The availability of support staff may influence the ability to provide child health surveillance.

Figure 5 also shows that London GPs provide this service to proportionately fewer children than their counterparts in the rest of the country. There is no gradient across types of socio-economic area in the rest of England; for each type of area, over 70 per cent of children aged under 5 receive surveillance.

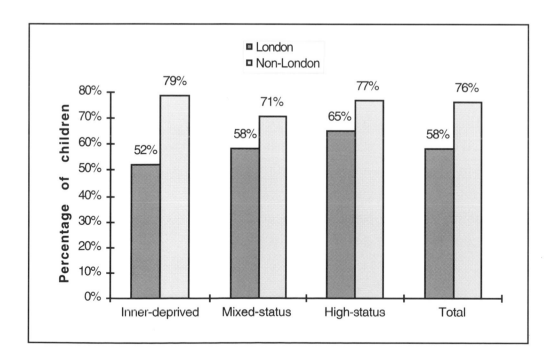

Figure 5: Provision of child health surveillance, London and England, 1994/95

Registration check-ups

(Technical note: data on registration check-ups are not available for 1994/95. Thus, incomplete data from 1993/94 are presented.)

Table 3 shows the number of registration check-ups in London DHAs per 1,000 resident population. Data are only available for eight of the 16 London DHAs. Two distinct groups emerge. Camden and Islington, East London and the City, Ealing, Hammersmith and Hounslow and Brent and Harrow have more than 100 registration check-ups per 1,000 resident population. By contrast, Barking and Havering, Bromley, Redbridge and Waltham Forest and Croydon have fewer than 80.

Differences are explained partly by the greater number of registrations per capita in the inner city DHAs. For example, in Camden and Islington there were 222 new registrations with a GP per 1,000 resident population; in Ealing, Hammersmith and Hounslow there were 237. By contrast, in Barking and Havering and Redbridge and Waltham Forest, there were respectively 118 and 117 new registrations. The higher rate of registration in central London suggests a more mobile population, and is also likely to lead to more registration check-ups.

Table 3: Registration check-ups per 1,000 resident population, by London DHA, 1993/94

DHA	Check-ups per 1,000 resident population
Camden and Islington	126
Ealing, Hammersmith and Hounslow	117
East London and the City	109
Brent and Harrow	103
Croydon	79
Redbridge and Waltham Forest	74
Bromley	71
Barking and Havering	56

Proportionately less data are missing on registration check-ups for the rest of England. Figure 6, based on the data available, suggests that London as a whole has a registration check-up rate that is 60 per cent higher than the rest of England; in mixed-status areas the difference in rate is 97 per cent. It is not surprising that higher rates are found in London given the mobility of the population in the capital. However, these findings should be treated with caution as some data are missing.

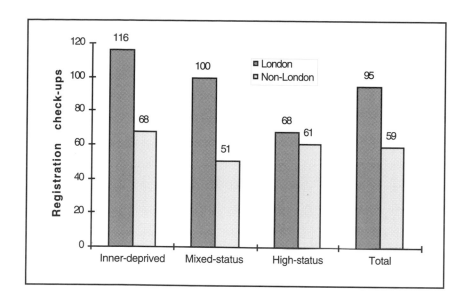

Figure 6: Registration check-ups per 1,000 resident population, London and England, 1993/94

Physical resources

This section considers the availability of physical resources for GPs in London to deliver primary health care. Two measures of the quality of physical resources are analysed: the proportion of GP premises that are considered to be below the minimum acceptable standard; and the proportion of practices that have no practice nurse. All data refer to 1994/95.

Premises below minimum standard

Figure 7 shows that in 1994/95 the condition of London GP premises as a whole was still very poor, with a quarter of premises below minimum standard. However, there is considerable variation across London. The east sector has the greatest proportion of poor premises, reflecting the fact that more than 30 per cent are below standard in all three DHAs in this sector. In total, there are six DHAs in London where more than 30 per cent of premises are below standard. By contrast, three DHAs have no premises below minimum standard: Bexley and Greenwich, Ealing, Hammersmith and Hounslow and Kingston and Richmond.

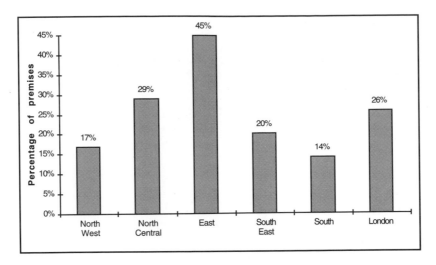

(Note: data for Kensington, Chelsea and Westminster are missing. In 1993/94, this DHA had 54 per cent of premises below minimum standard. Thus, it is likely that the proportion of premises below standard in the north-west sector and, to a lesser extent, London as a whole is underestimated.)

Figure 7: Proportion of GP premises below minimum standard, by sector of London, 1994/95

Figure 8 compares London with the rest of England: the proportion of premises below minimum standard in the rest of England is very low for all types of socio-economic area. In inner-deprived and mixed-status areas of London, over 25 per cent are below minimum standard. There has been a slight improvement since 1992/93, yet nevertheless, these figures suggest an even greater proportion of premises are below standard in 1994/95 than was the case in 1990/91 when 20 per cent of GP premises in London were below standard. These findings indicate the great challenge still facing primary care in London, even after two years of London Initiative Zone (LIZ) funding. It will be possible to gauge the full impact of this funding as data for subsequent years become available.

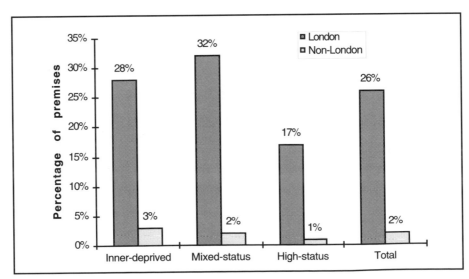

(Note: data for Kensington, Chelsea and Westminster are missing. In 1993/94, this DHA had 54 per cent of premises below minimum standard. Thus, it is likely that the proportion of premises below standard in inner-deprived London and, to a lesser extent, London as a whole is underestimated.)

Figure 8: Proportion of GP premises below minimum standard, London and England, 1994/95

Practices without a practice nurse

(Technical note: more data on the numbers of practice nurses are found in the section on human resources. This section considers the proportion of practices without a practice nurse.)

Figure 9 shows that the greatest proportion of practices without a practice nurse is in the east sector. This reflects the position of East London and the City in particular, where 28 per cent of practices do not have a practice nurse. There is no London DHA where all practices have access to a practice nurse.

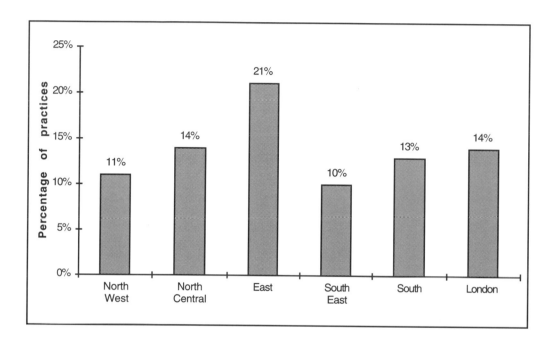

(Note: data for Kensington, Chelsea and Westminster are missing. In 1993/94, this DHA had 16 per cent of practices without practice nurses. Thus, the proportion of practices without practice nurses in north-west London may be underestimated.)

Figure 9: Proportion of GP practices without a practice nurse, by sector of London, 1994/95

Again, London compares badly with the rest of England, though the difference is not as great as for premises below minimum standard. Figure 10 shows a gradient across types of socio-economic area in London: fewer practices are without a nurse in high-status areas than in inner-deprived. Fourteen per cent of practices in London as a whole have no nurse compared with just four per cent outside the capital.

The position in London has improved since 1991/92 when 25 per cent of practices were without a practice nurse. However, there has also been an improvement throughout the rest of England, where the proportion has fallen from eight to four per cent. London has improved less quickly and remains substantially worse than the rest of the country. However, there is evidence of an increased rate of improvement in London between 1993/94 and 1994/95.

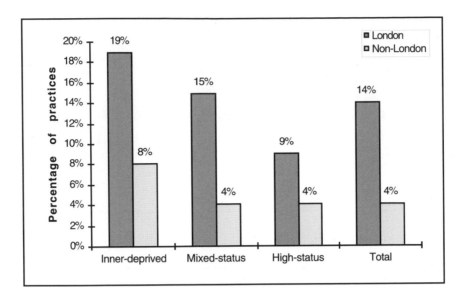

(Note: data for Kensington, Chelsea and Westminster are missing. In 1993/94, this DHA had 16 per cent of practices without practice nurses. Thus, the proportion of practices without a practice nurse in inner-deprived London may be overestimated.)

Figure 10: Proportion of GP practices without a practice nurse, London and England, 1994/95

Human resources

We turn now to look at various aspects of the human resources available for the delivery of GMS in London. All data in this section refer to 1994/95. An analysis of the availability of GPs is followed by consideration of key characteristics of the GP workforce. Finally, some detailed analysis of practice staff is provided.

GP availability

In London, the number of patients registered with a GP is often considerably more than the actual population served by the GP. Thus, the registered list size of GPs in London as a whole is greater than the actual population served. This phenomenon, known as 'list inflation', occurs elsewhere in the country but nowhere to the degree it does in London. It is due primarily to the time-lag in removing patients from GP lists: in some cases patients may not be removed at all. List inflation is considered in detail below.

Figure 11 shows the average resident population per GP, for each sector of London. This is established by dividing the resident population of an area by the number of GPs in that area. This average is greatest in the south and south-east sectors; however, with the exception of the north-central sector, there is comparatively little variation.

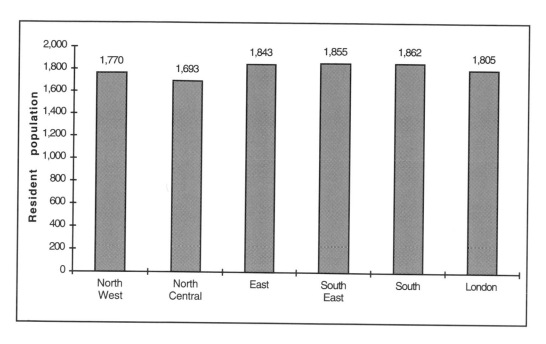

Figure 11: Average resident population per GP, by sector of London, 1994/95

However, there is more variation between types of socio-economic area. As Figure 12 shows, in London, the average resident population per GP is least in inner-deprived and greatest in high-status areas. The average in London as a whole is similar to that in the rest of England. However, the average in inner-deprived and mixed-status areas in London is less than that of comparable areas in the rest of the country; by contrast, in high-status areas the average in London is greater than that elsewhere.

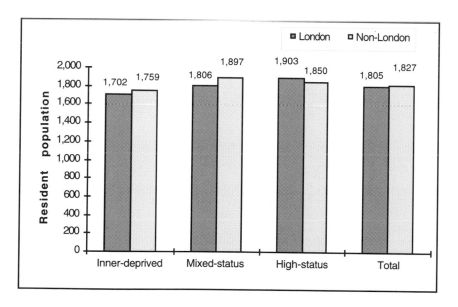

Figure 12: Average resident population per GP, London and England, 1994/95

However, registered list size – the total population registered with a GP divided by the number of GPs – gives a different impression. Registered list sizes in each sector of London are greater than the actual resident population. Based on the GP-registered population of London, the capital has 7.9 million residents, over 900,000 more than it actually has. DHAs with the greatest average resident population per GP are not always those with the greatest registered list size. The use of registered list size gives the impression that the provision of GPs per capita resident population in London is low compared with the rest of England. We now consider the phenomenon of 'list inflation' in more detail.

Figure 13 shows the level of list inflation across London is not uniform. List inflation is greatest in the north-west and north-central sectors, averaging twice the rate for London as a whole.

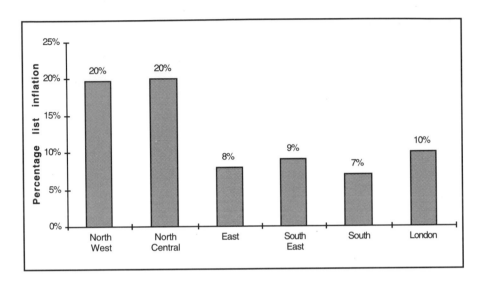

Figure 13: List inflation, by sector of London, 1994/95

Figure 14 compares the level of list inflation, both between types of socio-economic area in London, and with similar areas in the rest of the country. Inflation is greatest in inner-deprived areas of the capital reflecting the high level of population mobility. In London as a whole, registered list sizes are ten per cent greater than the average size of resident population per GP, compared with a difference of just two per cent in the rest of England. However, list inflation in London has fallen since 1990/91 when it was 19 per cent.

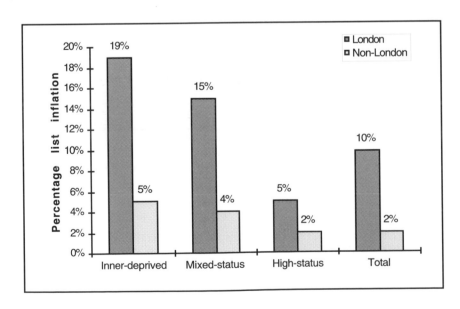

Figure 14: List inflation, London and England, 1994/95

GP characteristics

We now consider some basic characteristics of GPs in London. Sections are included on:

- GPs who are single-handed;

- GPs aged 65 years and over;

- GPs on the minor surgery list; and,

- the age profile of GPs.

While these indicators do not in themselves determine the quality of GP practice, taken as a whole they are a useful indication of how GPs in London differ from the rest of England.

■ Single-handed GPs

The proportion of single-handed GPs is a useful indicator of the level of service provided as they are often considered able to offer a more limited service than their counterparts in partnerships. Figure 15 shows the three sectors north of the river have a greater proportion of single-handed GPs: for all DHAs bar one in these three sectors, between 19 and 31 per cent of GPs practice single-handedly. However, in south and south-east London there is a lower proportion of single-handed GPs: no DHA has more than 18 per cent of single-handed GPs.

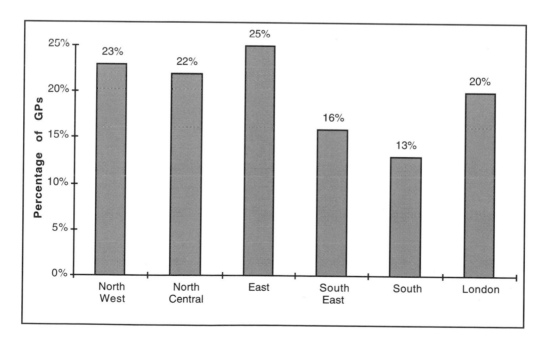

Figure 15: Proportion of single-handed GPs, by sector of London, 1994/95

As Figure 16 shows, London has more single-handed GPs than similar areas in the rest of the country, for each type of socio-economic area. The difference is greatest in high-status areas where, in London, 17 per cent of GPs are single-handed compared with seven per cent in the rest of the country.

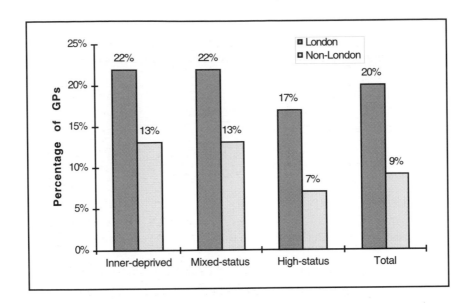

Figure 16: Proportion of single-handed GPs, London and England, 1994/95

■ GPs aged 65 years and over

Figure 17 shows that the proportion of GPs aged 65 years and over is approximately five per cent in each sector of London except north-central, where it is less than three per cent. Figure 18 compares London with the rest of England, showing that, for each type of socio-economic area, London has a higher proportion of GPs aged 65 years and over than is the case in comparable areas elsewhere in England. In London as a whole, 4.6 per cent of GPs are 65 years and over compared with just 2.7 per cent in the rest of England.

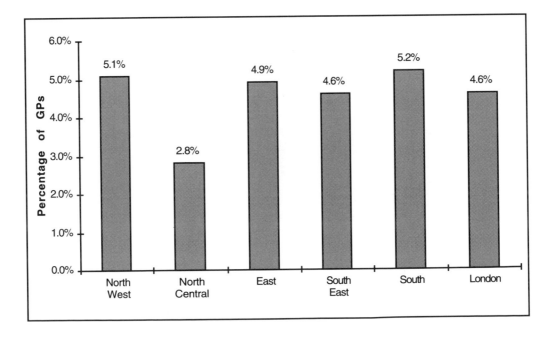

Figure 17: Proportion of GPs aged 65 years and over, by sector of London, 1994/95

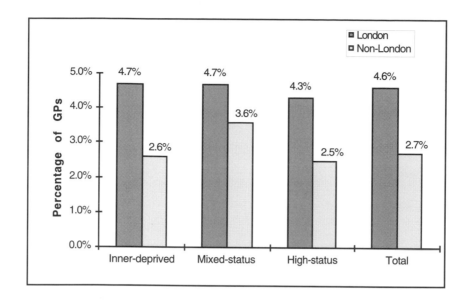

Figure 18: Proportion of GPs aged 65 years and over, London and England, 1994/95

■ Minor surgery

The provision of minor surgery by GPs is often cited as an example of a service traditionally offered in acute hospitals that can be provided in a primary care setting. Figure 19 shows that less than half the GPs in east London are on the minor surgery list, and just 52 per cent in the north west: in one DHA in the east only 26 per cent of GPs offer minor surgery. Although there has been a steady increase right across the capital, even Bromley with the highest proportion in London of GPs on the minor surgery list, 78 per cent, remains less than the national average.

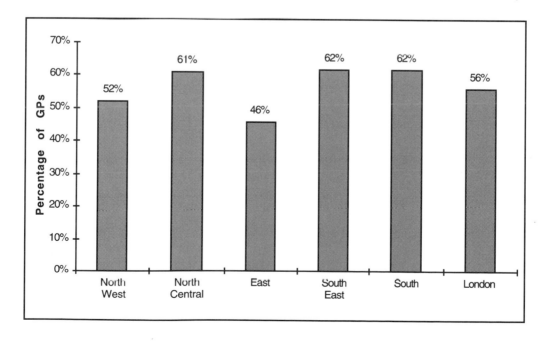

Figure 19: Proportion of GPs on the minor surgery list, by sector of London, 1994/95

Figure 20 shows, in both London and the rest of England, there is a gradient between inner-deprived and high-status areas with fewer GPs in more deprived areas providing minor surgery. However, for each type of socio-economic area, fewer GPs in London provide minor surgery than is the case in comparable areas elsewhere in England. Although there has been an increase in provision in London since 1993/94, the difference between London and the rest of the country remains similar, since provision in the rest of England has also expanded.

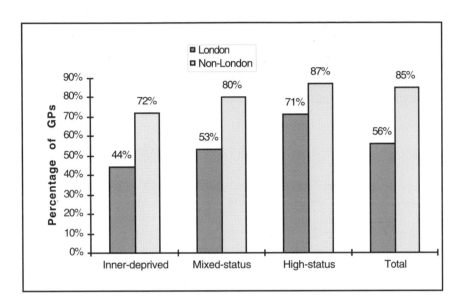

Figure 20: Proportion of GPs on the minor surgery list, London and England, 1994/95

■ Age profile of GPs

The age profile of GPs is a useful indicator of potential future changes in the provision of GPs in an area. For example, a greater proportion of GPs aged over 50 years, together with a comparatively low proportion of GPs under 35 years, could lead to shortages in the long term. Figure 21 compares the GP age profile in London with that of the rest of the country. GPs in London tend to be older, with 39 per cent of London GPs aged 50 years and over compared with just 29 per cent elsewhere. By contrast, only 27 per cent of London GPs are under 40 years compared with 35 per cent in the rest of England. This suggests there may be difficulty in recruiting younger GPs in London which could lead to future problems as the older cohorts of GPs retire over the next five to ten years. This would have to be tested in the light of more detailed local knowledge and data about GP recruitment and retention.

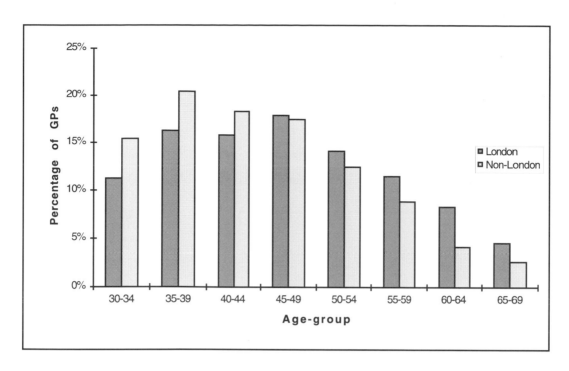

Figure 21: Age profile of GPs, London and England, 1994/95

Practice staff

This section compares the availability of nurses and 'other practice staff' in GP practices, both within London and between London and the rest of England. Data refer to whole time equivalent (WTE) staff per GP.

■ Practice nurses

Figure 22 shows that the greatest provision of practice nurses is in the north-west sector of London and the lowest in the east.

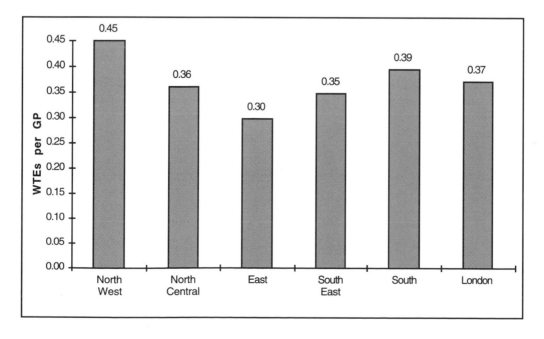

Figure 22: WTE practice nurses per GP, by sector of London, 1994/95

The provision of practice nurses per GP was slightly lower in London than in the rest of the country in 1990/91 – approximately 0.28 WTEs per GP in London compared with 0.3 in England as a whole. Figure 23 compares the level of provision, for different types of socio-economic area, in 1994/95, indicating a considerable increase in the provision of nurses throughout England. The rate of growth in London has exceeded that elsewhere, admittedly from a lower starting point: there is now little variation between types of area, either within London or between London and elsewhere.

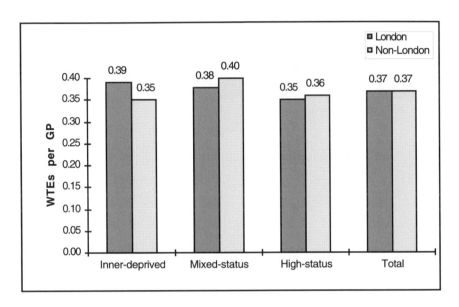

Figure 23: WTE practice nurses per GP, London and England, 1994/95

■ 'Other practice staff'

Other staff employed by GP practices include various professions allied to medicine such as chiropodists, counsellors and physiotherapists, and clerical and managerial staff. Figure 24 shows that the provision of these staff is greatest in the south-east sector of London. In one DHA in this sector there are over four WTE 'other practice staff' per GP.

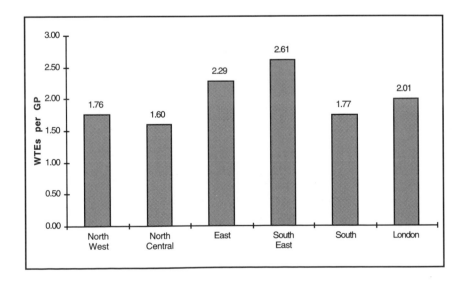

Figure 24: WTE 'other practice staff' per GP, by sector of London, 1994/95

Figure 25 shows that London as a whole has more 'other practice staff' per GP than elsewhere, approximately two WTEs per GP compared with 1.8. This is a significant change from 1990/91 when not only did London have a slightly lower provision of such staff than the rest of the country, but provision was much lower throughout England – approximately 1.45 in London and 1.48 in the rest of England. There is some variation between types of socio-economic area in London, but relatively little in the rest of the country.

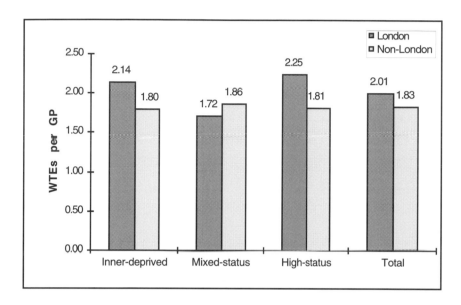

Figure 25: WTE 'other practice staff' per GP, London and England, 1994/95

4 Pharmaceutical Services

This section considers the provision of Pharmaceutical Services (PS) in London. An analysis is provided of the number of community pharmacies per capita resident population. We then compare the average number of prescriptions per pharmacy and pcr capita resident population across sectors of London, and between London and the rest of England. This represents most but not all prescriptions, since these can also be dispensed through hospital pharmacies or by GPs, although there are very few dispensing GPs in London.

Physical resources

Figure 26 shows the number of community pharmacies per million resident population varies between 231 in the south-east sector and 314 in the north-west. Most London DHAs have between 200 and 300 pharmacies per million resident population. However, Kensington, Chelsea and Westminster with 451 pharmacies per million population has 130 more than the next highest DHA in London. In the next section we show that Kensington, Chelsea and Westminster also has a considerably lower average number of prescriptions per pharmacy, suggesting that there are more small-scale pharmacies in this DHA.

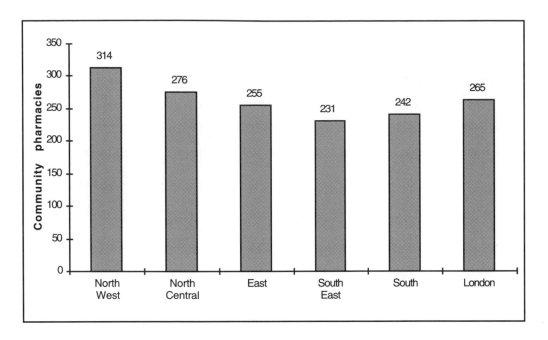

Figure 26: Community pharmacies per million resident population, by sector of London, 1994/95

Figure 27 shows that London has more pharmacies per capita resident population than the rest of England: this also holds for comparisons between similar types of socio-economic area in London and elsewhere. There are more pharmacies per capita resident population in inner-deprived areas when compared with other types of socio-economic area, both in the capital and in the rest of England.

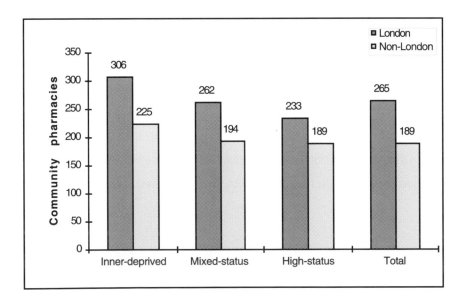

Figure 27: Community pharmacies per million resident population, London and England, 1994/95

Prescriptions per pharmacy

In this section we consider the number of prescriptions dispensed in pharmacies located in London DHAs: this is not identical to the number of prescriptions issued by London GPs. It was noted in *Primary Health Care in London: Quantifying the challenge (*Boyle and

Smaje, 1993), that the number of prescriptions dispensed includes some from non-London residents. This may be more of a factor in London with its large commuter population. However, Boyle and Smaje also note that this 'commuter effect' represents only two per cent of all drugs dispensed in the capital.

Figure 28 shows the average number of prescriptions per pharmacy per month varies between 2,144 in the north west and 3,100 in the east. The north-west average reflects the position referred to earlier in Kensington, Chelsea and Westminster DHA, where the average number of prescriptions per pharmacy is just 1,370.

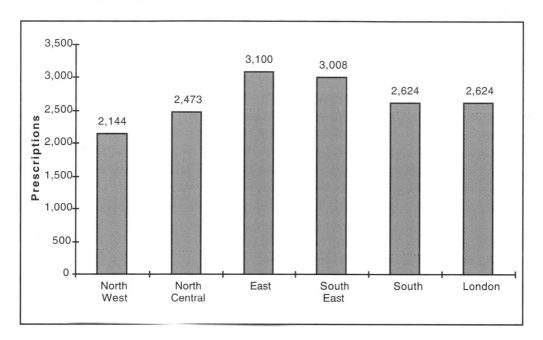

Figure 28: Average prescriptions per pharmacy per month, by sector of London, 1994/95

Figure 29 shows the average number of prescriptions dispensed per pharmacy is 45 per cent less in London than in the rest of England. The difference in inner-deprived and mixed-status areas of the capital is even greater: respectively, 69 and 54 per cent less than comparable areas elsewhere. Although more deprived areas of London have a lower average number of prescriptions per pharmacy than high-status areas, the average in all areas is considerably less than that of the rest of England. This may result in higher overhead costs associated with dispensing in the capital.

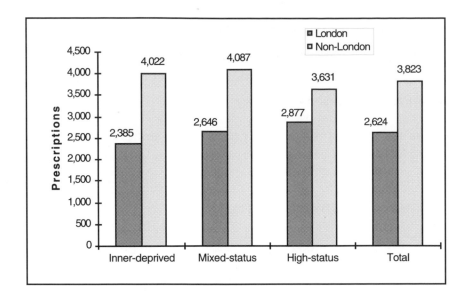

Figure 29: Average prescriptions per pharmacy per month, London and England, 1994/95

Prescriptions per capita

It has been established that there are fewer prescriptions per capita resident population in London than in the rest of the country (Boyle and Smaje, 1993). In 1990/91 the London average was 7.1 prescriptions per capita compared with eight in England as a whole. Figure 30 shows that, for 1994/95, prescriptions per capita vary between 7.6 in the south and 9.5 in the east, with a London average of 8.4, an increase of 18 per cent since 1990/91. The three London DHAs with the highest rates are in the east, whereas three of the four with the lowest rates are in the south sector.

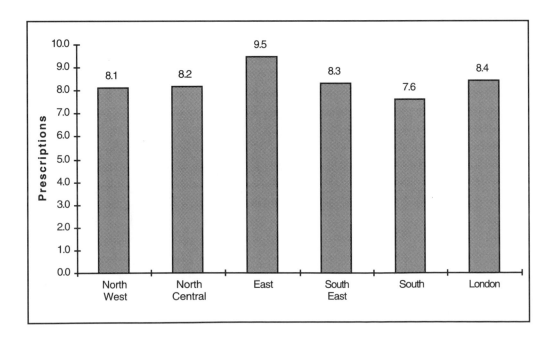

Figure 30: Annual number of prescriptions per capita, by sector of London, 1994/95

In comparison with London, the England average has increased less, by under eight per cent, to 8.6 prescriptions per capita. London now has approximately four per cent fewer prescriptions per capita than the rest of England. As Figure 31 shows, the difference between London and the rest of England increases with the level of deprivation of an area. London has a fairly small range across types of socio-economic area from 8.1 to 8.8, but rates in the rest of England increase with deprivation from 8.2 in high-status to 10.9 in inner-deprived areas.

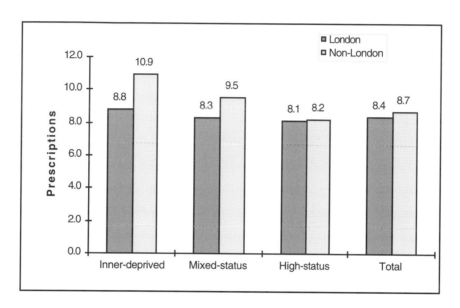

Figure 31: Annual number of prescriptions per capita, London and England, 1994/95

It is not surprising that the number of prescriptions per capita increases with the level of deprivation, given the negative relationship between deprivation and health. However, it is surprising that London has such a low rate in inner-deprived areas. An additional factor that may impact on the number of prescriptions per capita in inner-deprived areas is that residents are more likely to be exempt from prescription charges, and hence drugs commonly bought 'over the counter' in high-status areas may be prescribed. Analysis of average Net Ingredient Cost (NIC) per prescription gives some support to this hypothesis.

In 1990/91, NIC per prescription was £6.00 in London and £5.80 in the rest of the country. In both London and the rest of the country, NIC per prescription decreased as the deprivation level of an area increased. However, the gradient was more marked outside the capital, rising from £5.30 per prescription in inner-deprived areas to £6.20 in high-status; in London the range was from £5.90 to £6.10. The relative position has changed little since then.

In 1994/95, NIC per prescription was still slightly greater in London than in the rest of England – £7.50 compared with £7.40. Average NIC per prescription has remained less in deprived areas, in both London and the rest of the country. The difference between types of areas is still greater in the rest of the country than in London: NIC per prescription ranges from £6.70 to £7.90 outside the capital, compared with between £7.30 and £7.70 in London. Comparatively lower costs in inner-deprived areas lend credence to the hypothesis outlined above. However, greater differences between types of area, for both prescriptions per capita and NIC per prescription, suggest this may be a more significant factor outside London.

5 General Ophthalmic Services

This section considers the provision of General Ophthalmic Services (GOS), analysing both the level of activity and availability of human resources. Activity reflects the number of sight tests paid for by health authorities. NHS sight tests were restricted in April 1989 to certain eligible sectors of the population. These include: children aged under 16 years; students aged 16-18 years; adults on Income Support or Family Credit; adults on low income; and people with particular medical conditions, mainly relating to diabetes or glaucoma. The nature of the eligibility criteria means that relatively deprived areas or areas with a young population are likely to use more services, other things being equal.

Provision of services

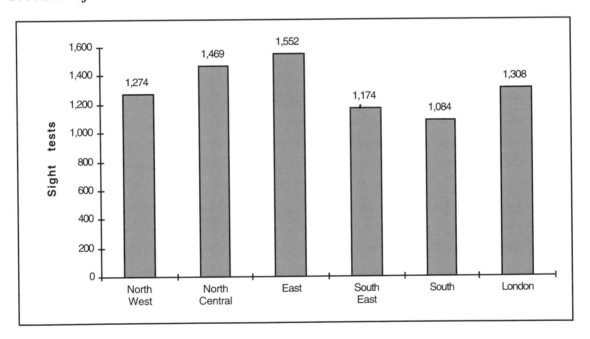

Figure 32: Sight Tests per 10,000 resident population, by sector of London, 1994/95

Figure 32 compares the number of sight tests funded per 10,000 resident population across sectors of London: this varies from 1,084 in the south sector to 1,552 in the east. Figure 33 shows that London has approximately the same number of sight tests per capita resident population as the rest of the country. There is a somewhat lower rate in inner-deprived areas of the capital compared with similar areas elsewhere in the country. In both London and the rest of England, as expected, there are more sight tests per capita as the level of deprivation increases, though the gradient is steeper in the rest of England.

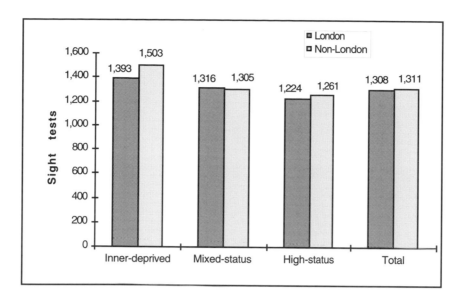

Figure 33: Sight Tests per 10,000 resident population, London and England, 1994/95

Human resources

Finally, in this section we consider the availability of human resources for the delivery of GOS. There are essentially two types of resource: ophthalmic opticians, who are qualified to test eyesight and to prescribe and dispense spectacles; and ophthalmic medical practitioners, who are qualified doctors specialising in eyes and eye care. In addition to their medical skills they are qualified to test eyesight and prescribe spectacles.

Ophthalmic opticians

Figure 34 compares the provision of ophthalmic opticians across sectors of London, showing that there are over four opticians per 10,000 resident population in the north-central sector, while the north-west and east both have less than three. In the north-west sector, at an individual DHA level, provision ranges from 5.6 per 10,000 resident population in Kensington, Chelsea and Westminster to less than two in Ealing, Hammersmith and Hounslow.

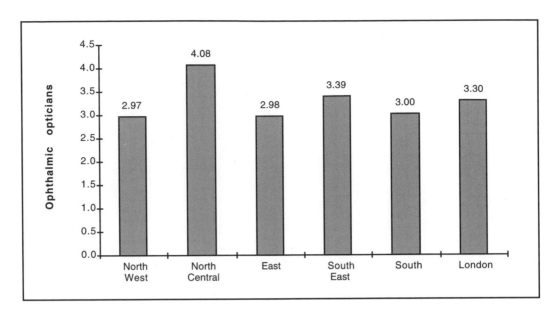

Figure 34: Ophthalmic opticians per 10,000 resident population, by sector of London, 1994/95

Figure 35 shows London has over 50 per cent more ophthalmic opticians per capita than the rest of the country. For each type of socio-economic area, there are more opticians per capita in London than elsewhere in England. The rate in inner-deprived London is over 50 per cent greater than that of inner-deprived areas elsewhere: this reflects in particular the position in Kensington, Chelsea and Westminster, and Camden and Islington, which, relative to population, have the greatest provision of ophthalmic opticians in the country.

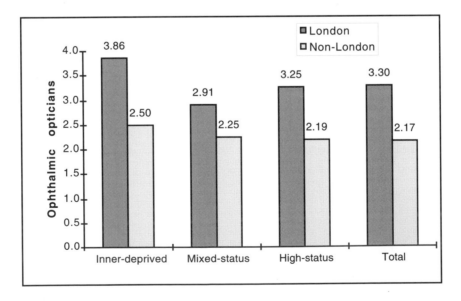

Figure 35: Ophthalmic Opticians per 10,000 resident population, London and England, 1994/95

Ophthalmic medical practitioners

Figure 36 shows that, in contrast to ophthalmic opticians, the highest provision of ophthalmic medical practitioners is in the south and south-east sectors of London, whereas north-central London has the lowest provision. Bromley has 1.74 ophthalmic medical practitioners per 10,000 resident population, by far the greatest provision in the capital, and indeed the country. This is ten times greater than that of Enfield and Haringey, for example.

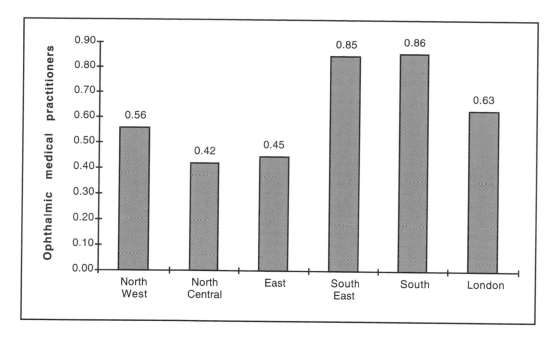

Figure 36: Ophthalmic medical practitioners per 10,000 resident population, by sector of London, 1994/95

Figure 37 shows London as a whole has over twice as many ophthalmic medical practitioners per capita as the rest of England. The eight DHAs in England with the greatest provision of ophthalmic medical practitioners relative to population, are in London. In both London and the rest of the country, the provision of ophthalmic medical practitioners per capita resident population decreases as the level of deprivation in an area increases.

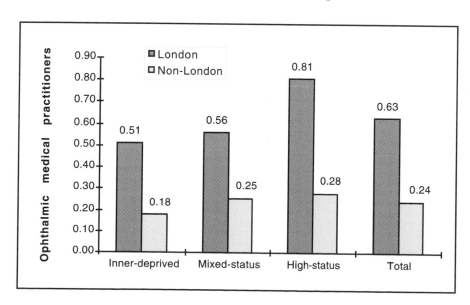

Figure 37: Ophthalmic medical practitioners per 10,000 resident population, London and England, 1994/95

Finally, if we compare the availability of ophthalmic professionals in the capital with the provision of sight tests, there appears to be a mismatch between the level of activity and the location of these professionals. However, a large proportion of sight tests are paid for privately: this varies according to the level of deprivation associated with an area. The apparent mismatch partially reflects a higher proportion of privately-funded sight tests in less deprived areas.

Chapter 8

Social Services

Summary

Provision of services

- Adult residential care consists of care for older people and care for 'other client groups' – people with physical disabilities, learning disabilities and mental health problems. There is considerably less provision of residential care in London, especially inner-deprived London, per capita resident population, compared with the rest of England. This is reflected in a lower admission rate to homes in London per capita resident population.

- Admissions of older people, per capita resident population aged 75 years and over, to residential homes in London is similar for each sector of the capital except the north west where a lower rate is observed. The admission rate to residential care for 'other client groups' varies considerably across London, from 24 per 10,000 resident population in the south east to 45 in the north west.

- The admission rate to residential care in London for older residents of the capital is just 60 per cent of the England average; it is less than 50 per cent in inner-deprived London.

- There is greater provision of all forms of community-based care per capita resident population in London than in the rest of the country. Per capita resident population, London as a whole provides twice as much day care, almost 30 per cent more home care and twice as many meals as the rest of England.

- There is considerable variation across sectors of London in the provision of community-based care with no one sector providing more in all respects. For example, compared with the London average, there are over 50 per cent more day care attendances per capita resident population in the south, the provision of home care is over 30 per cent greater in the east, and 40 per cent more meals are provided in the south east.

- There continues to be a significant difference in the balance between residential and community-based care in London when compared with the position in England as a whole: a similar situation to that in 1990/91.

- The proportion of adult residential care provided by the independent sector varies across London from 25 per cent in the east to 52 per cent in the north west. Although the proportion in London as a whole, 38 per cent, is similar to that in the rest of England, 37 per cent, there is substantial variation between types of area. In inner-deprived areas of London, 52 per cent of admissions are to the independent sector compared with just 24 per cent in similar areas outside the capital.

- The independent sector is *now* growing at a faster rate in London than elsewhere in England, but from a lower base.

- Forty per cent of meals in London are provided by the independent sector, compared with 47 per cent in England as a whole. In inner-deprived areas of London the proportion of meals provided by the independent sector is twice that of similar areas elsewhere.

- The provision of residential care for older people declined by 20 per cent in London between 1985 and 1995, but increased by a similar proportion in the rest of England. LA provision has decreased throughout England but has not been compensated by increased independent provision in London as elsewhere.

Utilisation of residential care

- In London as a whole, LAs support a similar number of older people, per capita resident population aged 75 years and over, in residential care, as the rest of England, though not necessarily in homes in London. LAs in inner-deprived areas of the capital support a greater number than similar areas elsewhere: 40 compared with 32 per 1,000 resident population aged 75 years and over.

- There is considerable variation across London in the number of people receiving LA-supported residential care per capita resident population aged 75 years and over: the highest level is in the east sector of the capital.

Physical resources

- There is some variation across London in the number of residential care places available for adult client groups and older people, driven by differences in independent provision. North-west London has the lowest provision of places; the north-central sector has the highest.

- In London as a whole over 60 per cent of residential care places are in the independent sector compared with over 75 per cent in the rest of England. Total provision in London, per capita resident population, is just 62 per cent of that elsewhere in England.

- There is considerable variation in the availability of nursing care places across London, ranging from nine per 1,000 population aged 75 years or over in the east to 38 in the south.

- London as a whole has 40 per cent less provision of nursing care places per capita resident population than the rest of England; in inner-deprived London there are just 20 per cent of the places available in similar areas outside the capital.

Human resources

- There is some variation in the number of WTE staff, relative to resident population, employed by LA social services to provide domiciliary, day centre and residential care: from 30 per 10,000 resident population in the south sector of London to 42 in the south east. Throughout London the greatest proportion of staff are involved in domiciliary care.

- London as a whole has a similar level of social services staff per capita population as the rest of England although there is some variation between types of areas. Inner-deprived and mixed-status areas in London employ fewer staff on average than similar areas elsewhere in the country.

Key Facts

Provision of services	*London*	*Rest of England*
Residential care		
Admission rate per 1,000 resident population aged 75+:	42	69
• Long-stay admission rate	13	21
• Short-stay admission rate	29	48
Admission rate per 10,000 resident population aged 18-64 years:	34	54
• Long-stay admission rate	14	17
• Short-stay admission rate	20	37
Community-based care		
Day centre attendance rate per 1,000 resident population aged 65+:	34	17
Households receiving home care per 1,000 resident population aged 65+:	71	55
Provision of meals per 1,000 resident population aged 75+:	405	211
Independent sector provision		
Proportion of admissions for all adult client groups to independent residential homes:	38%	37%
Proportion of meals provided by independent providers:	40%	47%

Utilisation of residential care

	London	Rest of England
LA-supported residents in homes for older people per 1,000 resident population aged 75+:	28	27

Physical resources

	London	Rest of England
Residential care places available for older people:	21,700	235,200
• Independent	13,200 (61%)	179,200 (76%)
• Local authority	8,450 (39%)	56,000 (24%)
Residential care places available for other adult client groups (learning and physical disabilities and mental health):	7,000	44,000
• Independent	5,500 (78%)	35,000 (79%)
• Local authority	1,500 (22%)	9,000 (21%)

Human resources

	London	Rest of England
WTE LA social services staff per 10,000 resident population aged 18 +, providing:		
• Residential care	14.5	14.7
• Day care	5.9	6.0
• Domiciliary care	16.9	14.6

1 Introduction

This chapter considers social services provision in London. The analysis is restricted to social services for adults. These are general health-related services, often provided to, or purchased on behalf of, their residents by local authority (LA) social services departments. However, wholly private funding of independent sector provision is now increasingly common, with social services departments assuming more the role of service facilitators.

Social services can be categorised as either residential or community-based. The former consists of long- and short-stay residential and nursing care in LA or independent homes, provided for older people and 'other client groups' – people with learning or physical disabilities or mental health problems. The latter are services provided in the community or client homes, such as meals on wheels, home care or day centres.

The analysis is limited to some extent by the nature of available data, particularly on the use of residential care services. In Section 3, residential care and community-based activity are considered in terms of admission or utilisation rate within an area, relative to resident population. This is essentially a provider-based perspective indicating the level of provision in an area, irrespective of where the client was (or is) originally resident. In the case of community-based care it is reasonable to assume that local provision serves local residents. However, residents of an area may use residential care facilities outside their locality, either through preference or, more commonly in London, because of a lack of local provision. The distinction between the provision of services by LAs and the independent sector is also examined in this section, including a brief analysis of changes since 1985 in the mix of provision of residential care for older people, between the LA and independent sectors.

Section 4 provides an analysis of the use of residential care, according to the area of residence of the recipient. However, as the data refer only to care which is wholly or partly funded by LAs, this allows but a partial view, taking no account of care which is not supported by a LA. Some discussion of the use of facilities outside the capital by London residents is provided, but it is not possible with existing data to map flows of care and people in a definitive way. In Section 5 we consider the availability of residential and nursing care places and, finally, in Section 6 the number of social services care staff per capita resident population is examined.

2 Data sources

The data in this section are drawn from two sources: the DoH report, *1996 Key Indicators of Local Authority Social Services*, (DoH, 1996f); and *Residential accommodation: Detailed statistics on residential care homes and local authority supported residents, England 1995* (DoH, 1996g). Both cover the financial year, 1994/95. In some cases, noted in the text, data are based on sample weeks in that year.

3 Provision of services

We compare residential care and community-based activity in terms of admission or utilisation rate, both across sectors of London and between London and the rest of the country. Data are based on the area of provision. Admissions to residential care in the course of the financial year are taken from the DoH return, RAC5.

Residential care

Adult residential care consists of care for older people, and care for people with physical disabilities, with learning disabilities, or with mental health problems. Figure 1 shows the admission rate to adult residential care is similar across London. This apparent similarity masks some substantial differences between individual LAs. Thus, one LA in north-west London with a particularly large proportion of short-stay admissions, has an admission rate of 155 per 10,000 adult residents, whereas another in the south has a rate of just ten.

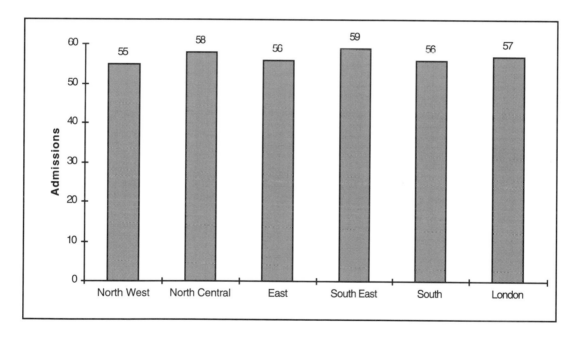

Figure 1: Residential care admissions per 10,000 resident population aged 18 years and over, by sector of London, 1994/95

Figure 2 compares London and the rest of England, both as a whole and by type of socio-economic area. There is a gradient observed in the capital, the level of admissions increasing as the level of deprivation falls: thus, inner-deprived areas of London have 48 admissions per capita, far fewer than the figure of 65 in high-status areas. London as a whole has over 40 per cent fewer admissions per capita than the rest of England. The difference is more marked in inner-deprived areas where the London admission rate is approximately half that of similar areas in the rest of the country, reflecting the lower level of provision of residential care places, particularly in the independent sector. This is considered further below.

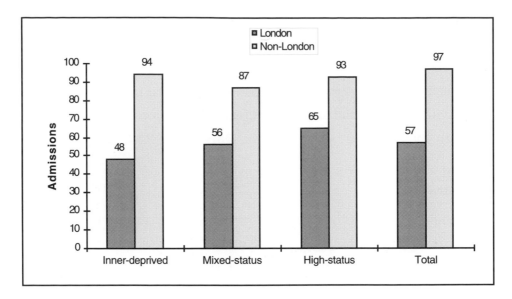

Figure 2: Residential care admissions per 10,000 resident population aged 18 years and over, London and England, 1994/95

We now consider in more detail the services described as adult residential care: care for older people, and care for 'other client groups' – physical disabilities, learning disabilities, and mental health.

Care for older people

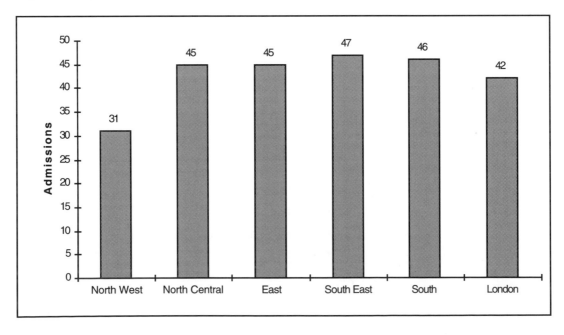

Figure 3: Residential care admissions per 1,000 resident population aged 75 years and over, by sector of London, 1994/95

Figure 3 shows some variation in the admission rate for older people across sectors of London, from 31 per 1,000 resident population aged 75 years and over in the north west to 47 in the south east.

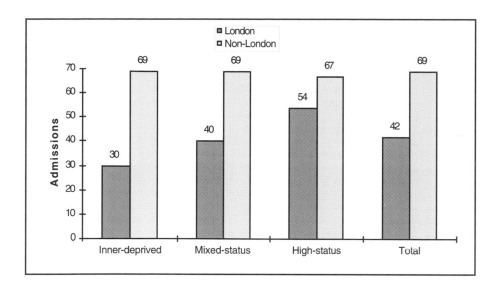

Figure 4: Residential care admissions per 1,000 resident population aged 75 years and over, London and England, 1994/95

Figure 4 compares London and the rest of England, showing that the rate of admission of older people to residential care in London is some 40 per cent less than that of the rest of England. Again, there is a particularly low rate in inner-deprived London. There is a similar admission rate across types of socio-economic area in the rest of the country, but in the capital there is a clear gradient: admission rate increases as level of deprivation falls. We show this gradient is not present for 'other client groups'. Thus, the gradient shown for adult residential care admission rates as a whole is driven by residential care for older people.

This lower admission rate in London reflects a relative shortage of residential care places for older people in the capital compared with the rest of England. The analysis is based on the use of local facilities. It is probably reasonable to assume, for the capital as a whole, that most of these places are occupied by Londoners; for individual LAs, on the other hand, there is likely to be some cross-boundary flow. It is important at this point to stress that London residents may also be using places in the rest of England. This is discussed further in subsequent sections. Nevertheless, the lack of local provision indicated here may make access to residential care more problematic for residents of London, and particularly inner-deprived London. Other things being equal, this would increase pressure on acute hospital services in the capital.

Care for 'other client groups'

Figure 5 shows considerable variation in the admission rate for 'other client groups' across sectors of London, from 45 per 10,000 adults aged 18-64 years in the north west, contrasting with the low rate in this sector for older people, to 24 in the south east. One LA in north-west London has a rate some four times the London average, largely driven by short-stay admissions for people with learning disabilities; at the LA level, admission rates in London vary from 10 to 152. There is also considerable variation in the proportion of admissions for constituent client groups: physical disabilities, learning disabilities and mental health.

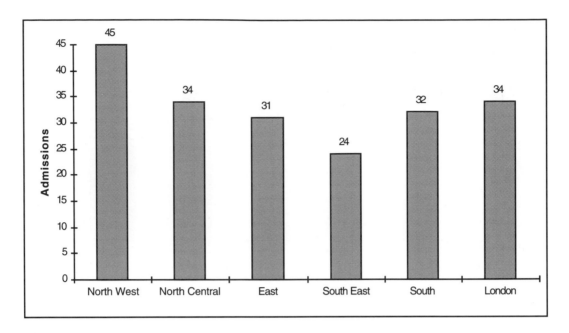

Figure 5: 'Other client groups' residential care admissions per 10,000 resident population aged 18-64 years, by sector of London, 1994/95

Figure 6 compares the admission rate for 'other client groups' in London with that of the rest of the country. Once again the admission rate in London as a whole, and in each type of socio-economic area, is substantially less than that of England: the average across all London LAs is just 63 per cent of that of the rest of England. However, there is no clear gradient of provision across type of socio-economic area, either within London or outside the capital.

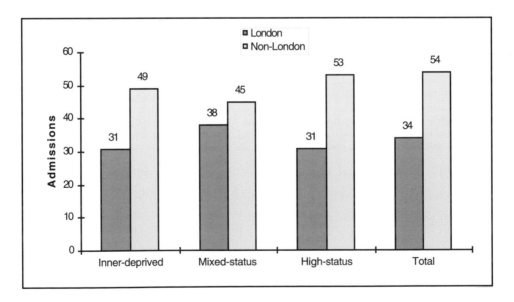

Figure 6: 'Other client groups' residential care admissions per 10,000 resident population aged 18-64 years, London and England, 1994/95

Community-based care

(Technical note: For each type of community-based service, activity data are missing for some LAs, in both London and the rest of England. In each case population data have been adjusted accordingly.)

We now consider the provision of community-based care by social services. This includes day care centres for older people, home care and the provision of meals, either in the client home or at luncheon clubs. These data are based on a sample week in October 1995.

Day care centres

Figure 7 shows considerable variation across London in the attendance rate per week at day care centres by residents aged 65 years and over: from 22 per 1,000 resident population in the north-west sector to 52 in the south. Attendance rates in four of the six LAs in the north-west sector are less than 20. By contrast, one LA in the south has an attendance rate of 117 per 1,000 residents aged 65 years and over. Attendance rates reflect the availability of day care centre places. In one north-west London LA there are only 14 day care places per 1,000 residents: this contrasts with the situation in the south London authority referred to above where there are 157.

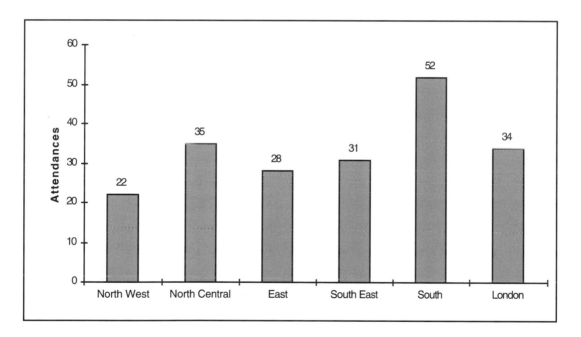

Figure 7: Day care centre attendances per week, per 1,000 resident population aged 65 years and over, by sector of London, October 1995

Figure 8 shows that the day care centre attendance rate in London as a whole is twice that of the rest of England: a comparison between inner-deprived areas in London and similar areas elsewhere shows the rate in the capital is more than twice that in the rest of the country. This contrasts vividly with the much lower rate of admission to residential care. There may be an element of substitution of day care for residential care in London.

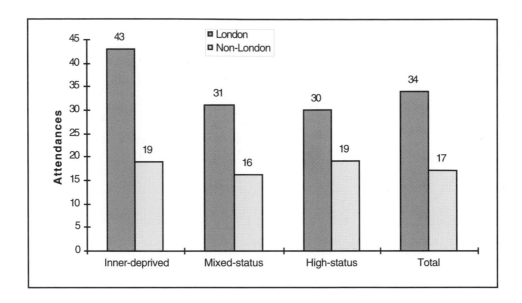

Figure 8: Day care centre attendances per week, per 1,000 resident population aged 65 years and over, London and England, October 1995

Home care

In this section the rate of provision of home care is analysed by relating the number of households contacted in a sample week where the oldest client is aged 65 years or over, to the resident population aged 65 years or over. Figure 9 compares the provision of home care across sectors of London, showing the greatest level of provision is in the east sector, at 94 households per 1,000 resident population aged 65 years or over, and the least in the north-central, at 56 households per 1,000. Even when, at a more detailed level, sub-age-groups are considered: 65-74, 75-84 and 85+ years; there remains a greater level of provision in the east sector.

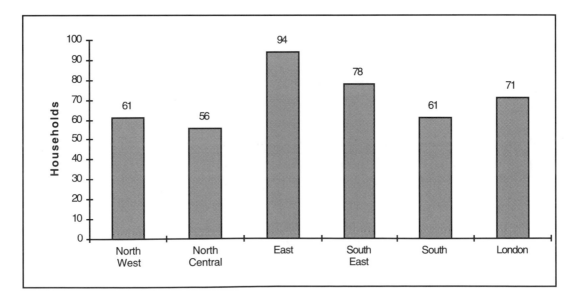

Figure 9: Households receiving home care per 1,000 resident population aged 65 years and over, by sector of London, October 1995

Figure 10 shows London as a whole provides almost 30 per cent more home care per capita than the rest of England. In both London and the rest of England, provision tends to increase with the level of deprivation. Inner-deprived and mixed-status areas outside the capital provide more home care than the average level in London as a whole. However, there is markedly more home care in inner-deprived areas of London where provision per capita approaches twice that in the rest of England as a whole.

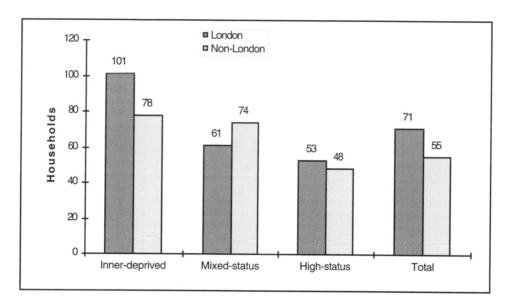

Figure 10: Households receiving home care per 1,000 resident population aged 65 years and over, London and England, October 1995

Provision of meals

Figure 11 shows some variation in the provision of meals for people aged 75 years and over in London: the north-west, north-central, and east sectors record similar levels per capita resident population; however, the south-east sector has considerably greater provision and the south somewhat lower. The day care attendance rate in the south sector is relatively high, suggesting that meals may be provided at day care centres, and hence not appear in these data.

Despite the variation, all sectors of London have considerably greater provision than elsewhere in England. London as a whole provides almost twice the average number of meals per capita as the rest of England. Figure 12 confirms that the relative provision of meals for older people by social services, whether in client homes or through 'luncheon clubs', is greater in London than the rest of the country. For each type of socio-economic area, London provides more meals per capita than similar areas outside the capital.

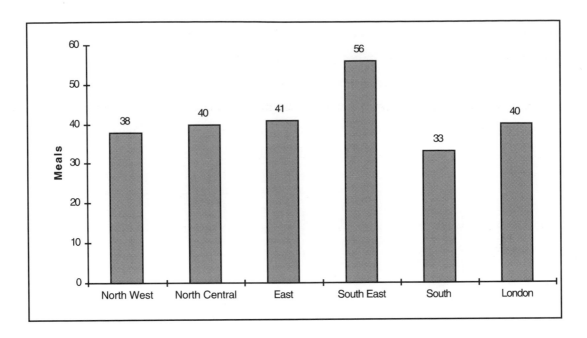

Figure 11: Meals per 100 resident population aged 75 years and over, by sector of London, October 1995

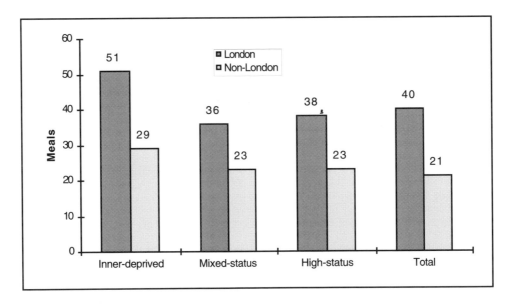

Figure 12: Meals per 100 resident population aged 75 years and over, London and England, October 1995

There is a clear contrast between the provision of community-based and residential-based services in London. Fewer residential services are provided in the capital than in the rest of the country, but more community-based services. To some extent community-based services in London have always tended to act as a substitute for residential-based ones. Factors such as the high cost of property in London may well have encouraged this pattern of provision to emerge. However, it fits also with a preferred approach to care for older people which stresses the importance of their independence, and hence provides services to maintain older people in their own familiar environment for as long as possible. Further detailed analysis using local data and knowledge would help to confirm and interpret these findings.

Independent sector provision

In recent years the distinction between the responsibility of LAs for ensuring that services are available to their local populations and the actual provision of those services has developed in ways similar to that which has been institutionalised in the 'purchaser-provider split' for health services. The independent sector has become increasingly important in the provision of social services and will become more so given the tenor of the recent announcement by the Secretary of State for Health that the LA should become an 'enabler and commissioner' of social services rather than a provider. We now compare the level of independent sector provision across sectors of London and between London and the rest of the country.

Adult residential care

Residential care may be provided in LA homes, which are those owned and staffed by the LA, or independent sector homes, which are those registered with the LA under the provision of the Registered Homes Act 1984. These include voluntary and private (for profit) homes. Figure 13 shows that the proportion of adult residential care provided by the independent sector varies across London from 25 per cent in the east to 52 per cent in the north west. There is greater variation across individual LAs, even within the same sector. For example, in the south all admissions to residential care in one LA are to independent providers, while in a neighbouring LA, the proportion is only 12 per cent.

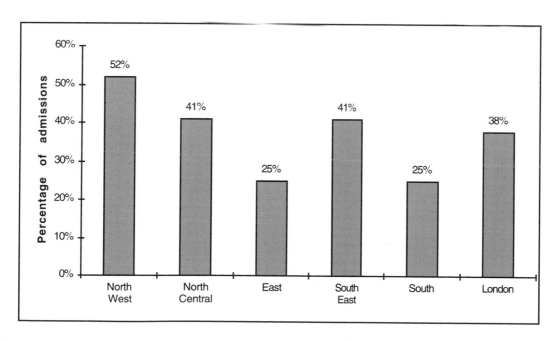

Figure 13: Proportion of adult residential care admissions to independent homes, by sector of London, 1994/95

Figure 14 shows the proportion of admissions to independent sector residential care in London as a whole is very similar to that of the rest of England. However, there is considerable variation between types of socio-economic area in London and similar areas in the rest of the country. In London the proportion of residential care provided by the independent sector increases with the level of deprivation in an area, whereas in the rest of England the reverse is true. The proportion of independent provision in inner-deprived London is twice that of similar areas elsewhere in the country, 52 compared with 24 per cent, but less in high-status London authorities when compared with similar areas outside the capital, 26 compared with 37 per cent.

The independent sector is now growing at a much faster rate in London than elsewhere in England: but from a lower base. This is shown by comparing the position in 1994/95 with that just one year previously. In 1993/94, 26 per cent of admissions were to the independent sector in London compared with 33 per cent in the rest of England. As Figure 14 shows, this had grown to 38 per cent in London in 1994/95, increasing by almost 50 per cent in a year; in the rest of the country it had grown to just 37 per cent.

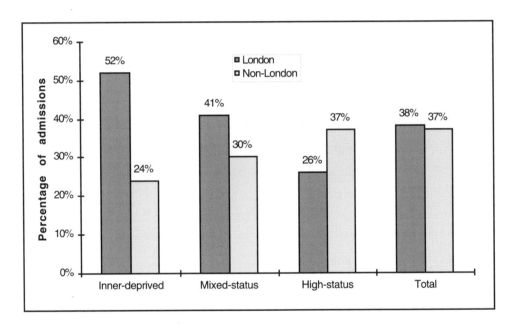

Figure 14: Proportion of adult residential care admissions to independent homes, London and England, 1994/95

Provision of meals

The independent sector is now even more important as a provider of meals, mainly for older people. Figure 15 shows that four out of ten meals in London are provided by the independent sector, with a range from 32 to 49 per cent across sectors. Again, there is substantial variation when individual LAs are examined, even within the same sector. For example, no meals are provided by the private sector in one east London LA whereas another has complete private provision of meals.

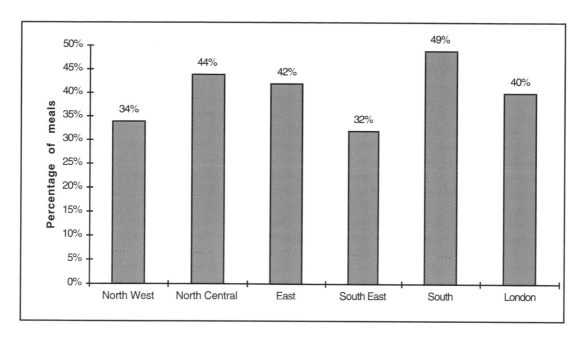

Figure 15: Proportion of meals provided by the independent sector under contract, by sector of London, 1994/95

Figure 16 compares the proportion of meals provided by the independent sector in London with that of the rest of the country. Although less is provided by the independent sector in the capital as a whole – 40 compared with 47 per cent in the rest of England – in inner-deprived London the proportion of meals provided by the independent sector is twice that of inner-deprived areas in the rest of the country.

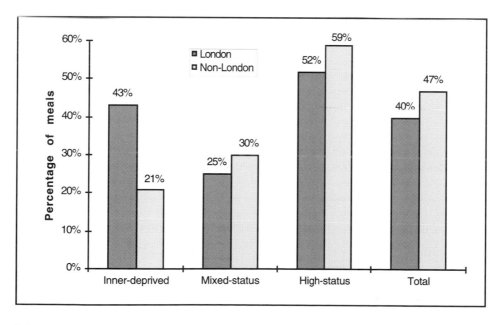

Figure 16: Proportion of meals provided by the independent sector under contract, London and England, 1994/95

Trends in independent sector residential provision for older people

There have been significant changes in the level and nature of provision of residential care for older people since 1985. Using DoH data (DoH, 1991a; DoH, 1996h), we show the increasing importance of the independent sector in the provision of residential care, and also highlight differences between London and the rest of the country.

Table 1: Residents in homes for older people, 1985-1995 (indexed to 1985 = 100)

Type of Area	1985	1986	1987	1988	1989	1990	1991	1992	1993	1994	1995
Inner-deprived											
London	100	97	100	91	90	88	76	74	72	71	64
Non-London	100	108	100	111	116	116	116	111	105	122	104
Mixed-status											
London	100	98	100	95	94	90	91	88	82	81	79
Non-London	100	109	100	120	129	134	137	134	133	133	133
High-status											
London	100	102	100	105	104	105	107	104	103	102	98
Non-London	100	107	100	115	124	176	128	126	126	126	131
London	100	99	98	97	96	94	92	89	86	85	81
England	100	106	108	113	120	137	122	120	118	120	119

Table 1 shows a decreasing trend in the number of residents in homes for older people located in each type of socio-economic area in London: the decline is greatest for inner-deprived and mixed-status areas. By contrast, in similar areas in the rest of England there have been increases in the number of residents, of four and 33 per cent since 1985.

Table 2: Residents in LA homes for older people, 1985-1995 (indexed to 1985 = 100)

Type of Area	1985	1986	1987	1988	1989	1990	1991	1992	1993	1994	1995
Inner-deprived											
London	100	87	93	89	84	79	75	67	62	59	46
Non-London	100	101	100	95	91	86	70	68	54	55	44
Mixed-status											
London	100	96	95	92	90	78	74	62	51	45	40
Non-London	100	101	99	96	95	84	82	71	62	60	52
High-status											
London	100	101	101	101	98	94	78	73	68	66	61
Non-London	100	102	95	99	98	93	89	71	67	62	58
London	100	94	96	93	90	83	75	67	60	56	48
England	100	100	97	96	94	87	80	69	61	58	52

Table 2 shows that the reduction in the number of residents in LA homes in London is similar to that in England as a whole – the number has halved. However, as Table 3 shows, there has been a substantial increase in the number of residents in independent sector homes in England, whereas the growth in the number of such residents in London has been modest, for example just ten per cent in inner-deprived areas of London, and certainly not sufficient to compensate for the reduction in LA provision.

Table 3: Residents in independent sector homes for older people, 1985-1995 (indexed to 1985 = 100)

Type of Area	1985	1986	1987	1988	1989	1990	1991	1992	1993	1994	1995
Inner-deprived											
London	100	120	117	98	103	110	79	92	96	102	110
Non-London	100	124	101	147	170	182	218	207	218	268	236
Mixed-status											
London	100	99	106	99	99	105	111	119	118	123	125
Non-London	100	125	102	172	202	242	258	272	287	292	309
High-status											
London	100	103	99	109	112	116	139	137	140	141	138
Non-London	100	113	105	131	150	258	166	181	184	188	204
London	100	105	101	102	105	110	115	120	122	126	127
England	100	113	120	132	148	193	170	178	182	188	195

Indices are useful for examining trends, but mask the actual level of provision. In 1985 the provision of residential care in London was already less than that of the rest of England. Thus, the number of residents in homes for older people per 1,000 resident population aged 65 years and over in London in 1985 was 24.2 compared with 27.5 in England. It is clear, therefore, that the provision of residential care for older people in London has declined from a lower starting point in comparison with the rest of England, where provision has actually increased.

4 Utilisation of residential care

The analysis thus far has taken primarily a provider perspective, identifying where care is provided, but not for whom. This distinction is fundamental in assessing the availability of residential care for Londoners. We have alluded to the fact that older Londoners in particular, but other client groups also, may obtain residential care in homes located in non-London LAs. In this section we consider in more detail the area of residence of those using residential care facilities.

Residents are defined as those in residence at a home on 31 March 1995, and are based on the DoH return, RAC5. Supported residents are those supported wholly or in part by a LA. These data are taken from the DoH return, SR1. A distinction is made between short- and long-stay residents: the former are those receiving short-term care who are normally resident elsewhere. In each case, residents in small homes with four or fewer residents are excluded from the analysis.

In the previous section we related the level of admissions to residential care in London to the resident population of the capital. This clearly does not reflect the totality of such care which Londoners use; at best it may provide some insight into the dislocation of Londoners which occurs in order to obtain care.

Three distinctions are important in this context: between supported and non-supported residents; between residents who are from the LA where the home is located and those who are not; and finally, between LA home residents and independent sector home residents. Thus, it is possible to classify people living in residential homes within a particular LA area in eight ways, as those in:

- LA homes, supported by the LA in which the home is located;

- independent sector homes, supported by the LA in which the home is located;

- LA homes, supported by other LAs;

- independent sector homes, supported by other LAs;

- LA homes, not supported by a LA, who were residents of the LA in which the home is located;

- independent sector homes, not supported by a LA, who were residents of the LA in which the home is located;

- LA homes, not supported by a LA, who were not residents of the LA in which the home is located;

- independent sector homes, not supported by a LA, who were not residents of the LA in which the home is located.

These distinctions are key to the determination of the quantity and location of care used by residents of London. However, national comparative data sets are not available which allow a definitive analysis. We provide what is essentially a purchaser-based analysis below, comparing the number of long-stay residents of homes for older people supported by LAs in London and England, irrespective of where the care is provided. Although it is not possible to produce similar results incorporating non-LA-funded provision, we outline the nature of the required analysis in Box 1.

Older people

Figure 17 shows considerable variation across London in the number of people receiving LA-supported residential care per 1,000 resident population aged 75 years and over. LA-supported residential care per capita is greatest in the east sector, reflecting very high levels of support by LAs in inner-deprived areas in this sector, rather than a consistent pattern across the sector as a whole.

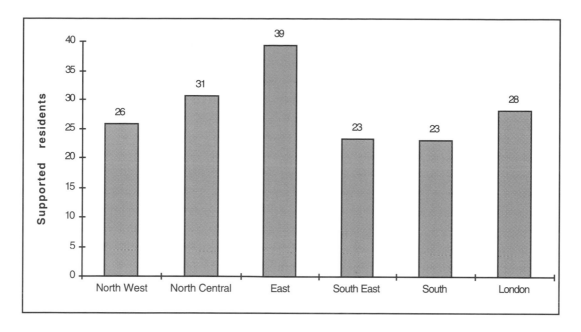

Figure 17: LA-supported residents of residential homes for older people per 1,000 resident population aged 75 years and over, by sector of London, 1995

Figure 18 shows that in London as a whole there are slightly more LA-supported older residents per capita than is the case in the rest of England: 28 per 1,000 resident population aged 75 years and over compared with 27. This is due to the higher level of LA-supported provision in inner-deprived areas of the capital compared with similar areas in the rest of the country: 40 compared with 32 per 1,000 resident population aged 75 years and over. By contrast, the level of LA-supported residential care for older people in mixed- and high-status areas of London is less than that in comparable areas elsewhere in England.

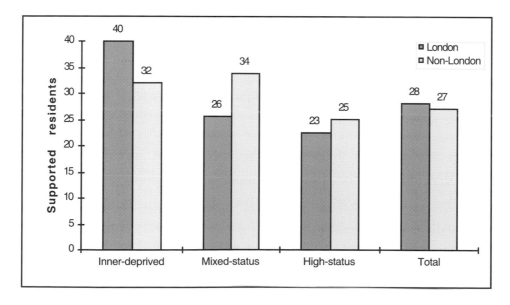

Figure 18: LA-supported residents of residential homes for older people per 1,000 resident population aged 75 years and over, London and England, 1995

However, as already noted, the above analysis excludes care that is not supported by LAs. It is likely that the ratio of this to LA-supported care is related to the level of deprivation in an area. Hence the picture when the totality of residential care for older people is compared between types of socio-economic area, both within London and between London and the rest of England, may change. For England as a whole we can estimate the ratio of LA-supported to total care. On the assumption that the number of people supported by LAs who are resident in homes outside England is negligible, and vice versa, the ratio of supported residents to total residents of England homes as a whole indicates the proportion, and hence number, of unsupported residents, as net flows around the country should cancel out.

For each LA area, the ratio of supported residents of that LA to total home residents in that area is affected both by the flow of people between areas, and the level of non-LA-supported provision. With current data it is not possible to distinguish these two effects. However some limits on flows can be established, as shown in Box 1.

For each LA area, if the number of LA-supported residents were greater than total residents of homes in that area, this would clearly imply there are flows of residents of that authority to homes in other areas. However, even if there are fewer LA-supported residents than total residents of homes in the LA area, there may be such flows, since a proportion of the total residents in homes in that area will not be funded by LAs. Moreover, it is possible some residents of homes within a LA may have originated from outside that authority.

In England as a whole, 56 per cent of older people in long-term residential care are not supported by LAs. The equivalent figure is not available for London. However, in London as a whole there are 13,042 LA-supported residents compared with a total of 19,357 residents of London homes; in inner-deprived areas of the capital the number of LA-supported home residents is slightly greater than the total number of people in homes in the area, 4,608 compared with 4,560. This strongly suggests some older people in London go outside the capital for long-term residential care, although we are not able to state a precise figure as there is no information, for the London population, on the level of non-LA-supported residents.

The position is even clearer in the case of 'other client groups', though precise figures are still not available. The number of LA-supported home residents for London is five per cent greater than the total number of residents of homes in the capital: clearly some Londoners must go outside London to obtain these forms of residential care.

This is as far as the analysis can be taken with the data currently available. However, Box 1 provides an example to illustrate the type of flow analysis and extra information required to understand the dislocation of older people from London to obtain residential (or nursing) care. Some fairly heroic assumptions are made for the purpose of illustration.

5 Physical resources

So far we have considered the use of services in various ways. In this section we analyse the availability of residential and nursing care places in London, first for all adult client groups and then for the subset of places for older people. A distinction is drawn between LA and independent sector provision.

Residential care places

Figure 19 shows, for all adult client groups, that north-west London has the lowest relative provision of residential care places in the capital: the neighbouring north-central sector has the greatest. This variation is driven mainly by differences in independent provision. The provision of LA residential care is slightly less in the north-central sector than that in the north west, but independent provision is over twice as great. In London as a whole, two out of every three residential care places are in the independent sector.

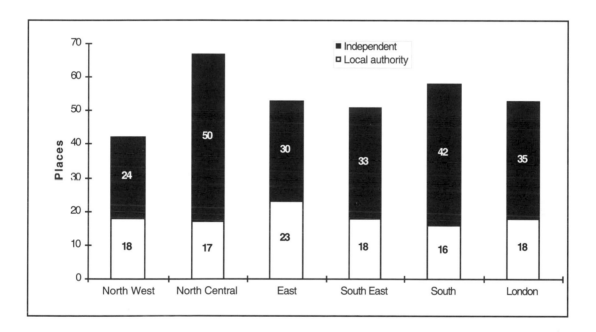

Figure 19: Residential care places per 10,000 resident population aged 18 years and over, all adult client groups, by sector of London, 1994/95

London as a whole has less residential care places per capita than England, particularly in the independent sector. Figure 20 shows that the shortfall in each type of socio-economic are in London is driven mainly by differences in the independent sector. LA provision in London as a whole is similar to that of the rest of the country, but independent provision is only half that outside the capital.

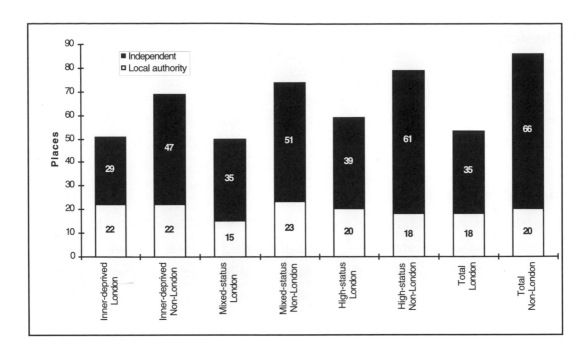

Figure 20: Residential care places per 10,000 resident population aged 18 years and over, all adult client groups, London and England, 1994/95

Figure 21 shows similar variation across London when just residential care places for older people are considered. The north-west sector has less places per capita population aged 75 years and over than the rest of London; the north-central sector has more: this variation is due to differences in independent sector provision. The proportion of total places for older people in the independent sector is slightly lower in London as a whole than was the case for all adult client groups: so, the independent sector is more important in the provision of residential care for 'other client groups' such as learning disability than it is for older people. However, with the current fast rate of growth of the independent sector, this position may be changing very rapidly.

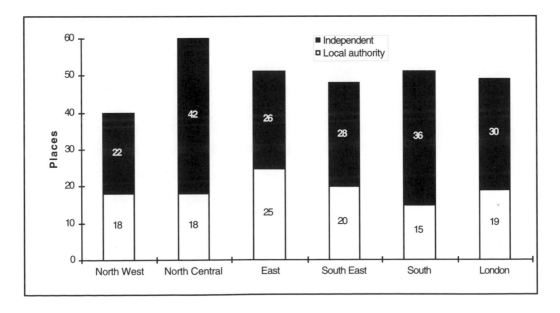

Figure 21: Residential care places per 1,000 resident population aged 75 years and over, by sector of London, 1994/95

Figure 22 compares the availability of residential care places for older people in London with that in the rest of England, showing that London as a whole has almost 40 per cent less places per capita: this is driven entirely by the difference in independent sector provision. London has only half as many places per capita as the rest of the country.

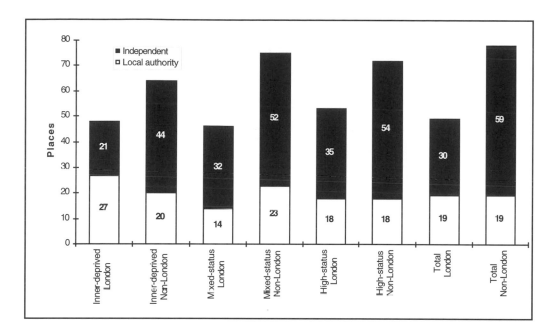

Figure 22: Residential care places per 1,000 resident population aged 75 years and over, London and England, 1994/95

Nursing care places

Figure 23 shows considerable variation in the provision of nursing care places across sectors of London: from nine per 1,000 resident population aged 75 years and over in the east to 38 in the south. In some LAs in the east sector, there are five or fewer places per 1,000, whereas there are LAs in the south of London where there are over 50 places.

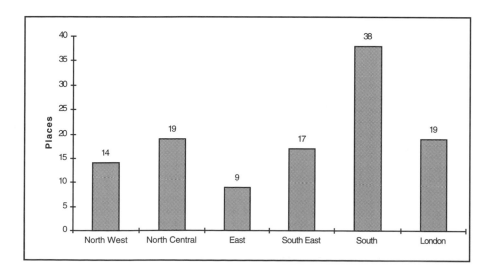

Figure 23: Nursing care places per 1,000 resident population aged 75 years and over, by sector of London, 1994/95

Figure 24 reveals the lack of nursing care places in London compared with the rest of England. Inner-deprived London has only one-fifth as many places available relative to resident population as inner-deprived areas outside the capital. The lack of nursing care places in London leads to an export of older people in need of nursing care from London to the rest of the country. Data are not available which allow flows from London to be mapped. However, it is known that 66 per cent of nursing care purchased by London LAs is in homes outside their own LA boundaries: this compares with an average of 18 per cent in England as a whole. However, we have no indication how much of this is outside the capital, and so at best this gives a very high upper limit. The lack of local nursing home places is also likely to increase pressure on other health care providers in London such as acute or community hospitals.

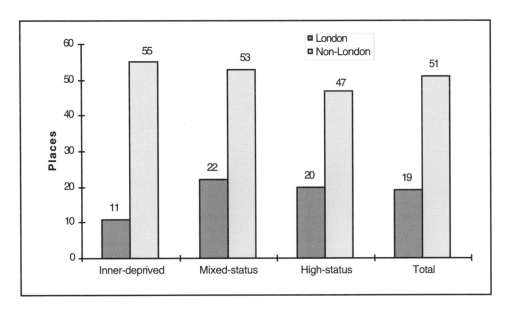

Figure 24: Nursing care places per 1,000 resident population aged 75 years and over, London and England, 1994/95

6 Human resources

We conclude by considering the provision of social services staff in London in 1994/95. Figure 25 shows the variation across sectors of London in the number of whole time equivalent (WTE) staff per 10,000 resident population aged 18 years and over, employed by LA social services departments to provide domiciliary, day centre and residential care: from 30 in the south to 42 in the south east. In each sector of London, a greater proportion of staff are involved in the provision of domiciliary than residential care.

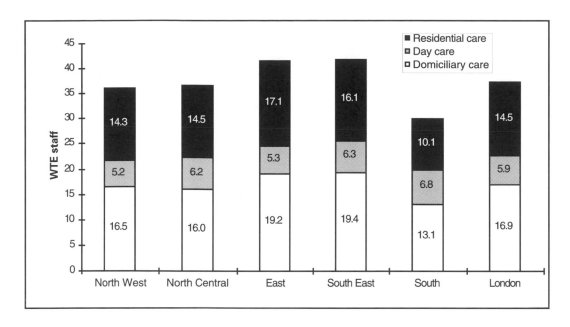

Figure 25: Social services staff per 10,000 resident population aged 18 years and over, by care type, by sector of London, September 1995

Figure 26, which compares London with the rest of England, shows slightly more WTE staff in the capital than is the case elsewhere in England. This reflects the position in high-status areas. In both inner-deprived and mixed-status areas, London has proportionately fewer staff than comparable areas of the rest of the country – 46 and 31 WTEs per 10,000 resident population aged 18 years and over respectively, compared with 52 and 41 outside the capital.

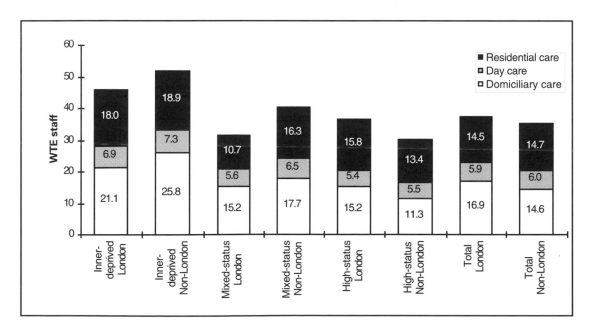

Figure 26: Social services staff per 10,000 resident population aged 18 years and over, by care type, London and England, September 1995

Box 1: An illustrative example of flows of older people for residential care

The provision of residential care in homes in London is less, relative to London's resident population, than in the rest of the country, but London LAs support slightly more residents per capita than those outside the capital. It is widely assumed that older Londoners receive residential care outside the capital. What is not known is how much. This is key to the determination of the total utilisation of residential care by older London residents, and also to understanding the level of dislocation of older Londoners taking place as a result of the lack of availability of residential care places in the capital.

Unfortunately, nationally available routine data do not allow flows of residential care across the country to be measured. Instead, we give a tentative indication of the nature of these flows.

Table 4: Illustrative flows of older people for residential care in England, 1995

| | SUPPORTED | | | | | | | | |
| | London | | | Non-London | | | England | | |
LOCATED	LA	Ind.	Total	LA	Ind.	Total	LA	Ind.	Total
London									
LA	6,899	0	6,899	0	0	0	6,899	0	**6,899**
Independent	3,487	8,971	12,458	0	0	0	3,487	8,971	**12,458**
Total	10,386	8,971	19,357	0	0	0	10,386	8,971	**19,357**
Non-London									
LA	0	0	0	45,892	0	45,892	45,892	0	**45,892**
Independent	2,656	6,833	9,489	42,235	108,651	150,886	44,891	115,484	**160,375**
Total	2,656	6,833	9,489	88,127	108,651	196,778	90,783	115,484	**206,267**
England									
LA	**6,899**	0	6,899	**45,892**	0	45,892	**52,791**	0	52,791
Independent	**6,143**	15,804	21,947	**42,235**	108,651	150,886	**48,378**	124,455	172,833
Total	**13,042**	15,804	28,846	**88,127**	108,651	196,778	**101,169**	124,455	225,624
Utilisation rate	28	35	63	27	34	61	27	34	61

(Table 4 does not include residents in small homes. Also national data suggest that there are more LA-supported residents in LA homes than there are total residents in these homes. This arises from a minor inconsistency in two data sources. The transfer of LA homes to the independent sector is picked up more completely in the return, RAC5, than in the SR1. In Table 4 the number of LA-supported residents in LA homes is reduced to equal the total number of residents in these homes. The overall number of supported residents in independent homes is increased appropriately.)

Table 4 illustrates how flows of residential care for older people between London and the rest of the country might be described, both for LA-supported and non-LA-supported care, to LA and independent sector homes. The flow matrix in Table 4 reflects the eight classifications previously applied to residents of homes. Only the bolded figures are actual data; the rest are estimates that are discussed below. The rows of the matrix reflect the location of care: whether in London LA or independent sector homes, or in non-London LA or independent sector homes. The columns of the matrix reflect the financing: whether London LA-supported or London non-LA-supported (independent), or non-London LA-supported or non-London non-LA-supported.

Data are available on the location of provision, which distinguish between LA and independent sector provision, by LA area. Thus, the England total column gives the actual number of residents in LA and independent sector homes in London and the rest of the country. These data are available for all LAs.

However, a comprehensive flow matrix cannot be created from existing data. For any particular LA, there is no indication where LA-supported residents are located, other than in that authority's area or not. Thus, for example, 24 per cent of residents supported by LAs in London are not resident in the supporting LA area but they may be in homes in another London LA. More fundamentally perhaps, data are not available for non-LA-supported residents at the individual LA level. At the national level it is known that such residents account for 56 per cent of total residents.

Data are available on financing, for individual LAs and England as a whole, showing the proportion of LA-supported residents, in LA and independent sector homes, separately. However, these data show which LA supports the resident, but not which authority the resident is located in. Thus, London and non-London supported residents are shown, but only for England as a whole. These actual data are used to provide part of the three England rows of the table.

As we have total residents in LA and independent sector homes for England as a whole, and total LA-supported residents, by type of home, for England, it is possible to calculate the independently supported residents, by type of home, for England. This is shown in the bottom three rows of the second last column. However, no further cells of this flow matrix can be provided from available data.

Instead, we propose a set of assumptions which allow the overall flow matrix to be calculated. These assumptions may be refined with further analysis or if alternative data sources are available. This approach makes clear the impact of various assumptions and also shows what additional information is required. The assumptions underlying the estimated part of Table 4 are:

- non-Londoner residents do not use residential care in London;

- for all LAs, there are no non-LA-supported residents of LA homes;

- for all LAs, the proportion of residents of independent sector homes that are LA-supported is the same as the England average, i.e. 28 per cent;

- the ratio of London non-LA-supported residents in independent homes in the capital to those outside the capital equals the ratio of LA-supported residents in independent homes in the capital to those outside the capital.

Under these assumptions, the flow matrix in Table 4 is calculated. These are very broad assumptions for which no particular validity is claimed. The last assumption in particular is necessary to provide *some* distribution of residents of independent sector homes between the London and non-London population. Nevertheless, it is possible to test the results against other information. As noted above, the number of London LA-supported residents not in own authority homes is 24 per cent, (DoH, 1996g). This establishes a maximum number of residents supported by London LAs in homes outside the capital. The assumptions would plainly be implausible if a figure emerged that was greater than the upper limit of 24 per cent.

In fact, the number of supported residents in LA homes outside the supporting LAs is 326 (DoH, 1996g), whereas our assumptions suggest the figure for outside London is 0. This implies that 326 residents supported by London LAs are in LA homes in other London LAs. Similarly the figure for independent homes of 3,091 (DoH, 1996g) compares with 2,656 from our analysis, implying that 435 residents supported by London LAs are in independent homes located in other London LAs.

The results of the analysis presented in this section must be treated with extreme caution as the assumptions determine largely the findings. However, the methodology gives a useful insight into the nature of provision of residential care for older people in London. On the basis of the above assumptions, the final row of the table indicates the rate of utilisation of residential care per capita resident population aged 75 years and over. Three possible findings emerge.

First, based on actual data, London LAs as a whole support slightly more residents of residential homes for older people, relative to population, than LAs in the rest of England. Second, on the basis of the above assumptions, there is more total per capita utilisation of residential care by Londoners, including that not funded by LAs, than in the rest of England, but unsupported residents are a slightly greater proportion of total residents outside the capital. Finally, also on the basis of the above assumptions, over 30 per cent of provision of residential care for older Londoners is provided outside the capital.

Chapter 9

Financial Resources

Summary

HCHS expenditure

- London providers account for 19 per cent of national HCHS expenditure compared with 16 per cent of FCE activity; 14 per cent of England's population is in London: these differences reflect both the use of services by non-residents and extra costs.

- The proportion of total expenditure accounted for by the medical specialties equals that by surgical specialties in all areas of the country except inner-deprived London where 36 per cent of expenditure is on medical specialties compared to just 26 per cent on surgical specialties.

- 15 per cent of HCHS expenditure accounted for by London DHAs as a whole is devoted to mental health compared with just 12 per cent in the rest of England. In both London and England 58 per cent of expenditure is devoted to general and acute services.

- London DHAs account for 17.5 per cent of total HCHS expenditure, less than the 19 per cent accounted for by London providers, reflecting the export of care from London providers to the rest of the country.

Provider finances

- The provision of health services accounts for 80 per cent of London provider income; 20 per cent comes from other sources such as education, training and research funding. By contrast, services income accounts for 90 per cent in the rest of the country.

- Services income is attributable to six sources: DHAs, GPFHs, other NHS trusts, the DoH, private patients, or other non-NHS sources. In London as a whole, 89 per cent of total services income is from DHAs.

- However, there is considerable variation between sectors in the relative importance of other sources. For example, GPFH income is most important in the south, where it accounts for seven per cent of services income. By contrast, private patient income is more important in the north-west and north-central sectors.

- Relatively less services income in London is from GPFHs and relatively more from the DoH and private patients, when compared with the rest of England: in inner-deprived London a total of 11 per cent of services income is from these two sources.

- The importance of other operating income, for example education, training and research funding, varies across London. It is most significant in the north west where it accounts for 27 per cent of total income.

- In three London trusts, education, training and research funding accounts for more than 50 per cent of total income.

- London trusts account for 18 per cent of total income from NHS patients, compared with 44 per cent of private patient income and 32 per cent of income from other sources.

- The average income of acute providers in London is £76 million compared with £63 million in the rest of England. Similarly, the average income of non-acute providers in London is greater than in the rest of the country.

- In each sector of London, the greatest proportion of expenditure is accounted for by staff: this varies from 59 per cent in the north west to 66 per cent in the south.

- Agency staff account for a greater proportion of staff expenditure in London than in the rest of England: six per cent of staff expenditure compared with two per cent.

- Average cost per member of staff in London is £22,400, 25 per cent more than the England figure of £17,900. The difference reflects higher wages costs in London, greater agency staff costs per member of staff, and, perhaps, a greater proportion of more highly paid employees in London.

- The total value of fixed assets owned by trusts in London is just over £4 billion, of which, buildings, fittings and installations account for 65 per cent. There are approximately £250 million worth of assets under construction in London.

- The value of land occupied by trusts in London is 21 per cent of their total fixed assets compared with 13 per cent for non-London trusts.

DHA expenditure

- DHA expenditure on HCHS per capita resident population varies across London from £423 in the south sector to £572 in north-central.

- Average DHA expenditure in London on HCHS per capita resident population is £462, over 30 per cent greater than the average in the rest of England of £353. Inner-deprived London DHAs spend over 40 per cent more per capita than comparable DHAs elsewhere in the country.

- In both London and England 96 per cent of DHA expenditure is devoted to health care and related services.

FHS expenditure

- FHS expenditure in London, at £141 per capita, is four per cent more than the average of £136 in the rest of the country: excluding administration costs and GPFH expenditure on hospital care. Average per capita expenditure varies between £130 in high-status areas of London and £158 in inner-deprived areas.

- Expenditure on pharmaceutical services per capita is less and expenditure on GMS is more in the capital than in the rest of the country.

- However, London benefits from DoH initiative funding of over £6 per capita: in inner-deprived areas this is more than £12 per capita. If this funding were removed, average per capita expenditure in inner-deprived London is just £3 more than similar areas in the rest of the country.

Social services expenditure

- London as a whole accounts for 21 per cent of total England expenditure on social services, which is considerably more than the proportion of national HCHS or FHS expenditure accounted by London DHAs.

- There is little variation in total gross social services expenditure per capita resident population in London with the exception of the south sector, where per capita spend is over 14 per cent less than the London average.

- Total gross social services expenditure per capita resident population in London is 60 per cent greater than that in the rest of England – £229 compared with £142; the average in inner-deprived London is 82 per cent greater than that in similar areas elsewhere.

- Since 1990/91, gross social services expenditure per capita resident population has increased by 37 per cent in London compared with 46 per cent in the rest of the country.

- Gross social services expenditure on older people per capita resident population aged 75 years and over is 16 per cent less in the south sector than the average in London as a whole.

- Gross social services expenditure on older people per capita resident population aged 75 years and over is over 50 per cent more in London than in the rest of England.

- Almost half of gross social services expenditure on older people in the rest of England is accounted for by residential or nursing care compared with 39 per cent in London as a whole; on the other hand, London spends 37 per cent on community-based care compared with 29 per cent in the rest of the country.

- Despite the different balance of expenditure, London LAs spend more per capita on most types of care for older people: the exception is nursing care where the London average is 13 per cent less than that of the rest of England.

Key Facts

HCHS expenditure	*London*	*Rest of England*
Provider HCHS expenditure		
Total provider HCHS expenditure:	£3.3 billion	£13.9 billion
Proportion in each expenditure category:		
• Medical	31.6%	28.1%
• Surgery	26.2%	28.9%
• Maternity	5.2%	4.9%
• Psychiatric	13.9%	14.2%
• Supra-district	1.5%	1.1%
• Supra-regional	1.2%	0.4%
• Other	1.6%	2.9%
• Day Care	1.4%	2.3%
• Community	17.3%	17.1%
Purchaser HCHS expenditure		
Total DHA health-care-related expenditure:	£3.2 billion	£14.7 billion
Proportion in each expenditure category:		
• General and acute	58%	58%
• Mental illness	15%	12%
• Primary care	10%	11%
• Mental handicap	6%	7%
• Maternity	5%	5%
• A&E	3%	3%
• Other contractual	2%	4%

Provider finances

	London	*Rest of England*
Total provider income:	£4.4 billion	£17.6 billion
Services income:	£3.6 billion	£15.7 billion
Other income (e.g. education, training and research):	£867 million	£1.8 billion
Proportion of services income, by source:		
• DHAs	89%	89%
• GPFHs	4%	8%
• NHS Trusts	1%	1%
• Department of Health	4%	<1%
• Private patients	2%	1%
• Other non-NHS	1%	1%
Acute provider average income:	£76 million	£63 million
• services income	£59 million	£56 million
• other income	£17 million	£8 million
Non-acute provider average income:	£38 million	£31 million
• services income	£34 million	£28 million
• other income	£4 million	£3 million

Provider finances (contd.)	*London*	*Rest of England*
Total provider expenditure:	£4.2 billion	£16.7 billion
Proportion in each expenditure category:		
• Services from other NHS bodies	3%	4%
• Board members remuneration	<1%	1%
• Staff costs	63%	65%
• Clinical supplies and services	12%	10%
• General supplies and services	2%	2%
• Establishment, transport and premises	10%	10%
• Financial costs	4%	4%
• Other	5%	3%

DHA expenditure

	London	Rest of England
Total DHA expenditure:	£3.4 billion	£15.4 billion
Health-care related services expenditure:	£3.2 billion	£14.7 billion
Total DHA expenditure per capita resident population:	£483	£368
Proportion of health-care-related expenditure, by expenditure category:		
• Trusts	93%	95%
• Other NHS providers	1%	1%
• Non-NHS providers	3%	2%
• Joint projects with local authorities	1%	1%
• Care in the Community	2%	1%

FHS expenditure

	London	Rest of England
Total expenditure on FHS:	£1.1 billion	£7.3 billion
FHS expenditure per capita resident population:	£141	£136
Proportion of FHS expenditure, by expenditure category:		
• GMS	40%	38%
• GOS	3%	3%
• PS	48%	56%
• DoH Initiative Funding	4%	<1%
• Administration	5%	3%

Social services expenditure

	London	Rest of England
Total expenditure on personal social services:	£1.6 billion	£5.9 billion
Proportion in each expenditure category:		
• Older people	39%	50%
• Children	31%	24%
• Learning disabilities	12%	13%
• Physical disabilities	7%	7%
• Mental health	6%	4%
• Central strategic	2%	1%
• Other	3%	1%

1 Introduction

This chapter considers the provision and use of financial resources for health-related services in London. Expenditure on Hospital and Community Health Services (HCHS) is analysed from both a provider and a purchaser perspective, outlining relative expenditure on individual health programmes and specialty groups. Analysis of provider HCHS expenditure allows comparisons between London and the rest of England of the proportion of total expenditure accounted for by individual specialties; analysis of purchaser HCHS expenditure allows comparisons of per capita spend on the various health care programmes.

Having presented this overview of health care expenditure, we provide more detailed analyses of provider finances based on summarised accounts. Data are presented relating to income source and expenditure type, staff costs and asset values. Further analysis of DHA expenditure is then presented, including some discussion of the formula for allocation of NHS financial resources. Using Family Health Services (FHS) accounts, we consider expenditure on the components of FHS. Finally, a financial analysis of social services expenditure is provided.

2 Data sources

This section is based on DoH data. These include data from the HFR22, HFR24 and TR2 returns that describe programme budgets in the NHS, as well as trust, DHA and FHSA summarised accounts. Social services data are taken from the Department of Health Local Authority Key Indicators (DoH, 1996f).

3 HCHS expenditure

In the past, it has been possible to present details of Hospital and Community Services (HCHS) expenditure, by DHA, on the basis of health care programme budgets, using data contained in the Health Service Indicators (Boyle and Smaje, 1992). These data are no longer available. Repeating the analysis is further complicated by the reorganisation of the NHS into purchasers and providers and the implications of this for the allocation of provider costs between purchasers. We are able to present data for providers, based on the DoH financial returns, HFR22 and TFR2, and for purchasers, based on the DoH financial return, HFR24. These returns aggregate expenditure differently, and this, combined with the effect of flows of cash and activity between purchasers and providers, makes reconciliation of the data impossible, particularly at a low geographical level.

Thus, we present separate analyses for purchasers and providers. These allow us to compare patterns of expenditure by hospitals in London and England, and to relate the expenditure by DHAs in the capital to that of DHAs in the rest of the country.

Provider HCHS expenditure

(Technical note: provider-based DoH financial returns allow an analysis of individual specialty expenditure at trusts (TFR2) and DMUs (HFR22) as well as total day care and community expenditure. These returns are not intended to reconcile to total NHS expenditure. They should reconcile to 'operating expenses less other operating income' as recorded in the provider income and expenditure account. In 90 per cent of cases the returns reconcile to within £100,000 of this.

The 'other' specialty group includes lines 501 to 599 of the financial return, comprising general practice non-maternity, radiotherapy, pathological, radiology, anaesthetics and A&E specialties. Total community comprises main code 73, lines 101-130, which detail expenditure on community nurses and other health programmes such as chiropody. Total day care comprises main code 70, lines 901 to 950, which detail expenditure on day hospital care, as opposed to acute day cases.)

A comparison is provided between types of socio-economic area in London and England. Table 1 compares absolute levels of expenditure. Table 2 considers these as a proportion of total expenditure. Specialty groups are those given in the DoH returns. Expenditures on in-patients and out-patients, where relevant, are combined.

Table 1: Provider HCHS expenditure, London and England, 1994/95

| Expenditure group | London | | | | Non-London | | | | England |
	Inner-deprived £m	Mixed-status £m	High-status £m	Total £m	Inner-deprived £m	Mixed-status £m	High-status £m	Total £m	£m
Medical	552	227	267	1,047	722	889	1,463	3,912	4,959
Surgical	396	212	259	868	703	930	1,506	4,037	4,904
Maternity	74	41	57	173	101	166	272	681	854
Psychiatric	187	157	117	461	209	421	835	1,985	2,446
Supra-district	32	7	11	50	67	26	47	156	206
Supra-regional	26	6	9	41	29	2	21	62	103
Other	30	9	14	52	79	60	156	408	461
Total day care	15	16	15	46	36	74	125	322	367
Total community	239	141	192	572	247	537	839	2,382	2,954
Total	1,552	816	942	3,310	2,193	3,104	5,265	13,944	17,253

Table 1 indicates the importance of providers in inner-deprived London: these account for 47 per cent of all London HCHS expenditure, 64 per cent of London supra-district expenditure, 63 per cent of supra-regional expenditure and 53 per cent of expenditure on medical specialties.

London providers account for 19 per cent of national HCHS expenditure. By comparison, 16 per cent of England's FCEs are provided in London and 14 per cent of England's population lives in the capital. This greater than proportionate expenditure by London hospitals reflects both the flow of non-Londoners to London hospitals and the higher costs of provision in London. However, there is variation between specialty groups. Whereas 40 per cent of supra-regional specialty expenditure is accounted for by London providers, just 13 per cent of total day care expenditure is in London and 11 per cent of 'other specialty' expenditure.

Table 2 demonstrates considerable variation in the proportion of total expenditure on different specialty groups, both between types of socio-economic area in London, and between London and the rest of the country. In England as a whole, approximately the same proportion is spent on medical and surgical specialties. This holds consistently throughout the country with the exception of inner-deprived London hospitals where 36 per cent of total expenditure is accounted for by medical specialties and just 26 per cent by surgical. Approximately the same proportion is spent on community services in both London and the rest of England, although there is some variation between types of socio-economic area. There is a lower proportion of total expenditure on community services in inner-deprived areas, which is more marked outside London.

Table 2: Composition of provider HCHS expenditure, London and England, 1994/95

Expenditure group	London				Non-London				England
	Inner-deprived %	Mixed-status %	High-status %	Total %	Inner-deprived %	Mixed-status %	High-status %	Total %	%
Medical	35.6	27.9	28.4	31.6	32.9	28.6	27.8	28.1	28.7
Surgical	25.5	26.0	27.5	26.2	32.1	29.9	28.6	28.9	28.4
Maternity	4.8	5.0	6.1	5.2	4.6	5.3	5.2	4.9	4.9
Psychiatric	12.0	19.3	12.4	13.9	9.5	13.6	15.9	14.2	14.2
Supra-district	2.1	0.8	1.2	1.5	3.0	0.8	0.9	1.1	1.2
Supra-regional	1.7	0.7	1.0	1.2	1.3	0.1	0.4	0.4	0.6
Other	1.9	1.1	1.4	1.6	3.6	1.9	3.0	2.9	2.7
Total day care	1.0	1.9	1.5	1.4	1.6	2.4	2.4	2.3	2.1
Total community	15.4	17.3	20.4	17.3	11.3	17.3	15.9	17.1	17.1
Total	100	100	100	100	100	100	100	100	100

Purchaser HCHS expenditure

(Technical note: HCHS expenditure by DHA is taken from the DoH financial return, HFR24. This total is divided between seven expenditure groups: mental handicap, mental illness, maternity, general and acute, A&E, primary care and other contractual expenditure. Total expenditure does not reconcile in each case with the total health-care-related expenditure figure in the DHA accounts. In England as a whole the difference is £186 million. Hence, tables based on this return do not reconcile exactly with those based on DHA accounts provided in Section 5. As data are missing for Barking and Havering, this DHA is excluded from this analysis. The total health-care-related expenditure of this DHA was approximately £135 million. The groups used to describe purchaser HCHS expenditure do not correspond to those used to describe provider expenditure. Primary care includes community services that are not part of another group, i.e. excluding community maternity, mental illness and mental handicap services. A&E refers to A&E department expenditure. Other contractual income is a catch-all for expenditure not classified elsewhere.)

A comparison is provided between types of socio-economic area in London and England. Table 3 compares absolute levels of total DHA expenditure, by health care programme. Table 4 relates DHA expenditure to resident population.

London DHAs, including Barking and Havering, are responsible for approximately 17.5 per cent of total HCHS expenditure by English DHAs. This compares with the 19 per cent of total national HCHS expenditure accounted for by London hospitals: the difference reflects the purchase of services from London hospitals by non-London purchasers.

Table 3: HCHS expenditure by DHA, by programme, London and England, 1994/95

Health programme	London				Non-London				England
	Inner-deprived £m	Mixed-status £m	High-status £m	Total £m	Inner-deprived £m	Mixed-status £m	High-status £m	Total £m	£m
General and acute	713	607	434	1,754	1,170	2,057	3,141	8,547	10,301
Mental illness	189	187	89	465	259	443	680	1,825	2,290
Primary care	119	121	77	317	173	432	602	1,568	1,885
Mental handicap	42	73	57	172	115	219	423	961	1,133
Maternity	52	59	38	150	94	211	317	806	956
A&E	37	44	24	105	72	124	186	506	611
Other contractual	16	49	7	73	65	118	241	526	598
Total	1,168	1,141	726	3,035	1,947	3,605	5,589	14,739	17,774

(Tables 3 and 4 contain no data for Barking and Havering.)

Figure 1 shows similar proportions of expenditure by programme in both London and the rest of the country. The general and acute group accounts for the greatest proportion of expenditure, 58 per cent of total in both London and the rest of England. The most notable difference is the additional expenditure on mental illness in the capital which accounts for 15 per cent of expenditure in London but only 12 per cent in the rest of the country. By contrast, expenditure on primary care and the 'other contractual' group in London is a smaller proportion of total expenditure than is the case in the rest of the country.

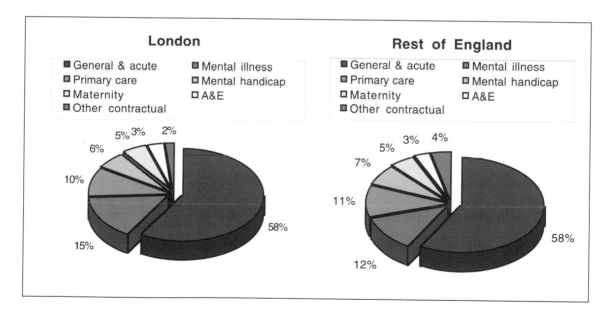

Figure 1: Proportion of expenditure, by programme, London and England, 1994/95

Table 4 compares per capita DHA expenditure, by programme, in London with the rest of the country. With the exception of other contractual income which accounts for only a small proportion of total, London DHAs spend more per capita on each programme than the rest of the country. Total expenditure per capita in London is 30 per cent greater than in the rest of the country. Individual programmes vary, with expenditure on mental handicap 13 per cent greater in London and mental illness 61 per cent greater.

Total expenditure per capita in inner-deprived London is 41 per cent greater than in similar areas in the rest of the country. On the other hand, comparing mixed- and high-status areas, expenditure in London is just 18 and 15 per cent more respectively. In both London and the rest of the country, expenditure increases with level of deprivation. However, this gradient is more pronounced in London. Inner-deprived London DHAs spend 52 per cent more per capita in total than high-status London DHAs. By contrast, total expenditure per capita is only 24 per cent greater in inner-deprived DHAs outside the capital than in DHAs in non-London high-status areas.

Table 4: HCHS expenditure by DHA, per capita resident population, by programme, London and England, 1994/95

Health programme	London				Non-London				England
	Inner-deprived	Mixed-status	High-status	Total	Inner-deprived	Mixed-status	High-status	Total	
	£	£	£	£	£	£	£	£	£
General and acute	352	229	227	266	247	207	186	205	213
Mental illness	93	70	47	71	55	45	40	44	47
Primary care	59	46	40	48	36	44	36	38	39
Mental handicap	21	28	30	26	24	22	25	23	23
Maternity	26	22	20	23	20	21	19	19	20
A&E	18	17	13	16	15	12	11	12	13
Other contractual	8	19	4	11	14	12	14	13	12
Total	577	430	380	460	410	363	331	353	368

Detailed comparisons with 1989/90 are not possible because of the different presentation of data since the introduction of the split between purchasers and providers. Boundary changes, mergers of DHAs and changes in the constituent members of the socio-economic groupings since 1989/90 further complicate comparisons.

Figure 2 shows HCHS expenditure per capita as a variation from the England average, across types of socio-economic area in London and the rest of England. Actual England expenditure is indexed to a value of 100.

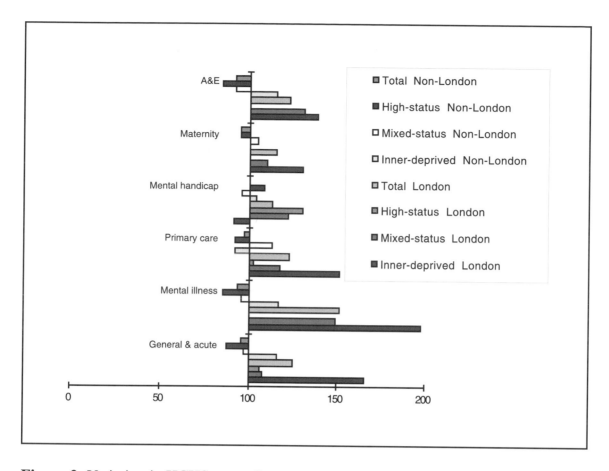

Figure 2: Variation in HCHS expenditure by DHA, per capita resident population, by programme, London and England, 1994/95 (England =100)

4 Provider finances

This section considers the financial position of trusts and directly managed units (DMUs) in London in more detail and provides comparisons with the rest of the country. Sections are included on:

- source of income and type of expenditure;

- a detailed breakdown of staff costs; and,

- an analysis of the value of fixed assets of London trusts, including estate, buildings and equipment, as well as assets under construction.

An assessment of the performance of trusts against the financial target of a six per cent return on capital employed is presented in Chapter 10, *'Measures of Efficiency'*.

Income and expenditure

Table 5 shows income and expenditure, in accordance with the NHS trust account summarisation schedules, for London providers – trusts and DMUs – by sector. Income is divided between 'services', which is essentially income for services purchased, and 'other' which includes funding for education and research, and for patient transport services as well as monies received from income generation and charitable contributions.

Understanding the various surpluses described in NHS accounts is important. Trusts incur costs other than operating expenses, largely connected with the transfer of ownership of capital assets to the trust. These costs must be met from income received. Thus, operating surplus does not equate to total surplus achieved by the trust. Box 1 considers the additional costs borne by NHS trusts.

Box 1: Understanding the surpluses

The operating surplus of a trust is modified by any profit or loss made on the disposal of fixed assets. It is also modified by any interest that the trust must pay or should receive. The interest payable will reflect the Interest Bearing Debt (IBD) that the trust owes the exchequer following the transfer of assets to the trust at its formation. The surplus is further modified by the payment of a dividend on Public Dividend Capital. The Public Dividend Capital (PDC) is a form of long-term government finance for the remainder of the value of the trust assets on which the trust must pay the government dividends. Dividends are only paid if the trust is in surplus after fixed interest obligations have been met. Further information is available in the *'Introductory Guide to NHS Finance in the UK', (HFMA/CIPFA, 1995).*

Table 5: Provider income and expenditure, by sector of London, 1994/95

Sector	Services income		Other income		Operating expenses		Operating surplus		Retained surplus	
	£m	%	£m	%	£m	%	£m	%	£m	%
North West	908	25	329	38	1,160	28	78	35	11	31
North Central	753	21	143	16	850	20	46	20	10	28
East	634	18	163	19	760	18	37	16	8	22
South East	751	21	154	18	865	21	39	17	2	6
South	517	15	78	9	569	14	26	12	5	14
London	3,563	100	867	100	4,204	100	226	100	36	100

(Tables 5-8 combine trust and DMU data.)

Table 5 shows that the north-west sector has the greatest proportion of provider income, expenditure, and surpluses in London, reflecting a greater level of activity. 'Other income' accounts for a greater proportion of total income in this sector, when compared with other parts of London: this is due to a higher than average proportion of research funding. The south sector has the smallest proportion of the capital's income, expenditure and operating surplus, although retained surpluses are greater in this sector than in the neighbouring south-east sector. Although the north-west sector has the greatest operating surplus expressed as a proportion of total income, the retained surplus is a smaller proportion of total income than that of either the north-central or east sectors. This reflects greater interest payments and PDC dividends payable in the north west.

Table 6 shows that providers in inner-deprived London account for nearly half of all income and expenditure in the capital. 'Other income' is particularly important in these areas: 59 per cent of 'other income' in the capital is received by inner-deprived providers compared with 47 per cent of services income. In comparison with the rest of England, London trusts have greater operating surpluses relative to total income – 5.1 compared with 4.8 per cent – but the retained surplus is identical in London and the rest of the country, at 0.8 per cent. Thus, the costs of interest and PDC dividends are proportionately greater in London than in the rest of the country. The proportion of income and expenditure accounted for by DMUs is greater in London than in the rest of the country – seven per cent in the capital compared to four per cent elsewhere. Trust income is considered in more detail in Box 2.

Table 6: Provider income and expenditure, London and England, 1994/95

Type of Area	Services income £m	Other income £m	Operating expenses £m	Operating surplus £m	Retained surplus £m
Inner-deprived London	1,666	512	2,070	108	21
Mixed-status London	970	256	1,158	69	7
High-status London	926	99	976	49	8
London	3,563	867	4,204	226	36
Inner-deprived Non-London	2,499	448	2,805	142	30
Mixed-status Non-London	3,475	317	3,605	187	42
High-status Non-London	6,091	752	6,522	321	45
Non-London	15,729	1,826	16,714	841	148
England	19,292	2,693	20,918	1,067	184

The source of provider income

We turn now to analyse services income in more detail. NHS accounts allow services income to be attributed to the following sources:

- health authorities (DHAs);

- general practice fundholders (GPFHs);

- NHS trusts;

- Department of Health (DoH);

- Non-NHS – private patients; and,

- Non-NHS – other.

Table 7 compares actual level of income from each source, and this as a proportion of total income, by sector of London. Although DHAs provide the majority of income in each sector, there is some variation between other sources. Providers in the north west have a greater proportion of income from private patients than other sectors. On the other hand, the Department of Health provides proportionately more income to the south-east and north-central sectors. The greater than average proportion of income from GPFHs in the south sector reflects the high proportion of fundholding practices in this area. Providers in the east sector are more reliant on DHAs for income. This is due in part to the number of DMUs in the sector which rely almost entirely on DHAs for funding.

Table 7: Source of services income, by sector of London, 1994/95

Sector	DHAs		GPFHs		NHS Trusts		DoH		Private Patients		Non-NHS Other		Total
	£m	%	£m	%	£m	%	£m	%	£m	%	£m	%	£m
North West	802	88	41	5	8	1	15	2	39	4	3	0	908
North Central	629	84	19	3	6	1	65	9	25	3	9	1	753
East	602	95	15	2	1	0	5	1	5	1	5	1	634
South East	653	87	28	4	2	0	51	7	13	2	3	0	751
South	471	91	36	7	2	0	2	0	4	1	2	0	517
London	3,158	89	140	4	20	1	138	4	86	2	22	1	3,563

Table 8, which compares London providers with those in the rest of England, shows that they receive a greater proportion of income from private patients – two compared with one per cent – and the Department of Health – four compared with virtually zero. The comparative importance of private patient income in London is demonstrated by the fact that London providers earn 44 per cent of total NHS income from private patients but only 18 per cent of total income from DHAs. By contrast, London, which has proportionately fewer GPFHs than the rest of the country, has a smaller proportion of income from fundholding practices – four against eight per cent.

Table 8: Source of services income, London and England, 1994/95

Type of Area	DHAs		GPFHs		NHS Trusts		DoH		Private Patients		Non-NHS Other		Total
	£m	%	£m	%	£m	%	£m	%	£m	%	£m	%	£m
Inner-deprived London	1,423	85	35	2	12	1	123	7	61	4	13	1	1,666
Mixed-status London	897	92	42	4	5	1	6	1	16	2	6	1	970
High-status London	838	90	64	7	3	0	10	1	9	1	3	0	926
London	3,158	89	140	4	19	1	138	4	86	2	22	1	3,563
Inner-deprived Non-London	2,273	91	148	6	26	1	26	1	19	1	7	0	2,499
Mixed-status Non-London	3,127	90	277	8	42	1	4	0	15	0	11	0	3,475
High-status Non-London	5,314	87	571	9	70	1	15	0	58	1	56	1	6,083
Non-London	13,948	89	1,323	8	198	1	46	0	109	1	96	1	15,721
England	17,106	89	1,462	8	217	1	185	1	195	1	118	1	19,284

(Table 8 excludes from the high-status non-London total, £7.9 million income at the North East Thames Regional Burns Unit which is not attributed in the account summaries.)

Providers in inner-deprived areas of London rely on different sources of income compared with those in similar areas in the rest of the country. They receive a greater proportion of income from the Department of Health – seven against one per cent – and private patients – four against one per cent – than providers in non-London inner-deprived areas. By contrast, DHAs – 85 compared with 91 per cent – and GPFHs – two compared with six per cent –

provide a smaller proportion of income. The difference between London and the rest of the country in mixed-status and high-status areas, while still evident, is more modest. Private patient income is examined in more detail in Box 3.

Box 2: Trust Income

Table 9: The ten NHS trusts in England with the greatest total income,1994/95

Trust	Total Income £m
Guy's and St Thomas's	256
The Royal Hospitals	229
Hammersmith Hospitals	208
Southampton University Hospitals	164
Royal Victoria Infirmary	163
United Leeds Hospitals	159
United Bristol Healthcare	157
South Manchester University Hospital	149
St George's Hospital	143
University College London Hospital	142
Central Manchester	140

Table 9 shows that the three trusts with the greatest income in England are large teaching hospitals in London. Two others feature in the top ten by income. Indeed, of 35 trusts with total incomes in excess of £100 million in 1994/95, ten are in London. The NHS trust with the smallest income is also in London. The Royal London Homeopathic has an income of just over £3 million.

Four of the top five trust operating surpluses are in London, although this reflects the greater total income of London trusts. However, taking operating surplus as a proportion of total income, London appears less dominant. Trusts with very large income and expenditure no longer predominate. Indeed, the smallest trust in the country, the Royal London Homeopathic, features in the top five shown in Table 10.

Table 10: The five NHS trusts in England with the greatest operating surplus as a proportion of total income, 1994/95

Trust	Total income £m	Operating expenses £m	Operating surplus £m	Surplus as % of income %
Heathlands Mental Health Services	30	25	5	16
Northgate and Prudhoe	31	27	4	14
Chelsea and Westminster	96	84	13	13
Royal London Homeopathic	3.2	2.8	0.4	13
East Surrey Learning Disability & Mental Health Services	30	26	4	12

Box 3: Private Patient Income

Table 11 shows that London providers dominate the list of providers with the greatest services income from private patients. Eight of the top ten are at least partly in inner-deprived London and five in the north-west sector. Although, for most trusts, services income provides by far the greatest proportion of total income, several of those listed from London rely heavily on education, research and training funds, as is shown in Table 18. Hence, the proportion of *total* income from private patients in such cases may be relatively small.

Table 11: The top ten NHS providers in England, by services income from private patients, 1994/95

Trust	*Private Patients* *£m*
Guy's and St Thomas's	10.0
Royal Marsden	9.5
Royal Free Hampstead	8.7
Hammersmith Hospitals	7.9
University College Hospitals	7.1
Great Ormond Street Hospital for Sick Children	6.2
St Mary's Hospital	5.8
Royal Brompton	4.7
Oxford Radcliffe	4.4
Northwick Park and St Mark's	2.9

Table 12 shows that London providers are among those which receive the greatest proportion of services income from private patients. Such trusts tend to obtain more income per private patient than income per NHS patient. For example, over half of services income at the Royal Marsden stems from private activity, yet less than 20 per cent of its FCEs are non-NHS. As for total private patient income, the north-west sector and inner-deprived London are well-represented on this list.

Table 12: The top ten NHS providers in England, by proportion of services income from private patients, 1994/95

Trust	*Proportion of services income from private patients* *%*
Royal Marsden	53
Royal Brompton	25
Nuffield Orthopaedic Centre	12
Wrightington Hospital	11
Harefield Hospital	10
Royal National Orthopaedic Hospital	9
Royal Free Hampstead	9
Great Ormond Street Hospital for Sick Children	8
Hammersmith Hospitals	8
Liverpool Cardiothoracic Centre	8

Other operating income

We now consider other operating income which includes funding for education, training and research, patient transport services, and monies received from income generation and charitable contributions. As Table 13 shows, such income is by no means negligible, totalling £867 million in London. This is 20 per cent of total provider income.

Over half of this £867 million is accounted for by 'education, training and research', with most of the remainder by 'other income'. In both cases the north-west sector has the greatest income. Almost 40 per cent of 'other operating income' in London is accounted for by providers in this sector. The situation at individual trusts may greatly affect the position of any given sector. For example, there is £3 million of charitable contributions in the southeast sector of which £2 million is accounted for by one trust.

Table 13: Other operating income, by type, by sector of London, 1994/95

Sector	Patient transport	Education, training & research	Charitable contributions	Transfers from donation reserve	Other income	Total other operating income
	£m	£m	£m	£m	£m	£m
North West	0	203	2	3	121	329
North Central	0	77	0	3	63	143
East	-	69	1	2	92	173
South East	0	86	3	3	61	154
South	-	38	0	1	39	78
London	1	473	6	12	375	867

(Table 13 combines trusts and DMUs. DMUs in London have £39 million of other operating income. All bar £400,000 is in 'other income'. However, this category may not be identical to the 'other income' category for trusts as there are fewer categories of other operating income recorded in DMU accounts.)

Table 14 shows that other operating income is most significant in the north-west sector where it accounts for 27 per cent of total income. Education, training and research is particularly important in this sector, accounting for 16 per cent of total income. This is a consequence of the location of several large teaching hospitals and former SHAs in the sector: see Tables 17 and 18.

Table 14: Other operating income as a proportion of total income, by sector of London, 1994/95

Sector	Patient transport	Education, training & research	Charitable contri- butions	Transfers from donation reserve	Other income	Total other operating income	Total income
	%	%	%	%	%	%	£m
North West	0.00	16	0.13	0.24	10	27	1,237
North Central	0.03	9	0.02	0.35	7	17	896
East	0.00	11	0.10	0.28	10	22	797
South East	0.03	9	0.34	0.37	7	17	905
South	0.00	7	0.06	0.14	6	13	595
London	0.01	11	0.14	0.28	8	20	4,430

(Table 14 combines trusts and DMUs.)

Table 15 shows that London providers receive £867 million, 32 per cent of all 'other operating income' in England. By contrast, they receive 18 per cent of 'services income'. In other words, London providers are less reliant on income from providing services than their counterparts in the rest of the country. Funding for education and research is particularly important in London. Forty-three per cent of national education and research income goes to London providers, 32 per cent to those in the three northern sectors of London, and 19 per cent to the north west sector alone. Outside London the 'other income' category is more important than education, training and research funding, accounting for 63 per cent of all 'other operating income'.

Table 15: Other operating income, by type, London and England, 1994/95

Type of Area	Patient transport	Education, training & research	Charitable contri- butions	Transfers from donation reserve	Other income	Total other operating income
	£m	£m	£m	£m	£m	£m
Inner-deprived London	0	304	4	9	194	513
Mixed-status London	0	128	0	1	127	257
High-status London	0	41	2	2	55	99
London	1	473	6	12	375	867
Inner-deprived Non-London	0	193	2	7	246	448
Mixed-status Non-London	1	109	4	4	200	317
High-status Non-London	1	249	15	10	477	752
Non-London	4	618	24	26	1,153	1,825
England	4	1,091	30	38	1,528	2,692

(Tables 15 and 16 combine trusts and DMUs; excluded from the high-status non-London total is £324,000 at the North East Thames Regional Burns Unit which is not attributed in the account summaries.)

Table 16 shows that in London as a whole, the proportion of total income arising from 'other operating income' is twice that in the rest of England – 20 compared with ten per cent. Moreover, in London, education, training and research funding represents 11 per cent of total income, compared with just four per cent in the rest of the country.

Table 16: Other operating income as a proportion of total income, London and England, 1994/95

Type of Area	Patient transport	Education, training & research	Charitable contri- butions	Transfers from donation reserve	Other income	Total other operating income	Total income
	%	%	%	%	%	%	£m
Inner-deprived London	0.00	14	0.19	0.42	9	24	2,146
Mixed-status London	0.00	11	0.00	0.08	10	21	1,220
High-status London	0.00	4	0.20	0.20	5	10	1,024
London	0.02	11	0.14	0.27	9	20	4,391
Inner-deprived Non-London	0.00	7	0.07	0.24	8	15	2,901
Mixed-status Non-London	0.03	3	0.11	0.11	5	8	3,788
High-status Non-London	0.01	4	0.22	0.15	7	11	6,808
Non-London	0.02	4	0.14	0.15	7	10	17,466
England	0.02	5	0.14	0.17	7	12	21,857

Education, training and research income

Education, training and research income is now considered in more detail. Table 17 shows that the eight trusts with the greatest income from education, training and research are in London (shown in bold type). These eight trusts account for 30 per cent of total income in England from this source. Indeed, the Hammersmith and Royal Hospitals trusts *together* account for ten per cent. Table 18 shows that income from education, training and research represents over half the total income of three London trusts. All ten trusts most dependent on such income are in London.

Table 17: The ten NHS trusts in England with the greatest income from education, training and research, 1994/95

Trust	Education, training and research £m
Hammersmith Hospitals	59.0
The Royal Hospitals	48.7
Guy's and St Thomas's	43.5
Royal Marsden	36.2
Royal Brompton	29.9
King's Healthcare	27.4
University College Hospitals	24.6
St George's Hospital	22.8
Central Manchester	22.3
Southampton University Hospitals	21.8

Table 18: The ten NHS trusts in England with the greatest proportion of total income from education, training and research, 1994/95

Trust	Education, training & research as a proportion of total income	
	%	£m
Royal Marsden	63	(57.6)
Tavistock and Portman	54	(7.1)
Royal Brompton	53	(56.9)
Hammersmith Hospitals	28	(207.6)
The Royal Hospitals	21	(228.7)
King's Healthcare	20	(138.5)
Moorfields Eye Hospital	18	(30.7)
University College Hospitals	17	(142.5)
Guy's and St Thomas's	17	(256.3)
Chelsea and Westminster Healthcare	17	(96.2)

(Table 18 gives total income in £ million in brackets.)

These figures reflect the position in 1994/95. However, changes to streams of research funding – often referred to as the Culyer reforms – may have significant implications for the distribution of funding described above. Trusts have been required to make assessments of the proportion of current levels of expenditure devoted to research.

Average provider income

We conclude our analysis of provider income by comparing average income for acute and non-acute providers between London and the rest of England. 'Acute' in this context is defined as acute, single specialty other than mental health, and combined providers; non-acute refers to community and mental health providers.

Figure 3 shows that acute providers in London as a whole have an average income 20 per cent greater than providers in the rest of the country – £76 million compared with £63 million. In each type of socio-economic area, the average income of acute hospitals is greater in London than in the rest of the country. Acute providers in inner-deprived areas have the highest average incomes, both in London and the rest of England – £82 million and £80 million respectively. The majority of large teaching hospitals are located in these areas.

Other income is more significant for acute providers in London, representing 22 per cent of total average income compared with 12 per cent in the rest of the country. This is a particularly important source of income in inner-deprived London. Indeed, on average, providers in inner-deprived areas of the capital derive less income from activity than those in high-status areas of London or in inner-deprived areas of the rest of the country. Nevertheless, due to the extent of other income, average total income in inner-deprived London is greater than that elsewhere in the country.

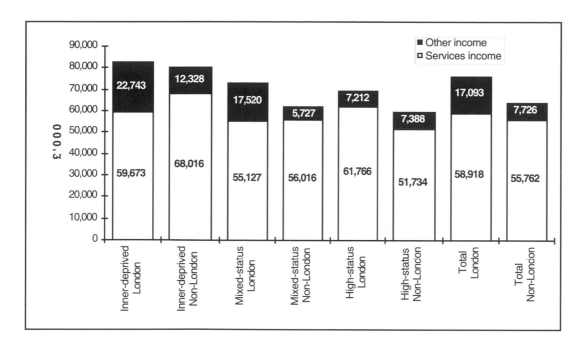

Figure 3: Average income of acute providers, London and England, 1994/95

Figure 4 shows that the average income of non-acute providers in both London and the rest of the country is a little under half that of acute providers. Average income in London is £38 million, compared with £31 million in the rest of England. Other income is less significant for non-acute providers. Even in inner-deprived London just 11 per cent of total income is derived from sources other than patient activity.

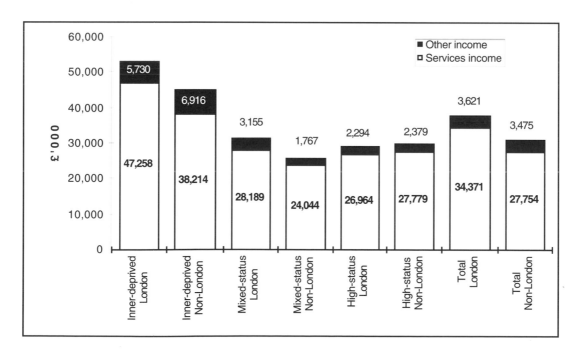

Figure 4: Average income of non-acute providers, London and England, 1994/95

The composition of expenditure

We now analyse operating expenditure according to expenditure type identified in the NHS accounts. Table 19 shows, by sector of London, the composition of expenditure in absolute and percentage terms. Total expenditure is greatest in the north west.

Sixty-three per cent of provider expenditure in London as a whole is accounted for by staff costs, ranging from 59 per cent in the north west to 66 per cent in the south. Clinical supplies and services and the costs of establishment, transport and premises each account for more than ten per cent of total expenditure in each sector. Other groups account for five per cent or less. Expenditure on board members' remuneration is relatively low throughout the country, at one per cent of total, accounting for £21 million in London and £127 million in England as a whole.

Table 19: The composition of provider operating expenditure, by sector of London, 1994/95

Sector	Services from other NHS bodies		Board members		Staff costs		Clinical supplies		General supplies		Establishment, etc.		Financial costs		Other		Total
	£m	%	£m	%	£m	%	£m	%	£m	%	£m	%	£m	%	£m	%	£m
North West	49	4	7	1	688	59	145	13	32	3	133	11	49	4	57	5	1,160
North Central	28	3	4	0	544	64	98	12	17	2	81	10	38	4	41	5	850
East	17	2	2	0	488	64	91	12	18	2	72	9	33	4	38	5	760
South East	22	3	4	0	545	63	111	13	18	2	88	10	33	4	44	5	865
South	17	3	3	1	375	66	55	10	14	2	58	10	25	4	23	4	569
London	133	3	21	0	2,638	63	500	12	100	2	433	10	174	4	201	5	4,204

Table 20 shows that 20 per cent of operating expenditure nationally is accounted for by London providers. The capital's providers spend a lower proportion on services from other NHS bodies and more on 'other' services than is the case in the rest of the country. Expenditure on staff in London at 63 per cent is less than the 65 per cent spent elsewhere in England. However, London providers spend 12 per cent of total expenditure on clinical services and supplies compared with ten per cent nationally.

Table 20: The composition of provider operating expenditure, London and England, 1994/95

Type of Area	Services from other NHS bodies		Board members		Staff costs		Clinical supplies		General supplies		Establish- ment, etc.		Financial costs		Other		Total
	£m	%	£m	%	£m	%	£m	%	£m	%	£m	%	£m	%	£m	%	£m
Inner-deprived London	68	3	8	0	1,257	61	280	14	43	2	208	10	91	4	115	6	2,071
Mixed-status London	36	3	7	1	733	63	156	13	32	3	125	11	45	4	57	5	1,158
High-status London	29	3	5	1	648	66	98	10	25	3	99	10	39	4	33	3	976
London	133	3	21	0	2,638	63	500	12	100	2	463	10	174	4	201	5	4,204
Inner-deprived Non-London	115	4	13	0	1,770	63	367	13	60	2	262	9	128	5	91	3	2,805
Mixed-status Non-London	150	4	22	1	2,386	66	340	9	83	2	364	10	142	4	118	3	3,605
High-status Non-London	284	4	44	1	4,186	64	650	10	144	2	686	11	262	4	257	4	6,509
Non-London	729	4	106	1	10,834	65	1,703	10	375	2	1,706	10	674	4	577	3	16,701
England	862	4	127	1	13,481	64	2,204	11	475	2	2,138	10	850	4	781	4	20,918

Staff costs

(Technical note: national total expenditure on staff costs is £10 million greater in the disaggregated staff expenditure table (TAC09) than it is in the total expenditure table (TAC06). This is not explained or accounted for in the DoH's figures. This discrepancy is only a fraction of total expenditure on staff, and is spread across trusts in all areas of the country. Thus, it is unlikely to invalidate the analysis.)

In this section we provide a more detailed analysis of expenditure on trust staff, showing a breakdown by costs of salaries and wages, social security contributions and other pensions, and agency staff. Staff costs are slightly less than those in Tables 19 and 20 as these were based on combined trust and DMU figures. Table 21 shows that London trusts spend over £2 billion on salaries and wages alone. In London as a whole, six per cent of total staff costs are accounted for by agency staff. Expenditure on agency staff in the three sectors north of the Thames is proportionately greater than that in the south sectors.

Table 21: Expenditure on trust staff, by sector of London, 1994/95

Sector	Salaries & wages		Social Security costs		Other pension costs		Agency staff		Total
	£m	%	£m	%	£m	%	£m	%	£m
North West	586	84	47	7	17	2	43	6	693
North Central	436	84	34	7	13	3	33	6	517
East	318	85	24	6	9	2	22	6	373
South East	472	86	35	6	14	3	27	5	547
South	296	87	23	7	9	3	13	4	340
London	2,107	85	163	7	61	2	138	6	2,470

Table 22 compares expenditure on staff in London with that in the rest of the country. Trusts in London account for around 19 per cent of the £13 billion spent on NHS staff in England. The proportion of total staff expenditure accounted for by agency staff in London, at six per cent of total, is a much more significant factor than elsewhere in England, where it accounts for just one per cent. Indeed, 49 per cent of national expenditure on agency staff takes place in London compared with only 18 per cent of national expenditure on salaries and wages. This would suggest that London has greater problems in recruiting and retaining staff, and possibly also with higher sickness rates.

Table 22: Expenditure on trust staff, London and England, 1994/95

Type of Area	Salaries & wages		Social Security costs		Other pension costs		Agency staff		Total
	£m	%	£m	%	£m	%	£m	%	£m
Inner-deprived London	944	84	72	6	27	2	76	7	1,119
Mixed-status London	606	85	47	7	18	3	39	5	710
High-status London	557	87	44	7	16	2	23	4	641
London	2,107	85	163	7	61	2	138	6	2,470
Inner-deprived Non-London	1,471	90	105	6	44	3	21	1	1,641
Mixed-status Non-London	2,118	90	153	6	64	3	20	1	2,355
High-status Non-London	3,655	89	268	7	109	3	74	2	4,107
Non-London	9,447	89	688	7	287	3	145	1	10,567
England	11,554	89	851	7	348	3	283	2	13,037

Nine of the ten trusts nationally with the greatest proportion of expenditure on agency staff are in London. In the case of one London trust, 15 per cent of the staff budget is devoted to agency staff, accounting for nine per cent of total trust expenditure. Furthermore, of the 40 trusts in England with the greatest proportional spend on agency staff, 37 are in London, suggesting that this is a widespread issue across the capital.

Table 23 shows that the average total cost associated with each member of staff in London trusts varies across sectors from £21,000 to £22,900. This is affected by the mix of staff, and location weighting. Data are not available on numbers of agency staff. However, expenditure on agency staff per salaried employee, which gives some indication of reliance on agency staff, is £1,300 in London as a whole, and varies from £900 in the south to £1,500 in the north-central sector.

Table 23: Cost per staff member, by sector of London, 1994/95

Sector	Salaries & wages £	Social Security costs £	Other pension costs £	Agency staff £	Total £
North West	19,400	1,600	600	1,400	22,900
North Central	19,300	1,500	600	1,500	22,800
East	19,500	1,500	500	1,400	22,900
South East	18,100	1,300	500	1,000	21,000
South	19,700	1,500	600	900	22,700
London	19,100	1,500	600	1,300	22,400

Table 24 provides a comparison of cost per staff member between London and England, showing that total expenditure on staff averages £4,500 – or 25 per cent – more per member of staff in London than in the rest of the country. This may be the result of a number of factors. These include: London weighting on salaries, a more highly-paid staff-mix, particularly medical staff, and greater use of agency staff. The overall cost of agency staff is nearly seven times greater in London than in the rest of the country. In inner-deprived London the cost of agency staff is equivalent to £1,600 per member of staff, compared with £200 in inner-deprived areas elsewhere in England.

Table 24: Cost per staff member, London and England, 1994/95

Type of Area	Salaries & wages	Social Security costs	Other pension costs	Agency staff	Total
	£	£	£	£	£
Inner-deprived London	19,200	1,500	500	1,600	22,800
Mixed-status London	19,100	1,500	600	1,200	22,400
High-status London	18,900	1,500	500	800	21,700
London	19,100	1,500	600	1,300	22,400
Inner-deprived Non-London	16,000	1,100	500	200	17,900
Mixed-status Non-London	15,800	1,100	500	100	17,600
High-status Non-London	16,300	1,200	500	300	18,300
Non-London	16,000	1,200	500	200	17,900
England	16,500	1,200	500	400	18,600

Fixed assets

We turn briefly to consider the value of assets held by London trusts: land, buildings and fittings, equipment, and assets under construction. We detail the value of donated and purchased assets.

Value of assets

Tables 25 and 26 provide a breakdown of the value of assets for acute and non-acute trusts in London. Definitions of acute and non-acute are given above. Table 25 reveals that the fixed assets of acute trusts in the north-west sector of London are 31 per cent of the total value of fixed assets in the capital. Buildings in this sector account for 72 per cent of the total value of fixed assets compared with 66 per cent in London as a whole. This reflects a number of trusts in the north west with highly valuable buildings – the Chelsea and Westminster, Hammersmith and St Mary's trusts. However, there are comparatively few assets under construction in this sector. By contrast, there are £148 million of assets under construction in the south east.

Table 25: Value of acute trust fixed assets, by type, by sector of London, 1994/95

Sector	Land	Buildings, fittings, installations	Equipment	Under construction	Total
	£m	£m	£m	£m	£m
North West	199	751	80	20	1,050
North Central	132	429	51	35	647
East	112	399	49	24	584
South East	110	406	48	148	711
South	83	240	34	19	376
London	635	2,225	261	246	3,368

Table 26 shows that land accounts for a greater proportion of the fixed assets of non-acute trusts – 32 per cent of the total value of fixed assets compared with 19 per cent for acute trusts. On the other hand, equipment is worth just two per cent of total fixed asset value, and assets under construction, just five per cent. This compares with eight and seven per cent respectively in the case of London's acute trusts.

Table 26: Value of non-acute trust fixed assets, by type, by sector of London, 1994/95

Sector	Land	Buildings, fittings, installations	Equipment	Under construction	Total
	£m	£m	£m	£m	£m
North West	85	141	5	6	237
North Central	61	116	2	6	185
East	-	-	-	-	-
South East	37	92	6	18	154
South	29	54	2	4	89
London	213	403	14	34	664

(Table 26 reflects the fact that there were no non-acute trusts, by our definition, in the east sector in 1994/95.)

Table 27 compares the value of the fixed assets of acute trusts in London with that in the rest of England. High land prices in London, and especially inner-deprived London, affect the value of London's fixed assets. The value of total fixed assets in London is 23 per cent of the England total but land values in the capital are 32 per cent of the national total. The value of land owned by the 18 acute trusts in inner-deprived London *alone* is equivalent to 13 per cent of the value of all land owned by acute trusts in England.

Land is a greater proportion of the total value of fixed assets in London than in the rest of England – 19 compared with 11 per cent. This is also true for assets under construction – seven compared with five per cent. By contrast, buildings and equipment in London account for a smaller proportion of total asset value – 66 and eight per cent respectively compared with 73 and ten per cent.

Table 27: Value of acute trust fixed assets, by type, London and England, 1994/95

Type of Area	Land	Buildings, fittings, installations	Equipment	Under construction	Total
	£m	£m	£m	£m	£m
Inner-deprived London	248	1,046	132	181	1,607
Mixed-status London	217	673	74	32	996
High-status London	171	506	55	33	765
London	635	2,225	261	246	3,368
Inner-deprived Non-London	132	1,231	204	114	1,681
Mixed-status Non-London	236	1,848	223	109	2,415
High-status Non-London	557	3,060	427	148	4,192
Non-London	1,137	7,592	1,068	561	10,358
England	1,772	9,817	1,330	808	13,725

Table 28 shows that a greater proportion of the total value of fixed assets in non-acute trusts in London is accounted for by land than is the case elsewhere in England. Thirty-two per cent of total assets is accounted for by land in London non-acute trusts compared with 20 per cent in the rest of the country.

Table 28: Value of non-acute trust fixed assets, by type, London and England, 1994/95

Type of Area	Land	Buildings, fittings, installations	Equipment	Under construction	Total
	£m	£m	£m	£m	£m
Inner-deprived London	89	193	8	20	310
Mixed-status London	68	95	4	10	177
High-status London	55	115	3	4	177
London	213	403	14	34	664
Inner-deprived Non-London	69	308	12	23	411
Mixed-status Non-London	112	364	17	26	519
High-status Non-London	285	827	50	73	1,235
Non-London	598	2,108	119	160	2,984
England	810	2,511	133	194	3,649

Changes in the value of fixed assets

Table 29, which combines figures for all trusts, shows that the value of land and buildings in London decreased in 1994/95, but that the value of assets under construction increased. The principle reason for the reduction in the value of land and buildings was indexation and depreciation rather than disposal. In fact, London trusts acquired land worth slightly more than that disposed of, and spent £63 million on new buildings while disposing of just £7 million worth.

Table 29: Changes in the value of fixed assets, by sector of London, 1994/95

Sector	Land			Buildings, fittings, installations			Under construction		
	1/4/94 £m	31/3/95 £m	Change £m	1/4/94 £m	31/3/95 £m	Change £m	1/4/94 £m	31/3/95 £m	Change £m
North West	312	284	-29	915	892	-23	13	27	14
North Central	214	193	-21	541	545	5	27	41	14
East	124	112	-12	405	399	-6	11	24	13
South East	160	147	-13	515	498	-18	147	166	19
South	123	112	-11	293	294	2	19	22	4
London	934	848	-86	2,669	2,628	-40	217	281	64

Table 30 shows that in both London and the rest of the country the value of land held by trusts declined while the value of assets under construction increased. However, there was an increase in the value of buildings outside the capital. Trust accounts suggest that the value of buildings acquired in the rest of England is greater than the reduction in value of existing assets through revaluation and indexation. That was not the case in London.

Table 30: Changes in the value of fixed assets, London and England, 1994/95

Type of Area	Land			Buildings, fittings, installations			Under construction		
	1/4/94 £m	31/3/95 £m	Change £m	1/4/94 £m	31/3/95 £m	Change £m	1/4/94 £m	31/3/95 £m	Change £m
Inner-deprived London	371	337	-35	1,247	1,239	-8	164	201	37
Mixed-status London	314	285	-29	768	768	-1	32	42	10
High-status London	249	226	-22	653	622	-31	21	37	16
London	934	848	-86	2,669	2,628	-40	217	281	64
Inner-deprived Non-London	230	209	-20	1,499	1,565	65	155	138	-17
Mixed-status Non-London	381	357	-24	2,212	2,234	22	124	138	14
High-status Non-London	944	868	-76	3,969	3,932	-37	168	222	54
Non-London	1,945	1,796	-149	9,810	9,891	81	607	731	124
England	2,878	2,643	-235	12,479	12,520	41	824	1,011	188

5 DHA expenditure

In this section we consider briefly expenditure by DHAs. Total actual expenditure is set alongside the allocation to DHAs of financial resources in 1994/95. Per capita expenditure is compared at a more detailed level, both across sectors of London and between London and the rest of England.

Total expenditure

Table 31 shows, for each sector of London, the absolute level of expenditure and income accounted for by DHAs. Income tends to equal expenditure: surplus or deficit is shown where applicable. Expenditure is greatest in the north-west sector of London, comprising 24 per cent of the London total. There is considerable variation in expenditure on DHA administration as a proportion of total spend. Thus, in the south-east sector DHA administration accounts for £9 million, just 1.3 per cent of total, whereas in the east, £32 million is spent on administration, some 4.6 per cent of total. However, this may partly reflect inconsistencies in the attribution of monies between expenditure categories.

The 'other' expenditure category comprises spending on Community Health Councils and other services not directly related to health care provision. In the north-west sector, 'other' expenditure accounts for £19 million or 2.3 per cent of the total; on the other hand, in the south less than £500,000 is spent in this way. Nevertheless, for all sectors, most expenditure is devoted to health care and related services, the proportion of total expenditure ranging from 95 per cent in the east to 97 per cent in the south east.

Table 31: DHA income and expenditure, by sector of London, 1994/95

Sector	Income £m	Health care & related services £m	DHA adminis- tration £m	Other £m	Total £m	Surplus £m
North West	819	779	18	19	815	3
North Central	648	622	22	8	651	-3
East	693	661	32	2	694	-1
South East	673	653	9	12	674	-1
South	535	507	22	0	530	5
London	3,368	3,222	102	41	3,365	4

(Table 31 excludes net surplus from DMUs and Common Services from the DHA surplus. If this were included, the surplus in London as a whole would increase from £4 million to £5 million.)

Table 32 shows that, in both London and the rest of England, 96 per cent of expenditure is devoted to health care and related services. Eighteen per cent of total England expenditure is accounted for by London DHAs. As Table 6 shows, this equals the proportion of provider services income in England accounted for by London trusts.

Table 32: DHA income and expenditure, London and England, 1994/95

| Type of Area | Income £m | Expenditure | | | | Surplus £m |
		Health care & related services £m	DHA adminis-tration £m	Other £m	Total £m	
Inner-deprived London	1,262	1,220	26	12	1,259	4
Mixed-status London	1,206	1,141	48	11	1,200	6
High-status London	900	861	28	17	906	-6
London	3,368	3,222	102	41	3,365	4
Inner-deprived Non-London	2,119	2,024	65	38	2,127	-7
Mixed-status Non-London	3,567	3,437	87	43	3,567	-1
High-status Non-London	5,871	5,612	191	52	5,855	15
Non-London	15,365	14,739	446	167	15,351	14
England exc. RHAs	18,733	17,961	548	208	18,716	18
RHAs	2,169	942	348	947	2,238	-68
England	20,903	18,903	896	1,155	20,953	-50

(Table 32 excludes net surplus from DMUs and Common Services from the DHA surplus. If this were included, the deficit in England as a whole including RHAs increases from £50 million to £53 million.)

Expenditure per capita

Table 33 provides a comparison of per capita DHA expenditure on health care across sectors of London. Total expenditure per capita is greatest in the north-central sector, some 18 per cent more than the London average. Expenditure in the south and south-east sectors is relatively less: per capita expenditure in the south sector, for example, is just 74 per cent of that in the north-central. Table 33 also shows variation in the proportion spent on health-related services, administration and 'other' services. Thus, expenditure on administration is greatest in the east sector, while relatively more is spent on 'other' services in the north west.

Table 33: DHA expenditure per capita resident population, by sector of London, 1994/95

Sector	Health care & related services £	DHA administration £	Other £	Total £
North West	460	10	11	481
North Central	546	19	7	572
East	463	22	1	486
South East	448	6	8	462
South	406	17	0	423
London	462	15	6	483

Table 34 compares expenditure per capita resident population in London with that in the rest of the country, showing per capita expenditure in London is over 30 per cent greater. This is particularly so in inner-deprived London where over 40 per cent more is spent per capita than in similar areas in the rest of the country. Differences between mixed- and high-status London and their comparator areas in the rest of the country are less but still significant. This comparison is based on expenditure for which DHAs are accountable, not all of which is devoted necessarily to the purchase of health care for local residents. This issue is discussed further in the next section.

Although, in absolute terms, greater per capita expenditure in London is primarily due to expenditure on health care, expenditure on DHA administration in London is also 36 per cent greater than that of the rest of England. However, expenditure per capita on DHA administration in inner-deprived areas of London is actually less than that of comparable areas elsewhere.

Table 34: DHA expenditure per capita resident population, London and England, 1994/95

Type of Area	Health care & related services £	DHA administration £	Other £	Total £
Inner-deprived London	602	13	6	621
Mixed-status London	430	18	4	452
High-status London	376	12	7	395
London	462	15	6	483
Inner-deprived Non-London	421	14	8	443
Mixed-status Non-London	356	9	4	369
High-status Non-London	333	11	3	347
Non-London	353	11	4	368
England	378	11	4	393

The allocation of financial resources

Financial resources are allocated to DHAs on the basis of a national formula known as 'weighted capitation', designed to distribute monies equitably between different parts of England, taking account of differences in levels of need and in the costs of providing similar services. In 1994/95 not all of the national HCHS budget was distributed on the basis of this formula as some monies were held back for specific purposes associated with particular types of service use, education or research: for example, supra-regional services and AIDS. This implies that not all funds for which DHAs are accountable, are devoted specifically to the purchase of health care for local residents. In 1994/95, £18.4 billion was allocated nationally using the capitation formula out of a total initial allocation of £20.4 billion. Also excluded at that time was capital charges which amounted to £1.8 billion.

Table 35 shows the allocation of financial resources to London DHAs on the basis of weighted capitation, both in absolute terms and per capita resident population, by sector of London. Actual allocations do not reflect perfectly the weighted capitation formula as the rate of adjustment of historical levels of expenditure is gradual. Thus, in London as a whole, DHAs receive £65 million, or three per cent, more than would have been the case if target allocations had been adhered to. Distance from target varies across sectors of London from the east where DHAs appear to be two per cent under target, to the north-central sector where they are nine per cent over target.

In per capita terms, the target allocation to London DHAs is less than the England average, although actual allocations are closer to the England figure. In other words, in 1994/95 the formula for allocating financial resources between different areas of the country assessed the level of funds required in London as a whole, per capita resident population, as less than the England average. This position has changed with the introduction of a new formula in 1995/96 and adjustments since then. However, a further complication arises since, throughout the 1990s, there has been a trend towards the distribution of a larger proportion of HCHS resources on the basis of the weighted capitation formula. In 1997/98 almost all HCHS funds will be allocated on this basis. This will change quite radically the position of some London DHAs.

Table 35: Total and per capita DHA budget allocations, by sector of London, 1994/95

Sector	Actual allocation		Target allocation		Difference		Percentage distance from target
	Total	Per capita	Total	Per capita	Total	Per capita	
	£m	£	£m	£	£m	£	%
North West	540	319	525	310	15	9	3
North Central	473	416	436	382	38	33	9
East	566	396	580	406	-14	-10	-2
South East	560	384	558	383	2	2	0
South	480	383	456	364	23	19	5
London	2,620	376	2,554	367	65	9	3
England	18,447	379	18,447	379	0	0	0

Health-care-related expenditure

We now consider health-care-related expenditure in more detail. Expenditure is broken down by five categories: NHS trusts; other NHS providers; non-NHS providers; joint projects with local authorities; and, care in the community. Table 36 shows that, in each sector of London, over 90 per cent of DHA expenditure is accounted for by NHS providers. Approximately three per cent of DHA expenditure in London is with non-NHS providers, ranging from five per cent in the south-east sector to two per cent in the south.

Table 36: DHA health-care-related expenditure, by sector of London, 1994/95

Sector	Trusts		Other NHS providers		Non-NHS providers		Joint projects with local authorities		Care in the Community		Total
	£m	%	£m	%	£m	%	£m	%	£m	%	£m
North West	722	93	8	1	33	4	4	0	12	2	779
North Central	593	95	1	0	16	3	2	0	10	2	622
East	604	91	8	1	20	3	3	1	26	4	661
South East	610	93	1	0	33	5	5	1	5	1	653
South	483	95	2	0	8	2	3	1	11	2	507
London	3,012	93	19	1	111	3	17	1	63	2	3,222

Table 37 shows that London DHAs spend proportionately less with NHS providers than their counterparts in the rest of the country, although the difference is just two per cent.

Table 37: DHA health-care-related expenditure, London and England, 1994/95

Type of Area	Trusts		Other NHS providers		Non-NHS providers		Joint projects with local authorities		Care in the Community		Total
	£m	%	£m	%	£m	%	£m	%	£m	%	£m
Inner-deprived London	1,132	93	9	1	45	4	7	1	27	2	1,220
Mixed-status London	1,067	94	8	1	35	3	5	0	26	2	1,141
High-status London	814	95	1	0	30	4	5	1	10	1	861
London	3,012	93	19	1	111	3	17	1	63	2	3,222
Inner-deprived Non-London	1,931	95	26	1	31	2	11	1	25	1	2,024
Mixed-status Non-London	3,290	96	26	1	45	1	21	1	55	2	3,437
High-status Non-London	5,332	95	35	1	134	2	33	1	78	1	5,612
Non-London	14,052	95	101	1	281	2	89	1	215	1	14,739
England exc. RHAs	17,064	95	120	1	392	2	107	1	278	2	17,960
RHAs	794	84	41	4	107	11	0	0	-	0	942
England	17,858	94	160	1	499	3	107	1	278	1	18,903

6 FHS expenditure

In this section we consider expenditure on family health services (FHS). These consist of general medical services (GMS), general ophthalmic services (GOS) and pharmaceutical services (PS). A small proportion of FHS expenditure is devoted to general dental services (GDS), but payments are mainly administered by the Dental Practices Board. In 1994/95, the Dental Practices Board expenditure was £800 million in England as a whole. Data are not available to allow comparisons between London and the rest of the country.

General Practice Fundholder (GPFH) expenditure on primary and hospital care is included with FHS expenditure in DoH accounts. In total, around £8.4 billion is spent on FHS in England, including £200 million on FHSA administration. London accounts for approximately £1.1 billion of this, almost 13.5 per cent of the total. In 1990/91, London accounted for just under 15 per cent of national FHS expenditure. However, GPFH expenditure on hospital services is now included in the FHS total. As there are less fundholders in London than elsewhere in England, this makes FHS spend in the capital appear proportionately less. If GPFH expenditure were excluded, London's share of national FHS expenditure is unchanged since 1990/91.

Expenditure per capita

We compare expenditure per capita, by type of socio-economic area in London, with similar areas in the rest of the country. Figure 5 shows that London as a whole has a lower expenditure per capita than the rest of the country. However, as already noted, the inclusion of GPFH expenditure on hospital services creates the apparent underspend on FHS in London, as there are fewer fundholding practices in London than the rest of the country, especially in inner-deprived areas. If GPFH expenditure is excluded, as Figure 6 shows, per capita expenditure on FHS in London is greater than in the rest of the country – £141 compared with £136. Inner-deprived and mixed-status London spend more per capita than their counterparts in the rest of the country, while expenditure per capita is less in high-status areas of the capital than in similar areas elsewhere.

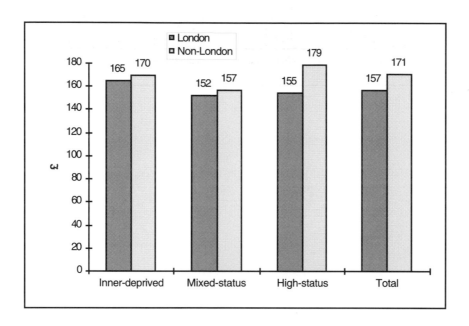

Figure 5: FHS expenditure per capita, excluding administration, London and England, 1994/95

This reverses the position in 1990/91 when per capita expenditure on FHS was less in London than in the rest of the country. However, as we shall see, this reflects the provision of non-recurring DoH initiative funding for primary care in London.

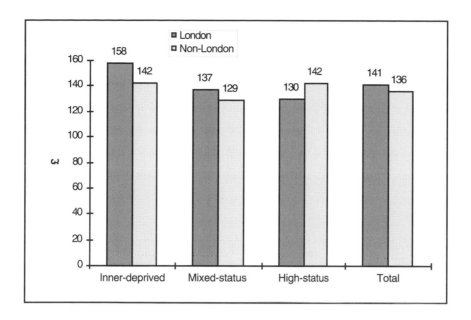

Figure 6: FHS expenditure per capita, excluding administration and GPFH expenditure on hospital care, London and England, 1994/95

The components of FHS expenditure

This section compares expenditure in London on various elements of FHS with that in the rest of England. These include:

- general medical services (GMS), comprising payments to GPs;

- general dental services (GDS);

- general ophthalmic services (GOS), comprising payments to NHS opticians;

- pharmaceutical services (PS), principally comprising payments for drugs prescribed by GPs and dispensed by community pharmacists; and,

- administration.

Figure 7 shows the proportion of total FHS expenditure accounted for by these categories, for London and the rest of England. GPFH hospital expenditure is excluded. Four per cent of FHS expenditure in London arises from DoH initiative funding (primarily related to London Initiative Zone expenditure), an element which is virtually non-existent in the rest of the country. London spends more on administration – five compared with three per cent; a greater proportion is spent on GMS in London than is the case in the rest of the country, but a significantly smaller proportion of FHS expenditure is accounted for by PS. Since 1990/91 the proportion of expenditure on administration has increased from two to three per cent of FHS expenditure nationally.

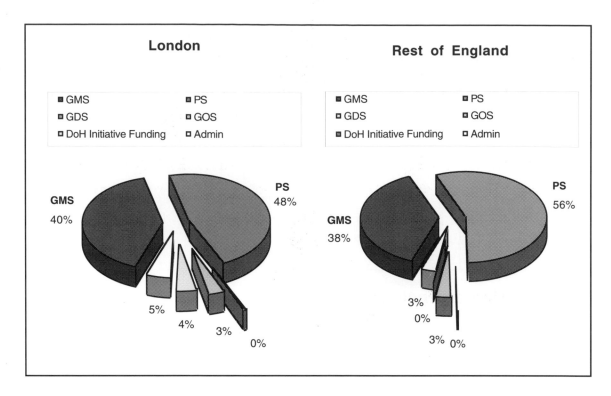

Figure 7: Proportion of FHS expenditure, by type, London and England, 1994/95

Table 38 provides a breakdown of expenditure per capita resident population on the various elements of FHS including administation. Expenditure per capita by GPFHs for hospital services is excluded. Total expenditure per capita on FHS in London is £148, five per cent greater than in the rest of the country. However, this difference is more than accounted for by the greater administration costs and non-recurring DoH initiative funding in London: together these represent nine per cent of the capital's FHS budget.

Table 38: A breakdown of FHS expenditure per capita resident population, London and England, 1994/95

Type of Area	GMS	GDS	GOS	PS	DoH Initiative funding	Total health care	Admin- istration	Total
	£	£	£	£	£	£	£	£
Inner-deprived London	66.6	1.5	5.3	72.1	12.2	157.8	8.6	166.3
Mixed-status London	57.7	0.3	4.4	69.3	5.0	136.7	6.2	143.0
High-status London	55.8	0.5	3.8	67.8	2.3	130.2	6.2	136.4
London	59.7	0.7	4.5	69.6	6.2	140.7	6.9	147.6
Inner-deprived Non-London	53.8	0.2	6.0	82.1	0.1	142.2	5.1	147.3
Mixed-status Non-London	48.8	0.2	4.5	75.2	0.0	128.8	4.0	132.8
High-status Non-London	58.4	0.4	4.2	79.5	0.0	142.5	4.0	146.5
Non-London	53.2	0.3	4.4	78.4	0.0	136.3	4.0	140.3

There is considerable variation across types of socio-economic area. Expenditure per capita resident population in inner-deprived and mixed-status areas of London is 13 and eight per cent more than that in similar areas in the rest of the country, while in high-status areas of the capital, expenditure is seven per cent less. However, these comparisons are affected by DoH initiative funding. If this is excluded, expenditure in inner-deprived and mixed-status London is closer to that of comparable areas elsewhere in England.

London as a whole spends more on GMS than the rest of the country – £60 per capita resident population compared with £53. Comparing per capita expenditure on GMS in inner-deprived areas of London with that in similar areas in the rest of England, greater differences emerge. Expenditure on GMS in inner-deprived London is 24 per cent greater than in non-London inner-deprived areas. However, the position is reversed for PS, where, in inner-deprived London, expenditure per capita is just 88 per cent of that in similar areas elsewhere in the country.

7 Social services expenditure

We turn now to consider local authority (LA) expenditure on social services in 1994/95. Total gross social services expenditure is presented for London and England, classified by client group, and shown as total and per capita expenditure. We also consider per capita expenditure on services for older people and adult client groups – learning disabilities, mental health and physical disabilities – in greater detail.

Gross social services expenditure

Table 39 shows that approximately £1.6 billion is spent on social services in London. Expenditure is classified by five distinct client groups, central strategic expenditure and a catch-all 'other' group. In London as a whole, 40 per cent of gross social services expenditure is accounted for by services for older people, 31 per cent by children's services and 25 per cent by adult client groups. There is comparatively little variation across sectors of London, although those with greater proportions of expenditure on services for older people tend to have a smaller proportion on services for children and vice versa.

Table 39: Gross social services expenditure, by client group, by sector of London, 1994/95

Sector	Central Strategic		Children		Learning Disabilities		Mental Health		Older People		Physical Disabilities		Other		Total
	£m	%	£m	%	£m	%	£m	%	£m	%	£m	%	£m	%	£m
North West	7	2	122	32	47	12	23	6	147	38	25	6	12	3	384
North Central	6	2	78	29	32	12	16	6	112	41	18	7	7	3	269
East	6	2	101	30	40	12	17	5	141	42	20	6	10	3	334
South East	8	2	119	33	45	12	17	5	141	39	26	7	7	2	363
South	4	2	69	28	32	13	16	6	102	42	17	7	4	2	245
London	32	2	489	31	197	12	89	6	642	40	106	7	41	3	1,595

Table 40 shows that, in comparison with the rest of England, a smaller proportion of total social services expenditure is on services for older people in London as a whole, but relatively more is spent on services for children. The proportion of expenditure on adult client groups in both London and the rest of the country is similar. In London, a slightly greater proportion of gross social services expenditure is accounted for by the central strategic and 'other' classifications. London as a whole accounts for 21 per cent of total England expenditure on social services. This is considerably more than the proportion of national HCHS or FHS expenditure accounted for by London DHAs. Figure 8 shows graphically, for London and the rest of England, the proportion of gross social services expenditure in each category.

Table 40: Gross social services expenditure, by client group, London and England, 1994/95

Type of Area	Central Strategic		Children		Learning Disabilities		Mental Health		Older People		Physical Disabilities		Other		Total
	£m	%	£m	%	£m	%	£m	%	£m	%	£m	%	£m	%	£m
Inner-deprived London	12	2	228	35	71	11	37	6	248	38	37	6	23	3	654
Mixed-status London	11	2	160	29	72	13	32	6	219	40	38	7	12	2	544
High-status London	9	2	101	25	53	13	20	5	176	44	32	8	6	2	397
London	32	2	489	31	197	12	89	6	642	40	106	7	41	3	1,595
Inner-deprived Non-London	12	1	247	29	97	11	42	5	390	46	56	7	7	1	852
Mixed-status Non-London	20	1	372	25	181	12	63	4	749	51	88	6	10	1	1,482
High-status Non-London	34	2	539	24	313	14	92	4	1,097	49	162	7	17	1	2,254
Non-London	88	1	1,442	24	760	13	252	4	2,926	50	400	7	40	1	5,908
England	120	2	1,931	26	956	13	341	5	3,568	48	507	7	81	1	7,503

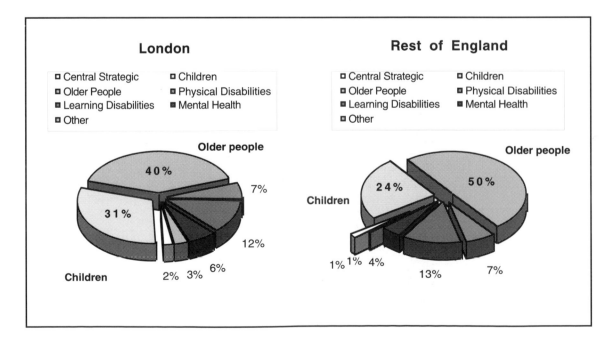

Figure 8: Social services expenditure, by client group, London and England, 1994/95

Gross social services expenditure per capita

Figure 9 compares total gross social services expenditure per capita resident population across sectors of London. For London as a whole, per capita expenditure is £229, varying from £196 in the south to £249 in the south east. North of the Thames there is comparatively little variation in per capita total expenditure.

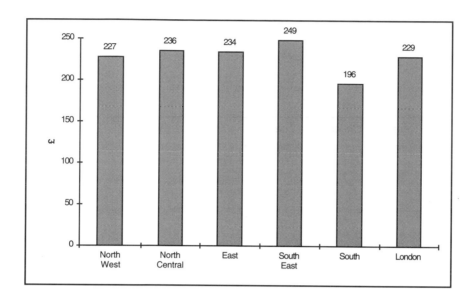

Figure 9: Gross social services expenditure per capita resident population, by sector of London, 1994/95

Figure 10 shows that per capita gross social services expenditure is some 60 per cent greater in London than in the rest of England – £229 compared with £142. This disparity is most noticeable in inner-deprived London where expenditure on social services is 82 per cent greater than in similar areas of the rest of the country. The differences between mixed- and high-status areas of London and their comparators in the rest of the country are still substantial, but less – 34 and 29 per cent respectively.

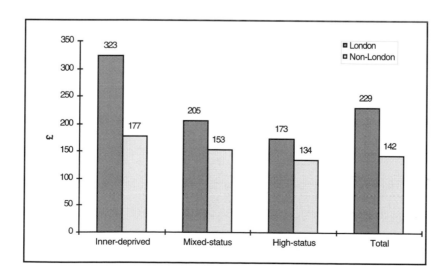

Figure 10: Gross social services expenditure per capita resident population, London and England, 1994/95

Since 1990/91, gross social services expenditure per capita resident population has increased by just 37 per cent in London as a whole compared with 46 per cent in the rest of the country. For all types of socio-economic area, the increase in expenditure in London has been proportionally less than that in the rest of England. However, expenditure in the capital was, and remains, much higher.

Services for older people

We now consider gross expenditure on services for older people per capita resident population aged 75 years and over. Figure 11 shows per capita expenditure on social services for older people in London as a whole is £1,464, ranging from £1,231 in the south sector to £1,641 in the east, almost a third as much again.

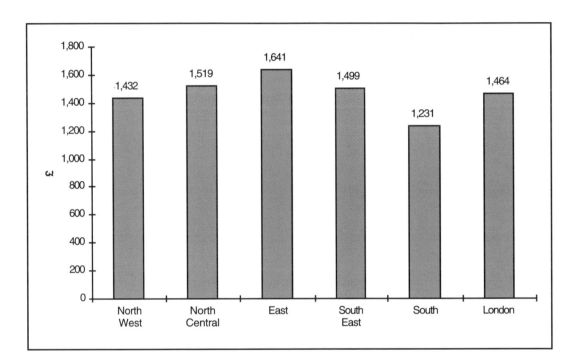

Figure 11: Gross expenditure on social services for older people, per capita resident population aged 75 years and over, by sector of London, 1994/95

Figure 12 shows that per capita expenditure on services for older people is over 50 per cent more in London than in the rest of the country. The difference is even more marked when inner-deprived areas of London are compared with similar areas in the rest of the country. Although expenditure increases with the level of deprivation, both in London and outside, the amount spent on social services for older people in inner-deprived areas outside the capital is just 58 per cent of that in similar areas of London. Once again, the difference is much less significant when mixed- and high-status areas of London and England are compared.

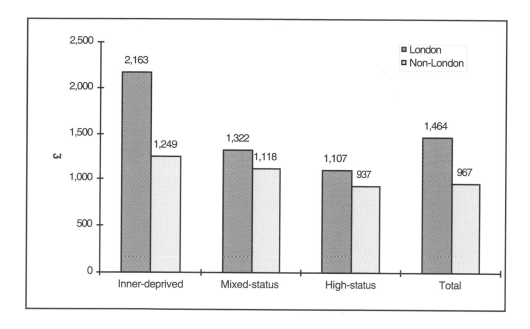

Figure 12: Gross expenditure on social services for older people, per capita resident population aged 75 years and over, London and England, 1994/95

As Figure 13 shows, there are considerable differences between London and the rest of the country in the proportion of social services expenditure for older people spent on various care categories. Almost half of total expenditure on older people in the rest of England is accounted for by either residential or nursing care. By contrast, the proportion of such expenditure in London is just 39 per cent.

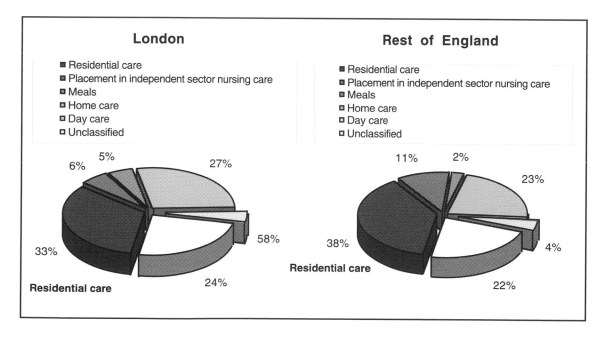

Figure 13: Gross social services expenditure for older people, by care type, London and England, 1994/95

On the other hand, the proportion of community-based expenditure in London – on home care, day care and the provision of meals – is 37 per cent compared with 29 per cent in the rest of the country. In London an almost equal proportion is spent on residential and community-based care, whereas elsewhere in England the proportion spent on residential care is almost twice that on community-based categories. Finally, the unclassified category – which includes management of residential and domiciliary care, provision of field social workers, occupational therapists and outreach care – is slightly greater in London than in the rest of the country.

Despite this different balance of expenditure, London LAs as a whole spend more per capita resident population than the rest of England on most types of care, as Table 41 indicates. Thus, expenditure per capita in London is just over 25 per cent more on residential care, and almost twice as much on various forms of domiciliary care: the exception is nursing care where the London average is 13 per cent less than that of the rest of the country.

Table 41: Gross expenditure on services for older people, by care type, per capita resident population aged 75 years and over, London and England, 1994/95

Type of Care	London				Non-London				England
	Inner-deprived £	Mixed-status £	High-status £	Total £	Inner-deprived £	Mixed-status £	High-status £	Total £	£
Residential care	720	392	373	471	431	431	377	372	384
Nursing care	120	89	83	95	150	119	94	109	107
Meals	112	67	47	72	33	28	19	20	27
Home care	541	365	303	389	315	258	214	221	242
Day care	118	68	63	79	51	38	33	34	40

Services for adult client groups

Adult client groups comprise learning disabilities, physical disabilities and mental health. Data are available showing per capita expenditure on residential care and on domestic and domiciliary care for the combined adult client groups.

Residential care

Figure 14 shows some variation between the sectors of London in per capita expenditure on residential care for adult client groups, from £31 in south London to £36 per capita in the north-central sector, with an overall London average of £33.

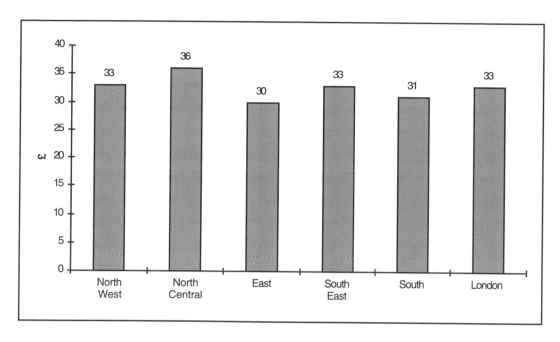

Figure 14: Gross expenditure on residential care for adult client groups, per capita resident population aged 18-64 years, by sector of London, 1994/95

Figure 15 shows substantial variation in per capita expenditure, both between types of socio-economic area in London, and between London and the rest of the country. Expenditure per capita resident population in inner-deprived areas of London is over 50 per cent greater than that in either mixed- or high-status areas of the capital; and, over twice that of the rest of the country, even when compared with similar areas elsewhere. There is a consistent pattern of greater expenditure throughout London, with a London average of £33 per capita compared with £18 in the rest of England.

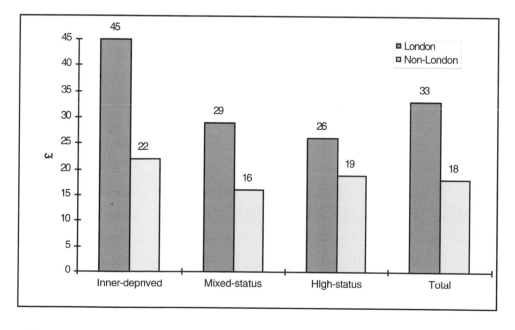

Figure 15: Gross expenditure on residential care for adult client groups, per capita resident population aged 18-64 years, London and England, 1994/95

Day care

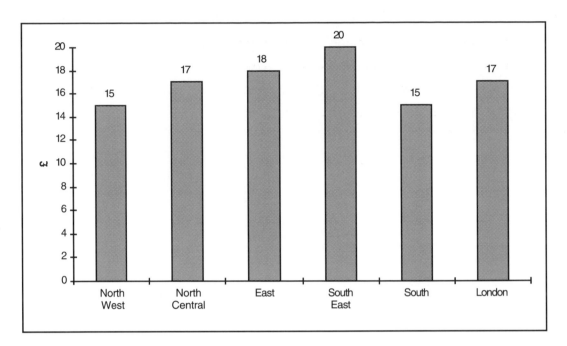

Figure 16: Gross expenditure on day care for adult client groups, per capita resident population aged 18-64 years, by sector of London, 1994/95

Figure 16 shows greater proportionate variation across London in expenditure per capita resident population on day care than was the case for residential care, shown in Figure 14. Expenditure per capita in the south-east sector is over 30 per cent greater than that in the north-west or south sectors. No relationship is apparent between levels of expenditure on residential care and on day care.

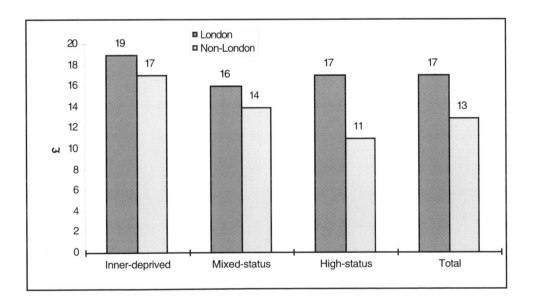

Figure 17: Gross expenditure on day care for adult client groups, per capita resident population aged 18-64 years, London and England, 1994/95

As Figure 17 shows, the difference between London and the rest of England in expenditure per capita on day care services is considerably less than is the case for residential care, shown in Figure 15. Whereas expenditure per capita for residential care in inner-deprived areas of London is twice that of similar areas in the rest of the country, it is just 12 per cent greater in the case of day care. In contrast with the pattern noted for residential care, the greatest difference between London and the rest of the country occurs in high-status areas.

Chapter 10

Measures of Efficiency

Summary

Hospital services

- Average length of stay (LOS) for acute in-patients varies between 5.1 days in east London and 6.9 days in the north west. There is greater variation in some individual specialties, particularly the non-acute. Thus, the average psychiatric LOS in the north west is twice that of the south-east sector.

- Average LOS for the acute specialties group in London as a whole is 5.7 days compared with 4.9 in England. Average LOS is greater in London for medicine, obstetrics and gynaecology, surgery and urology, trauma and orthopaedics, ENT and paediatrics.

- Average geriatric LOS in London is ten per cent greater than the England average; on the other hand, average psychiatric LOS is 13 per cent less.

- Average acute LOS in London has increased slightly, from 5.6 to 5.7 days, since 1989/90. However, the proportion of admissions treated as day cases in London has increased substantially over this period, which is likely to lead to an increase in the complexity of in-patient cases.

- Turnover interval is a measure of the average time each hospital bed remains empty between in-patient FCEs. There is considerable variation in acute turnover interval in London, from 0.8 days in the east to 1.5 in the north west.

- Acute turnover interval in London as a whole is 18 per cent less than that of the rest of England. In 1989/90 the difference was even greater at 33 per cent.

- Throughput is a measure of the number of FCEs per available bed per year. London as a whole has a throughput of 76 FCEs per bed, including day cases, compared with 75 in the rest of England. There is some variation across London with a considerably greater throughput of 86 in the south. This reflects both a high day case rate and a low in-patient length of stay in that sector.

- Bed occupancy rates can be both a measure of efficient use of resources and an indicator of pressure on scarce resources. London as a whole has a higher occupancy rate for combined acute and geriatric beds compared with the rest of England – 86 as opposed to 79 per cent.

Financial efficiency

- Average cost per acute case varies by over 50 per cent across London: from £762 in the east to £1,194 in the north-central sector.

- Average cost per acute case is over 20 per cent greater in London than in the rest of England. Average cost per psychiatric episode in inner-deprived London is over 40 per cent greater than that of similar areas in the rest of the country.

- Average cost per out-patient attendance varies between £57 in the south and £82 in the north-central sector of London.

- Average cost per out-patient attendance is 17 per cent greater in London than in the rest of England.

- The average cost of staff relative to total FCEs delivered varies across London: the greatest costs are in the south east and the lowest in the east.

- The average cost of staff relative to total FCEs delivered is considerably higher in London than in the rest of England. This is particularly true of medical staff: the cost of consultants is 40 per cent more per FCE in London compared with the rest of the country; the cost of non-consultant medical staff is 58 per cent more.

- Trusts are expected to achieve a six per cent return on their net assets. In 1994/95 a quarter of London trusts failed to achieve this target. The greatest proportion of these were in the east and south-east sectors.

- The proportion of trusts failing to achieve a six per cent return on net assets was greater in London than in the rest of England, particularly in high-status areas where 44 per cent failed to achieve the target.

NHS performance targets

- In 1995/96 London trusts performed well against Patient's Charter standards.

- London hospitals performed particularly well in terms of day case rates compared with hospitals outside the capital: for example 41 per cent of inguinal hernias in London were treated as day cases compared with 31 per cent in the rest of England.

- London providers performed worse in achieving guaranteed admission within one month following last-minute cancellation of an operation: the failure rate in the capital was 14 per provider compared with seven in the rest of England.

Key Facts

Hospital services	*London*	*Rest of England*
Average length of stay:		
• acute specialties	5.7 days	4.9 days
• all specialties	9.6 days	8.3 days
Acute turnover interval:	1.2 days	1.4 days
Throughput per acute bed excluding day cases:	51 FCEs	53 FCEs
Throughput per acute bed including day cases:	76 FCEs	75 FCEs
Combined acute and geriatric bed occupancy:	86%	79%

Financial efficiency

	London	Rest of England
Cost per FCE:	£1,264	£1,058
Cost per acute FCE:	£962	£791
Cost per out-patient attendance:	£68	£58
Proportion of trusts failing to make a six per cent return on net assets:	26%	21%

NHS performance targets

	London	Rest of England
Proportion of out-patients seen within 30 minutes of appointment time:	91%	92%
Proportion of A&E attenders assessed within 5 minutes of arrival:	94%	94%
Average number of patients, per provider, not admitted within a month of last-minute cancellation of an operation:	14	7
Day case rate:		
• inguinal hernia repair	41%	31%
• arthroscopy of knee	73%	66%
• cataract extraction	53%	50%
• laparoscopy with sterilisation	81%	75%
Proportion of out-patients seen within 13 weeks:	85%	87%
Proportion of out-patients seen within 26 weeks:	97%	98%
Proportion of patients admitted from waiting-list within 3 months:	69%	71%
Proportion of patients admitted from waiting-list within 12 months:	95%	97%

1 Introduction

Previous chapters have provided an analysis of the health needs of Londoners and the delivery and resourcing of health services in the capital. These data are now used to determine measures of efficiency for the provision of health services in London. We present measures of the utilisation of resources in the capital using several standard indicators of bed utilisation. Financial measures of efficiency, including average cost per unit of activity, as well as an analysis of staff costs per FCE, are also provided. We detail trust performance against the financial target of a six per cent return on assets. A discussion of trust operating surplus is provided in Chapter 9. Finally, performance against Patient's Charter standards on in- and out-patient waiting lists, A&E department waiting times and day case rates is also provided.

2 Data sources

Unless otherwise stated, activity data for patients using a hospital bed are taken from the analysis of HES data for 1994/95: see previous chapters. Bed availability figures are based on the data underlying the DoH report, *'Bed availability for England, 1994/95'* (DoH, 1995d). Financial data are based on the DoH financial returns, TFR2, TFR3 and HFR22. The analysis of performance against financial targets is based on data presented in *'The Fitzhugh Directory of NHS Trusts Financial Information 1996'* (Fitzhugh, 1996). Performance against Patient's Charter targets is based on the DoH report, *'The NHS Performance Guide 1995-96'* (DoH, 1996i).

3 Hospital services

We consider the efficiency of provision of hospital services in terms of a number of measures associated with the delivery of in-patient care: these include average length of stay (LOS), turnover interval, throughput and bed occupancy levels.

Average length of stay

We consider first the variation across London in average length of stay (LOS) per FCE, for the main specialty groups. Average LOS is defined as the average duration, in days, of a finished in-patient consultant episode – that is, the number of days a patient occupies a bed, on average. Hence, day cases are excluded.

Table 1 shows some variation in average LOS between sectors of London, both for the acute specialty group as a whole, and for individual specialties. Thus, acute average LOS varies between 5.1 days in the east and south and 6.9 days in the north-west sector. There is even greater variation in the non-acute specialties: for example, the psychiatric average LOS in the north west is twice that of the south-east sector of London.

Taken over all specialties, the south sector, at 11.2 days, has the greatest average LOS. This compares with a range of 8.4 to 10.8 days in the other sectors. This is due to a substantially greater average LOS in non-acute specialties. In particular, the average psychiatric LOS for trusts in one DHA in the south is 156 days compared with a London average of 74.

Table 1: Average LOS, by specialty group, by sector of London, 1994/95

Specialty Group	North West	North Central	East	South East	South	London
Anaesthetics	2.5	2.3	0.8	6.4	2.5	3.8
Dental	1.5	1.8	2.4	1.8	2.3	1.9
ENT	2.7	2.4	2.2	2.1	2.1	2.3
Geriatrics	20.2	23.7	27.2	15.7	23.5	22.1
Haematology	8.8	8.8	4.0	7.3	7.2	6.9
Medicine	9.7	7.3	6.7	8.4	6.3	7.9
Obs. and Gynae.	2.8	1.9	2.5	2.5	2.0	2.4
Ophthalmology	2.1	1.4	1.9	2.1	2.1	1.9
Orthopaedics	8.4	6.9	7.6	8.3	9.4	8.1
Paediatrics	3.6	3.4	3.2	4.1	3.1	3.5
Psychiatric	97.1	72.5	69.7	47.2	82.4	74.3
Surgery/Urology	6.3	5.9	6.3	6.1	5.6	6.1
Acute group	6.9	5.2	5.1	6.0	5.1	5.7
All specialties	10.8	9.1	8.6	8.4	11.2	9.6

Figure 1 shows that, with the exception of ophthalmology, the average LOS for each of the seven major acute specialties is greater in London than in England as a whole. In general, average LOS is greatest in inner-deprived London: providers in high-status London have an average LOS closer to the England figure. For the acute specialty group, average LOS in London is 5.7 days, compared with 4.9 in England as a whole.

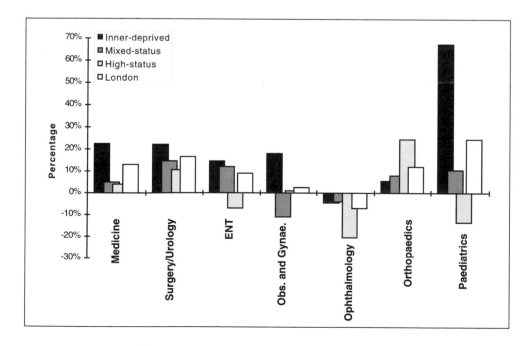

Figure 1: Percentage variation from the England average LOS for seven acute specialties, London, 1994/95

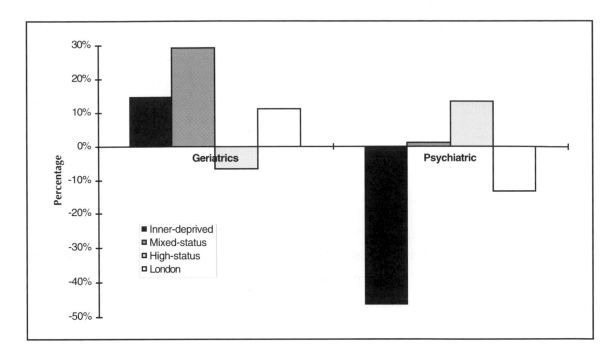

Figure 2: Percentage variation from the England average LOS for non-acute specialties, London, 1994/95

Figure 2 shows that the average geriatric LOS in London is ten per cent greater than that in England as a whole; conversely, the average psychiatric LOS in the capital is 13 per cent less. In inner-deprived London the average psychiatric LOS is 46.1 days, considerably less than other parts of London, as well as the national average. Providers in all four inner-deprived DHAs in London have a short psychiatric LOS. This may reflect differences in the nature of care being offered in these areas; for example, that it is intended to be more short-term. A better insight into the meaning of this finding would be provided by more detailed investigation at a local level.

Compared with 1989/90, average acute LOS has increased very slightly in London from 5.6 to 5.7 days. However, taken on its own this is potentially misleading, for no account is taken of the effect of increased day cases. In Chapter 2 it was shown that London providers have increased their proportion of day cases significantly. When these are included in the analysis, London appears more efficient than the rest of the country, at least in terms of overall hospital throughput. Much of the work carried out as day cases in 1994/95 may consist of less complex cases which would have been treated as in-patients with a short LOS in 1989/90. Thus, the in-patient casemix may be more complex than previously. A comparison with 'similar' cases in 1989/90 might be expected to reveal a *reduction* in average LOS despite the increase in the headline figure.

The above discussion reflects the fact that average LOS is a relatively crude measure of efficiency. It does not take into account the complexity of case-mix within a specialty, nor the proportion of activity carried out as day cases. An apparent lack of efficiency may simply reflect a more complex casemix.

For a more complete picture, we consider three other measures of the use of available bed resources: turnover interval; throughput; and bed occupancy. All three depend on information concerning available beds. Unfortunately, data concerning available beds by specialty are not available, and in any case their reliability may be questionable. Turnover interval and throughput are measured using data for acute beds only. In measuring bed occupancy, data on acute and geriatric specialties are combined.

Turnover interval

Turnover interval is a measure of the average time that each hospital bed remains empty between episodes of care. It is calculated by dividing total unoccupied bed days by total FCEs (excluding day cases). Table 2 provides a comparison across sectors of London of turnover interval and throughput – including and excluding day cases. Turnover interval for acute beds ranges from 0.8 days in the east, to 1.5 days in the north-west sector.

Table 2: Measures of efficient use of acute beds, by sector of London, 1994/95

Measure	North West	North Central	East	South East	South	London
Turnover Interval	1.5	1.3	0.8	1.2	1.4	1.2
Throughput	46.7	49.8	55.5	52.2	56.6	51.4
Throughput including day cases	74.6	70.3	78.2	76.4	86.0	76.3

Figure 3 compares acute turnover interval between London and England showing that, with the exception of inner-deprived areas, London has a shorter turnover interval than comparable areas elsewhere.

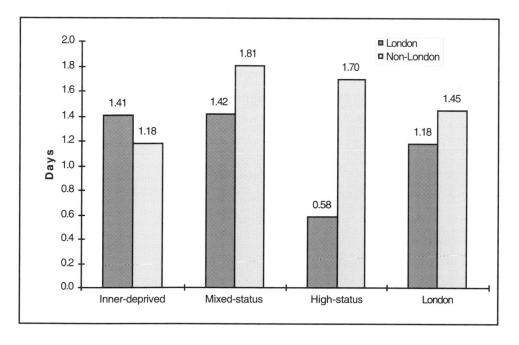

Figure 3: Acute turnover interval, London and England, 1994/95

The turnover interval for acute beds has fallen in both London and the rest of England since 1989/90, but at a faster rate outside the capital: turnover interval in London as a whole is now 18 per cent less than that of the rest of the country whereas five years ago it was 33 per cent less. Turnover interval may be a better measure than average LOS of the efficient use of hospital beds as it is not affected so much by differences in casemix. It tends rather to reflect better bed management procedures.

Throughput

Throughput is another measure of the rate of utilisation of hospitals beds; it is defined as the number of FCEs per available bed per year, and depends on two factors, average LOS and turnover interval. Day cases may also be included in a measure of throughput, though strictly speaking such cases do not relate to available beds in the sense used here. The day case rate provides a simple multiplicative factor which can be applied to produce throughput including day cases. As noted, this distinction is important in the case of London which has a higher day case rate than the rest of the country. When day cases are included, throughput in London is greater than that in the rest of England.

Table 2 shows that acute throughput is greatest in the south and east sectors of London when day cases are excluded. The greater level of throughput in these sectors is driven by a short average LOS – 5.1 days in both sectors. In the east there is also a low turnover interval of less than one day, while in the south, turnover interval exceeds the London average. Thus, a less complex casemix rather than inherently more efficient use of acute beds may be responsible for the greater throughput in these sectors. This explanation is partially supported by the fact that these sectors have a higher proportion of 'DGH-type' hospitals and a lower proportion of teaching and specialist hospitals than other parts of London. However, firm conclusions cannot be drawn without more detailed analysis of the HES database, linked to local knowledge and data.

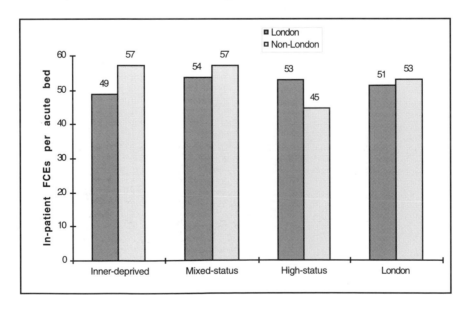

Figure 4: Acute throughput, London and England, 1994/95

Figure 4 shows that throughput in London is less than that in England – 51 FCEs per acute bed compared with 53. There is some variation across providers in different types of socio-economic area. Thus, in London the greatest level of throughput is achieved by providers in mixed-status areas; in the rest of England, hospitals in both inner-deprived and mixed-status areas show a high level of throughput – 57 FCEs per year. The picture changes somewhat when day cases are included.

Referring back to Table 2, it is shown that when day cases are included in the analysis, the south sector has by far the greatest throughput in London – 86 FCEs compared with a range of 70 to 78 in other sectors. Throughput in the south becomes significantly more than in the east, reflecting the greater day case rate of 34 per cent compared with 29 per cent in the east. When day cases are included, as Figure 5 shows, London outstrips the rest of England with a throughput of 76 FCEs compared with 75 in the rest of the country. Only providers in inner-deprived areas of London achieve a lower throughput than similar areas in the rest of England.

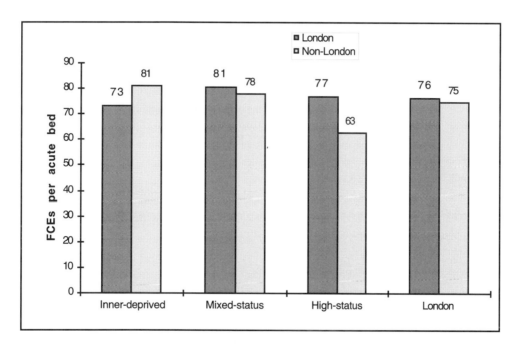

Figure 5: Acute throughput, including day cases, London and England, 1994/95

Bed occupancy

Bed occupancy is an alternative measure of efficient use of hospital resources. It can also be an indicator of pressure on scarce resources. A report from the inner London health authority chief executives in February 1995 (Inner London Chief Executives, 1995) suggested that an average 85 per cent bed occupancy rate was to be preferred.

Bed occupancy is a measure of the proportion of hospital bed stock which is occupied over a given period of time, often a year. However, calculating bed occupancy accurately is not straightforward. A fundamental issue is the inclusion of unfinished episodes as well as finished episodes. Most analysis in this report is in terms of finished episodes or FCEs. The inclusion or exclusion of unfinished episodes may have a significant impact on results.

This issue is considered in more detail in Box 1. For the purposes of this analysis, unfinished episodes are included: this takes account of beds occupied by a single unfinished episode throughout the year, i.e. for 365 days. Although such episodes account for just 0.3 per cent of all episodes, finished or unfinished, that occur in London hospitals, this is equivalent to 14 per cent of occupied bed days.

However, analysis of unfinished episodes in individual hospitals produces some unlikely results. Most significantly, for several hospitals in the Trent region, sufficient unfinished consultant episodes lasting a year are recorded on the HES database, to imply a bed occupancy rate of over 100 per cent *even if no other activity were performed*. Such unlikely results at individual hospitals can easily skew results at a relatively disaggregated level. For this reason we do not attempt to present our usual analysis by socio-economic grouping or sector. Also, Trent region data are excluded from the rest of England figure.

Further, and in contrast with other analyses in this section, acute and geriatric episodes are combined. Detailed analysis of the situation in individual providers suggests that there is not always a clear distinction in the recording of acute and geriatric patients, especially for episodes lasting more than a year. Combining acute and geriatric bed days is likely to give a more accurate representation. Thus, Figure 6 presents data for London and the rest of England alone, showing that London has a greater occupancy rate than the rest of the country – 86 compared with 79 per cent.

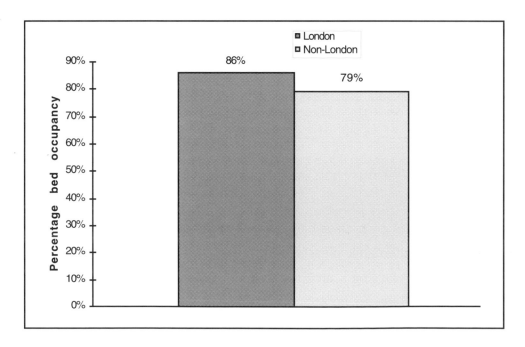

Figure 6: Occupancy rate for acute and geriatric beds, London and England, 1994/95

Of particular value in any understanding of the pattern of utilisation of hospital beds is a measure of the variation of occupancy rates on a daily basis. A hospital with an average bed occupancy of 85 per cent may still register high occupancy rates on any given day. However, for any given provider, the HES dataset may not allow more detailed analysis of bed occupancy.

There are missing records in the HES dataset when measured against the DoH KP70 return of hospital activity. These are compensated for by the use of 'grossing factors', which are applied to FCEs by specialty and region. When these are applied to individual records, the number of FCEs on the HES database for any given specialty and region approximates to the KP70 figure. Unfortunately, analysis of daily bed use in London implies that missing data are not usually spread evenly throughout the year, but occur at particular times, especially at the beginning and end of the financial year. Thus, use of the grossing factors, applied evenly throughout the year, does not rectify problems of missing data when considered at a daily level.

Box 1: Calculating bed occupancy

Table 3 shows occupied bed days and episodes of care in London hospitals in 1994/95. Four types of episode can be identified in any given financial year: finished episodes which started that year (shown in Table 3 as 1994-95/finished); unfinished episodes which started that year (1994-95/unfinished); finished episodes which started before that year (pre-1994-95/finished); and unfinished episodes which started before that year (pre-1994-95/unfinished). The first type accounts for the great majority of episodes. There are considerably less episodes in the second and third categories and they are of a similar order of magnitude. By far the smallest category is the last – pre-1994-95/unfinished. 1,146 of these 3,762 are acute episodes.

Table 3: Occupied bed days and episodes, all specialties, London, 1994/95

	Occupied Bed Days				Episodes		
	Episode start				Episode start		
Episode Type	1994/95	Pre-1994/95	Total	Episode Type	1994/95	Pre-1994/95	Total
Unfinished	728,048	1,373,130	2,101,178	Unfinished	20,721	3,762	24,483
Finished	6,750,392	663,411	7,413,803	Finished	1,451,631	16,338	1,467,969
Total	7,478,440	2,011,989	9,490,429	Total	1,472,352	20,100	1,492,452

However, the number of occupied bed days associated with each of these categories varies considerably. This can be seen most clearly in Table 4 which expresses these results as a proportion. While pre-1994-95/unfinished episodes account for only 0.3 per cent of total episodes in London, 14 per cent of bed days are associated with them. In contrast, 97.3 per cent of episodes are in the 1994-95/finished category but only 71 per cent of bed days. This reflects the difference in the average number of bed days occupied by each category of episode in the financial year. In the case of the former, this is 365 days, although total LOS may be much longer, while for the latter the average is only 9.6 days.

Table 4: Proportion of occupied bed days and episodes, all specialties, London, 1994/95

Episode Type	Occupied Bed Days			Episode Type	Episodes		
	Episode start		Total		Episode start		Total
	1994/95	Pre-1994/95			1994/95	Pre-1994/95	
	%	%	%		%	%	%
Unfinished	8	14	22	Unfinished	1.4	0.3	1.6
Finished	71	7	78	Finished	97.3	1.1	98.4
Total	79	21	100	Total	98.7	1.3	100

Table 5 shows a similar situation in the rest of the country. Only 0.2 per cent of episodes are in the pre-1994-95/unfinished category, but 11 per cent of total occupied bed days are associated with these.

Table 5: Proportion of occupied bed days and episodes, all specialties, rest of England, 1994/95

Episode Type	Occupied Bed Days			Episode Type	Episodes		
	Episode start		Total		Episode start		Total
	1994/95	Pre-1994/95			1994/95	Pre-1994/95	
	%	%	%		%	%	%
Unfinished	6	11	16	Unfinished	1.2	0.2	1.4
Finished	76	8	84	Finished	97.2	1.4	98.6
Total	82	18	100	Total	98.5	1.5	100.0

These findings have implications for the calculation of efficient use of resources. For example, if ten per cent of beds are only notionally available because they are occupied by long-stayers then the throughput of FCEs in beds that are effectively available for use is that much greater.

However, this effect can also lead to the overstating of pressure on beds. For example, if overall bed occupancy is 85 per cent but ten per cent of beds are occupied constantly because of long-staying unfinished episodes, the occupancy rate of the remaining 90 per cent of beds is only 83 per cent. The greater the proportion of total bed stock associated with long-staying unfinished episodes, the greater this effect is.

This issue of apparent long-stay patients in acute hospital beds certainly merits further analysis.

4 Financial efficiency

In this section, the financial efficiency of London trusts is considered in terms of the overall cost per unit of two types of hospital activity – FCEs and out-patient attendances. We also provide an analysis of various staff costs per FCE. Both in-patients and day cases are included in FCEs. Finally, we consider the performance of London trusts against their financial target of a six per cent return on assets employed.

Trust and DMU financial returns, TFR2 and HFR22, contain both financial and activity data at a disaggregated specialty level. These allow the calculation of specialty costs per FCE and cost per out-patient attendance. Unfortunately, the data on activity contained in the financial returns are not consistent with other NHS sources of activity data, in particular the HES dataset and KH09 returns for out-patient activity.

This suggests two alternatives for estimating unit costs: using activity and financial information from the financial returns; or combining the expenditure figure in the financial return with activity data from the HES database to provide the cost per FCE, or from the KH09 return to provide cost per out-patient attendance.

Both approaches have arguments in their favour. The former ensures consistency in the sense that the same data source provides both numerator and denominator. Furthermore, this also ensures consistency with published figures produced by the DoH. However, the activity data in the financial returns is inconsistent with the HES dataset and is, therefore, of questionable accuracy. Using an activity figure derived from HES data may be more accurate, but gives a different cost per FCE figure from those contained in the financial returns.

Cost per case

For cost per case, we present an analysis based just on data from the financial returns. Table 6 compares average cost per acute FCE across sectors of London, showing the highest average cost of £1,194 in the north-central sector, followed by £1,106 in the south east. There is considerable variation across individual specialty groups. Hospitals in the north-central sector have among the lowest average cost per FCE for the non-acute specialties – geriatrics and psychiatric.

Average cost per acute FCE in London, at £962, is 41 per cent more than the equivalent figure for 1989-90, which was £681. However, total expenditure on acute in-patients has grown by 61 per cent in London over the same period. This implies that FCEs are now provided more efficiently than before, although this conclusion does not take account of possible changes in recording practice.

Table 6: Cost per FCE, by specialty group, by sector of London, 1994/95

Specialty Group	North West £	North Central £	East £	South East £	South £	London £
Anaesthetics	137	331	180	587	191	362
Dental	384	604	350	440	542	475
ENT	565	867	496	575	655	657
Geriatrics	3,517	2,643	2,965	2,586	1,991	2,727
Haematology	1,208	1,351	466	735	1,190	987
Medicine	819	1,390	656	1,390	892	978
Obs. and Gynae.	617	699	650	843	649	690
Ophthalmology	360	714	602	488	546	546
Orthopaedics	1,516	1,443	1,321	1,299	1,569	1,430
Other non-acute	660	1,549	1,162	3,068	-	1,112
Paediatrics	750	1,073	744	954	784	863
Psychiatric	11,760	10,014	7,148	11,379	11,075	10,332
Surgery/Urology	1,200	1,539	1,099	1,347	1,075	1,260
Acute	892	1,194	762	1,106	888	962
Total	1,190	1,456	996	1,452	1,295	1,264

Table 7 shows average cost per acute episode in London as a whole is over 20 per cent greater than that in the rest of the country; average cost per psychiatric episode is over 40 per cent greater than that in the rest of England. In both London and the rest of the country, the highest costs per acute episode occur in hospitals in inner-deprived areas.

Table 7: Cost per FCE, by specialty group, London and England, 1994/95

| Specialty Group | London | | | | Non-London | | | | England |
	Inner-deprived £	Mixed-status £	High-status £	Total £	Inner-deprived £	Mixed-status £	High-status £	Total £	£
Anaesthetics	440	222	306	362	891	344	468	547	522
Dental	422	445	573	475	430	535	480	487	485
ENT	716	607	596	657	630	542	560	570	582
Geriatrics	3,588	2,974	2,005	2,727	2,346	2,052	2,292	2,222	2,295
Haematology	1,053	1,047	723	987	1,263	528	631	734	790
Medicine	1,038	836	984	978	828	800	816	819	850
Obs. and Gynae.	780	590	678	690	641	572	584	594	610
Ophthalmology	521	609	571	546	569	628	595	607	597
Orthopaedics	1,334	1,562	1,397	1,430	1,293	1,171	1,239	1,232	1,257
Other non-acute	1,810	1,328	514	1,112	574	983	1,119	976	987
Paediatrics	1,140	614	754	863	926	588	687	670	701
Psychiatric	10,369	9,915	10,867	10,332	7,285	6,476	8,022	7,205	7,622
Surgery/Urology	1,621	1,084	997	1,260	1,178	817	867	899	955
Acute	1,073	862	892	962	904	743	777	791	820
Total	1,367	1,239	1,141	1,264	1,045	986	1,077	1,058	1,092

Cost per out-patient attendance

We now consider cost per out-patient attendance. Again, there are two potential sources of activity data: the financial returns and the KH09 activity return. These are presented simultaneously in Table 8 below. With the exception of north-central London, using activity data from the financial returns produces a slightly greater cost per attendance. Regardless of which activity data are used, the ordering across sectors of London of cost per attendance is the same, with the greatest cost recorded in the north-central sector and the least in the south sector. Several providers with high costs per out-patient attendance are located in the north-central sector.

Table 8: Cost per out-patient attendance, by sector of London, 1994/95

Activity data source used	North West £	North Central £	East £	South East £	South £	London £
Financial returns	69	80	68	70	59	70
KH09	67	82	65	66	57	68

Table 9 shows that cost per out-patient attendance is greater in London than in the rest of England, regardless of which set of activity data are used. Using the KH09 activity data (which appears more reliable: the financial returns activity data reveal some unlikely costs per attendance for individual providers) the average cost of an out-patient attendance in London, at £68, is 17 per cent greater than that in the rest of the country. In London the greatest cost per attendance is in inner-deprived areas where 11 providers have a cost per out-patient attendance greater than £100.

Table 9: Cost per out-patient attendance, London and England, 1994/95

Activity data source used	London				Non-London				England
	Inner-deprived £	Mixed-status £	High-status £	Total £	Inner-deprived £	Mixed-status £	High-status £	Total £	£
Financial returns	82	61	58	70	65	57	56	57	60
KH09	78	65	54	68	67	55	57	58	60

Staff costs per FCE

In this section we present an analysis which relates the total cost of various staff groups to the number of FCEs produced, comparing trusts in London with those in the rest of the country. Data are from trust financial returns (TFR3) and the HES dataset. These allow a comparison of the cost per FCE in terms of four staff groups: consultants, other medical staff, nurses and professions allied to medicine (PAM). FCEs are the main output of most trusts and as such are indicative of total output. Hence, the ratio, cost per FCE, is useful for comparative purposes.

Table 10 compares, across sectors of London, average staff costs per FCE, for each staff group. The average cost of medical staff and nurses per FCE is greatest in the south-east sector. Total staff costs per FCE are substantially lower in the east.

Table 10: Staff costs per FCE, by sector of London, 1994/95

Staff group	North West £	North Central £	East £	South East £	South £	London £
Consultants	143	147	119	157	123	139
Non-consultants	168	169	140	171	151	161
Nurses	663	696	502	709	651	647
PAM	94	87	50	88	85	82
Total	1,732	1,895	1,278	1,926	1,597	1,690

(Tables 10 and 11 exclude DMU activity and costs.)

Table 11 shows that the cost of staff per FCE is greater in London, for each staff group, than in the rest of the country. This is particularly true of medical staff: the cost of consultants is 40 per cent more per FCE in London than in the rest of the country, and 58 per cent more for other medical staff. The difference between the cost of nurses and other professions is less marked but the total cost of staff per FCE in London is still over 30 per cent greater than elsewhere in England. Trusts in inner-deprived areas of London have greater medical staff costs per FCE delivered than those elsewhere in the capital.

Table 11: Staff costs per FCE, London and England, 1994/95

Staff group	London Inner-deprived £	Mixed-status £	High-status £	Total £	Non-London Inner-deprived £	Mixed-status £	High-status £	Total £	England £
Consultants	165	127	116	139	100	100	112	99	105
Non-consultants	193	152	126	161	98	103	118	102	111
Nurses	662	662	609	647	489	594	652	580	590
PAM	81	91	73	82	59	72	80	71	73
Total	1,858	1,671	1,462	1,690	1,101	1,287	1,469	1,285	1,348

Trust financial targets

Trusts are expected to meet annual financial targets. As well as breaking even on income and expenditure, they should achieve a real, pre-interest return of six per cent on average net assets. This is calculated as the proportion of net assets that the surplus represents. Figure 7, based on *'The Fitzhugh Directory NHS Trusts Financial Information 1996'* (Fitzhugh, 1996), shows that, in 1994/95, a quarter of trusts in London failed to achieve this target. The greatest proportion of these are in the east and south-east sectors.

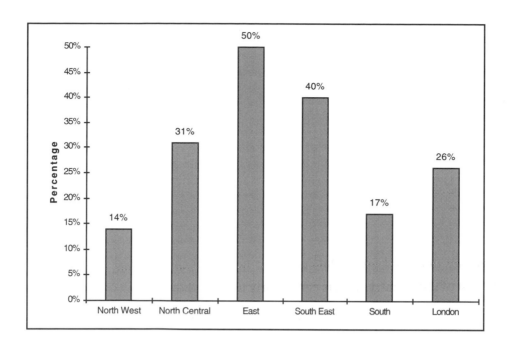

Figure 7: Proportion of trusts failing to make a return of six per cent or more on net assets, by sector of London, 1994/95

Figure 8 shows that the proportion of trusts failing to make a return of six per cent or more is greater in London than in the rest of the country. The proportion of trusts failing to make the target was greatest in high-status areas of London: approximately three times as many as in inner-deprived areas of the capital.

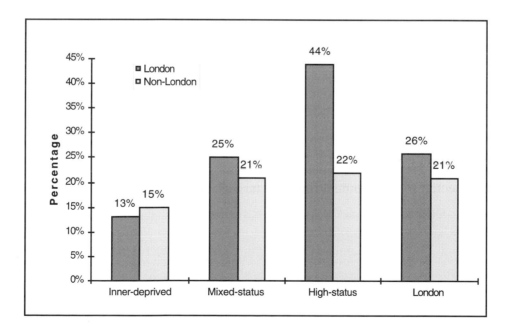

Figure 8: Proportion of trusts failing to make a return of six per cent or more on net assets, London and England, 1994/95

5 NHS performance targets

This section considers the performance of trusts in London against standards set in the Patient's Charter. These are categorised into four groups. The first is: the proportion of out-patients seen within 30 minutes of appointment time; the proportion of A&E attenders seen within five minutes of arrival; and the number of patients not admitted within a month of an operation being cancelled. The second group concerns day case rates for a set of four procedures. The third group is the proportion of out-patients seen within 13 weeks and 26 weeks of being placed on a waiting list. Finally, the fourth group is the proportion of patients admitted within three months and 12 months of being placed on a waiting-list for in-patient or day case treatment.

There has been some scepticism both about the value of these targets as indicators of the quality of health services delivered, and about the validity of the results produced. However, these are official measures and as such merit consideration.

Table 12: Average performance against Patient's Charter targets, London and England, 1995/96

Standard	London				Non-London				England
	Inner-deprived %	Mixed-status %	High-status %	Total %	Inner-deprived %	Mixed-status %	High-Status %	Total %	%
Out-patients	91	92	90	91	93	92	92	92	92
A&E	93	94	92	94	95	96	93	94	94
Operations cancelled*	9	26	14	14	4	2	12	7	8
Day case rate:									
inguinal hernia	40	40	42	41	24	32	34	31	34
arthroscopy	70	78	72	73	64	69	64	66	66
cataracts	47	53	66	53	52	42	53	50	50
laparoscopy	81	85	80	81	68	79	77	75	77
% O-Ps seen in 13 weeks	88	84	87	85	90	87	85	87	83
% O-Ps seen in 26 weeks	98	96	98	97	99	98	98	98	97
% patients admitted									
in 3 months	71	60	70	69	73	73	68	71	71
in 12 months	95	96	95	95	98	98	96	97	97

(* In the case of operations cancelled, the figure shown is the average number per provider, not a proportion.)

Table 12, which compares London with similar areas in the rest of the country for each standard in 1995/96, shows London performs slightly worse than similar areas outside the capital for the first group of targets. In particular, hospitals in mixed-status areas of London perform worse against the cancelled operations target.

Hospitals in London generally perform better in relation to the day case targets than those outside the capital. This is consistent with the higher day case rate noted in Chapter 2. In particular, the rate for inguinal hernia is 41 per cent in London compared with 31 per cent in the rest of the country. The only exception is cataracts in inner-deprived London where 47 per cent are day cases compared with 52 per cent in inner-deprived areas of the rest of the country.

The performance of London hospitals against both in-patient and out-patient waiting-time targets appears to be very slightly worse than for hospitals in similar areas outside of the capital; nevertheless there is a compliance rate of 95 per cent or more for both lower targets.

However, these results conceal great variation in performance between individual London trusts. For example, the proportion of in-patients admitted in three months, which averages 69 per cent in London as whole, varies between 45 and 100 per cent at individual hospitals. Variation in performance as measured by standard deviation from the mean is slightly greater in London than is the case nationally, for most standards.

APPENDICES

Appendix 1

Geographical classifications

Sectors of London

District Health Authorities

North West
Kensington, Chelsea & Westminster
Ealing, Hammersmith & Hounslow
Brent & Harrow
Hillingdon

North Central
Camden & Islington
Enfield & Haringey
Barnet

East
East London & the City
Redbridge & Waltham
  Forest
Barking & Havering

South East
Lambeth, Southwark & Lewisham
Bexley & Greenwich
Bromley

South
Merton, Sutton & Wandsworth
Kingston & Richmond
Croydon

Socio Economic Area

London District Health Authorities

Inner-deprived London
Kensington, Chelsea & Westminster
East London & the City
Camden & Islington
Lambeth, Southwark & Lewisham

Mixed-status London
Brent & Harrow
Ealing, Hammersmith
  & Hounslow
Redbridge & Waltham Forest
Enfield & Haringey
Merton, Sutton & Wandsworth

High-status London
Barnet
Hillingdon
Barking & Havering
Bromley
Bexley & Greenwich
Croydon
Kingston & Richmond

London Providers

Inner-deprived London
Camden & Islington Community Health
CELFACS
Chelsea & Westminster Healthcare
Eastman Dental Hospital
Guy's & St Thomas's Hospital
King's Healthcare
Lewisham & Guy's Mental Health
Moorfields Eye Hospital
National Hospital for Neurology & Neurosurgery
Newham Healthcare
Optimum Health
Queen Elizabeth Hospital for Children
Riverside Community Health
Riverside Mental Health
Royal Brompton Hospital
Royal Free Hampstead
Royal London Homeopathic Hospital
Royal Marsden
St Mary's
Tavistock and Portman
The Bethlem & Maudsley
The Gt Ormond St Hospital for Sick Children
The Homerton Hospital
The Lewisham Hospital
The Royal Hospitals
University College London Hospitals
West Lambeth Community
Whittington Hospital

Mixed-status London
Central Middlesex Hospital
Chase Farm Hospitals
Ealing Hospital
Enfield Community Care
Forest Healthcare
Hammersmith Hospitals
Haringey Community
Harrow & Hillingdon Healthcare
Hounslow & Spelthorne Community
Merton & Sutton Community
North Middlesex Hospital
North West London Mental Health
Northwick Park & St Marks
Parkside
Pathfinder Mental Health Services
Redbridge Healthcare
Royal National Orthopaedic
  Hospital
St George's Healthcare
Wandsworth Community Health
The St Helier
West London Healthcare
West Middlesex University Hospital

High-status London
Barnet Healthcare
Bexley Community
  Health
Bromley Hospitals
Croydon Mental Health
Greenwich Healthcare
Harefield Hospital
Havering Hospitals
Hillingdon Hospital
Kingston and District
  Community
Kingston Hospital
Lifecare
Mayday Healthcare
Mount Vernon and
  Watford Hospitals
Queen Mary's, Sidcup
Ravensbourne
Richmond Twickenham
  & Roehampton
Teddington Memorial
  Hospital
Wellhouse

Non-London District Health Authorities

**Inner-deprived
Non-London**
Sunderland
South of Tyne
Newcastle & North Tyneside
Bradford
Leeds
Sheffield
South Birmingham
Liverpool
Manchester

**Non-London
combined DHAs**
North Birmingham:
  64% Inner-deprived,
  36% High-status

Salford & Trafford:
  51% Inner-deprived,
  49% High-status

Northamptonshire:
  45% Mixed-status,
  55% High-status

Bury & Rochdale:
  46% Mixed-status,
  54% High-status

**Mixed-status
Non-London**
North Durham
South Durham
Tees
Grimsby & Scunthorpe
West Yorkshire
Wakefield
Southern Derbyshire
Leicestershire
Barnsley
Doncaster
Rotherham
North Nottinghamshire
North Staffordshire
Coventry
Dudley
Sandwell
Walsall
Wolverhampton
North Cheshire
St Helens & Knowsley
Bolton
Wigan
East Lancashire
West Pennine

**High-status
Non-London**
Nottingham
Cambridge
Huntingdon
Bedfordshire
North West Hertfordshire
South West Hertfordshire
East & North Hertfordshire
North Essex
South Essex
East Kent
West Kent
East Surrey
Mid Downs
North West Surrey
South West Surrey
Mid Surrey
Portsmouth & SE Hants
Southampton & SW Hants
North & Mid Hampshire
Wiltshire & Bath
Berkshire
Buckinghamshire
Oxfordshire
Bristol & District
Gloucestershire
Solihull
North Worcestershire
South Staffordshire
Warwickshire
Chester
South East Cheshire
Sefton
Wirral
Stockport

London Local Authorities

Inner-deprived London
City of London
Hackney
Tower Hamlets
Newham
Camden
Islington
Kensington and Chelsea
City of Westminster
Lambeth
Southwark
Lewisham

Mixed-status London
Ealing
Hammersmith and Fulham
Hounslow
Brent
Harrow
Enfield
Haringey
Redbridge
Waltham Forest
Merton
Sutton
Wandsworth

High-status London
Hillingdon
Barnet
Barking
Havering
Kingston upon Thames
Richmond upon Thames
Croydon
Greenwich
Bexley
Bromley

Appendix 2

Standardised mortality ratio

The following explanation of the calculation of the Standardised Mortality Ratio is taken from the Health Service Indicator Handbook (DoH, 1996a).

The ratio is of actual number of deaths of residents of an area (regardless of where death occurred) to the number of deaths that, from England and Wales death rates, one would expect given the age and sex structure of the local population.

To produce the expected number of deaths the England and Wales rates are applied to the number of male and female residents in the following age bands:

< 1	30-34	65-69
1-4	35-39	70-74
5-9	40-44	75-79
10-14	45-49	80-84
15-19	50-54	85 +
20-24	55-59	
25-29	60-64	

In algebraic terms, using the notation:

$D(na)$ is the number of deaths of residents of England and Wales in age band **a** from a condition in a given calendar year

$D(i)$ is the number of deaths from that condition in that year among the residents of district **i**

$P(na)$ is the population of England in age band **a** in the given calendar year

$P(ia)$ is the population of district **i** in age band **a** in that year

the SMR for any given condition is:

$$\frac{D(i) \times 100}{\sum D(na) \times \frac{P(ia)}{P(na)}}$$

Because England *and Wales* average death rates are used, the all-England SMR for most causes of death is not 100 as might be expected but actually slightly more or less.

Appendix 3

Types of socio-economic area in London, 1989/90

Inner-Deprived
Riverside
Parkside
Hampstead
Bloomsbury & Islington
City and Hackney
Newham
Tower Hamlets
Haringey
West Lambeth
Camberwell
Lewisham & North Southwark
Wandsworth

Urban
Hounslow & Spelthorne
Ealing
Waltham Forest
Greenwich

High-Status
Barnet
Harrow
Hillingdon
Barking, Havering & Brentwood
Enfield
Redbridge
Bexley
Bromley
Croydon
Kingston & Esher
Richmond, Twickenham & Roehampton
Merton and Sutton

Appendix 4

The composition of specialty groups

Anaesthetics group
190 Anaesthetics

Dental group
140 Oral Surgery
141 Restorative Dentistry
142 Paediatric Dentistry
143 Orthodontics

Geriatrics group
430 Geriatric Medicine

Haematology group
303 Haematology
823 Haematology

Medicine group
300 General Medicine
301 Gastroenterology
302 Endocrinology
304 Clinical Physiology
305 Clinical Pharmacology
310 Audiological Medicine
311 Clinical Genetics
312 Clinical Cytogenetics
313 Clinical Immunology
314 Rehabilitation
315 Palliative Medicine
320 Cardiology
330 Dermatology
340 Thoracic Medicine
350 Infectious Diseases
360 Genito-Urinary Medicine
361 Nephrology
370 Medical Oncology
371 Nuclear Medicine
400 Neurology
401 Clinical Neurophysiology
410 Rheumatology
450 Dental Medicine
460 Medical Ophthalmology

Obs. and Gynae. group
501 Obstetrics
502 Gynaecology

Ophthalmology group
130 Ophthalmology

Orthopaedics group
110 Trauma and Orthopaedics
180 Accident and Emergency

Other non-acute group
610 General Practice – Maternity
620 General Practice – Other than Maternity
800 Clinical Oncology
810 Radiology
820 General Pathology
821 Blood Transfusion
822 Chemical Pathology
824 Histopathology
830 Immunopathology
831 Medical Microbiology
832 Neuropathology
900 Community Medicine
901 Occupational Medicine

Paediatrics group
420 Paediatrics
421 Paediatric Neurology

Psychiatric group
700 Mental Handicap
710 Mental Illness
711 Child and Adolescent Psychiatry
712 Forensic Psychiatry
713 Psychotherapy
715 Old Age Psychiatry

Surgery/Urology group
100 General Surgery
101 Urology
50 Neurosurgery
160 Plastic Surgery
170 Cardiothoracic Surgery
180 Paediatric Surgery

Appendix 5

The composition of diagnosis groups

Infectious Diseases	ICD9 Codes 001-139
Cancer	ICD9 Codes 140-239
Endocrine	ICD9 Codes 240-279
Blood	ICD9 Codes 280-289
Mental	ICD9 Codes 290-319
Nervous	ICD9 Codes 320-389
Cardiac	ICD9 Codes 390-429
Cerebrovascular	ICD9 Codes 430-439
Vascular	ICD9 Codes 440-459
Respiratory/Thoracic	ICD9 Codes 460-519
Oral	ICD9 Codes 520-529
Digestive	ICD9 Codes 530-579
Urinary	ICD9 Codes 580-629
Childbirth	ICD9 Codes 630-676
Skin	ICD9 Codes 680-709
Musculo-Skeletal	ICD9 Codes 710-739
Congenital	ICD9 Codes 740-759
Perinatal	ICD9 Codes 760-779
Ill-defined	ICD9 Codes 780-799
Trauma	ICD9 Codes 800-999
V code	ICD9 Codes V01-V82

Appendix 6

The composition of provider-type groups

Specialist group
Queen Elizabeth Hospital for Children*
Royal National Throat, Nose & Ear Hospital
Royal National Orthopaedic Hospital
Harefield Hospital
Royal London Homeopathic Hospital
The Great Ormond Street Hospital
  for Sick Children*
Moorfields Eye Hospital*
The Bethlem & Maudsley*
Royal Brompton Hospital*
Royal Marsden*
National Hospital for Neurology & Neurosurgery*
Eastman Dental Hospital*

(denotes former SHA)*

Teaching group
Royal Free Hampstead
Guy's & St Thomas's Hospital
St Mary's
St George's Healthcare
King's Healthcare
The Royal Hospitals
Chelsea & Westminster Healthcare
Hammersmith Hospitals
University College London Hospitals

Border group
Hillingdon Hospital
Kingston Hospital
The St Helier
Wellhouse
Havering Hospitals
Chase Farm Hospitals
Queen Mary's, Sidcup
Kingston & District Community

Other acute group
The Homerton Hospital
North Middlesex Hospital
Central Middlesex Hospital
Ealing Hospital
Forest Health Care
West Middlesex University Hospital
Northwick Park & St Mark's
Greenwich Healthcare
Bromley Hospitals
Redbridge Health Care
Richmond, Twickenham & Roehampton
  Healthcare
The Lewisham Hospital
Mayday Healthcare
Whittington Hospital
Newham Healthcare

Other non-acute group
CELFACS
Parkside
West London Healthcare
Enfield Community Care
Harrow & Hillingdon Healthcare
Pathfinder Mental Health Services
Ravensbourne
Riverside Community Health Care
Riverside Mental Health
Camden & Islington Community Health Services
Merton & Sutton Community
North West London Mental Health
Lewisham & Guy's Mental Health
Bexley Community Health
Wandsworth Community Health
West Lambeth Community
Hounslow and Spelthorne Community
  and Mental Health
Tavistock and Portman
Teddington Memorial Hospital
Barnet Healthcare
Haringey Healthcare
Croydon Community
Lifecare
Optimum Health

References

Audit Commission (1992), *All in a day's work*, HMSO, London

M. Bone, A. Bebbington, C. Jagger, K. Morgan and G. Nicolass (1995), *Health expectancy and its uses*, HMSO, London

S. Boyle and C.Smaje (1992), *Acute Health Services in London: An analysis*, King's Fund, London

S. Boyle and C.Smaje (1993), *Primary Health Care in London: Quantifying the challenge*, King's Fund, London

R. Carr-Hill, G. Hardman, S. Martin, S. Peacock, T. Sheldon and P. Smith (1994), *A formula for distributing NHS revenues based on small area use of hospital beds*, Centre for Heath Economics, University of York, York

A. Clarke and M. McKee (1992), 'The consultant episode: an unhelpful measure', *British Medical Journal*, **305**, 1307-1308

DHSS (1977), *The National Health Services Act 1997*, HMSO, London

DoH (1991), *Health of the Nation*, Department of Health, London

DoH (1991a), *Residential Accommodation for Elderly and Younger Physically Handicapped People: All Residents in Local Authority Voluntary and Private Homes Year ending 31 March 1985 to Year ending 31 March 1990*, Department of Health, London

DoH (1994), *NHS operating theatres availability and use, England 1993/94*, Department of Health, London

DoH (1995a), *Health Service Indicators Dataset 1995*, Department of Health, London

DoH (1995b), *Out-patients and ward attenders, England 1994/95*, Department of Health, London

DoH (1995c), *NHS day care facilities, England 1993/94*, Department of Health, London

DoH (1995d), *Bed Availability for England, 1994/95*, Department of Health, London

DoH (1995e), *Private hospitals, homes and clinics registered under Section 23 of the Registered Homes Act 1984, Volume 2, 1994/95*, Department of Health, London

DoH (1995f), *Patient care in the community – community psychiatric nursing summary information for 1994/95*, Department of Health, London

DoH (1995g), *Patient care in the community – district nursing summary information for 1994/95*, Department of Health, London

DoH (1995h), *Patient care in the community – community mental handicap nursing summary information for 1994/95*, Department of Health, London

DoH (1995i), *Speech therapy services summary information for 1993/94*, Department of Health, London

DoH (1995j), *Dietetic services summary information for 1993/94*, Department of Health, London

DoH (1995k), *Chiropody services summary information for 1993/94*, Department of Health, London

DoH (1995m), *Ophthalmic Statistics for England 1984/85 to 1994/95*, Department of Health, London

DoH (1995n), *General Pharmaceutical Services in England 1994/95*, Department of Health, London

DoH (1996a), *Health Service Indicators Handbook*, Department of Health, London

DoH (1996b), *Patient care in the community – specialist care nursing summary information for 1994/95*, Department of Health, London

DoH (1996c), *Professional advice and support programmes summary information for 1994/95*, Department of Health, London

DoH (1996d), *Health Service Indicators Dataset 1996*, Department of Health, London

DoH (1996e), *GMS Base Statistics, October 1995*, Department of Health, London

DoH (1996f), *1996 Key Indicators of Local Authority Social Services*, Department of Health, London

DoH (1996g), *Residential accommodation: Detailed statistics on residential care homes and local authority supported residents*, Department of Health, London

DoH (1996i), *The NHS Performance Guide 1995-96*, Department of Health, London

Fitzhugh (1996), *The Fitzhugh Directory of NHS Trusts Financial Information 1996*, Health Care Information Services, London

A. Harrison, R. Hamblin and S. Boyle (1995), *Analysing changes in emergency medical admissions, Trust Federation*, London

Health Committee (1995), *London's Ambulance Service, Health Committee Second Report*, HMSO, London

Health Committee (1996), *Public Expenditure on Health and Personal Social Services: Memorandum received from the Department of Health containing Replies to a Written Questionnaire from the Committee*, HMSO, London

HFMA/CIPFA (1995), *Introductory Guide to NHS Finance in the UK*, HFMA, London

Hillingdon Health Agency (1994), *Proposals to change services at Mount Vernon and Watford Hospitals NHS Trust*, Hillingdon Health Agency, London

King's Fund London Commission (1992), *London Health Care 2010*, King's Fund, London

OPCS (1994), *General Household Survey 1992*, OPCS, London

OPCS (1995), *General Household Survey 1993*, OPCS, London

C. Seng, L. Lessof, M. McKee (1993), 'Who's on the fiddle?', *Health Service Journal*, **103** (5334), 16-17

B. Williams and J. Nicholl (1995), 'Patient characteristics and clinical caseload of short stay independent hospitals in England and Wales, 1992/93', *British Medical Journal*, **308**, 1699-1701